Studying Persons and Lives

STUDYING PERSONS AND LIVES

A. I. Rabin
Robert A. Zucker
Robert A. Emmons
Susan Frank

Editors

SP SPRINGER PUBLISHING COMPANY

New York

Springer Publishing Company, Inc.
536 Broadway
New York, NY 10012

90 91 92 93 94 / 5 4 3 2 1

ISBN: 0-8261-6870-1

Printed in the United States of America

Contents

4 Psyche Embedded: A Place for Body, Relationships, and Culture in Personality Theory   86
Carol Gilligan, Lyn Brown, and Annie Rogers

5 Unity and Purpose in Human Lives: The Emergence of Identity as a Life Story   148
Dan P. McAdams

6 Studying Lives in a Changing Society: Sociological and Personological Explorations   201
Glen H. Elder and Avshalom Caspi

Preface

In 1978, the Department of Psychology at Michigan State University inaugurated the Henry A. Murray Lectures in Personality. At that first conference we celebrated the fortieth anniversary of the publication of Murray's groundbreaking book, *Explorations in Personality*. Subsequently, the Murray Lectures became a regular triennial event at which outstanding researchers and theoreticians in the field of personality were invited to present and discuss their latest creative efforts. Three books, based on the past three lectureships, have appeared during the past 10 years.

The present volume, the fourth in the series, *Studying Persons and Lives*, represents the contributions to the latest Murray Lectures, which were held on the campus of Michigan State University in the spring of 1988. Our intention was to focus on persons, not primarily on personality traits or variables; and on *lives*, not on cross-sectional views of the human personality, but on the life process traversed over time. Of special importance is the fact that Henry Murray died, in his ninety-fifth year, in the summer of 1988. The biographic essay, written by James Anderson (Chapter 8) and the memoir, in the form of an epilogue, by Robert Zucker, appropriately conclude the present volume which is dedicated to the memory of Henry A. Murray.

The editors continue to be grateful to Gordon Wood, chairperson of the Department of Psychology, for his sustained interest in and support of this series. We also thank the doctoral alumni of the department for their continued financial contributions which help to sustain the lectureship. These meetings also were supported in part by contributions from the co-sponsoring department of Psychiatry, Family and Child Ecology, and the Counseling Center, chaired by Drs. Donald H. Williams, Robert Griffore, and Lee June, respectively. Of special note is the grant from the Michigan State University Development Fund, and the personal support and commitment of one of its' directors, Dr. John Cantlon, also Michigan State University's Vice President for Research and Graduate Studies. From the very beginning, Dr. Cantlon has been a strong and interested supporter of this series; we are grateful for his continued interest and enthusiasm.

An enterprise of this magnitude, whose planning takes place over several years, is dependent upon the help of many individuals. We thank Drs. C. L. Winder, Dozier Thorton and Robert Noll, all of Michigan State University, and Professor Emeritus Ross Stagner of Wayne State University, for their contributions to the success of the meetings. Last, the Lectureship committee is most grateful for the efforts of the Kellogg Conference Center staff for their sustained work in bringing this lectureship to fruition. In particular, we especially thank Marc Van Wormer for his continuing foresight, sensitivity and skill; we regret that we will not be working with him hereafter, and wish him well in his new position.

Introduction to the Series

The Henry A. Murray Lectures in Personality, presented by Michigan State University, are designed to advance our understanding of personality in depth, across situations, and over the range of the human life-span. The lectures offer a spacious forum in which leading psychologists can explore the most difficult questions in personality theory and research from the perspective of their own work. It is hoped that this series will encourage the conceptual risk-taking that will lead to the imaginative, strong, and theoretically organized work that is needed to advance the science of personology.

These lectures are named in honor of Henry A. Murray in order to draw upon a spirit of inquiry that has directed much of the best contemporary work on personality. Throughout his distinguished career, Murray dealt with the most difficult theoretical and methodological questions with all the skills available to the scientist and the humanist. His wide-ranging mind took him across the gulfs that separate alternative approaches to the study of human beings. Murray argued for a science of personology that would include the physiological and the phenomenological, that would rely on the specialties of test construction as well as of literary scholarship, that saw the need for the taxonomist of personality as well as the psychotherapist of persons, that studied the isolated incident as well as entire lives, and that could encompass subjects as diverse as the study of mythology and the study of personnel selection. It is hoped that the series of Murray lectures may continue to draw upon all these sources in order to advance the science of personology and to contribute to human welfare.

Contributors

Albert I. Rabin is Professor of Psychology Emeritus at Michigan State University. He is currently Institute Professor at the Wright Institute, Berkeley. He has taught at Boston University, City University of New York, Hebrew and Bar-Ilan Universities (Israel), and the University of Aarhus (Denmark). Dr. Rabin has published numerous articles and reviews in various professional and scientific journals. He also has contributed chapters to more than 30 edited books, and published a number of books in the areas of assessment, personality development, and kibbutz childrearing.

Robert A. Zucker received his Ph.D. in clinical psychology from Harvard University. He is currently Professor of Psychology and Co-Director of Clinical Training at Michigan State University. He has taught at Rutgers University and at the University of Texas at Austin and has been a visiting scholar at the National Alcohol Institute. His long-term research interests are stability and change over the life course, with a particular focus on developmental psychopathology. As part of this work he also directs the Michigan State University Longitudinal Study and the Prevention of Conduct Disorders Program. He has edited three books and has published extensively on the relationship of psychopathology to personality and to developmental processes.

Robert A. Emmons is Assistant Professor of Psychology at the University of California, Davis. He received his Ph.D. from the University of Illinois at Champaign-Urbana, and formerly taught at Michigan State University. His major research interests are in human motivation, with a particular focus on goal approaches to personality, and personality and physical health.

Susan J. Frank received her Ph.D. in clinical Psychology from Yale University. She has taught at the University of Maryland and the Illinois Institute of Technology. Her interests are in parent/child relationships throughout the life course and their influence on individual development. Recent studies have focused on antecedents and outcomes of adolescents' and young adults' experience of attachment and autonomy in relation to their parents.

James William Anderson, Ph.D., is an Assistant Professor of Clinical Psychology at Northwestern University Medical School, a Research Fellow at the Chicago Institute for Psychoanalysis, and a psychotherapist in private practice. His research specialty is psychobiography; he has published papers on the methodology of psychological biography and has written psychological studies of Woodrow Wilson, William James, the English analyst D. W. Winnicott, and Henry A. Murray. The first recipient of the Heinz Kohut Memorial Fellowship, he also was awarded a fellowship by the National Endowment for the Humanities.

Lyn Mikel Brown, Ed.D., is a research associate at Harvard University Graduate School of Education.

Avshalom Caspi received his Ph.D. in developmental psychology from Cornell University. He is Assistant Professor of Psychology at Harvard University, where he contributes to the social, personality, and developmental psychology training programs. He is currently involved in several longitudinal studies investigating the causes and consequences of continuity and change in social behavior across the life course.

Glen H. Elder, Jr. is Howard W. Odum Distinguished Professor of Sociology and Research Professor of Psychology at the University of North Carolina, Chapel Hill. He has also served on the faculties of the University of California-Berkeley and Cornell. Over the past 25 years he has been engaged in a program of longitudinal studies of social change and human development within a life course framework. Former co-chair of the SRCC Committee of the Life Course and Human Development, he is currently a co-director of the Carolina Consortium on Human development of the Chapel Hill campus.

Carol Gilligan received her Ph.D. from Harvard University and currently holds a professorship in Harvard's Graduate School of Education. She has written numerous papers on ego and moral development during adolescence and early adulthood. The focus of much of her work, including her recent book, *In A Different Voice: Psychological Theory and Women's Development*, is on differences between females and males in concepts of self and morality throughout the course of development.

Dan P. McAdams received his Ph.D. from Harvard University in Personality and Developmental Psychology and taught at Loyola University of Chicago from 1980 to 1989. He is currently Professor of Education and Psychology at

Northwestern University. He is author of *Power, Intimacy, and the Life Story* and (with Richard Ochberg) *Psychobiography and Life Narratives.* He is also associate editor of the *Journal of Personality.* His research has focused on intimacy and power motivation, identity and the development of self, and personality development during the adult years.

Paul E. Meehl received his Ph.D. in clinical psychology at the University of Minnesota, where he is Regents' Professor of Psychology, Professor of Psychiatry, and Member of the Center for Philosophy of Science. He is a past president of the American Psychological Association (1962) and recipient of its Distinguished Contributor Award, and he is a member of the National Academy of Sciences. Engaged in part-time practice of psychotherapy (psychoanalytic and RET), his current research interests are quantitative metatheory, and development of new taxometric methods for studying the genetics of schizophrenia.

John R. Nesselroade is Research Professor of Human Development at the Pennsylvania State University. He received his Ph.D. from the University of Illinois at Urbana-Champaign. He is a Fellow of Divisions 5, 7, and 20 of the American Psychological Association and a Past President of Division 20. In 1972 he received the Cattell Award for Distinguished Multivariate Research from the Society of Multivariate Experimental Psychology. Nesselroade is a Visiting Senior Fellow of the Max-Planck-Institute for Human Development and Education, West Berlin, and editor (with R. B. Cattell) of the 2nd edition of the *Handbook of Multivariate Experimental Psychology.*

Annie G. Rogers, Ph.D. is a research associate at Harvard University Graduate School of Education.

William McKinley Runyan received his Ph.D. in Clinical Psychology and Public Practice from Harvard University, and is currently Associate Professor, School of Social Welfare, and Associate Research Psychologist, Institute of Personality Assessment and Research, University of California at Berkeley. One of his missions in life is to help clarify and develop relationships between the study of lives and other traditions in personality psychology. A recipient of the Henry A. Murray Award for contributions to personality psychology, he is the author of *Life Histories and Psychobiography: Explorations in Theory and Method,* and editor of *Psychology and Historical Interpretation.*

1

Concerning the Study of Persons and Lives

A. I. Rabin, Robert A. Zucker,
Robert A. Emmons, and Susan Frank

When Robert White made his plea for "studying personality the long way" (White, 1981), he implied two meanings for the term "long." First, the reference was regarding the need to take one's time in studying personality, to view it multidimensionally and not be satisfied with single-shot investigation and brief forays in the field. The second meaning corresponds to Murray's notion of the "long units" of personality, consisting of whole lives—not mere episodes or variables studied cross-sectionally at some point along the temporal continuum.

The papers in the present Murray Lectures volume, whether in substance or method, are studies of approaches to the investigation of long units of personality. Consonant with Murray's dictum that "the psychologist must attempt to discover as much as he can about the life histories of his subjects" (Murray, 1938, p. 741), the contributors to this volume have been learning and discovering much about their subjects in sundry and rather novel and sophisticated ways. They have studied completed lives with much archival and published data offering significant guidance, or lives in progress with intensive interview and test materials as their substantive support. Furthermore, they have been concerned with the biological substratum as well as with the impact of history and of social and cultural change upon personality.

In this introductory chapter an effort is made to interrelate the different contributions and point to their advances in personality theory and research.

ON INQUIRY IN PERSONALITY PSYCHOLOGY

It is perhaps fitting that, after this introduction, the first chapter in this volume is written by William McKinley Runyan. Runyan's widely acclaimed book, *Life Histories and Psychobiography* (1982), is probably most responsible for the recent upswing of interest in the study of lives. His first volume examined a number of conceptual and methodological challenges encountered in the study of individual lives. This time around, Runyan outlines the agenda that personality psychology has set for itself. According to Runyan, personality psychology is characterized by four lines of inquiry: developing general theories, accounting for individual and group differences, studying specific personality processes, and understanding individual persons and lives. Runyan has argued that personality psychology needs to be concerned with three different levels of understanding: (1) what is true of all human beings, (2) what is true of groups of human beings, and (3) what is true of individual human beings in particular social and historical contexts. This can be seen as an embellishment of Kluckhohn and Murray's (1953) classic dictum "Every man is in certain respects (a) like all other men, (b) like some other men, and (c) like no other man" (p. 53). While Runyan's work on psychobiography has focused on the last of these goals of inquiry, the remaining chapters in this volume represent an adequate sampling of the other domains as well.

Lives and persons can be studied from a variety of vantage points. One way in which to partition these approaches is in terms of where they stand along a dimension of firmness, anchored at opposite ends by what could be called the "hard" and "soft" extremes of the discipline. The hard end of the discipline is typically associated with a rigorous methodology, strict adherence to hypothesis testing, and point predictions. The "soft" end of the discipline is typically not as interested in making specific predictions nor in restricting inquiry to phenomena amenable to rigorous methodologies. This distinction is an important one, as it informs the types of theoretical conjectures possible, which in turn designate the types of data seen as permissible. Traditions at the "hard" end include the behaviorist, the cognitive, the psychometric, and the biological. At the "soft" end are the psychoanalytic, phenomenological-humanistic, and narrative-interpretive approaches. Framed in Runyan's terms, the major objective of the hard traditions is studying specific processes and classes of behavior. The major objectives of the soft traditions are in understanding lives in social-historical contexts. Cutting across the two traditions are the objectives of developing general theories of personality and analyzing group and individual differences. In terms of methods, the hard traditions are associated with experimental and quantitative methods (e.g., psychometric, taxonomic) whereas the soft traditions are associated with interpretive and historical-contextual methods (e.g., narratives and case studies).

Using this distinction as a springboard, the other contributors to this volume can be located along a "hard versus soft" dimension. From hardest to softest, the ordering would proceed as follows: Meehl, Nesselroade, Elder and Caspi, McAdams, and Gilligan. Meehl's work on the development of taxonomic methods for the assessment of schizophrenia, coupled with his belief in taxonomic categories as ontologically "real" entities, has long been the epitome of a quantitative, biological approach to psychopathology. Meehl has been described as "a dust-bowl empiricist who endorses actuarial methods and rigorous research" (Rorer & Widiger, 1983, p. 443). Nesselroade's mathematical approach to modeling personality constancy and change also places him within the hard tradition. Elder and Caspi's search to understand lives under changing historical conditions qualifies them for the softer end of the continuum, although their adherence to empirically based methodology moves them back a bit on this dimension. McAdams's depiction of identity as a life story places him squarely in the narrative-interpretive tradition. Identity, that which binds together past, present, and future, lends coherence to personality. The narrative-interpretive tradition is perhaps best exemplified in the chapter by Carol Gilligan and her colleagues. Both McAdams and Gilligan listen in an attempt to identify the central themes in the stories that their subjects tell.

As will be evident throughout the volume, the study of persons and lives requires input from both traditions, and complete understanding is unattainable without such a combined effort.

ON THE YIN AND YANG OF CONFLICT

Another way of considering several of the papers is in terms of what they have to say about the central role that conflict plays in persons' lives. Although framed differently, the clash between agentic and communion orientations permeates both McAdams's and Gilligan's theorizing. This "duality of human experience," to use Bakan's (1966) terminology, has been used by Gilligan and McAdams to highlight the central role of conflict in shaping the lives of their subjects. For Gilligan, the conflict is moral—framed in terms of opposing imperatives of justice versus care and responsibility. For McAdams, conflict occurs between the superordinate thematic lines of power and intimacy motivation, in that these orientations will often yield contradictory prescriptions for behavior. In each case, conflicts stem from differential emphases on connectedness versus separation in interpersonal relationships.

It is ironic that inasmuch as conflict is normally viewed as pathological, particularly within psychoanalytic perspectives, it is also a positive influence in people's lives. Developmental theorists have long contended that it is only through such a dialectical tension between these conflicting orientations that personal growth is possible (Kagan, 1982; Loevinger, 1976; Riegel, 1976). Development involves a continuous resolution or balance of conflicting demands throughout the life course. Resolution of such conflict is also regarded as of utmost importance for the writers of this volume. For McAdams, one way in which intimacy and power motivations are reconciled is through the generativity script—the leaving of a legacy to the succeeding generation. Generativity involves the creative synthesis of power and intimacy. Gilligan relies on the musical metaphor of a "fugue" to describe the harmonious resolution of the justice and caring orientations to moral conflicts, which according to them is the hallmark of moral maturity.

The theme of conflict reappears in Elder and Caspi's chapter as well. These authors point to the influence of historical events on the genesis of role conflicts in young adults growing up during the Great Depression and World War II. Economic hardship engendered role conflicts by prematurely requiring children to fulfill adult work roles while simultaneously balancing the demands of familial and educational tasks. Interestingly, war had the opposite effect of minimizing such role conflict by instituting, in effect, a moratorium. Entry into military service removed individuals from the context in which conflicting demands were cultivated. Implicit in Elder and Caspi's work is the notion that the types of intrapsychic and interpersonal conflict studied by Gilligan and McAdams can be shaped by historical forces and social change.

Evidence of Harry Murray's anticipatory vision can be found in these formulations also. Individuality is played out in the choices one makes, and since life is inherently complex, choosing between conflicting alternatives is unavoidable. Murray contended that some of the primary functions of personality are to reduce conflicts between needs (by the creation of serial programs) through substitution, integration, compartmentalization, and social conformity (Murray & Kluckhohn, 1953).

A TEMPORAL PERSPECTIVE ON PERSONALITY

The title of this volume makes a distinction between the study of "persons" and the study of "lives." This and other distinctions that it brings to mind—"stability" and "change," "structure" and "process," "personality" and "development"—are difficult to maintain, a difficulty that follows from a temporal framing of personality. Temporality as a basic assumption in personality theory is far more commonplace today than when Murray first published *Explorations* in 1938. In defining personality as a constantly changing configuration, Murray did not shy away from the inherent difficulties of capturing a process that "will not stop and allow itself to be examined repeatedly and at leisure by the experts" (Murray & Kluckhohn, 1953, p. 3). The challenge, as he saw it, was to seek unity and organization in process—in the processes associated with a single psychological event, in the "successive developments which occur through a long series of events or through the entire series of occurrences which constitute a life" (Murray & Kluckhohn, p. 4), in conflict and choice, in development and change, and in the dynamic transactions between a changing human organism and its changing environment. This same challenge—the challenge posed by a dynamic vision of persons and lives—gives focus and shape to several of the chapters in this volume, in particular those by Dan McAdams, Carol Gilligan, John Nesselroade, and Glen Elder and Avshalom Caspi.

McAdams and Gilligan, both groomed in the traditions of Henry A. Murray and Robert W. White, rely on the narrative to do justice to the temporal nature of personality. McAdams seeks to capture integrative themes, whereas Gilligan listens for patterned ways of dealing with moral conflict in the stories of persons living out and reflecting on their lives. But while these two theorists employ the same medium, their emphases are quite different. For McAdams, what is most interesting about a life story is what it reveals about the subject's "imagos." Functionally, imagos are thematic threads, weaving perception of stability and unity into a narrative of changing events and experiences— theoretical tools that raise the person into topographical relief from the surface of a life story, that project structure from a background of development. In comparison, Gilligan, in examining her subject's narrative, is more attuned to change than stability. Not only does she listen for transformations in her subject's experiences of self and self-in-relation-to-others, but she also attends to and actively attempts to manipulate changes in the relationship between the psychological investigator and the research participant. For Gilligan, the person (qua narrator) emerges through several guided readings of her descriptions of the choices she makes between conflicting moral imperatives of "justice" and "care"—choices that are made in the context of relationships and that are shaped and reshaped by events and experiences in personal, social, and developmental time.

Nesselroade, in his efforts to uncover stability and organization in "state" (as well as traits), confronts the challenge of "capturing a constantly changing configuration" at a more micro level of analysis. Nesselroade's reliance on affect rating scales and (p-) factor analytic techniques sharply contrasts with McAdams's quasi-literary analysis of far more qualitative data. Yet there is an affinity of purpose that links the work of these two investigators—a search for consistency and structure in what might appear to the less disciplined observer as a randomly occurring, shapeless hodgepodge of psychic events. Although Nesselroade does not cite Murray (as he outlines in his chapter, his training is in the psychometric tradition), his quest for order and organization in "changing properties and configurations [of behavior]" and his assertion that personality consistency is likely to be found "in the general prototypical approaches and strategies by which people construct particular behavior patterns" cannot but have a familiar ring to those who trace their scholarly heritage back to the work begun at the Harvard Psychological Clinic.

Finally, Elder and Caspi confront the challenges inherent in a temporal framing of personality by imposing structure not only on the course of individual lives over time but also on the ways in which lives are affected by variations in the historical and social/relational contexts in which they are embedded. In examining the effects of economic depression and war on the life courses of members of successive cohorts, they place persons and lives in "family, historical and lifetime." These theorists find constancy in change itself, and organization in higher order processes that link historical and social variation to the trajectories of individual lives: increases in and subsequent efforts to diminish the discrepancy between claims and resources; new situational imperatives that demand new behavioral and social arrangements; and the accentuation of preexisting personal and relational characteristics. Although Elder and Caspi speak less to cultural than to historical and social variation, they offer a provocative and dynamic approach for closing in on what Murray and Kluckhohn referred to as the "person in and of environments" (1953, p. 6).

FILLING IN THE BLACK BOXES (ALIAS FILLING IN LITTLE ORPHAN ANNIE'S EYES)

Our final comments in way of introducing the works in this volume focus on two papers that bring a psychobiological perspective on one hand, and a sociohistorical perspective on the other, to bear on the study of personality— and as such, fill in some of personality theory's most infamous "black boxes."

A Biopsychological Perspective

Paul Meehl notes in his chapter that

> the long-term aim of much research is to be able to offer an explicit definition of the theoretical entities that in the early stages are defined implicitly or "contextually" by their role in th[e] network of connections among observables. . . . In drawing a diagram to illustrate the nomological network . . . , where one connects the concepts represented by open circles with lines or strands of the net, . . . I was struck by an analogy between those open circles and the vacuous eyes that used to appear in the Little Orphan Annie cartoons of my youth. So I dubbed this . . . kind of openness "Orphan Annie's Eyes," meaning that one of our long-term scientific aims is to learn enough about the *innards* of an implicitly defined theoretical entity . . . so that . . . we can . . . provide an explicit theoretical definition of the entity in terms of its inner nature. (see pp. 291–292)

In his chapter, Meehl delves into the black box of schizophrenia with care and precision. He rejects a constructionist view of the concept; he wrestles with the history of the construct and with the question of whether this is an arbitrary class or a true taxon.

> When we attribute empirical taxonicity to a concept, we have in mind something stronger than [a region or a quantitative dimension]. . . . In ordinary language we say that we are intending to refer to a *natural kind*, such as a biological species, a disease entity, a personality type, a Mendelizing mental deficiency syndrome, a "qualitative" as contrasted with a merely "quantitative" difference between groups of individuals. To use an expression from Plato, "We want to carve nature at its joints." (see p. 253)

Meehl's treatment, and his eventual conclusion that the schizotypic taxon— the sine qua non of the disorder—is masked by the qualitative diversity of the clinical display but is best understood as "a quantitative aberration in the synaptic transmission function," is a detailed and closely reasoned example of the practice of hard science at its best. Meehl traces the derivatives of this neural deficit and carefully spells out the ways that the schizotaxic diathesis can manifest itself in a variety of seemingly unconnected domains.

At the same time, despite the theory's invocation of social learning history as part of the process, one may still ask the question, is this a theory of variables or of persons? We turn to Meehl again:

> All that is, strictly speaking, inherited is the schizotaxic brain, upon which the schizotypal personality develops by a complicated process of social learning. . . . I would assign a crucial role to the occurrence of certain sorts of adverse events, some of which are essentially independent of the personal characteristics . . . of the individual, literally matters of "bad luck" or "pure chance." . . . Something takes place . . . a pure happenstance that altered [the individual's] momentary psychological state and hence his readiness to misperceive along certain lines; then something else takes place, equally independent, in both the causal and statistical senses, of the first event, which impacts him because of an ideographic significant *that it would not have for another equally schizoid person*, and that it would not even have for this individual, despite its special idiographic content, if he were not in the state he's currently in. (see pp. 278, 284)

Although this description of process is not incompatible with personological theory, the reader might see it as far removed from the fabric of life histories that Murray and his co-workers attempted to piece together. But if we turn to other of Murray's works, the theoretical distance is not so great. In discussing the creative process and the structure of life compositions, Murray reiterates Whitehead:

> His conception is that of a procession of overlapping and interdependent events, or actual concrete occasions, in space-time. . . . A fine, microanalysis would yield a sequence of occasions, or actual entities, each of which . . . would perish at the instant

of its composition and be immediately succeeded by another actual occasion. A grosser analysis would take a whole act, or endeavor, as the "real thing" (White-head), the direction and quality of which has imposed itself on it constituent parts. (1959, pp. 100–101)

The critical difference, then, between Meehl and Murray is what drives the action sequence as it cumulates. Meehl, the biophile, sees the neural deficit as central; Murray, the psychophile, sees intentionality as central.

A Historical/Social Perspective on Filling in Orphan Annie's Eyes

Elder and Caspi's chapter, while in many ways worlds apart from Meehl's, similarly draws our attention to open circles that personologists traditionally have made little effort to define in an explicit way. Elder and Caspi's theorizing and sociohistorical influences is less positivistic and more interactionist than Meehl's treatment of schizophrenia—intellectual differences that are as much a function of differences in level of explanation (biological vs. sociological) as of personal preferences. Nevertheless, Meehl's metaphoric reference to Orphan Annie's eyes is an apt way of describing the gaping conceptual holes confronting investigators seeking to extend the study of lives to "the study of lives in a changing society."

For Elder and Caspi, hidden deep in Annie's eyes are the secrets of historical and social influences on persons and lives. Although demonstrations of systematic differences between individuals born in different birth cohorts have made it more difficult for personologists to ignore the relevance of these influences, as Elder and Caspi point out, "Period effects remain a black box." They outline what is essentially a four-step approach to shedding light on the contents of this box and examining their implications for persons and lives.

Elder and Caspi begin by operationalizing what they assume to be most essential about a historical event or time period for the course of individual lives (for example, in studying the effects of the Great Depression, they begin with a measure of family income loss). They then attempt to identify multiple behavioral and personality outcomes, both proximal and distal, associated with the (operationalized) event and, next, offer explicit definitions of the processes that link the event to outcomes. Finally, they seek to identify and study factors such as the individual's life stage that potentially moderate the link between processes and outcomes.

Notably, while both Elder and Caspi's and Meehl's investigations are theoretically driven, they approach their nomological networks from opposite directions. Elder and Caspi begin with the historical event, or more specifically, its operationalization, as a given. There is little discussion as to whether they have correctly identified what is most essential about the event or period in history, or whether there would be any notable differences in the ensuing nomological network had they begun with a different operationalization. Because their focus is on examining the processes that link the event to multiple outcomes, unasked questions about the initial operationalization recede into the background as the network of connections to persons and lives takes on added complexity and conceptual richness. In contrast, Meehl, in seeking to discover the "inner nature" of schizophrenia, begins with the network of connections between observable "outcomes" and works his way back through the nomological network to uncover the sine qua non of the disorder.

These sorts of differences in direction as well as level of explanation exert competing pulls on the field of personology. Although it has become somewhat faddish to speak of a biopsychosocial approach to studying persons and lives as the ideal, the conceptual distance that separates Meehl's from Elder and Caspi's work illustrates what may be insurmountable hurdles standing in the way of a holistic understanding of persons in "nature" as well as in "society and culture."

REFERENCES

Bakan, D. (1966). *The duality of human existence: Isolation and communion in Western man.* Boston: Beacon Press.

Kagan, R. (1982). *The evolving self: Problem and process in human development.* Cambridge, MA: Harvard University Press.

Loevinger, J. (1976). *Ego development.* San Francisco: Jossey-Bass.

Murray, H. A. (1938). *Explorations in personality.* New York: Oxford University Press.

Murray, H. A., & Kluckhohn, C. (1953). Outline of a conception of personality. In C. Kluckhohn & H. A. Murray (Eds.), *Personality in nature, society, and culture* (2nd ed., pp. 3–49). New York: Alfred A. Knopf.

Riegel, K. F. (1976). The dialectics of human development. *American Psychologist, 31,* 689–698.

Rorer, L. G., & Widiger, T. A. (1983). Personality structure and assessment. *Annual Review of Psychology, 34,* 431–463.

Runyan, W. M. (1982). *Life histories and psychobiography: Explorations in theory and method.* New York: Oxford University Press.

White, R. (1981). Exploring personality the long way: The study of lives. In A. I. Rabin, J. Aronoff, R. A. Zucker, & A. Barcley (Eds.), *Further explorations in personality.* New York: John Wiley.

2

Individual Lives and the
Structure of Personality Psychology

William McKinley Runyan

INTRODUCTION

There is striking disagreement about the current state of personality psychology. Those in other branches of psychology often believe that the personality area is in bad shape. You hear questions like "What of interest has happened in personality psychology in the past 20 or 30 years?" Or the view is expressed that personality theory is all right, but nobody is doing it any more, in that there aren't many chapters to add to Hall and Lindzey's influential *Theories of Personality* (1957) textbook. Or some critics believe that there initially were a number of plausible global conceptualizations of personality, such as those advanced by Freud, Adler, Jung, Horney, and others, but that hard empirical research has shown that they just don't hold up.

On the other hand, people within personality psychology are often much more positive about the field. Many have spoken in recent years about a renaissance or revitalization of personality psychology (cf. Craik, 1986; Hogan, 1985; Maddi, 1984; Millon, 1984; Tomkins, 1981). A simplified version of these positive views is that personality psychology used to be a vibrant and exciting intellectual enterprise when it was launched by Gordon Allport, Henry Murray, and others in the 1930s and 1940s, but that the field fell on hard times in the 1960s due to an overemphasis on the measurement of traits, the neglect of important theoretical issues, and the impact of critiques such as Mischel's widely cited *Personality and Assessment* (1968). However, the field is now productive and vital again, having responded to the unjustified criticisms, learned from the valid ones, and come to appreciate more deeply the virtues of person-situation interactionism (Block, 1977; Endler & Magnusson, 1976; Kenrick & Funder, 1988; Magnusson & Endler, 1977). From this perspective, the field of personality is now thriving and on the move again with a variety of theoretically interesting and practically important research programs (cf. Aronoff, Rabin, & Zucker, 1987; Rabin, Aronoff, Barclay, & Zucker, 1981; Zucker, Aronoff, & Rabin, 1984). There is now an "expansionist spirit" (p. x), with a broadening of the scope of personality psychology, with advances coming from multiple bases such as biological-evolutionary, cognitive-motivational, and social-cultural approaches to personality (Cantor & Kihlstrom, 1987).

One problem in assessing the state of personality psychology is that it is difficult to comprehend the range of research enterprises in the field and their relationships to one another. This is certainly true for outsiders to the field, and, I believe, often for insiders as well.

A central issue I want to address in this paper is the cognitive structure of the field of personality psychology, focusing on the place of the study of lives in relation to the wider field. The second section will propose a way of conceptualizing the structure of the field in terms of four primary tasks or objectives: developing general theories of personality, analyzing individual and group differences, studying specific processes or classes of behavior, and, finally, studying individual persons. In the third section, I will discuss the appropriate criteria for evaluating work in the study of individual lives and discuss the concept of progress as a way of addressing methodological and epistemological problems. The fourth section will explore relationships between the study of lives and other traditions in personality psychology. Finally, I will suggest how a clearer conception of the structure of personality psychology can be useful both internally and in relation to the wider field of psychology.

Before beginning the substantive discussion, this would be an appropriate place to provide a short autobiographical comment on my own relationship to the Murray tradition, as is customary in these Murray lectures. When I entered graduate school at Harvard in 1969 in clinical psychology and public practice, I said at an opening weekend retreat with faculty and fellow graduate students that I wanted to work on applying scientific methods to the study of lives, examining problems in the description, explanation, prediction, and intentional change of lives. I eventually completed a dissertation on that topic in 1975.

I first met Henry Murray in the summer of 1970, after I had sent him a rough initial paper sketching ideas about a scientific approach to the study of lives. He responded graciously to this early stumbling effort, and even though he had retired in 1962, my contacts with him were most important throughout graduate school and after. His encouragement and infectious enthusiasm made it easier to pursue the study of lives in face of the opposition of many who didn't see it as a worthwhile endeavor. It was reassuring that someone who seemed a more complex and complete human being felt that the study of lives was worth pursuing, in spite of the professional and intellectual difficulties involved.

I felt a deep sympathy and resonance with what I took to be Murray's stance toward psychology, appreciating the breadth and wealth of human experience; standing against dogma and orthodoxy, against oversimple formulations and the pursuit of trivial problems; moving toward the study of whole persons functioning in their natural environments, toward inquiry of practical utility, and with respect for inner experience as well as objective methods. He inspired me in some way almost every time I talked with him, from our first meeting in 1970 through the next 17 years, until a final visit in December, 1987 about 6 months before his death at age 95.

In retrospect, I've often tried to understand what was so special about Henry Murray. He seemed to me a person of unusual stature, who gave me a sense of what it might have been like to know Freud or Jung. Compared with most contemporary psychologists, he seemed more alive, to have greater depth, greater awareness of inner experience, greater wit and expressiveness, and greater sensitivity to the nuances of social interaction; he opened your eyes to layers of mental and social functioning that you were previously unaware of. His influence on generations of personality psychologists is, I suspect, as much from these personal characteristics as from his publications.

I will return in the next section of this paper to the intellectual structure of personality psychology. These reflections on Murray, though, remind me that a biographical and institutional analysis of the galaxy of characters that constitute the field—ranging from stars to black holes—is also warranted, but that is a task for another occasion.

THE INTELLECTUAL STRUCTURE OF PERSONALITY PSYCHOLOGY

It is very difficult to get a conceptual grasp on the structure of the field of personality psychology, due to the enormous range of things going on within it. What common ground, if any, is there between theories of psychosexual stages, factor analytic studies of questionnaire responses, experimental studies of aggression, assessment and prediction studies, behavior genetics, and psychobiography? How to understand the structure of a field that includes such bewildering diversity?

A first common way of organizing the field of personality psychology is in terms of major theoretical orientations or traditions, such as psychoanalysis, behaviorism or learning theory, trait and psychometric approaches, and humanistic psychology. These are the "Big Four," which are almost always discussed, while other traditions sometimes discussed are culture and personality, behavior genetics and sociobiology, the study of lives, and cognitive approaches to personality. This approach is frequently used in undergraduate personality courses and is adopted in undergraduate texts such as Liebert and Spiegler's *Personality: Strategies and Issues* (1987), Pervin's *Personality: Theory, Assessment, and Research* (1980), or Peterson's *Personality* (1988). A variant of this is a biographical analysis of the work of major theorists in the field, such as found in Hall and Lindzey's *Theories of Personality* (1957, and subsequent editions) or Monte's *Beneath the Mask: An Introduction to Theories of Personality* (1987).

A second way of dividing up the field is in terms of core conceptual issues that cut across theoretical orientations, including topics such as the structure of personality, the dynamics of personality, the development of personality, the assessment of personality, and the change of personality. This strategy was used by Gordon Allport in his foundational text *Personality: A Psychological Interpretation* (1937) and is used in the preface to the 40-plus volumes of the Wiley Series on Personality Processes.

A third way of dividing up the field is in terms of different methodological traditions or techniques. The most influential version of this is probably given by Lee Cronbach in his "The Two Disciplines of Scientific Psychology" (1957), and "Beyond the Two Disciplines of Scientific Psychology" (1975), where he argues that the field of psychology could be seen as developing along an experimental tradition and a quantitative-correlational tradition, which need to be integrated into a more comprehensive interactional tradition examining the interaction of individual differences with responses to experimental and situational conditions. These correlational, experimental, and interactional research designs have all been important in personality psychology, along with longitudinal, cross-cultural, archival, and case study methods. Another approach to conceptualizing the field of personality from a methodological perspective is provided in Kenneth Craik's (1986) analysis of the history of personality psychology in terms of the rise, fall, and resurrection of seven different methodological traditions, which he identifies as biographical/archival, field studies, laboratory methods, naturalistic observational assessment, observer judgments, personality scales and inventories, and projective techniques.

A fourth way of dividing up the field of personality is in terms of empirical research on substantive processes and classes of behavior, with examples such as aggression, sexual behavior, creativity, altruism, anxiety, psychopathology, locus of control, delay of gratification, achievement motivation, stress and coping, and so on. Many textbooks combine a discussion of four or five major theoretical traditions with a number of specific personality processes (e.g., Mischel, 1981; Phares, 1988; Wiggins, Renner, Clore, & Rose, 1976). Textbooks are, of course, also organized according to various combinations of these four principles, such as a discussion of four theories followed by a set of substantive processes; a review of four or five major theoretical orientations, with research and applications discussed under each; the placement of theory, empirical research, and applications in separate sections; and so on.

In this paper I want to propose a fifth way of conceptualizing the structure of personality psychology, one that cuts across the prior conceptual frameworks and that raises intriguing questions about the degree of interrelatedness of the disparate intellectual enterprises that constitute the field. If successful, this framework may bring into view aspects of the structure of the field not previously visible.

The central idea is that the field of personality psychology is concerned with four major tasks or objectives: (1) developing general theories of personality, (2) studying individual and group differences, (3) analyzing specific processes and classes of behavior, and (4) understanding individual persons and lives.

The relationships between these four objectives and the development of each of them over time are outlined in Figure 2.1. Starting with the top row, "General Theory," we can trace the development of a number of the major theoretical programs in personality psychology, beginning with the advent of psychoanalysis around 1900 with the publication of Freud's *Interpretation of Dreams* (1900); behaviorism around 1913 with John B. Watson's "Psychology as the Behaviorist Views It"; culture and personality in the 1930s with Margaret Mead, Ruth Benedict, Edward Sapir, and others; the psychometric approach in the 1940s with the early publications of Hans Eysenck and R. B. Cattell; the humanistic-phenomenological approach with Carl Rogers and Abraham Maslow in the 1950s; cognitive approaches with the work of George Kelley in 1955, but then more extensively with cognitive-experimentalists such as Mischel, Bandura, Cantor, and Kihlstrom; and ending with work in behavior genetics and sociobiology becoming more prominent in the 1970s and 1980s, with Wilson, Arnold Buss, David Buss, and others. It should be emphasized that these historical datings are highly approximate, and for more specific research purposes, they might be dated somewhat differently, but the primary point is to outline the historical emergence of each theoretical tradition and then be able to raise questions about its relations to developments in studies of individual and group differences, of specific processes and classes of behavior, and of individual persons and lives, as represented in the bottom three rows of Figure 2.1.

The second row, that of studying individual and group differences, is represented with a sample of relatively influential programs of this type, such as studies of intelligence by Binet, Terman, Wechsler, Eysenck, Howard Gardner, and others; studies in psychodiagnostic categories by Kraepelin, Karl Menninger, and as found in the *Diagnostic and Statistical Manual* (DSM-I, DSM-III); and studies of personality traits, dimensions, and types, as with studies of extroversion-introversion by Jung and others, Henry Murray's studies of needs, the development of the MMPI, Meehl's analysis of clinical versus statistical prediction, the California Psychological Inventory, the work of Cattell, Eysenck, Block, Cronbach, Wiggins, and others on personality measurement, and recent discussion of the "Big Five" dimensions of personality. The study of group differences according to gender, age, race, social class, culture, and historical period may also be included in this row, but for purposes of simplicity in the diagram I have focused on studies of individual differences.

The third row is concerned with studies of specific processes and classes of behavior, such as a set of phenomena examined in psychoanalysis, including dreams, slips, jokes, and anxiety; the study of phobias by Watson and other late behaviorists; the famous study of "honesty" by Hartshorne and May (1928); the study of frustration and aggression at Yale by Dollard et al. (1939); the study of sexual behavior by Kinsey and colleagues (1948, 1953); the study of anti-Semitism in conjunction with research on the authoritarian personality; the study of achievement motivation by McClelland et al. (1953); studies of creativity at the Institute of Personality Assessment and Research, University of California at Berkeley, by Donald MacKinnon (1978) and others; studies of delay of gratification by Walter Mischel in the 1960s and later (Mischel, 1966); and a variety of other more recent studies of different classes of behavior. The items noted on the chart are obviously only selections from a much larger set.

The fourth and bottom row deals with studies of individual persons and lives, which have been divided into the four subgroups of studies in self-understanding, of clinical patients, of research subjects, and of biographical figures. A few of the items included in the diagram are Freud's famous clinical case studies of Dora, Little Hans, the Rat Man, Dr. Schreber, et al.; Freud's psychobiographical analyses of Leonardo da Vinci, Dostoevsky, and Moses; the study of intelligence in 300 historical geniuses by Catherine Cox (1926) in association with Lewis Terman; the case study of "Earnst" written by Robert White in Henry Murray et al. *Explorations in Personality* (1938); the study of Adolf Hitler by the Office of Strategic Services (OSS) in World War II and many other subsequent psychobiographies; Henry Murray's studies of Herman Melville; the study of three normal lives in *Lives in Progress* (White, 1952); Gordon Allport's analysis in *Letters from Jenny* (1965); the influential edited collection, *Case Studies in Behavior Modification* (Ullmann & Krasner, 1965); Erik Erikson's psychobiographical studies *Young Man Luther* (1958) and *Gandhi's Truth* (1969); a personality research study in *Cocaine Users* (Spotts & Shontz, 1980); case studies in the DSM-III casebook; and psychobiographical studies of Henry James, Joseph Stalin, Emily Dickinson, Vincent Van Gogh, and many others (see Gilmore, 1984; Runyan, 1982, 1988a, 1988b).

Although methodological approaches are not explicitly included in this diagram, it may be noted that different methodological approaches tend to be associated with particular objectives and thus with particular rows in the chart. Most simply, the bottom row, studying individual persons and lives, tends to rely on case study, archival, historical, and interpretive methods; the third row,

FIGURE 2.1 The history of four interrelated types of inquiry in personality psychology.

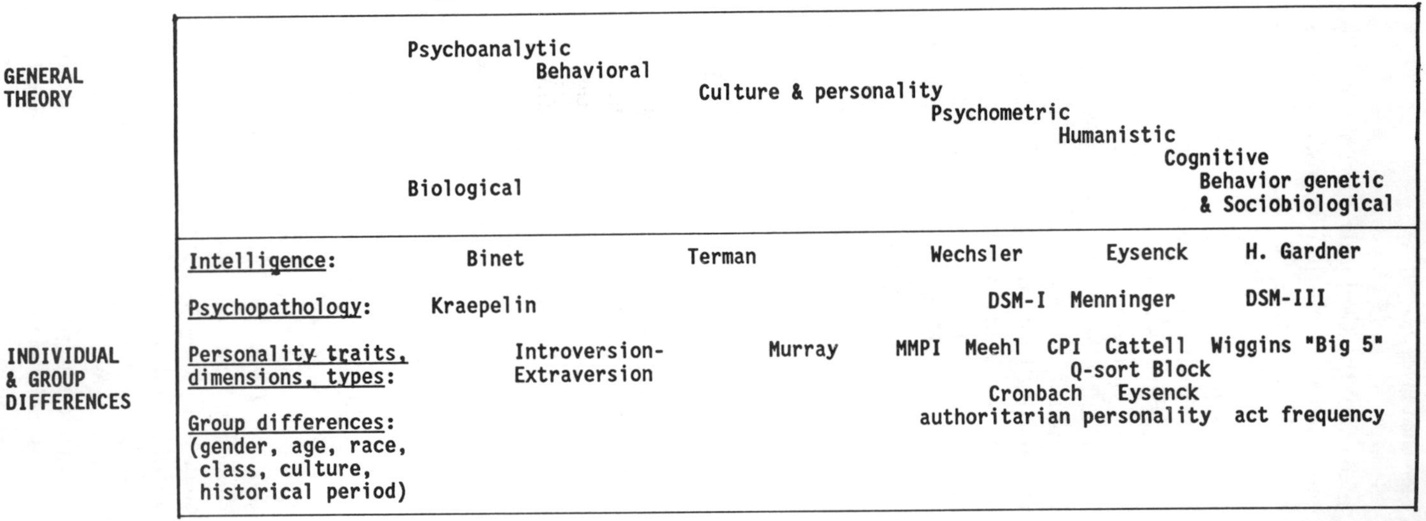

GENERAL THEORY

Psychoanalytic
    Behavioral
        Culture & personality
           Psychometric
             Humanistic
               Cognitive
                 Behavior genetic
                  & Sociobiological

Biological

INDIVIDUAL & GROUP DIFFERENCES

Intelligence: Binet   Terman   Wechsler   Eysenck   H. Gardner

Psychopathology: Kraepelin   DSM-I   Menninger   DSM-III

Personality traits, dimensions, types: Introversion-Extraversion   Murray   MMPI   Meehl   CPI   Cattell   Wiggins "Big 5"   Q-sort   Block   Cronbach   Eysenck   authoritarian personality   act frequency

Group differences: (gender, age, race, class, culture, historical period)

SPECIFIC PROCESSES & CLASSES OF BEHAVIOR	1900	1940	1980
	dreams, slips, jokes, anxiety, phobias, honesty	frustration & aggression, sexual behavior, anti-Semitism, achievement motivation, altruism, creativity, delay of gratification	social cognition, stress & coping, self-monitoring, goal-seeking, drug use, suicide, symptoms

INDIVIDUAL PERSONS AND LIVES

	1900	1940	1980
Self-understanding:			
Clinical patients:	Freud's case studies: Dora, Little Hans, Rat Man, Dr. Schreber, et al.	"Earnst"	Case Studies in Behavior Modification, DSM-III Casebook, Cocaine Users
Research subjects:		Lives in Progress, Letters from Jenny	
Biographical figures:	Leonardo da Vinci, Dostoevsky, Moses; The Early Mental Traits of 300 Geniuses	George III, Melville, Hitler, Wilson, Young Man Luther, Gandhi	H. James, Stalin, E. Dickinson, Van Gogh, etc.

17

studying specific processes and classes of behavior, tends to rely more heavily on experimental methods; the second row, studying individual and group differences, tends to rely more on psychometric, correlational, and factor analytic methods. The top row of general theory may draw on varying combinations of methodological approaches.

This conceptual partitioning of the field of personality psychology into four different objectives or streams of work is useful from a number of different perspectives. First, it makes clear some of the very different kinds of objectives pursued by different investigators. It is across these lines that different individuals and groups in personality psychology sometimes have little interest in, respect for, or even knowledge of one another's research. These differences have led at times to severe criticisms of one another's work, such as experimentalists being unhappy with the relatively grand or untestable claims of general theorists or, conversely, general theorists being uninterested in the more microexperimental studies of specific behaviors or the quantitative measurement of particular dimensions. Some such analysis of the internal lines of division and criticism within the field is necessary for understanding its intellectual and interpersonal structure.

A second issue suggested by this diagram is that of the fascinating epistemological question of the very possibility of knowledge in each of these four enterprises. What kinds of knowledge are and are not possible in each of these four lines of inquiry, from developing general theory down to studying individual lives? The next section of this chapter will focus on the issue of intellectual progress in the study of individual lives, but similar questions may be raised about each of the other levels.

Third, laying out the historical evolution of work within each of these four tasks raises interesting empirical and historical questions about what connections, if any, there are between them over time. What influence has the development of general theory had upon the study of specific individual and group differences, upon specific processes and classes of behavior, or upon the study of individual lives? How, for example, has psychoanalysis as a general theory had an influence upon diagnostic classifications, upon the study of specific classes of behavior such as dreams, jokes, or psychiatric symptoms, or upon the study of individual lives such as Leonardo da Vinci's or Martin Luther's? In turn, what influence has research at each of these three levels had upon the development of psychoanalytic theory? Or, to take an example from the individual and group difference level, how have the diagnostic categories in the current *Diagnostic and Statistical Manual* (DSM-III) been influenced by advances in psychoanalytic theory, behavioral theory, cognitive theory, or biological theory (Millon & Klerman, 1986)? How have diagnostic categories such as schizophrenia or borderline disorders been related to the study of specific symptoms or clusters of symptoms and to the interpretation of individual clinical or historical figures? In short, a whole research agenda is opened up by examining the degree of interconnectedness or not between research within each of these four partially independent streams of work.

At a minimum, this conceptualization of the structure of personality psychology in terms of four distinct tasks or objectives and their relationships to one another is *one* of the useful ways of conceptualizing the structure of the field of personality, along with the previously discussed conceptualizations in terms of theoretical orientations, core conceptual issues, methods, and classes of substantive phenomena. My hunch is that this conceptualization reveals something fundamental about the structure of the field, although I will only begin to be able to argue that in this paper.

APPROPRIATE CRITERIA AND PROCEDURES FOR MAKING PROGRESS IN THE STUDY OF INDIVIDUAL LIVES

It has been argued thus far that the structure of personality psychology can fruitfully be conceptualized in terms of the four different objectives of developing general theory, analyzing individual and group differences, studying specific classes of behavior, and developing an understanding of individual persons. This third section will address the issue of appropriate criteria and procedures for studying individual lives and will examine how "progress" occurs in the study of individual lives and the processes that contribute to it. The fourth and following section will examine in more detail the relationships between progress in the study of individual lives and advances in other areas of personality psychology.

Either explicitly or implicitly, many psychologists have a number of objections to the detailed study of individuals. We have been trained to think about social science in a way that makes the study of individuals seem somehow trivial, irrelevant, or misguided. Typical concerns are that the study of individuals is not rigorous enough, is too subjective, isn't generalizable enough, or isn't sufficiently scientific. A number of investigators have written about methods for conducting more rigorous studies of individuals (e.g., Bromley, 1977, 1986; Chassan, 1979; Horowitz, 1979; Runyan, 1982, 1983), but a prior question is whether it is worth doing at all. This section reviews a number of common objections to the study of individual persons and assesses their persuasiveness.

Perhaps the most widespread criticism of studies of particular lives is that it is difficult to generalize from them. Staub (1980) suggests that "if we *focus* on the uniqueness of every human being, we cannot generalize from one person to another. Since the aim of science is to discover laws or principles—applicable at least to some, if not to all people—what we will learn will not contribute to a science of psychology" (p. 3). Allport's summary of such criticisms is that "we'd have to generalize to other people or else we'd have nothing of any scientific value" (Allport, 1962, p. 406).

These criticisms seem to be based on the unwarranted assumption that the goal of personality psychology is solely to produce generalizations at the highest possible level of abstraction, preferably universal generalizations. As argued earlier, personality psychology needs to attend to at least four different kinds of objectives, ranging from general theory through the study of individual differences and specific classes of behavior to the study of individual persons. Although there is some transfer between these four levels, they are at least partially independent of one another. To the cry of "How can you generalize from that idiographic study?" the equally appropriate response is "How can you particularize from that group or population study?" Work on all four tasks is necessary, and the fact that inquiry at one level does not automatically answer questions at the other levels is not a telling criticism.

A second objection is that interpretations of individual cases are seen as too arbitrary or subjective. For example, "The events of most people's lives are sufficiently variegated and multifarious that virtually any theoretical template can be validated. The case study simply allows the investigator freedom to locate the facts lending support to his or her preformulated convictions" (Gergen, 1977, p. 142). Is interpretation of the single case little more than an arbitrary application of one's theoretical prejudices? It may be possible to interpret any life with any theory, but often only at the cost of distortion or selective presentation of the evidence. Any explanatory conjecture can be made, but not all of them stand up under rigorous cross-examination. Similarly, in legal proceedings, self-serving explanations of the course of events by a guilty defendant often crumble under rigorous cross-examination. This problem of critically evaluating alternative explanations within studies of individual lives is examined in greater detail elsewhere (Crosby, 1979; Runyan, 1981).

A third criticism is that the study of individuals is useful for generating hypotheses but not for testing them. For example, "We can surmise (or, if you will, intuit) general laws from a single case in the hypothesis-forming phase of scientific endeavor, but we can verify them only by resorting to experimental or statistical inquiry or both. . . . As excellent a way as it is to make discoveries, the study of an individual cannot be used to establish laws" (Holt, 1962, pp. 196–197).

This criticism seems to be based on several misunderstandings. First, it assumes that there are only general laws and not laws applying to particular cases (Herbst, 1970). Second, it seems to imply that experimental and statistical inquiry cannot be carried out at the level of the individual case. It is true that universal laws usually cannot be established through the study of a particular individual, but laws of the individual can be formulated and tested through rigorous experimental and statistical methods at the level of the individual (e.g., Chassan, 1979; Hersen & Barlow, 1976).

A fourth objection is that it is not only impractical but also literally impossible to conduct an idiographic study of every individual. If individuals are largely dissimilar, then "every sparrow would have to be separately identified, named and intuitively understood" (Murray, 1938, p. 715). If all individuals are unique, then it would be necessary to formulate "as many theories as there are persons in the universe" (Levy, 1970, p. 76). This criticism raises an important question about the costs and benefits of detailed studies of individuals. Granted that there are not sufficient resources for studying every individual in the universe, it is still entirely feasible to conduct detailed idiographic studies of individuals of particular interest to us, including historical figures such as Adolf Hitler, Sigmund Freud, or Virginia Woolf, particular clinical patients, or other individuals of interest. We don't have the time and money to study all individuals, but neither do we have the resources to test all possible theories. It is necessary to be selective, both in theoretical inquiries and in studies of specific individuals.

A fifth objection, and the final one to be discussed here, is that there is nothing wrong with the idiographic study of individuals, but it is not science. Levy (1970), for example, argues that the meaning of data about individual cases "can only be found within the context of laws that hold for all individuals. . . . It is not possible to go beyond this and remain within the confines of science" (p. 76). Nunnally (1978) states that "the idiographists may be entirely correct, but if they are, it is a sad day for psychology. Idiography is an antiscience point of view: it discourages the search for general laws and instead encourages the description of particular phenomena (people)" (p. 548).

Is there some genuine conflict or contradiction between the study of individual persons and the scientific endeavor? Is the study of individual persons more properly the concern of the novelist, the biographer, the historian, or perhaps the clinician? It is undeniably true that historians and biographers are concerned with the description and interpretation of individual lives. There are, however, many tasks of generalizing about, systematically describing and measuring, explaining, predicting, and attempting to change the course of individual lives that seem properly to fall within the domain of the social and behavioral sciences. If the thrust of this criticism is that it is impossible to apply systematic, reliable, quantitative, or experimental methods to the study of individual cases, this criticism has been refuted by the proliferation of quantitative and experimental studies of the single case (e.g., Davidson & Costello, 1969; Hersen & Barlow, 1976; Kratochwill, 1978).

The suggestion that science as a whole is not concerned with the study of particulars is clearly untenable, as this criterion would rule out significant portions of geology, astronomy and cosmology, and evolutionary biology. These sciences are concerned not solely with general principles and processes but also with topics, such as, respectively, the structure and evolution of this particular earth, the structure and origins of our solar system, and the particular sequence of species leading to the evolution of man.

A Note on Criteria and Methods

One of the more problematic issues in the study of individual lives within psychology has been the question of appropriate criteria and methods for assessing the adequacy of studies of individual lives. Far too frequently, work in this area is judged on criteria or standards derived from other domains, such as a psychometric criterion of "reliability" or an experimental criterion of efficacy in ruling out alternative causal explanations.

The application of inappropriate evaluative criteria has had damaging consequences in several ways, both in leading to disparagement of the study of individual lives and to its neglect in favor of larger-scale quantitative and experimental studies, and in a failure to develop and apply those criteria and procedures that can lead to meaningful improvements in the study of individuals. Progress in the study of lives requires the use of evaluative criteria that are relevant to its primary functions of presenting, organizing, and interpreting information about the course of experience in a single life. It is essential to move away from the attitude that case studies of individual lives can be used to prove anything or can be interpreted just as effectively with one theory as any other, and to move instead toward appropriately rigorous standards and criteria for the study of individual cases (cf. Meehl, 1973). A valuable development along these lines is the quasi-judicial approach (Bromley, 1977, 1986) in which evidence, inferences, and arguments are subjected to critical assessment by those holding opposing points of view. Rigorous use of the case study method requires that studies of individuals be assessed not only on the internal criteria of coherence and interest but also on the external criteria of correspondence with the full range of available facts, with their ability to stand up under tests of attempted falsification, and plausibility when weighed against alternative accounts and interpretations.

According to Bromley (1977), "A psychological, 'case-study' is a scientific account, in ordinary language, of an individual person in normal or problematic circumstances" (p. 163) and "is essentially a reconstruction and interpretation, based on the best evidence available, of part of the story of a person's life" (p. 164). A case study is undertaken in response to a problem in understanding and/or a problem requiring practical action and usually focuses on a small number of issues, which determine the relevance of the evidence and arguments to be considered. It is impossible for a case study to tell the whole story of a person's life and circumstances, because the whole story is overwhelmingly complex and detailed. Rather, a more appropriate goal is to tell the story in such a way that the omitted information makes little or no difference in understanding the main structure of the events and arguments in question.

A central feature of Bromley's argument is that the preparation of case studies follows a quasi-judicial procedure. A case study presents a theory about how and why a person behaved as he or she did in particular circumstances, and this theory needs to be tested by collecting evidence and formulating arguments relevant to the claims put forward in the theory. This quasi-judicial method is based on methods evolved in law for ascertaining truth and conducting fair trials and requires that evidence, inferences, and arguments be critically examined by those with conflicting points of view.

The judicial analogy seems apt in that it suggests that alternative parties engaged in interpretation may have competing interests (whether legal, theoretical, or practical interests) that often seem relevant to understanding debates surrounding particular cases, whether in courts of law, historical-political controversies, or scientific debates. For example, Freud's case of the Wolf Man was written partly in order to further his side of the argument with Adler and Jung about the importance of childhood sexual disturbance in adult neurosis. Or, Wolpe and Rachman's (1960) critique of Freud's Little Hans case was written in order to criticize the evidential foundations of psychoanalytic interpretation, as well as to argue for the superiority of learning theory formulations. Such competing theoretical interests often seem to lie behind and to motivate the collection of evidence, the drawing of inferences and conclusions, and the critical analysis of alternative formulations of individual cases in clinical and scientific work.

The quasi-judicial construal of case studies, which considers both the logical-empirical and social-political aspects of the process of formulating and critically evaluating case studies, also seems appropriate from contemporary philosophy of science perspectives, which suggest that science cannot be understood solely through rational reconstruction of its logical procedures (e.g., Hempel, 1965; Nagel, 1961) or primarily as a social phenomenon (Kuhn, 1970), but rather must be seen as a joint interplay of both logical-empirical and social-political considerations (Suppe, 1977).

Progress in Psychobiographic Inquiry

A useful way of looking at methodological and epistemological problems in the study of individual lives is to consider the extent to which such research programs are "progressive" or not. What constitutes progress in our knowledge and understanding of an individual life? To the extent that progress occurs, what processes bring it about? And finally, how do advances in other areas of personality psychology relate to progress in the study of individual lives?

For example, what progress, if any, has there been in our psychological understanding of Adolf Hitler during the course of research on his life, from the OSS study in World War II (Langer, 1972) through Alan Bullock's classic biography in 1952 through Robert Waite's *The Psychopathic God: Adolf Hitler* (1977)? What progress, if any, has there been in our knowledge and understanding of Sigmund Freud, from an early biography by Wittels (1924) through Ernest Jones's standard three-volume biography (1953–1957) through more recent studies by Roazen (1975), Sulloway (1979), Gay (1988), and others? Finally, in the clinical realm, what advances, if any, have there been in our knowledge and understanding of Freud's classic case studies of Little Hans, the Wolf Man, the Rat Man, Dora, and others through decades of reanalysis and reinterpretation (e.g., Bernheimer & Kahane, 1985; Ellenberger, 1970; Gardiner, 1971; Kanzer & Glenn, 1980; Obholzer, 1982; Sherwood, 1969)?

Conceptualizing Progress in Biography

To respond to questions about whether certain sequences of life history studies are progressive or not requires a clarification and definition of the concept of progress. The literature on the concept of progress is surprisingly extensive, from studies of the history of the idea of progress, to analyses of progress in physics, biology, the social sciences, history, and other disciplines, to progress in technology and material benefits, to economic progress, to progress in morals, and, finally, to progress in human welfare as a whole (cf., Almond, Chodorow, & Pearce, 1982; Laudan, 1977; Munz, 1985; Nisbet, 1980).

Underlying these many uses of the concept of progress, the idea may be defined most simply as change over time in a direction perceived as desirable or preferable. Thus it involves a temporal or historical component and a valuative component. A third possible component of the idea of progress, which is sometimes but not necessarily implied, is that of progress as *inevitable*. Let me make clear that I am *not* claiming that a sequence of biographical studies is necessarily progressive. Some are, and some aren't. Rather, the concept of progress is introduced as a way of addressing epistemological issues in the study of lives, as a way of comparing life history studies not to some absolute standard of truth, which can be impossibly difficult to specify, but rather to prior studies in terms of a variety of specifiable criteria.

Consider, for example, the case of Lincoln biography. Lincoln's death was followed by a stream of idealized and hero-worshiping biographies. One of the first realistic biographies was published by Herndon and Weik in 1889. It dealt with issues such as Lincoln's uncertain ancestry, the development of his character, and his changing religious beliefs. Was this progress or not? A review in the *Chicago Evening Tribune* in 1889 said of the book, "It vilely distorts the image of an ideal statesman, patriot, and martyr. It clothes him in vulgarity and grossness. . . . It brings out all that should have been hidden. . . . It is not fit for family reading. . . . In all its parts and aspects—if we are a judge, and we think we are, of the proprieties of literature and human life—we declare that this book is so bad, it could hardly have been worse."

Clearly, from their perspective, the book was not an improvement over the earlier hero-worshipping biographies. The point? "Progress" always has to be assessed in reference to a particular frame of reference, to particular valuative criteria. Thus the same work may be judged as progressive in light of one set of criteria, such as historical realism, and regressive in light of other criteria, such as religious or moral purity.

Furthermore, the same work may be progressive in some aspects and regressive in others. Lytton Strachey's influential *Eminent Victorians*, published in 1918, was an advance in terms of criteria such as selectivity, wit, and debunking, but regressive in terms of historical accuracy and compassion in its portraits of Florence Nightingale, Matthew Arnold, and other Victorian heroes. In short, the same work may be seen as progressive or regressive in terms of different criteria and may also be progressive in some aspects but regressive in others.

How then should we look at progress in our knowledge and understanding of individual lives? It seems to me that progress in psychobiographical studies can be meaningfully assessed in terms of criteria such as (1) the comprehensiveness of the evidential base, (2) the insightfulness and persuasiveness of interpretation, and (3) the literary or aesthetic appeal of the narrative account. This paper focuses on the first two of these criteria, the quality of evidence and of interpretation; other works have focused on literary appeal (Novarr, 1986; Petrie, 1981). Advances in understanding can occur through a variety of processes, such as collecting additional evidence, developing more powerful background theory and research to draw on, proposing and testing new interpretations, and so on.

The processes involved in advancing our knowledge and understanding of individual lives can, for the sake of simplicity, be divided into eight steps or components, as in Figure 2.2. This set of processes is related to the specific criteria I am proposing. Other criteria of progress, such as moral rectitude, metaphoric expressiveness, or political correctness, would suggest a somewhat different set of processes.

The components in Figure 2.2 have been numbered from 1 to 8 for purposes of identification rather than to identify any rigidly fixed sequence of steps. The top left-hand box, which is labeled "Evidence and Processes of Data Collection," includes things such as finding additional letters or diaries, conducting further interviews, or finding additional archival records or physical evidence. In research on Hitler, for example, this would include material such as *Mein Kampf*, interviews with and documents by those who knew him, the discovery of his burned corpse, records of his personal physician, and the alleged discovery of previously unknown "Hitler diaries." The second step is the critical examination of evidence and sources, including activities such as detecting forgeries or falsifications in the evidential base and learning how much weight to give to the testimony of different witnesses. In the case of Hitler research, dental records supported the claim that the partly burned body found by Russian soldiers outside the Fuhrer's air raid shelter in Berlin was that of Hitler (Waite, 1977), while a study of the paper used in the alleged Hitler diaries revealed that it was produced after his death.

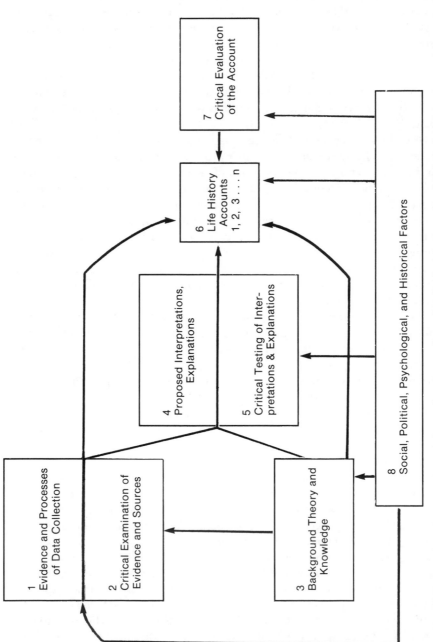

FIGURE 2.2 Advances in our knowledge and understanding of individual lives: a simplified model of component processes.

The third component is background theory and knowledge, which is drawn upon in interpreting the individual case and would include theories of personality development, an understanding of the relevant cultural and historical background, and knowledge of relevant medical conditions and biological processes. In particular, this background theory and knowledge would include advances in all other areas of personality, such as general theories of personality, research on individual and group differences, and studies of specific processes and classes of behavior. The fourth step is the generation of new interpretations and explanations of the individual case, while the fifth step is the critical evaluation and attempted falsification of proposed interpretations (cf. Runyan, 1981).

The sixth component is the production of a narrative account of the life, which incorporates a number of specific interpretations and explanations, organizes a substantial amount of data about the life, and draws on theoretical and background knowledge. The numbered subscripts indicate a whole sequence of accounts that might be produced about the same life, such as a biography of Hitler produced in 1944, one in 1952, and another in 1977. All of the preceding five processes used in constructing the account can be repeated in an iterative cycle.

The seventh step is the critical evaluation of the narrative account, as in the form of a book review for a biography or a case conference for a clinical presentation, considering factors such as the adequacy of the evidence, the appropriateness of the background theory, and the credibility of the proposed interpretations. The eighth and final component is social, political, psychological, and historical factors, which influence each of the other processes. They influence what data are collected and seen as relevant and how critically they are scrutinized. These factors influence the kinds of background theory and knowledge that are drawn upon, the interpretations that are proposed and how critically they are evaluated, the shape and structure of the finished narrative account, and the critical reception that the finished work receives. As one example of such political and social influences upon the course of biographical interpretation, King George III's political supporters argued for a physical interpretation of his symptoms, suggesting that they were temporary, while his political opponents argued for an interpretation in terms of a mental disturbance that might well be permanent and make him unfit to rule.

The impetus for a new psychobiographical study can come from developments in any one of the eight components in Figure 2.2, such as the discovery of new sources of evidence, advances in theoretical knowledge that make possible the interpretation of previously inexplicable events, or the critique and dismissal of earlier interpretations and the proposal of new ones. The next section will examine how developments in different areas of personality theory and research have been utilized in advancing our understanding of individual lives.

RELATIONSHIP BETWEEN THE STUDY OF LIVES
AND OTHER AREAS OF PERSONALITY PSYCHOLOGY

What relations are there between progress in the psychological analysis of individual lives and advances in other branches of personality psychology? What relations, if any, are there between progress in the study of individual lives and progress in general personality theory, research on individual and group differences, or research on specific processes and classes of behavior? In terms of Figure 2.1, this is equivalent to asking what connections there are between the study of individual persons in row 4 with developments in the top three rows.

Studies of individual lives can have implications for inquiry at each of the other three lives. Methodology texts often state that the study of single cases can provide hypotheses, which then need to be tested with quantitative or experimental methods (as in Figure 1, rows 2 and 3). Or, general theories of personality can be influenced by their personal or subjective origins in the lives of individual personality theorists, as Stolorow and Atwood (1979) have argued is true in the work of Sigmund Freud, Carl Jung, Wilhelm Reich, and Otto Rank. Or, Abraham Maslow has reported that his ideas about self-actualization came initially from reflections about the similarities of two of his mentors, Max Werthmeier and Ruth Benedict (Maslow, 1971). Or, Rae Carlson (1988) has discussed how psychobiographical research can contribute to the development of general theories of personality.

Unquestionably, the study of individual lives influences other lines of research in personality, but for the present discussion, I will focus on influences going in the other direction, or on the ways in which progress in the study of individual lives has been influenced by advances in other areas of personality psychology. Most simply: How is the course of research on individual lives influenced by advances in general theories of personality, by studies of individual and group differences, and/or by research on specific processes and classes of behavior?

In terms of Figure 2.2 on processes contributing to progress in the study of lives, all of these developments in personality theory and research would be channeled through the third component, "Background Theory and Knowledge." This background theory and knowledge would include developments in all other areas of personality psychology and would not, of course, be restricted to advances in personality psychology, and would also include advances in other areas of psychology and contributions from other disciplines such as history, sociology, anthropology, political science, and biology.

The contributions of other areas of personality psychology to the study of lives will be reviewed under four different headings: (1) influences of general personality theory upon the study of lives, including psychoanalytic, neo-analytic, and nonanalytic theories of personality; (2) influences of research on individual and group differences upon the study of lives, such as research on intelligence or categories of psychopathology; (3) influences of research on specific processes and classes of behavior, such as altruistic behavior; and (4) influences of all different kinds of personality theory and research as they are funneled into the study of a single life, such as that of Adolf Hitler.

First, what influences have there been from advances in general theories of personality upon psychobiography and the study of individual lives? The first and most extensive influence upon the study of individual lives is certainly from psychoanalysis, beginning with Freud and his Viennese followers, spreading out through Europe and the United States, and taking another step forward with Erik Erikson's work in *Young Man Luther* (1958) and *Gandhi's Truth* (1969). Recent discussion and reviews of the influence of psychoanalytic theory upon biography and psychobiography are contained in Edel (1984), Mack (1971), and Moraitis and Pollock (1987).

Within psychoanalysis, the influence of different schools or traditions of psychoanalytic theory upon biography and psychobiography can be analyzed in more detail, such as moving from traditional Freudian drive theories to ego psychology, object relations theory, and self-psychology. Developments in ego psychology and object relations theory approaches to psychobiography are reviewed by Loewenberg (1988), who uses examples such as Richard Nixon and Adolf Hitler to illustrate how changing theoretical frameworks within psychoanalysis have led to revised interpretations of the same historical figures. On the applications of self-psychology, Strozier (1985) covers applications of Kohutian self-psychology to biography and history, and Strozier and Offer (1985) examine a number of applications of self-psychology to political leaders such as Abraham Lincoln, Woodrow Wilson, Kaiser Wilhelm II, and Mahatma Gandhi. At a clinical level, the implications of changes in psychoanalytic theory for the reinterpretation of Freud's case studies of Dora, Little Hans, the Rat Man, the Schreber Case, and the Wolf Man are explored in a volume edited by Kanzer and Glenn (1980).

What, though, about the uses of personality theories other than psychoanalysis in psychobiography? In principle, any theory of personality could be drawn on in interpreting an individual life history, so psychoanalytic psychobiography could be supplemented with behavioral psychobiography, phenomenological-humanistic psychobiography, cognitive psychobiography, and so on. What, though, has actually been done in using these other theoretical frameworks in psychobiography?

Perhaps the most extensively developed behavioral interpretation of a life is found in the three volumes of B. F. Skinner's autobiography (1976, 1979, 1983), in which he attempts to describe his own life in terms of changes in the external environment and their effect on his overt behavior, without reference to inner experiences or feelings. One rare attempt to apply social learning theory in a book-length psychobiography is a study of Elizabeth Cady Stanton in terms of Bandura's social learning theory (Griffith, 1984). In the clinical realm, a far greater number of individual cases have been interpreted in terms of behavioral or learning theory (e.g., Turkat, 1985; Ullmann & Krasner, 1965; Wolpe & Rachman, 1960).

Uses of phenomenological-humanistic personality theory may also occasionally be found, such as Carl Rogers's reinterpretation of the case of Ellen West (1980), who suffered from anorexia nervosa and eventually committed suicide, or a study of Clarence Darrow in terms of Charlotte Buhler's theory of stages of goal seeking (Horner, 1968), or Sartre's use of existential theory as well as psychoanalysis in his study of Flaubert (1981).

The uses of alternative theoretical perspectives in the study of lives are also indicated in a recent special issue of the *Journal of Personality* titled "Psychobiography and Life Narratives" (McAdams & Ochberg, 1988), which illustrates the application of Silvan Tomkins's script theory to the lives of Nathaniel Hawthorne and Eleanor Marx (Carlson, 1988) and to the analysis of personal documents and clinical material (Alexander, 1988); the quantitative analysis of Eriksonian themes of identity, intimacy, and generativity in the writings of Vera Brittain (Stewart, Franz, & Layton, 1988); and a study of achievement, affiliation, and power motives in Richard Nixon (Winter & Carlson, 1988). In spite of the growing number of applications of other personality theories in psychobiography, it still seems fair to say that far more psychobiographical studies have been influenced by some version of psychodynamic theory than by any other personality theory, or even by all the others in combination. Elsewhere I have speculated on different possible explanations for the relative contributions of psychoanalytic and nonanalytic theory in psychobiography (Runyan, 1988b).

Moving down to the second row of Figure 2.1, what developments in the study of individual and group differences have been used in advancing our understanding of individual lives? To mention just a few examples, let us start with the example of intelligence. Lewis Terman began trying to estimate the IQs of historical figures such as Francis Galton (Terman, 1917), and Terman's student, Catherine Cox, with the help of a grant obtained by Terman from the Commonwealth Fund, estimated the childhood IQs of 300 famous men and women in *The Early Mental Traits of Three Hundred Geniuses* (1926). For example, on IQ ratings for recorded behavior up to age 17, the estimate for John Stuart Mill was 190; for Goethe, 185; Pascal, 180; Voltaire, 170; David Hume, 155; Descartes, 150; Thomas Jefferson, 145; and Napoleon, 135. Cox and Terman are explicit that these estimates are only for early *recorded* behavior and may or may not accurately reflect the individual's actual IQ. I am not trying to vouch for the adequacy of these analyses but rather to indicate how advances in the study of individual differences (in this case, IQ) were used in the study of particular historical figures. Terman points out how biographers' ignorance of age norms in the development of intelligence led them to misinterpret the behavior of their subjects. For example, Karl Pearson's biography of Francis Galton reports data on Galton's childhood performance and then says that they give no significant indication of his future genius, whereas Terman assesses the same material and says it indicates a childhood IQ of nearly 200.

Staying at the level of individual differences, consider the implications of advances in psychodiagnostic categories for our understanding of individual lives. George III, king of England during the American Revolution and from 1760 to 1820, suffered from a perplexing combination of physical and psychological disorders periodically throughout his later life, including symptoms such as delirium, excitement, sleeplessness, painful weakness of the arms and legs, visual and auditory disturbances, delusions, and agitated talking and hyperactivity. How is such a puzzling array of symptoms to be explained? To simplify, the history of different explanations of the king's disorders can be roughly divided into five stages: (1) contemporaneous explanations, which fell back on the theory of an imbalance between the four humors of black bile, yellow bile, phlegm, and choler; (2) classification according to nineteenth-century descriptive psychiatry, in which he was diagnosed as having "ordinary acute mania"; (3) a psychodynamic explanation in 1941, in which his breakdowns were understood as breakdowns of his vulnerable defenses under the pressure of stressful political and domestic events; (4) explanations in the 1960s in terms of the metabolic disease porphyria, which leads to physical and psychological disorders similar to those of George III; and (5) finally, criticisms of the porphyria hypothesis, in that the genetic evidence seems inconsistent with it, and a search for alternative explanations, with lead poisoning being one possibility consistent with both George III's symptoms and with the genetic evidence. Details of these symptoms and the changing classifications and diagnostic assessments of the king's disorders are presented elsewhere (Runyan, 1988a), but the point for present purposes is to show how understanding of an individual case is dependent upon changing background knowledge in the form of available diagnostic systems and categories. As new diagnostic categories emerge, such as borderline disorders or narcissistic disorders, they are then applied to a host of historical and clinical cases, such as Adolf Hitler, Thomas Wolfe, or Pablo Picasso.

Moving down to the third row of Figure 2.1, how has research on specific processes and classes of behavior affected our knowledge and understanding of individual lives? What contributions to biographical and case study analyses have been made through research on such classes of behavior as specific psychiatric symptoms, sexual behavior, anti-Semitism, creativity, obedience to authority, bystander intervention, altruism, stress and coping, drug use, or suicide? To mention one example, Samuel and Pearl Oliner in *The Altruistic Personality: Rescuers of Jews in Nazi Europe* (1988) draw on the extant literature on altruism, pro-social behavior, moral reasoning, interpersonal attachment, and empathy in their study of more than 400 rescuers of Jews in Nazi-occupied Europe.

As a second example, consider that Woodrow Wilson did not learn his letters until age 9 and could not read until he was 11. Alexander and Juliette George (1956/1964) originally suggested that as a boy Wilson was filled with rage at his demanding and perfectionistic father, which he could not openly acknowledge or express, and that this failure to learn was motivated by unconscious resentment at his father. In response, Weinstein, Anderson, and Link (1978) argued that Wilson's delay in reading was not due to emotional difficulties but to developmental dyslexia, which is caused by a delay in the establishment of dominance of one hemisphere, usually the left, for language.

In rebuttal, the Georges (1981-1982) drew on details of recent research on this class of behavior, dyslexia. In particular, they argued that it is not established that the absence of cerebral dominance is responsible for dyslexia, that many specialists continue to believe that emotional factors are responsible for some reading disorders, and that details of Wilson's life—such as the amount of his reading, the neatness of his handwriting, and his excellent spelling—are all inconsistent with a diagnosis of developmental dyslexia. In this debate they draw on a specialized body of psychological theory and research on a particular class of behavior in order to critique an alternative explanation and to argue that the bulk of the evidence is consistent with their original interpretation. (This debate is not yet finished and has continued in subsequent years, with references cited in Link et al., 1986.)

Adolf Hitler

Thus far I've indicated how advances in the areas of general theory, the study of individual differences, and research on specific processes and classes of behavior have been used in the study of individual lives. The array of uses of other areas of personality psychology in the study of lives can also be illustrated from the bottom up, as it were, by examining the course of research on a specific life and seeing how it has been affected by theory and research from different areas of personality psychology. The individual life can be used as a lens with which one can view the range of uses of psychology. This array of uses of psychological theory and research will be illustrated with the psycho-biographical study *The Psychopathic God: Adolf Hitler* (1977) by Robert Waite.

At the level of general theory, Waite draws most heavily on psychoanalytic theory, with discussions of the anal stage in Hitler's development (pp. 148-149), of a "primal scene trauma" and its consequences (pp. 162-168), of Hitler's Oedipus complex (pp. 162-165), and of the operation of defense mechanisms such as displacement and projection in his anti-Semitism (p. 190). Waite also draws on the psychosocial theory of Erik Erikson in discussions of trust and mistrust in Hitler's childhood, with pervasive feelings of mistrust remaining consequential throughout his life (pp. 383–386), and in discussions of identity development and identity crisis in Hitler's adolescence and early adulthood (pp. 184–205).

At the level of individual and group differences, research on a number of groups that Hitler could be classed with was drawn upon in interpreting his life, such as borderline personalities, monorchids (males with one testicle), anal characters, and anti-Semites. For example, on the basis of Soviet autopsy reports on Hitler's partially burned body, Waite believes there is convincing evidence that Hitler's left testicle was missing. Hitler also had a wide variety of psychological characteristics that match those of studies of other patients with this characteristic, such as feelings of social inadequacy, concerns with bowel movements and feces, belief in themselves as special persons, and passive tendencies, with a reaction formation against them in an insistence on hardness, toughness, and ruthlessness. Another study suggests that monorchid patients often have an intense concern with redesigning and reconstructing buildings, as if to quell anxieties about defects in their own bodies, which is consistent with Hitler's preoccupation with designing and redesigning elaborate architectural plans for Linz, Vienna, and Berlin (pp. 150–162).

Hitler's psychodiagnostic and medical classification has been a subject of extensive debate, and Waite reviews at least six different diagnostic possibilities, including Parkinson's disease with psychiatric side effects, medical poisoning (from an incompetent physician), rapidly progressive coronary arteriosclerosis, syphilis, damage to his left cerebral hemisphere, and borderline personality (pp. 349–359). Waite finds the last of these diagnoses most persuasive, as it best fits many (though not all) of Hitler's behavior patterns.

At the level of research on specific classes of behavior and experience, Waite draws on studies in areas such as anti-Semitism (pp. 359–373); survivor guilt (which Hitler felt over the death of his brother; pp. 171–172), sexual perversion (Waite argues that Hitler had women urinate or defecate on his head; pp. 237–243), masochistic or self-destructive behavior (which Waite argues was partially responsible for some of Hitler's disastrous military decisions such as the invasion of the Soviet Union or declaring war on the United States; pp. 391–411), and, finally, research on suicide in attempting to understand Hitler's end (pp. 411–426).

This discussion is not an exhaustive analysis of Waite's use of psychology in interpreting Hitler, but it does illustrate how our understanding of an individual life can be informed by theory and research at the three levels of general theories of personality, studies of individual and group differences, and research on specific processes and classes of behavior. An intriguing question for future inquiry is what additional advances in personality and other branches of psychology could be drawn upon to further illuminate Hitler's behavior and career.

CONCLUSION

To summarize, this chapter argued that the structure of personality psychology can usefully be seen as involving four central tasks or objectives, namely, developing general theories of personality, analyzing individual and group differences, studying specific classes of behavior, and developing a better understanding of individual persons.

I then briefly reviewed and responded to several common criticisms of the study of individual lives and sketched the dynamics of "progress" in the study of individual lives and the processes that contribute to it. The last section explored relationships between the study of lives and other lines of work within personality psychology. A whole universe swings into view when one begins to consider the multidirectional relationships between progress in our understanding of individual lives and advances in each of the other forms of psychological inquiry.

The study of lives was one of the central concerns and motivating agendas for early founders of personality psychology, such as Gordon Allport, Henry Murray, or Sigmund Freud, but was then lost track of in the 1950s and 1960s (with some exceptions, as in the work of Robert White or Erik Erikson), as far greater attention was given to psychometric concerns and the experimental study of particular processes. These are important programs of research, but it is a deadly loss for the field if the study of lives is lost sight of, or is totally crowded out by these other interests.

The study of individual persons is one of the important tasks of psychology in general and of personality psychology in particular. There are encouraging signs that the study of lives is emerging again as an important line of research within personality psychology (e.g., Anderson, 1981; Bromley, 1986; Craik, 1986; Elms, 1988; McAdams, 1985, 1987; Runyan, 1982, 1988a, 1988b).

This new spirit is well represented in a recent special issue of the *Journal of Personality* (March 1988) entitled "Psychobiography and Life Narratives" and edited by Dan McAdams and Richard Ochberg. As stated in the introduction, "Today, personality psychologists seem less ashamed than they did 20 years ago to admit that the subject of their study is human lives. . . . Once again, it is okay to study the 'whole person.' Better, contemporary personologists insist, as did pioneers like Gordon Allport and Henry Murray, that such an endeavor is the personologist's *raison d'être*" (McAdams & Ochberg, 1988, p. 1). The volume effectively represents a sample of the current interests of personality psychologists in the study of lives, including papers by Dan McAdams overviewing the field; Alan Elms analyzing why Freud's study of Leonardo went wrong; Abigail Stewart, Carol Franz, and Lynn Layton applying quantitative measures of Eriksonian stages to the writings of Vera Brittain; David Winter and Leslie Carlson using motive scores in the study of Richard Nixon; Rae Carlson using Silvan Tomkins's script theory in analyzing the lives of Eleanor Marx and Nathaniel

Hawthorne; James Anderson conducting an original psychobiographical study of Henry Murray; Richard Ochberg analyzing the narratives that middle-aged businessmen tell about their careers; Jacquelyn Wiersma digging beneath the stereotyped stories that women tell about their career changes; George Rosenwald arguing for the values of multiple-case research in revealing shared social conditions; Irving Alexander outlining methods for analyzing personal data in psychobiography and in personality assessment; and William Runyan reviewing intellectual and historical progress in psychobiography.

My aspiration in this paper has been to help clarify relationships between the study of lives and other programs of inquiry in personality psychology. It can be useful in each of our own lines of research, whether psychometric, experimental, theoretical, or life-historical, to have a clearer vision of the overall structure of the field and of the relationship of these different enterprises to one another.

There are important contributions from each of these four enterprises but also real limitations in the extent and possibilities of knowledge within each. If pushed far enough, there are limitations to how theoretical-nomothetic one can get, as group and historical differences in phenomena start to emerge. There are limitations in how causal and experimental one can get, as chains of causal influence are soon swallowed up in mists of historical indeterminacy. There are even limitations in how quantitative one can get, as there is a finite population of persons and other entities to study and historical or evolutionary changes occur in every relationship we examine (Runyan, 1988b). And finally, there are limitations from economic, ethical, and theoretical sources in how far we can go in knowing and understanding an individual life. As each form of inquiry pushes against the boundaries of its possibilities and begins fading into uncertainty, its limitations can sometimes be supplemented by contributions from the others. In the long run, it may be possible to fit the potentials and limitations of each of these programs of inquiry into a larger and more comprehensive understanding of the field of personality psychology. For the present, we would do well to renew the integrative breadth and vision advocated by founding parents of the field such as Murray and Allport.

Quantitative, causal-experimental, theoretical, and historical-interpretive forms of inquiry are all necessary parts of the whole. The study of individual lives is, at a minimum, one of the legitimate programs of research in psychology and, in collaborative tension with other approaches, a vital part of the structure of personality psychology.

REFERENCES

Alexander, I. E. (1988). Personality, psychological assessment, and psychobiography. *Journal of Personality*, 56, 265–294.

Allport, G. W. (1937). *Personality: A psychological interpretation.* New York: Holt.

Allport, G. W. (1962). The general and the unique in psychological science. *Journal of Personality, 30,* 405–422.

Allport, G. W. (1965). *Letters from Jenny.* New York: Harcourt, Brace & World.

Almond, G., Chodorow, M., & Pearce, R. (Eds.). (1982). *Progress and its discontents.* Berkeley: University of California Press.

Anderson, J. W. (1981). Psychobiographical methodology: The case of William James. In L. Wheeler (Ed.), *Review of personality and social psychology* (Vol. 2, pp. 245–272). Beverly Hills, CA: Sage.

Aronoff, J., Rabin, A. I., & Zucker, R. A. (Eds.). (1987). *The emergence of personality.* New York: Springer.

Bernheimer, C., & Kahane, C. (Eds.). (1985). *In Dora's case: Freud-hysteria-feminism.* New York: Columbia University Press.

Block, J. (1977). Advancing the psychology of personality: Paradigmatic shift or improving the quality of research? In D. Magnusson & N. S. Endler (Eds.), *Personality at the crossroads: Current issues in interactional psychology.* Hillsdale, NJ: Lawrence Erlbaum Associates.

Bromley, D. B. (1977). *Personality description in ordinary language.* New York: Wiley.

Bromley, D. B. (1986). *The case-study method in psychology and related disciplines.* Chichester: Wiley.

Cantor, N., & Kihlstrom, J. F. (1987). *Personality and social intelligence.* Englewood Cliffs, NJ: Prentice-Hall.

Carlson, R. (1988). Exemplary lives: The uses of psychobiography for theory development. *Journal of Personality, 56,* 105–138.

Chassan, J. B. (1979). *Research design in clinical psychology and psychiatry* (2nd ed.). New York: Irvington.

Cox, C. (1926). *The early mental traits of three hundred geniuses.* Stanford, CA: Stanford University Press.

Craik, K. H. (1986). Personality research methods: An historical perspective. *Journal of Personality, 54,* 18–51.

Cronbach, L. J. (1957). The two disciplines of scientific psychology. *American Psychologist, 12,* 671–684.

Cronbach, L. J. (1975). Beyond the two disciplines of scientific psychology. *American Psychologist, 30,* 116–127.

Crosby, F. (1979). Evaluating psychohistorical explanations. *Psychohistory Review, 7,* 6–16.

Davidson, P. O., & Costello, C. G. (Eds.). (1969). *N = 1: Experimental studies of single cases.* New York: Van Nostrand Reinhold.

Dollard, J., Doob, L. W., Miller, N. E., Mowrer, O. H., & Sears, R. R. (1939). *Frustration and aggression.* New Haven: Yale University Press.

Edel, L. (1984). *Writing lives: Principia biographica.* New York: W. W. Norton.

Ellenberger, H. R. (1970). *The discovery of the unconscious.* New York: Basic Books.

Elms, A. C. (1988, August). *The psychologist as biographer.* Paper presented at the Henry A. Murray Award Lecture, American Psychological Association Annual Convention, Atlanta, GA.

Endler, N., & Magnusson, D. (Eds.). (1976). *Interactional psychology and personality.* Washington, DC: Hemisphere.

Erikson, E. H. (1958). *Young man Luther*. New York: W. W. Norton.

Erikson, E. H. (1969). *Gandhi's Truth*. New York: W. W. Norton.

Freud, S. (1900/1958). *The interpretation of dreams*. In J. Strachey (Ed. and Trans.), *The standard edition of the complete psychological works of Sigmund Freud* (Vols. 4-5, pp. 1-621). London: Hogarth Press. (Original work published 1900)

Gardiner, M. (Ed.). (1971). *The wolf-man*. New York: Basic Books.

Gay, P. (1988). *Freud: A life for our time*. New York: W. W. Norton.

George, A. L., & George, J. (1956; 1964). *Woodrow Wilson and Colonel House: A personality study*. New York: Dover.

George, J. L., & George, A. L. (1981-82). *Woodrow Wilson and Colonel House*: A reply to Weinstein, Anderson, and Link. *Political Science Quarterly*, 96, 641-665.

Gergen, K. J. (1977). Stability, change, and chance in understanding human development. In N. Datan & H. Reese (Eds.), *Life-span developmental psychology: Dialectical perspectives on experimental research*. New York: Academic Press.

Gilmore, W. J. (1984). *Psychohistorical inquiry: A comprehensive research bibliography*. New York: Garland.

Griffith, E. (1984). *In her own right: The life of Elizabeth Cady Stanton*. New York: Oxford University Press.

Hall, C. S., & Lindzey, G. (1957). *Theories of personality*. New York: John Wiley.

Hartshorne, H., & May, M. A. (1928). *Studies in deceit*. New York: Macmillan.

Hempel, C. G. (1965). *Aspects of scientific explanation*. New York: Free Press.

Herbst, P. G. (1970). *Behavioural worlds: The study of single cases*. London: Tavistock Publications.

Hersen, M., & Barlow, D. H. (1976). *Single case experimental designs*. New York: Pergamon Press.

Hogan, R., & Jones, W. (1985). Preface. In R. Hogan & W. Jones (Eds.), *Perspectives in Personality* (Vol. 1, pp. ix-xiii). Greenwich, CT: JAI Press.

Hogan, R., & Jones, W. (1985). *Perspectives in personality* (Vol. 1). Greenwich, CT: JAI Press.

Holt, R. R. (1962). Individuality and generalization in the psychology of personality. *Journal of Personality*, 30, 377-404.

Horner, A. (1968). The evolution of goals in the life of Clarence Darrow. In C. Buhler & F. Massarik (Eds.), *The course of human life* (pp. 64-75). New York: Springer.

Horowitz, M. J. (1979). *States of mind: Analysis of change in psychotherapy*. New York: Plenum Medical.

Jones, E. (1953-1957). *The life and work of Sigmund Freud* (Vols. 1-3). New York: Basic Books.

Kanzer, M., & Glenn, J. (Eds.). (1980). *Freud and his patients*. New York: Jason Aronson.

Kenrick, D. T., & Funder, D. C. (1988). Profiting from controversy: Lessons from the person-situation debate. *American Psychologist*, 43, 23-34.

Kinsey, A., Pomeroy, W. B. & Martin, C. E. (1948). *Sexual behavior in the human male*. Philadelphia: W. B. Saunders.

Kinsey, A., Pomeroy, W. B., Martin, C. E., & Gebhard, P. H. (1953). *Sexual behavior in the human female*. Philadelphia: W. B. Saunders.

Kratochwill, T. R. (Ed.). (1978). *Single subject research*. New York: Academic Press.

Kuhn, T. S. (1970). *The structure of scientific revolutions* (2nd ed.). Chicago: University of Chicago Press.

Langer, W. C. (1972). *The mind of Adolf Hitler.* New York: Basic Books.

Laudan, L. (1977). *Progress and its problems: Towards a theory of scientific growth.* Berkeley: University of California Press.

Levy, L. (1970). *Conceptions of personality.* New York: Random House.

Liebert, R. M., & Spiegler, M. D. (1987). *Personality: Strategies and issues* (5th ed.). Chicago: Dorsey Press.

Link, A. et al. (Eds.). (1986). Introduction. In *The papers of Woodrow Wilson* (Vol. 54, pp. vii–xiii). Princeton, NJ: Princeton University Press.

Loewenberg, P. (1988). Psychoanalytic models of history: Freud and after. In W. M. Runyan (Ed.), *Psychology and historical interpretation* (pp. 126–156). New York: Oxford University Press.

Mack, J. E. (1971). Psychoanalysis and historical biography. *Journal of the American Psychoanalytic Association, 19,* 143–179.

MacKinnon, D. W. (1978). *In search of human effectiveness: Identifying and developing creativity.* Buffalo, NY: Creative Education Foundation.

Maddi, S. (1984). Personology for the 1980s. In R. Zucker, J. Aronoff & A. I. Rabin (Eds.), *Personality and the prediction of behavior.* New York: Academic Press.

Magnusson, D., & Endler, N. (Eds.). (1977). *Personality at the crossroads: Current issues in interactional psychology.* Hillsdale, NJ: Lawrence Erlbaum Associates.

Maslow, A. (1971). *The farther reaches of human nature.* New York: Viking Press.

McAdams, D. P. (1985). *Power, intimacy, and the life story: Personological inquiries into identity.* Homewood, IL: Dorsey Press.

McAdams, D. P. (1987). A life-story model of identity. In *Perspectives in Personality* (Vol. 2, pp. 15–20). Greenwich, CT: JAI Press.

McAdams, D., & Ochberg, R. (Eds.). (1988). Psychobiography and life narratives [Special issue]. *Journal of Personality, 56.*

McClelland, D. C., Atkinson, J. W., Clark, R. A., & Lowell, E. G. (1953). *The achievement motive.* New York: Appleton-Century-Crofts.

Meehl, P. E. (1973). Why I do not attend case conference. In P. E. Meehl, *Psychodiagnosis: Selected papers* (pp. 255–302). Minneapolis: University of Minnesota Press.

Millon, T. (1984). On the renaissance of personality assessment and personality theory. *Journal of Personality Assessment, 48,* 450–466.

Millon, T., & Klerman, G. (Eds.). (1986). *Contemporary directions in psychopathology.* New York: Guilford Press.

Mischel, W. (1966). Theory and research on the antecedents of self-imposed delay of reward. In B. A. Maher (Ed.), *Progress in experimental personality research* (Vol. 3, pp. 85–132). New York: Academic Press.

Mischel, W. (1968). *Personality and assessment.* New York: Wiley.

Mischel, W. (1981). *Introduction to personality* (3rd ed.). New York: Holt, Rinehart & Winston.

Monte, C. (1987). *Beneath the mask: An introduction to theories of personality* (3rd ed.). New York: Holt, Rinehart & Winston.

Moraitis, G., & Pollock, G. H. (Eds.). (1987). *Psychoanalytic studies of biography*. New York: International Universities Press.

Munz, P. (1985). *Our knowledge of the growth of knowledge: Popper or Wittgenstein?* London: Routledge & Kegan Paul.

Murray, H. A. (1938). *Explorations in personality*. New York: Oxford University Press.

Nagel, E. (1961). *The structure of science*. New York: Harcourt, Brace & World.

Nisbet, R. (1980). *The history of the idea of progress*. New York: Basic Books.

Novarr, D. (1986). *The lines of life: Theories of biography, 1880–1970*. West Lafayette, IN: Purdue University Press.

Nunnally, J. C. (1978). *Psychometric theory* (2nd ed.). New York: McGraw-Hill.

Obholzer, K. (1982). *The wolf man—sixty years later: Conversations with Freud's controversial patient*. New York: Continuum.

Oliner, S. P., & Oliner, P. M. (1988). *The altruistic personality: Rescuers of Jews in Nazi Europe*. New York: Free Press.

Pervin, L. A. (1980). *Personality: Theory, assessment, and research*. New York: Wiley.

Peterson, C. (1988). *Personality*. San Diego: Harcourt Brace Jovanovich.

Petrie, G. (1981). *Ultimately fiction: Design in modern American literary biography*. West Lafayette, IN: Purdue University Press.

Phares, E. J. (1988). *Introduction to personality* (2nd ed.). Glenview, IL: Scott, Foresman.

Rabin, A. I., Aronoff, J., Barclay, A., & Zucker, R. (Eds.). (1981). *Further explorations in personality*. New York: Wiley-Interscience.

Roazen, P. (1975). *Freud and his followers*. New York: Alfred A. Knopf.

Rogers, C. R. (1980). Ellen West—and loneliness. In C. R. Rogers, *A way of being* (pp. 164–180). Boston: Houghton Mifflin.

Runyan, W. M. (1981). Why did Van Gogh cut off his ear? The problem of alternative explanations in psychobiography. *Journal of Personality and Social Psychology, 40*, 1070–1077.

Runyan, W. M. (1982). *Life histories and psychobiography: Explorations in theory and method*. New York: Oxford University Press.

Runyan, W. M. (1983). Idiographic goals and methods in the study of lives. *Journal of Personality, 51*, 413–437.

Runyan, W. M. (1988a). Progress in psychobiography. *Journal of Personality, 56*, 295–326.

Runyan, W. M. (Ed.). (1988b). *Psychology and historical interpretation*. New York: Oxford University Press.

Sartre, J. P. (1981). *The family idiot: Gustave Flaubert, 1821–1857* (Vol. 1). (C. Cosman, Trans.). Chicago: University of Chicago Press.

Sherwood, M. (1969). *The logic of explanation in psychoanalysis*. New York: Academic Press.

Skinner, B. F. (1976). *Particulars of my life*. New York: Alfred A. Knopf.

Skinner, B. F. (1979). *The shaping of a behaviorist*. New York: Alfred A. Knopf.

Skinner, B. F. (1983). *A matter of consequences*. New York: Alfred A. Knopf.

Spotts, J. V., & Shontz, F. C. (1980). *Cocaine users: A representative case approach*. New York: Free Press.

Staub, E. (1980). *Personality: Basic aspects and current research.* Englewood Cliffs, NJ: Prentice-Hall.

Stewart, A. J., Franz, C., & Layton, L. (1988). The changing self: Using personal documents to study lives. *Journal of Personality, 56*(1), 41–74.

Stolorow, R. D., & Atwood, G. E. (1979). *Faces in a cloud: Subjectivity in personality theory.* New York: Jason Aronson.

Strachey, L. (1918). *Eminent Victorians.* New York: Harcourt Brace Jovanovich.

Strozier, C. (Ed.). (1985). *Self-psychology and the humanities.* New York: W. W. Norton.

Strozier, C., & Offer, D. (Eds.). (1985). *The leader: Psychohistorical essays.* New York: Plenum Press.

Sulloway, F. J. (1979). *Freud, biologist of the mind: Beyond the psychoanalytic legend.* New York: Basic Books.

Suppe, F. (1977). *The structure of scientific theories* (2nd ed.). Urbana, IL: University of Illinois Press.

Terman, L. (1917). The intelligence quotient of Francis Galton in childhood. *American Journal of Psychology, 28*, 209–215.

Tomkins, S. S. (1981). The rise, fall and resurrection of the study of personality. *Journal of Mind and Behavior, 2*, 443–452.

Turkat, I. D. (Ed.). (1985). *Behavioral case formulation.* New York: Plenum Press.

Ullman, L. P., & Krasner, L. I. (Eds.). (1965). *Case studies in behavior modification.* New York: Holt, Rinehart & Winston.

Waite, R. G. L. (1977). *The psychopathic god: Adolf Hitler.* New York: Basic Books.

Watson, J. B. (1913). Psychology as the behaviorist views it. *Psychological Review, 20*, 158–177.

Weinstein, E., Anderson, J., & Link, A. (1978). Woodrow Wilson's political personality: A reappraisal. *Political Science Quarterly, 93*, 585–598.

White, R. W. (1952). *Lives in progress.* New York: Holt, Rinehart & Winston.

Wiggins, J. S., Renner, K. E., Clore, G. L., & Rose, R. J. (1976). *Principles of personality.* Reading, MA: Addison-Wesley.

Winter D. G., & Carlson, L. (1988). Using motive scores in the psychobiographical study of an individual: The case of Richard Nixon. *Journal of Personality, 56*, 75–104.

Wittels, F. (1924). *Sigmund Freud: His personality, his teaching, and his school.* New York: Dodd, Mead.

Wolpe, J., & Rachman, S. (1960). Psychoanalytic "evidence": A critique based on Freud's case of Little Hans. *Journal of Nervous and Mental Disease, 131*, 135–148.

Zucker, R. A., Aronoff, J., & Rabin, A. I. (Eds.). (1984). *Personality and the prediction of behavior.* New York: Academic Press.

3

Adult Personality Development: Issues in Assessing Constancy and Change

John R. Nesselroade

Though all could tell them reasons why they'd fail,
not one could tell them they shouldn't sail.
—Anonymous

INTRODUCTION

The Quest

Despite the ebb and flow of the quality of ideas that have influenced its direction, the study of personality continues to beckon new recruits from each succeeding generation of behavioral scientists. Countless resources have been invested in searching little known seas to find the fabled continent of lawful relationships and predictable events, and yet, as one puzzles over the charts and maps of established findings, it seems the expedition has scarcely begun. Although many of the perils are more clearly marked for the contemporary navigator than they were for our hardy forebears, the shape and the location of the sought-after landmass remain only rudely suggested. Still, the threatening storms of the 1960s and 1970s have been weathered, albeit with alterations of course and, perhaps, some shortening of sail, and as we venture on through the 1980s, the horizon once more seems to hold the promise of a substantial landfall. The logs of those early explorers in personality, such as Henry A.

Murray, whom we honor today are at once irreplaceable historical documents, valuable guides to as yet uncharted waters, and irresistible challenges to sail boldly on.

Why This Perspective on the Issues?

A conscientious attempt to reconstruct the developmental trajectory through which I passed in reaching the point of writing this chapter would heavily credit good luck, good mentors, good colleagues, good students, and good friends. My parents, John S. and Emma E. Nesselroade, who were both native West Virginians, were virtuous, religious people. Although in my family there was no tradition of attending college, there was something of an intellectual emphasis, not the least important aspects of which were the appreciation of learning and strong encouragement to bring home high marks from school to prove it. I became aware of the value of "going on to college" while in secondary school. In 1958, funded by GI Bill educational benefits purchased with three post high school years of active duty in the United States Marine Corps, I followed my older brother, Edward, and a younger brother, Dale, to college. Subsequently all the rest of my siblings—Kenneth, David, and Nancy—earned at least baccalaureate degrees.

I was accepted at Marietta College, 10 miles from where I grew up, and registered in the electrical engineering curriculum. Electrical engineering (EE) was both a natural extension of my military occupational specialty and a promising career direction. Thanks to Marietta's insistence on a liberal education, in my second year I enrolled in Professor Bruce Blackburn's introductory psychology course. When I subsequently confessed a waning regard for EE and proclaimed a growing interest in psychology, Professor Blackburn startled me by saying, "I think it's terrific that you want to major in psychology. My advice to you is to take all the mathematics that you can get. I don't care whether or not you take my psychology courses. We'll get you into a good graduate program." I married Carolyn Boyles, followed Blackburn's advice, and in July 1961, one BS in mathematics and a daughter later, and just prior to beginning graduate classes at the University of Illinois, I was in Champaign-Urbana, learning to submit factor analysis runs on the Iliac for Raymond B. Cattell.

The combination of a half-time research assistantship with Cattell and the proseminar for 1st-year graduate students in the Lloyd Humphreys-led Department of Psychology at Illinois in the early 1960s made basic training at Parris Island seem like an idyl in comfort and self-indulgence. With unending gratitude to my patient and supportive Carolyn and our daughters, Cindy and Jenny, I managed to complete my Ph.D. and to take some advantage of the incredibly rich intellectual opportunities in psychology that Illinois provided in those days. Apprenticing with Cattel, for whom I still have great admiration and with whom I continue to collaborate (e.g., Nesselroade & Cattell, 1988), was exciting. His fearsome intellect, scientific audacity, unflagging energy, and general irreverence made each day an adventure. It was in that brisk milieu that a spark of interest in personality change and stability, at both the group and individual levels, was first struck and then fanned into flame through the course of a master's thesis and doctoral dissertation. Thus ignited, in 1967 I was hired into the Department of Psychology at West Virginia University.

At West Virginia, I joined the small subset of faculty comprising the personality-social component of the program. Soon, another new assistant professor named Paul Baltes joined the faculty and became a member of the developmental group. In very short order, Baltes and I became intellectual confidantes and close friends. We have remained so for over 20 years. At that time at West Virginia, a small group led by K. Warner Schaie and Baltes was beginning to forge some key links in a chain of events that gave new life to life-span development. Coincidentally, the senior member of the personality-social program took a position elsewhere, and Schaie, who was then department chairman, disbanded the personality-social unit and let other program areas absorb the survivors. When he told me my options were to join the clinicians, the experimentalists, or the developmentalists, I became a developmentalist.

My good fortune has continued through 16 exciting years of association with colleagues, students, and friends at Penn State and around the country and the world. Now at *age* 52, looking back on a formative *period*, I am lucky to have been a member of a *cohort* so committed to the articulation of a life-span orientation to the study of development. I have been encouraged to pursue old concerns of structuring and measuring personality change and stability and stimulated to approach interesting phenomena from a life-span development perspective. These two central thrusts, along with a renewed and vital appreciation for the multidimensional character of generalizing from the data one has to the data one might have obtained, have weighed heavily in the production of this chapter.

Constancy and Change Reflect Order and Organization

There are several assumptions that guide the discussion to follow. One of the central ones is that the phenomena of interest to students of personality reflect an order and organization in behavior that we need to study, model, and approximate. Thereby we can, more or less, understand those phenomena. Moreover, the underlying order and organization include dynamic features that are reflected in natural phenomena. Therefore the phenomena that we study manifest changing properties and configurations. To the extent that such changes are driven in an orderly, organized manner, it is appropriate to try to understand them as well as constancy. Thus the purpose of empirical inquiry is to describe and explain the dynamic and changing, as well as the static, properties of nature's order and organization. To ignore the study of dynamics and change and to look only to those features that are more or less constant and stable is to stop too soon and to settle for too little in the pursuit of scientific knowledge and understanding.

Organization in nature makes the pursuit of empirically based knowledge a sensible activity, but it also creates some hazards. The very order and organization that we are trying to understand can interfere with our attempts to do so. Experimental design, for example, represents an attempt to separate events into two subsets: Those in which we are interested, and those events that happen concomitantly and that confound our interpretation and understanding of the ones in which we are interested (e.g., as retest effects confound repeated measurements in longitudinal research). In a similar vein, choosing one subset of variables on which to focus indirectly involves other variables that are related to the selected subset because of organization in systems of variables. Obviously, not all potentially relevant variables can be examined in studying a particular phenomenon. How should we choose a subset on which to focus? Perhaps in past research we have not answered this question well, and that, at least in part, might account for why students of personality do not yet dominate their subject matter. Perhaps we would be more effective if we attended more to strategies involving comprehensive and intensive measurement such as were advocated by Henry Murray and others. This is a matter that will receive further emphasis.

Consistency in Personality

The criteria by which one selects focal variables reflect assumptions about the target phenomena and their organization. For example, the belief that the behavior of an individual is understandable only in a context is central to many theories of personality. Indeed, it seems hopeless to try to understand personality in bits and pieces taken out of context. The same piece of behavior may have quite different functional significance in different person/context combinations, and different pieces of behavior may have the same functional significance in different person/context combinations. Individuals develop and contexts change. To study personality from a developmental perspective requires examining both differences and similarities in the ways individuals' functioning is organized over spatial and temporal coordinates (Baltes & Nesselroade, 1973).

From the perspective of studying behaviors in individual/context combinations, it is difficult to make a case for personality consistency in the specifics of people's actions, feelings, or thoughts. People have the capability to vary their behavior across varying conditions to produce the same outcomes (Ford, 1987). Thus the specific "pieces" of behavior derive their meaning from the context. However one labels them, it seems to be in the general prototypical approaches and strategies by which people construct particular behavior patterns that personality consistency is likely to be found.

PURPOSES OF CHAPTER

I have in mind three major objectives for this chapter: (1) to examine the merits of approaching adult personality from a developmental perspective and to identify some of the gains to the study of personality being contributed by students of adult developments, (2) to identify and discuss selected methodological concepts and issues that have important implications for the study of personality and personality development, and (3) to examine critically but constructively the use of individual differences approaches to studying personality and its development.

Adult Personality Development

Personality concepts, especially temperament ones, have received a great deal of close scrutiny in the past couple of decades. Despite vigorous attacks and sustained debate (e.g., Block, 1977, 1981; Epstein & O'Brien, 1985; Mischel, 1979; Mischel & Peake, 1982), the study of personality continues to attract interest and to prompt considerable research activity (e.g., Leventhal & Tomarken, 1986; Miller & Turnbull, 1986; Singer & Kolligian, 1987).

As long as both new and revamped ideas and concerns are being brought to bear to meet challenges and criticisms, the outlook for the study of personality will continue to be positive. Work that has been fostered by the life-span (e.g., Baltes, 1987; Lerner, 1988) and life course (e.g., Caspi, 1987; Elder, 1985) perspectives on development has, in the writer's view, helped to give new impetus to personality research. For example, the importance of context (Baltes, 1987; Caspi; Elder & Liker, 1982; Lerner, 1984) for the developing individual and the study of the range of plasticity (Baltes & Schaie, 1976; Lerner, 1984) are having a marked impact on the study of adult personality development (Featherman & Lerner, 1985). Similarly, new formulations of systems approaches and methodology (e.g., Ford, 1987; Ford & Ford, 1987) provide a framework with which to structure both constancy and change in personality and behavior. Recent work in behavior genetics (Plomin, 1986) has brought a new emphasis to that approach to the study of personality and personality change that includes the elderly as well as younger subjects and emphasizes contextual as well as genetic influences on development (McClearn, Pedersen, Plomin, Nesselroade, & Friberg, 1988). A growing research emphasis on the nature, determinants, and correlates of *successful aging* (Rowe & Kahn, 1987) reflects these important theoretical and methodological thrusts. In sum, the fact that developmental researchers of different specialities are studying personality at the adult level offers reason to continue to be optimistic about the future of personality research.

Methodological Issues and Theory

One of the themes running through this paper is the assessment of constancy and change in adult personality development. More to the point, I will be concerned primarily with a selected set of methodological issues that bear on the topics of constancy and change in personality research. An emphasis on methodological issues, however, should not be construed as antithetical or irrelevant to substantive and theoretical concerns. Indeed, the value of substantive research and theory is not in the least at question, but I hasten to assert, empirical inquiry in a given domain does not advance through theory development alone (Baltes & Reese, 1984; Cattell, 1966). Improved measurement instruments and techniques, innovations in design, and creativity in modeling and data analysis also contribute in major ways. In one of his last papers my great and good colleague, the late Jack Wohlwill (1988), emphasized how method and theory are teamed in a curious dance where each has the possibility of leading at one time or another.

I have been fortunate to have been involved with several thoughtful collaborators (Baltes, Reese, & Nesselroade, 1977; Nesselroade & Ford, 1985, 1987; Nesselroade & Labouvie, 1985) in attempts to examine critically the relationship between methodology and theory in developmental research. In many instances it is difficult, if not impossible, to separate the two. Regardless of the interdependence of substantive and methodological concepts, it is important to realize their differences and when one has and when one has not separated them. Behavioral scientists have not always done this well. For example, experimentalists usually swaddle their favorite concepts in the fabric of analysis of variance, while differential psychologists clothe their favorites in the textiles of factor analysis and, now, structural modeling. Conflicting opinions between camps may represent method differences as much or more than fundamental substantive differences concerning phenomena.

In spite of the sometimes fuzzy boundary between theory and method, the writer believes that it is useful to try to disentangle the two for discussion purposes. By bringing key methodological issues into a sharper focus and accompanying them with substantive illustrations, I hope to help create syntheses that will advance the field of personality research.

Individual Differences

As discussed by Cronbach (1957), the study of individual differences has long been viewed by many as the appropriate path to the understanding of behavioral principles. Historically, the study of individual differences has been associated strongly with human abilities, general personality traits, and measurement and prediction activities. The approach leaned heavily on a conception of relatively stable attributes of individuals and contexts. With an emerging enthusiasm to account for change as well as stability becoming more evident, it seems timely to scrutinize the use of individual differences in relation to that end. In this paper, the individual differences approach will be examined with regard to how it might better serve the objectives of students of developmental phenomena and other kinds of change.

SEVEN FOCAL ISSUES

The title of this paper implies a large number of significant issues bearing on the study of personality that might be identified and discussed herein. As a way of organizing discussion related to the three purposes identified above, I have chosen seven issues that I believe are of particular salience to the general topic of the paper and that I hope will pique the curiosity and interest of the reader. The issues of concern, which will be presented as assertions that I shall try to defend subsequently, will be identified explicitly here and again in later portions of the text.

The first issue is largely substantive. It both sets the stage for the presentation and discussion of more methodological issues and testifies to the interdependence of method and theory mentioned earlier. The focal issues are as follows:

1. *Adult personalities manifest important changes that are construable as developmental.* Often adults are coping with three generations; their own, their children's, and their parents'. Adults face transitions that are physical, psychological, and social in nature, and in many cases, they are plumbing the depths of their reserves to deal with events. At the same time they are undergoing biochemical, physiological, and physical changes as their roles and role expectations are being altered. As one considers the nature of the demands, both endogenous and exogenous, being placed on the adult, perhaps the real puzzle is not that there are systematic changes but rather that there is recognizable continuity and the maintenance of coherence and identity at the individual level.

2. *Constancy and change are advantageously considered together rather than in isolation from each other.* Many personality researchers tend to focus on constancy, whereas many developmentalists interested in personality tend to emphasize matters of change. For several reasons, however, change should not, indeed cannot, be identified without some attention being paid to matters of constancy (see, e.g., Brim & Kagan, 1980). Nor should change be excluded from concern in focusing on constancy. Life-span developmentalists (e.g., Lerner, 1984) have argued how critical it is to attend to both kinds of phenomena. In addition to the complementary roles in which constancy in some form is required as a backdrop against which to chart change, there are supplemen-

tary relationships between the two, attention to which leads to a more complete portrayal of adult personality and its development.

3. *Changes can be either qualitative or quantitative, and the two possibilities should be recognized and allowed for.* Changes can take a variety of forms. Sometimes changes can be represented in terms of mere gains or losses on one or more measurable dimensions, for example, physical growth; other times, they may be best construed as qualitative shifts in the phenomenon of interest, for example, stagewise progressions in cognitive or personality development. Both kinds of changes are deeply entrenched in the literature of behavioral development (Lerner, 1988). Rendering the distinction between the two operational is not always easy, but some methodological tools such as the common factor model have made such a distinction possible for a long time and, with new developments, it is now quite rigorous.

4. *Empirical data are inherently multimodal, and it is critical to recognize the implications of that fact in collecting and analyzing them.* Data gathered and analyzed to study adult personalities or, for that matter, any other behavioral phenomenon are simultaneously classifiable in multiple modes. In conducting empirical inquiry, we are inevitably limited by design constraints to meager representation of one or more of the possible modes of classification, such as persons, variables, and occasions of measurement. In other words, the act of data collection forces choices on the investigator concerning not only subject samples but also variables, occasions of measurement, observers, and so on. Once made, the choices foreclose some possibilities even as they provide for others. These choices should be made explicitly and with a view to their implications for the conclusions and generalizations to which the researcher aspires.

5. *An idiographic orientation to studying phenomena can well serve a nomothetic science.* I believe strongly in the merit of developing general laws that are applicable to many or all entities of interest. The level of abstraction at which nomothetic relationships can be established, however, is a matter that requires careful examination. Apprehending intraindividual change patterns may require extensive data collection and analysis at the individual level prior to aggregating information across individuals if aggregation is to lead to nomothetically useful relationships (Cairns, 1986; Lamiell, 1981; Lerner, 1988; Nesselroade & Ford, 1985; Zevon & Tellegen, 1982).

6. *Related to the measurement of personality attributes, there is a fundamental distinction to be made between the concepts of reliability and stability.* Failure to make a clear distinction between the psychometric properties of a measurement instrument and the temporal characteristics of the psychological phenomenon being measured has helped to foster confusion in both substantive and methodological literature focused on change. Reliable measurement can be performed on both stable and changing phenomena. Thus high reliability does not necessarily result in high stability.

7. *The distinction between stable individual differences and individual differences (and similarities) in intraindividual change is critical for developmental research.* For the developmentalist, change is a basic phenomenon. If a differential approach to the study of personality development is to be taken, it needs to be focused on differences and similarities in change patterns, which provide a more appropriate basis for understanding development than does studying differences and similarities in relatively stable scores. In many cases the two kinds of variability (intraindividual change and interindividual differences) are confounded and need to be disentangled if progress is to be made in understanding developmental phenomena.

Line of March

The seven foci are listed in Table 3.1, with a concrete example for each of them. The first six issues will be examined in the process of dealing with the first two purposes of the chapter, that is, examining adult development and selected methodological and theoretical issues. Subsequently, I shall examine in some detail the seventh issue, which involves the individual differences approach to the study of development and developmental changes. Finally, I will try to look briefly toward a methodological agenda for the next decade or so in the study of adult personality development.

STUDYING PERSONALITY DEVELOPMENTALLY

Adult Personality Development

Assertion: Adult personalities manifest important changes that are construable as developmental.

When does personality develop? For some students of personality, the processes so named cease with the end of childhood. For others, development ends as soon as the organism moves from the adolescence into adulthood. For still others, personality development is a lifelong phenomenon and, as with any other age, adulthood is a time of transition and change (e.g., Erikson, 1959). As Baltes and Reese (1984, p. 493) remarked, "A life-span perspective is one based on the belief that the changes (growth, development, aging) shown by people from the time of their conception, throughout their lives, and until the time of their death are usefully conceptualized as developmental." Troll (1982), for example, recently has summarized the features of a number of theories, both qualitative and quantitative, of adult development.

On the one hand, it may seem sometimes that adult personalities are fairly expressed as a set of more or less stable true scores, a situation implied by an undue preoccupation with computing and reporting test-retest stability coeffi-

TABLE 3.1 Focal Issues and Examples

Issue	Example
1. Adult personality development	Adaptation (systematic functional change) to loss of spouse
2. Constancy and change as supplementary	Irascibility (stable, trait-like) and momentary anger (changing, state-like) in same person
3. Distinction between quantitative vs. qualitative change	Growing 5 pounds heavier vs. moving from married to widowed status
4. Multimodal nature of data	Mary's (person) weight (variable) at age 30 (occasion) as guessed (method) by a carnival huckster (rater) on Saturday (occasion) when it's raining (ambient stimulus condition)
5. Idiographic data can serve nomothetic aims	Each individual's relative investment of his spare time in social vs. solitary activities (an idiographic measure) used as a measure of gregariousness to be related to other variables across persons (a nomothetic comparison)
6. Distinction between reliability and stability	How a physicist tries to measure the location of a particle (reliability) vs. the location at different times (stability)
7. Distinction between stable individual differences and individual differences in intraindividual change	Staying at the head of the class through high school and college (stable individual differences) as opposed to recovering or not recovering from an attack of influenza (individual differences in intraindividual change)

cients over intervals of, say, 1 year or less to several decades, as is the case in many studies of adult personality characteristics. On the other hand, even when such coefficients are substantial, the variables under scrutiny do not reflect the variety and scope of adult behavior, nor do the stability coefficients represent all the variation for which one might account. Thus regardless of the occasional test-retest stability coefficients in the .70s (or even higher), adulthood is also a time of interesting, systematic changes, many of which are age related.

The life-span orientation to the study of ontogenetic change has had an important impact on the way many of us think about the concept of development. It emphasizes processes that may extend across the individual's life-span and encourages the study of both continuity and discontinuity as well as plasticity in individuals' lives. Recently Baltes (1987) presented a contemporary statement of what it means to approach the subject matter of intellectual development from a life-span orientation. His discussion is equally pertinent to the study of personality.

Baltes identified several features of development as viewed from a life-span orientation. Among them were (1) multidirectionality (and multidimensionality); (2) historical embeddedness and susceptibility to other structural cultural factors; (3) dynamic, continuous interplay between gains and losses; and (4) plasticity in development. These aspects of life-span developmental study identified by Baltes will briefly be considered to set the stage for examining the set of methodological issues.

Multidirectionality and Multidimensionality

Development involves *patterns* of change. These change patterns occur over time and are defined on multiple variables. Increases or gains on some variables are almost invariably concurrent with decreases or losses on other variables (Baltes, 1987; Lerner, 1988). Thus multidirectionality and multidimensionality reflect concern for both multiple variables and multiple occasions of measurement. The kind of complexities in change suggested by Baltes (1987) puts a huge demand on empirical data if adequate description and modeling of developmental phenomena are to be achieved.

Historical Embeddedness

Personality development can be conceived as a product of properties of the person and properties of the context. It follows that some of the consistencies and changes in personality are primarily functions of the consistencies and changes in the person's context, and others are primarily functions of consistencies and changes in the person. Three categories of influences that impinge on individuals' development were mentioned by Baltes (1987): age-graded influences, history-graded influences, and non-normative influences. The three sources, which operate through the life-span, shape the development of lives. *Age-graded influences*, as the term signifies, are rather closely related to chronological age, although considerable interindividual differences in actual timing are often observed. They include both person and context influences such as the biological (e.g., hormonal) and social (e.g., role) events traditionally identified as key features of development and their interactions. *History-graded influences*, which represent contextual consistencies that may differ from one generation to the next, also involve both biological and environmental determinants and help to define the larger context in which individuals develop. *Nonnormative influences* are biological and environmental events the occurrence and/or sequencing of which may differ unsystematically from one person (or group of persons) to another. They are not generally applicable, nor are they closely tied to ontogenesis or historical change, yet they can have a profound effect on an individual's developmental trajectory (see, e.g., Bandura, 1982).

Historical embeddedness concerns also dramatize the comprehensiveness of the operations needed to produce appropriate data for developmentalists. For example, the study of historical embeddedness calls for a different time perspective in the design and conduct of research than does ontogenetic development. For example, using only one cohort in a longitudinal study leaves ontogenetic development and historical change completely confounded (Baltes, et al., 1977). Following a second cohort may be redundant as far as ontogenetic change components are concerned, but not with respect to historical/cultural change components.

Interplay Between Gains and Losses

The dynamic between gains and losses (in adaptive capacity) integrates in one individual the multidirectionality and multidimensionality mentioned above. It brings patterns of change associated with aging and patterns of change associated with child development into one comprehensive scheme of change over the human life-span. Thus although the attributes may differ from age to age, the relative relationship between gains and losses represents a derived characteristic that varies with age. For instance, in some respects children are experiencing many gains and few losses, while the converse holds for older adults. But the dynamic between gains and losses across the life-span represents a pertinent attribute whatever the age levels under consideration. *Selective optimization with compensation*, which is a prototypical change mechanism for successful cognitive aging (Baltes, 1987; M. Baltes, 1986), surely has its counterparts in the adaptation adults must make to changing personality characteristics and contextual demands. To identify such patterns of changes and adaptations in behavior requires information on intraindividual change and stability in personality as well as information concerning similarities and differences in those change patterns.

Developmental Plasticity

Individuals show an impressive array of developmental outcomes (e.g., Baltes, 1987). This very diversity leads to other important questions. How else might a given individual have developed had conditions and circumstances been different? What new patterns of behavior can an individual accomplish? Explorations of plasticity have taken several forms and involve a variety of disciplines (Lerner, 1984). The conception of many possible trajectories, only one of which is actually realized, makes a clear link to the emphasis on interindividual differences in intraindividual changes mentioned earlier in the seventh issue.

Summary

Adults undergo systematic changes. This has been proposed at the level of elaborate theories of development (e.g., Erikson, 1959) and shown in a variety of descriptive work on age trends (e.g., Nesselroade, Schaie, & Baltes, 1972; Schaie, 1983). There exists sufficient theory and research to sustain the usefulness of a conception of personality and personality development that views adulthood as a time of systematic and meaningful changes embedded in a larger framework of stability (Ford, 1987). The kinds of changes involved and their different patterns across individuals, variables, and time are complex and require "heroic" design, data collection, and analysis efforts. Understanding these changes and how they are involved in the transactions of the individual with his or her environment for the last three quarters of the life-span is a challenge to personality researchers. The study of adult personality can scarcely be said to be complete without attending to these systematic changes that occur in adulthood and undertaking the rigorous empirical work needed to refine conceptions such as those identified above. Accepting this, a host of interesting methodological issues become salient.

Constancy and Change

Assertion: Constancy and change are advantageously considered together rather than in isolation from each other.

Concepts of constancy and change (e.g., Brim & Kagan, 1980; Costa & McCrae, 1980; Nesselroade, 1987) are central to the work of developmentalists. Constancy receives much attention in the adult personality literature (e.g., Costa & McCrae). In many cases, this results in part from viewing development as an infancy through adolescence phenomenon that is followed by a long period of relative stability and then decline.

In this section, I want to characterize change and stability in a manner suitable to the purposes of this chapter. The characterization is not meant to be complete, comprehensive, or permanent—only useful as an heuristic. Rather than use the concepts of change and stability as mutually exclusive, I want to focus on the interdependence between the two and will give three illustrations of the ways that they can be profitably used together in studying adult development.

Constancy as a Backdrop for Change

It seems to me that more than ever before in the social and behavioral sciences, there is a concern for understanding change and intraindividual variability and other manifestations that suggest dynamic as opposed to static aspects of the organism. This shows up not only in the frequent criticism and denigration of static concepts but also in a growing emphasis on methodologies and modeling procedures that purport to represent dynamic features of systems of variables. Admittedly, the steps are still simple, but, for example, the recognition of the importance of longitudinal research if one is to learn about change (McCall, 1977; Wohlwill, 1973) and the call for modeling probabilities of transitions from state to state (Allison, 1984; Tuma & Hannan, 1984) focus on changes (however, on the regularities or invariants of change phenomena). This increase in the level of abstraction—from static concepts to regularities in intraindividual change—is a point to which we will return later.

Defining and measuring change requires a reference frame. If "Bob grew 2 inches last year" is a valid assertion, it implies that we have information that extends over time about Bob. It also implies that we have information that extends over time about the attribute height. We would not measure Bob at Time 1 and Mary at Time 2 and identify the difference as an increment in Bob's height. Nor would we measure Bob at Time 1, weigh him at Time 2, and identify the difference as a height difference. In a fundamental sense, then, change derives its meaning and interpretation from associated concepts of constancy (see, e.g., Lerner, 1984).

Coexistent Constancy and Change

Elsewhere I have presented, revised, and discussed a variety of both substantive and methodological topics concerning the trait-state distinction in personality research (Nesselroade, 1987). An essential argument was that individual differences on observable attributes that exist at any given point in time are decomposable into two kinds of variability: that characterizing relatively stable score components and that characterizing relatively changeable score components. Figure 3.1 illustrates the conception of both stable and changing contributions to observable variables. Here two distinct sources of variance, one representing stable individual differences (traits) and one representing a dimension of intraindividual change (states), are implicated in the observed differences among individuals. Such "coordinate" sources of variance have been demonstrated for many temperament dimensions (Cattell & Scheier, 1961; Hooker, Nesselroade, Nesselroade, & Lerner, 1987; Roberts & Nesselroade, 1986), and there is some evidence that the conception applies to human abilities as well (e.g., Horn, 1966).

Teaming up stable and fluctuant attributes to characterize important concepts has a long history. Indeed, the historical development of language pays mute tribute to the notion. Eysenck (1983) pointed out that in 45 BC Cicero made a distinction between irascibility (the trait) and anger (the state; see Table 3.1 and Figures 3.1 and 3.2). Contemporary work on trait and state anxiety (Cattell & Scheier, 1961; Nesselroade, 1987; Speilberger, Lushene, & McAdoo, 1977; Zuckerman & Lubin, 1965) has further clarified the linkages as well as the distinction between the two kinds of concepts.

Cattell (1963), for example, argued for the importance of triangulating on the more general concepts by using different slices of the data box. Important dimensions of individual differences can be manifested both in terms of variation among people at one point in time and in changes within persons

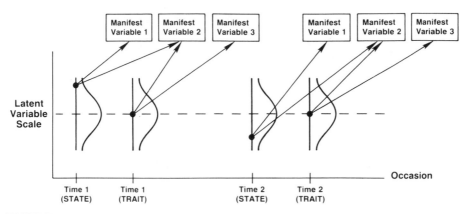

FIGURE 3.1 Constancy and change sources of interindividual differences (after Nesselroade, 1987).

across time. This formulation expands the range of phenomena to which individual differences approaches can be applied in critical ways for the developmentalist, as will be argued later.

Change as Substance for Constancy

Students of behavior have long focused on stability, even in trying to cope with the problems of describing changeable attributes of the organism (e.g., the emphasis on test-retest coefficients by developmentalists). Change can also be the "stuff" of which stability is made. Nesselroade and Ford (1987), for example, in examining the study of intraindividual variability in the elderly, discussed the concepts of steady state and changes in steady state. Figure 3.2 illustrates the essential idea. Intraindividual variability can manifest stable attributes such as a between persons difference in the mean level around which the variability occurs. This is how some researchers have elected to define trait (e.g., Zuckerman & Lubin, 1965). Other possibilities of stable differences between persons in characteristics of change patterns include amplitude and periodicity of change. More important, perhaps, one can focus on the structure or stability in intraindividual change patterns specified across multiple variables and time points and compare and contrast parameters defining the patterns for the individuals. The concept of developmental trajectory, for example, illustrates a kind of stability in an ongoing change process. In a subsequent section, the determination of structure in intraindividual change by P-technique factor analysis will be examined in detail.

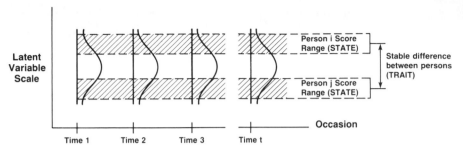

FIGURE 3.2 Change as substance for constancy: steady state "hum" (after Nesselroade, 1987).

Summary

Developmentalists are interested in both constancy and change. Constancy,
which fits well with the objective of prediction, does not begin to account for
the differences one observes among individuals. Nor is the absence of constancy or stability necessarily reflective only of error in the classical test theory
sense. Change concepts are needed if we are to realize the richness of interindividual differences. Formulations that can accommodate both constancy and
change features are attractive in light of the considerable variation that remains to be accounted for in most predictive and explanatory systems.

Qualitative Versus Quantitative Changes

*Assertion: Changes can be either qualitative or quantitative, and the two
possibilities should be recognized and allowed for.*

The kinds of changes attended to by developmentalists have led to various
classifications. One that has proven quite general in categorizing developmental phenomena, and which Lerner (1988) tied to metatheoretical concerns,
distinguishes between qualitative and quantitative changes (Baltes & Nesselroade, 1970; Wohlwill, 1973). The contrast between systems for developmental scaling, stage theories, and other qualitative descriptive schemes versus the
models of quantitative differences and changes exemplifies the distinction.

A variety of analytical tools are available for dealing with the different kinds
of data that reflect the quantitative versus qualitative distinction (e.g., factor
analysis and regression techniques, configural frequency analysis, monotonicity
analysis, etc.; see Nesselroade & Cattell, 1988). What has helped to make the
distinction work in the adult development and aging literature is the common
factor model and the associated concept of factor invariance (e.g., Cunningham

& Birren, 1980; Fitzgerald, Nesselroade, & Baltes, 1973; Hertzog & Schaie, 1986; Nesselroade et al., 1972). The concept of factor invariance and mathematical and statistical tools now available for testing for it offer a basis for organizing patterns of change in both group and individual data (Cunningham & Birren, 1980; Hooker et al., 1987; Mortimer, Finch, & Kumka, 1982; Nesselroade, Mitteness, & Thompson, 1984; Zevon & Tellegen, 1982) in terms of the qualitative versus quantitative change distinction.

In the context of factor analyzing difference scores to study patterns of growth and change (Cattell, 1963; Nesselroade & Bartsch, 1977; Nesselroade & Cable, 1974), quantitative and qualitative changes can be distinguished in terms of the factor analytic model as follows (see also Nesselroade, 1970). Let

$$a_{jit} = b_{j1t} \, F_{1it} + b_{j2t} \, F_{2it} + \ldots + b_{jkt} F_{kit} + U_{jit} \tag{1}$$

where a_{jit} is the observed score for person i on variable j at occasion t, the bs are the weights (factor loadings) that define the values of the a_{jit} in terms of the F's, the unmeasured variables or factors. The U_{jit} are the unique factors, one for each observed a. Let

$$a_{jit^1} = b_{j1t^1} \, F_{1it^1} + b_{j2t^1} \, F_{2it^1} + \ldots + b_{jk^1t^1} \, F_{k^1it^1} + U_{ijt^1} \tag{2}$$

represent a similar breakdown of the observed scores at a later occasion (t^1) in terms of k^1 factors (k may or may not equal k^1). Each equation provides a specification of an individual's score on a_j at a particular occasion of measurement in terms of the factors. Each individual's change score on the observed variables can be obtained by subtracting a_{jit} from a_{jit^1}. The changes can be represented in terms of the right-hand sides of Equations 1 and 2 (the factors) by subtraction also. However, depending on the temporal characteristics of the bs, the changes on the right-hand side can take quite different forms. If the bs are invariant (same numbers of factors [$k = k^1$] and same patterns of loadings) at t and t^1, then the difference between a_{jit^1} and a_{jit} can be represented as

$$a_{jit^1} - a_{jit} = b_{j1}(F_{1it^1} - F_{1it}) + b_{j2}(F_{2it^1} - F_{2it}) + \ldots + b_{jk}(F_{kit^1} - F_{kit}) + (U_{jit^1} - U_{jit}). \tag{3}$$

If the bs are not invariant, the simplicity of 3 does not obtain and the differences are

$$a_{jit^1} - a_{jit} = b_{j1t^1}F_{1it^1} \, b_{j2t^1} \, F_{2it^1} + \ldots + b_{jkt^1} \, F_{k^1it^1} + U_{jit^1} - b_{j1t}$$
$$F_{1it} - b_{j2t} \, F_{2it} - \ldots - b_{jkt} \, F_{kit} - U_{jit}. \tag{4}$$

The situations contrasted in (3) and (4) exemplify the kind of changes that have been identified as *quantitative* change and *qualitative* change, respectively. As shown in (3), changes in factor scores account for changes in observed scores. According to equation (4), however, there is no simple representation of the observed changes. They are functions of both the occasion t and occasion t^1 factors. To describe the individual's observed changes requires one to explicitly identify both the occasion t and the occasion t^1 factors. In Figure 3.3 this basic distinction between the two kinds of changes is illustrated graphically. There, in the case of the invariant factor, the corresponding factor score distributions are located on single continuum. This in turn implies the possibility of estimating individual level change scores if repeated measurements are involved *or* doing group mean comparisons if independent samples are involved. Neither possibility obtains for the factors that are not invariant. Obviously, the distinction between qualitative and quantitative changes can be made in other than factor analytic terms. For our purposes here, however, the factor model provides a precise illustration of the two kinds of changes. The statistical developments in assessing factor invariance of the past couple of decades have put such determinations on a firm and rigorous footing.

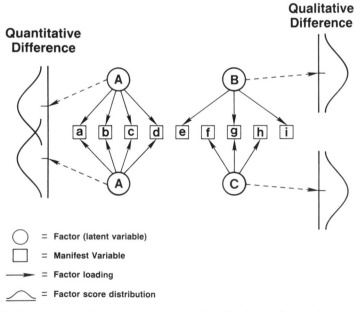

FIGURE 3.3 Factor-analytic representation of qualitative and quantitative changes (after Nesselroade, 1970).

Traditional use of the factor model involves groups of individuals rather than individuals. As will be noted subsequently when single-subject (P-technique) factor analysis is discussed, the investigation of qualitative versus quantitative change at the individual level offers a promising approach to the identification of individual differences in personality.

Summary

Developmentalists have made much of the distinction between qualitative and quantitative changes. For example, by appropriate techniques longitudinal data can be examined to determine whether or not changes from occasion to occasion can be conceptualized as quantitative or qualitative. This in turn dictates the kinds of analyses that are appropriate to capture and represent the change information. The operational possibilities of the common factor model have brought this distinction into the study of development in a relatively powerful way. By making the distinction applicable at either the individual or group level, it promises to be an even more useful tool in the study of personality development and change.

SOME METHODOLOGICAL IMPLICATIONS OF STUDYING PERSONALITY DEVELOPMENTALLY

Selection: A Multimodal View of Empirical Inquiry

Assertion: Empirical data are inherently multimodal, and it is critical to recognize the implications of that fact in collecting and analyzing them.

In earlier sections I have emphasized the burden placed on data by the many and complex expectations that developmentalists are interested in testing. In this section some of the design and data collection issues will be formalized, and the consequences of design choices identified and discussed.

Consider a score (datum) of 130. It might be Smith's IQ as measured by the WAIS at age 20 years, White's systolic blood pressure as measured by the team physician 10 minutes after running the mile indoors, or Jones's weight in street clothes on the morning of his fourteenth birthday. In each example, the score of 130 is identified by three different classification modes: person, variable, and occasion.

For the developmentalist, a broad goal is to ask about whole persons possessing an amazingly rich behavioral repertoire and existing in a panoply of contexts over their lifetimes. Doable empirical inquiry, however, is so limited that we are simply unable to "capture" the whole organism and its context in all their temporal variation and translate those operations into a set of data that can then be parsed either to discover lawful relationships or to provide support for conjectured ones. Rather, in practice, we can acquire only a subset of the potentially available information, a subset that represents the various modes of classification more or less well. For instance, with one or possibly two exceptions, the subset of data obtained in a given study probably involves a paucity of measures, a limited number of observers, relatively few persons, and a smattering of conditions, occasions, or situations.

In practice, one sees exquisitely representative national samples of persons measures only *once* on attributes on which individuals can manifest systematic change. Or, frequently repeated measurements providing adequate information about change are obtained on small convenience samples of persons that are of dubious value from the standpoint of generality. In either case, the measurement instruments used might be relatively precise and valid tools, or they might be hastily thrown together test batteries or pools of items of unknown (and, alas, unquestioned) substantive and psychometric properties.

From such limited subsets of data, the choice of which is guided by an implicit, if not explicit, view of nature, we attempt to apprehend the complete organism and its context by enunciating and establishing relationships that are generalizable to the unobtained data of which the realized subsets are but limited representations. The consequences of these limitations are not neutral in regard to the substantive conclusions one can draw; rather, they dictate to a considerable extent what view of nature we will obtain. On the one hand, as alluded to earlier, we can use our resources to measure individuals in the most exquisite detail at one measurement occasion. But an individual changes, and by the next hour, next day, or next year, many of the scores would no longer accurately characterize that person. Thus if we used them to describe the individuals subsequently, the portrayal could be largely erroneous. On the other hand, resources could be expended in measuring the individuals over and over again to determine the course of change. This emphasis, however, can result in measuring only a few persons or, if the sample size is maintained, only a few variables instead of the rich variety that might be needed to represent the content domain of interest.

In the social and behavioral sciences, the constraints inherent in collecting data have stimulated valuable discussion of such matters as external validity or generalizability of research designs (Campbell & Stanley, 1966; Cook & Campbell, 1979), representative design of experiments (Brunswick, 1956; Cattell, 1966), and dependability of measurements (Cardinet, Tourneur, & Allal, 1981; Cronbach, Gleser, Nanda, & Rajaratnam, 1972). In the study of development and change, the questions and reservations concerning measurement and design issues have been further emphasized (Baltes, Reese, & Nesselroade, 1977; Hultsch & Hickey, 1978; Nesselroade, 1983, 1988; Wohlwill, 1973). From the hordes of uncertainties signified by these complex characterizations of data, some researchers have flown to the safety of concentrating on the relatively simple, stable, and therefore seemingly more predictable attributes of living organisms—those that are easily measured and that change in an orderly, if not grudging, manner. As noted elsewhere, this perspective misses the richness of both changes within the individual and differences between individuals in those change patterns.

The limiting characteristics of the way empirical inquiry must be conducted force us to make choices concerning which observations or measurements we will obtain in a given research study. Explicit decisions concerning persons, variables, occasions, and so forth, are necessary in order to fashion an experimental design. Once one array of choices involving persons, variables, and occasions have been implemented in a particular design, other possible arrays have, of necessity, been rejected.

It is important to be able to justify the design choices made in a given instance. Despite the convincing rationales reflecting measurement and design concerns that can be mustered to justify the choices that specify the nature of a given data collection scheme, these choices invariably carry with them certain costs. Those costs are exacted in the form of restrictions on the nature and scope of the generalizations that one is able to make from the particular subset of data gathered and analyzed. For example, one familiar argument involves contrasting laboratory and field research with regard to rigor versus generality. Someone once phrased it as the choice between "knowing more and more about less and less or less and less about more and more."

The Data Box and Selection Operations

Elsewhere in a series of discussions (Nesselroade, 1983, 1986, 1988; Nesselroade & Ford, 1987), a general framework for thinking about empirical inquiry in developmental study has been sketched out that rests on the concepts of selection and selection effects. The ideas bear on the design, measurement, and modeling decisions one makes in conducting research. They also have important implications for the conduct of meta-analyses, although that will not be discussed here. There are three central ideas: (1) Empirical inquiry amounts to drawing subsets of observations from a generalized data box of the kind described by Cattell (1966), (2) the experimental arrangements and design features that define the selected subset of observations inevitably are multimodal selection operations, and (3) selection leads to selection effects that, although they reflect nature's organization, can distort the conclusions one can draw concerning the nature and generality of relationships reflected in the data.

In simple terms, selection involves choosing or picking a subset from a number of elements by some natural or artificial process. The entities on which selection takes place can be either concrete or abstract. The elements are the scores we assign (or might have assigned had we chosen to do so) to a given person on a given variable at a given occasion of measurement.

Obviously, the very act of selection implies the possibility of at least one difference (values on the selection variable or variables) between those entities selected and those not selected. But under selection conditions, there are likely to be other differences between the selected elements and those not selected or between the elements from two different selections. The point is that attributes are organized (interrelated across elements in the universe), and subgroups will differ on those variables that are related to the selection variable or variables on which the subgroups were formed. The systematic differences between selected subgroups on variables other than the selection attributes are referred to as *selection effects*. Thus selection involves the process or operation of separating into groups, and selection effects are the results of the separating operation. The more and the greater the differences between subsets of selected elements, the less valid will be attempts to generalize from one subset to another.

Figure 3.4 illustrates the essential selection ideas using a version of the data box (Cattell, 1966). The figure conveys the multimodal selection notion and emphasizes the restricted nature of data actually selected in relation to the "universe" from which it is drawn. Although they are not exhaustive by any means (Cattell, 1966), here we will consider three data box modes: persons, variables, and occasions of measurement. We will focus on the concept of generalization and take each of these three modes in turn and examine the nature of selection and selection effects with respect to it.

The Persons Dimension and Generalizability

Discussions of generalizability with respect to matters of research design, data analysis, and interpretation most often focus on the persons mode of the data box. With some exceptions (e.g., Brunswick, 1956), the concept of representative sampling is usually applied to data classifications along the persons mode. Well developed mathematical and statistical concepts associated with sampling procedures and inference have enabled us to structure this aspect most unambiguously and to give something solid to fall back on in criticizing studies.

The kinds of selection effects that are due to selection operations with respect to the persons mode are relatively familiar. These include reduced variances and attenuated correlations due to restricted score ranges, as illustrated by Figure 3.5 The objections that many researchers voice to single-subject designs reflects the deep-seated beliefs concerning person sampling and generalizability that are taught early on in the training of social and behavioral scientists. The point I want to emphasize is that persons is only one of several modes that need to be considered in assessing generalizability.

The Variables Dimension and Multidimensionality

Selection operations involving the variables mode seem to be less appreciated and are certainly less well understood than are those involving the persons mode. Those espousing a "multivariate orientation" (Baltes & Nesselroade,

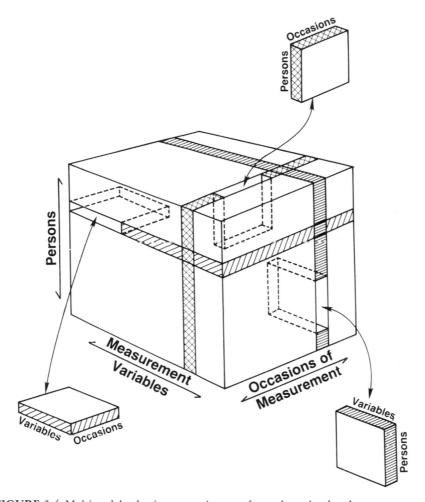

FIGURE 3.4 Multimodal selection operations performed on the data box.

1973; Nesselroade & Ford, 1987) have identified the important issues and have offered some exemplary attempts to define and representatively sample with respect to the variables mode (e.g., Cattell, 1952; Nunnally, 1967). However, defining and representatively sampling from content domains is not something that has been well worked out (Humphreys, 1962). In line with the considerations of this chapter, the variables mode includes both person and context variables, which can futher complicate matters.

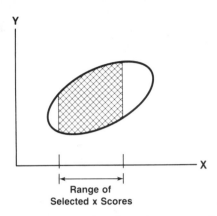

FIGURE 3.5 Selection and generalization along the persons dimension.

The choice of variables that, in turn, helps to define the selection of observations actually drawn in an empirical study involves some notion, although it may be quite vague, of a domain of possible measures. Yet which particular variables are used determines the selection of data that will be examined. How validly do the variables chosen represent the concepts of interest? To use a spatial metaphor, as illustrated in Figure 3.6, some variables fall close the center of a domain, representing some latent variable; others fall on the periphery. One can get a very different perspective on a latent variable or concept (say, anxiety or extraversion), depending on which manifest observables are used to index it.

Modeling with latent variables (Bentler, 1980), which has become an important part of personality research, demands that careful attention be paid to the variables mode. The distinction between measurement and structural model made within the structural modeling literature attests to the singular importance of the variables mode and of selection with respect to it. The relationships among latent variables lie at the heart of theory building in the personality domain. One's selection of data with regard to the manifest or observable variables that represent important latent variables influences the estimation of those relationships via selection effects. Inadequate selections can be disastrous in both basic and applied situations. An example from my own recent experience illustrates the problems of inadequate representations of indicators. A loved one became ill for unidentified reasons. Clinical examination with a stethoscope revealed no heart abnormality. However, x-ray examination by another physician revealed that the person was within 2 weeks of dying from congestive heart failure. Use of the second indicator (the x-ray examination) saved her life.

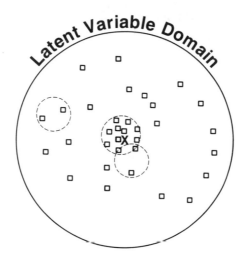

X = Centroid of domain

□ = Manifest variable

◌ = Selection of manifest variables
     to define latent variable

FIGURE 3.6 Selection and generalization along the variables dimension.

The Occasions Dimension for Developmentalists

The occasions mode is a central one for developmentalists. Here we will not differentiate between the occasions mode as representing time and the occasions mode as representing different contexts or situations, although, admittedly, in some cases it is important to make that distinction (e.g., Epstein, 1979; Mischel, 1979).

Questions involving notions of constancy and change imply that the occasions mode of the data box is involved in the characterization of one's data. Tests of stability require multiple occasions of measurement, as do assessments of change. Thus cross-sectional studies do not represent well the occasions mode of the data box. Measuring only once does not provide a basis for inferences about the amount and direction of changes on the variables being measured. The cross-sectional design is an extreme, of course, but measuring only twice may not be much of an improvement (Rogosa, Brandt, & Zimowski, 1982). The point, more generally, is that selection effects resulting from selection operations involving the occasions mode can be especially damaging to the developmentalist. So called "sleeper effects," for example, are only identified when a generous representation of the occasions mode is involved in

Occasion

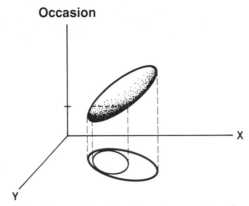

FIGURE 3.7 Selection and generalization along the occasions dimension.

data collection. Figure 3.7 illustrates how relationships extended through time can remain undetected unless the data selection operations work to manifest these relationships (e.g., delayed effects).

Summary

The empirical study of developmental phenomena places complex demands on data. Valid generalizations about differential change patterns of important theoretical concepts depend on obtaining (selecting) data that represent the persons mode (differential patterns), the occasions mode (temporal patterns), and the variables mode (markers of the theoretical concepts) simultaneously. Selection effects created by design restrictions (even though restrictions are necessary to make a design workable) jeopardize the conclusions one draws from a given set of data. Just as one seeking to establish nomothetic laws can ill afford to ignore the persons mode, and the theoretically oriented person who deals with latent variables cannot safely ignore the variables mode, the developmentalist must sooner or later be certain to represent the possibilities of the occasions mode. The developmentalist who aspires to contribute to theory and the establishment of nomothetic relationships must attend to all three modes. In a given study, at best, some aspects of Nature's data box will be poorly represented, and the conclusions reached will reflect the selection effects that result, whether or not they are explicitly acknowledged.

Idiographic Approaches in Nomothetic Science

Assertion: An idiographic orientation to studying phenomena can well serve a nomothetic science.

The distinction between idiographic and nomothetic approaches to lawfulness has received much of its currency in the domain of personality research (Allport, 1937, 1950). Although the approaches have been presented as antithetical, contemporary writers have suggested a synthesis of the two wherein idiographic conceptions are put into the service of seeking nomothetic laws (Cairns, 1986; Lamiell, 1981; Lebo & Nesselroade, 1978; Lerner, 1988; Nesselroade & Ford, 1985; Zevon & Tellegen, 1982).

The essential argument I want to champion here is that the aggregation of data across individuals to develop nomothetic statements can be done prematurely. Understanding the nomothetic processes of human development involves an appreciation of the lawful individuality of each person (Lerner, 1988). Studying the individual thoroughly before aggregating information across individuals (Nesselroade & Ford, 1985; Zevon & Tellegen, 1982) or measuring what the individual does in relation to what he could do (Lamiell, 1981) can produce a more appropriate basis for constructing nomothetic relationships. Thus the objective of determining nomothetic laws remains; what differs is the nature of the data (variable, person, and occasion selection) on which such lawful statements rest. Such an emphasis on a thorough selection of data in regard to variable and occasion modes is consistent with the practices and recommendations of Henry Murray and his collaborators in, for example, *Assessment of Men* (Office of Strategic Services Assessment Staff, 1948).

As a result of genetic and experiential differences, for instance, the manifestations of abstract dimension x in Individual A may involve somewhat different observables than in Individual B. Martha might manifest her anxiety in shortness of breath and a racing pulse, and Eric might manifest his in an elevated systolic blood pressure and increased palmar sweat. Or, Mary might respond "very true for me" to the stimulus adjective "anxious" because she feels anxious, whereas Joan might respond the same way to "anxious" because she feels eager. In addition, they might share other observable attributes of x. However, any lack of equivalence of meaning of observable response patterns confuses the aggregation of data across individuals even though there might be great similarity in, for example, the eliciting stimulus, the course of change, or the patterning of other covariates of a latent attribute of interest such as anxiety. The point is that if we rigidly key on the observed variables (either the indicators or the independent variables), important relationships may be adulterated or missed altogether. One approach to this problem is to analyze each person's data into more abstract patterns that eliminate idiosyncrasies and thereby facilitate comparisons of similarities and differences. One such method will now be discussed.

P-technique Factor Analysis

One of the more interesting (for me) methodological techniques I have explored is the structured examination of intraindividual change by using multivariate, replicated, single-subject, repeated measures (MRSRM) designs and

P-technique factor analysis. The general approach has been around for 4 decades (e.g., Cattell, Cattell, & Rhymer, 1947; for review see Luborsky & Mintz, 1972), and a recent spate of papers suggest that there is increased interest in, if not full acceptance of, the methodology.[1]

The approach rests on two distinct kinds of invariance, both of which are sought within the context of intraindividual variability. One refers to defining a pattern or structure that characterizes the changes within the individual over some significant period of time. It is a form of the concept of stationarity discussed in time series analysis (e.g., Molenaar, 1985). In other words, is the structure (e.g., factor pattern) of relationships within which changes are to be constructed invariant over the period of observation? The other kind of invariance has to do with the extent to which these patterns of intraindividual variation are invariant (replicate) across different individuals. Depending on the extent to which patterns of intraindividual variation replicate (display factorial invariance) across different individuals, Zevon and Tellegen (1982) and Nesselroade and Ford (1985) have discussed the importance of using intraindividual change information to identify characteristics of differences and similarities between individuals that might be used more effectively to study nomothetic lawfulness.

To illustrate the approach and link it to the individual differences tradition, I want to briefly report on a recent study by Corneal and Nesselroade (1988). We conducted an MRSRM study that involved frequently repeated measurements of self-reported emotional behavior. The subjects were two 12-year-old boys. Both youngsters lived with their respective mothers, who were divorced. Both boys also spent significant amounts of time in the homes of their remarried fathers. Quite independently of each other, using a standardized format, each boy reported his emotional reactions to events that occurred on a day-to-day basis. Each boy's responses were factor analyzed; one factor analysis was done of the responses in the home of the mother, and one of the responses in the remarried father's home. In the mother-only context, occasion-to-occasion variability (steady state "hum") in reported intensity of emotions was characterized by a person-specific number of factors (two factors for one boy, three factors for the other). In the remarried-father context, the data were characterized by three factors for the first boy and four factors for the second boy. There was always a difference of one factor between the two boys, but in moving from one family context to the other, for both boys an additional factor was required to describe the occasion-to-occasion variability manifested on the same set of measurement variables. Even though the measurement system was ostensibly the same for both boys in both situations, their response patterns not only showed intraindividual changes as they changed contexts, but they

---

[1]Connie Cannon and I are currently working on a review of MRSRM studies conducted since 1970. Thus far, we have found more than 30 in the behavioral science literature.

also showed consistent interindividual differences in the numbers of dimensions involved in those changes. This is a more abstract kind of individual difference (interindividual differences in intraindividual change patterns) than one typically studies (interindividual differences in score level on one or more attributes).

For each boy, changing family context involved change in the dimensionality of his response patterns. To the extent that switching back and forth between contexts consistently invokes the same changes in patterns of response differentiation, one has predictable patterns of change in steady state. If the pattern of changes in steady state is regular as changes in contact occur, then a more abstract steady state "hum" is involved. That in turn provides "stuff" for identifying a more abstract constancy, such as predictable patterns of change in steady state.

Summary

Psychologists have not done as well as one would like in establishing nomothetic laws that represent impressive predictions. Among the lines of investigation that promise to improve matters is the thorough, intensive study of the individual case as a preliminary to aggregating data across individuals. Single-case analysis, however, tends to prompt immediate and profound concerns about generalizability. We argue that the skepticism in this line of criticism should be tempered long enough to test the gains that can accrue from using replicated single-subject designs. In fact, some key developments in behavioral science have already resulted from this general strategy, for example, operant learning theory.

The more vigorous the repudiation of MRSRM designs, the greater the assurance of their value. Critics who cry "What about generalizability?" and demand large numbers of participants are in effect asserting that people differ from one another in nontrivial ways, thus emphasizing one selection mode without proper regard, perhaps, for others. MRSRM designs are aimed at careful selection on multiple modes which eventually produces a stronger inferential base by sharpening those differences among individuals, rather than trying to even out differences to the point that they no longer matter in a given research design. Careful attention to the various selection modes may reveal that for particular purposes, less wide representation on one mode (e.g., persons) may be offset by broad representation on another (e.g., occasions), as in, for instance, the establishment of a new disease syndrome.

Reliability Versus Stability

Assertion: Related to the measurement of personality attributes, there is a fundamental distinction to be made between the concepts of reliability and stability.

One of many unresolved problems in measuring behavioral phenomena is the separation of measurement instrument or measurement characteristics and behavioral attribute or process characteristics. There are numerous discussions of properties of measurement instruments, such as validity and reliability, and coefficients by which to characterize instruments and applications with respect to these properties (e.g., Nunnally, 1967). The roles played by such coefficients in, say, the assessment of change have been somewhat in dispute for decades (Bereiter, 1963; Cronbach & Furby, 1970).

A distinction that has been usefully made, especially in the context of the trait-state distinction mentioned earlier, is that between *reliability* of the measurement instrument and *stability* of the phenomenon being measured (Nesselroade, Pruchno, & Jacobs, 1986). For example, if one tries to measure a phenomenon at two points in time with a measuring instrument that measures *reliably* both at Time 1 and at Time 2, and there is a lack of correlation (low test-retest stability) between the two sets of measurements, the lack of correlation can be attributed to the nature of the phenomenon. Turning the interpretation around somewhat, the test-retest stability coefficient provides a poor estimate of the reliability of the instrument, even though it properly indicates that the phenomenon being measured changes differentially over time. Test-retest coefficients have worked reasonably well in the case of human abilities, to the extent that such attributes manifest a great deal of stability and the measuring instruments are reliable. But even with abilities a very long interval between test and retest produces a somewhat ambiguous interpretation if the coefficients are only moderately high.

One can attempt to measure a highly stable phenomenon with an instrument that might have high reliability or low reliability. If the instrument is highly reliable and the phenomenon is quite stable, then test-retest coefficients over some interval will tend to be high. If the instrument is unreliable and the phenomenon is quite stable, the test-retest coefficient would tend to be low because of attenuation due to error. Suppose, however, that the instrument is reliable but the phenomenon is not highly stable (e.g., emotional states compared with a 2-week interval between). The test-retest correlation would also tend to be low in this case. Finally, with an unreliable measure of an unstable phenomenon, the test-retest coefficient is again low. Thus by test-retest coefficient alone one cannot distinguish logically between the last three cases. Yet test-retest coefficients are often used to estimate reliability (of the instrument). Von Eye (1982), for example, has systematically investigated the relationship between reliability and test-retest stability.

I will briefly illustrate the points raised with two examples. The first involves an analysis of repeated measurements reflecting scores on two parallel forms of a state anxiety scale (Nesselroade et al., 1986). A model fitting procedure was used to estimate how reliably the two forms measured the latent variable—state anxiety—and the stability of the latent variable scores over three time intervals. The outcome is shown in Figure 3.8.

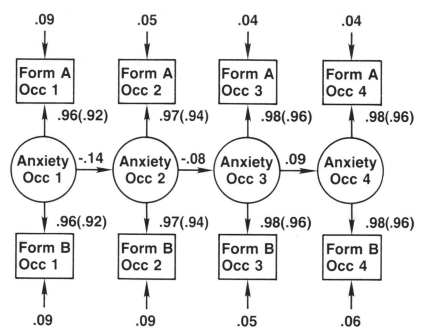

FIGURE 3.8 Reliability and stability (after Nesselroade, Pruchno, & Jacobs, 1986). Numbers at each occasion of measurement are (from top to bottom): unique variance-Form A, loading (and estimated reliability)-Form A, loading (and estimated reliability)-Form B, and unique variance-Form B. Numbers between pairs of occasions are estimates of stability of the latent variable, state anxiety. Fit of model to data ($X^2 = 23.87$; $df = 21$; $p = .30$).

Reliability estimates for the forms are .92, .94, .96, and .96 at occasions 1, 2, 3, and 4, respectively. The stability coefficients for the three intervals vary around zero. These data illustrate that it is possible to measure an unstable phenomenon in a reliable manner. They also show the possible inappropriateness of using a test-retest coefficient as an estimate of test form reliability.

The second example is drawn from a paper by Nesselroade and Cable (1974) that involved factor-analyzing scores on state and trait anxiety variables at two occasions of measurement separately and also the factoring of the between-occasion differences to test the model that the trait anxiety factor should be present at each separate occasion of measurement but should drop out of the difference score solution, whereas the state anxiety factor should be present in all three analyses (Nesselroade & Bartsch, 1977). Again, the argument is essentially that both state and trait scores are reliably measured at a given occasion of measurement. The trait factor, however, is stable, and the act of taking differences removes the stable interindividual differences information from the change scores. To the extent that the trait anxiety test scores represent the stable trait anxiety factor (latent variable) and unsystematic error, only the latter is left in the difference score factor analysis, and thus no trait factor is required to account for the common variance. The outcome of this analysis is presented in Table 3.2. It closely resembles theoretically based expectations and bears witness to the possibility of separating trait-like and state-like sources of variance.

Summary

Reliability of measurement and stability of individual differences are not the same phenomenon even though familiar recommendations to use test-retest correlations to estimate reliability obscure this fact. Work with state measurement has clearly shown the fallacy in this recommendation by demonstrating that highly reliable measurements may show little or no stability over quite short time intervals. For developmentalists, the implications of this distinction between reliability and stability can be summarized in three major points: (1) Variance (individual differences) at a given point in time is not necessarily reflective of stable attributes, (2) changeable attributes can (and should) be reliably measured by instruments that are sensitive to changes, and (3) test-retest correlations should not be used to estimate reliability unless the attribute being measured is a highly stable one.

IMPLICATIONS FOR INDIVIDUAL DIFFERENCES STRATEGIES

The Study of Individual Differences

Assertion: The distinction between stable individual differences and interindividual differences (and similarities) in intraindividual change is critical for developmental research.

The use of individual differences has been the general approach of many students of behavior, including life-span developmentalists (Cronbach, 1957), to their subject matter. It is acknowledged, however, that cogent arguments have been made for experimental methods to understanding development (e.g., Baer, 1973), but this discussion will focus on applications of the individual differences orientation and approaches to the study of systematic changes.

Here, the individual differences approach will be given a critical examination using some of the concepts presented earlier. My own intellectual origins and nurturance have depended heavily on the study of individual differences and associated conceptions, and I realize the risk of intellectual indigestion incurred when one "bites the hand that feeds." Therefore I shall critique with more than a pinch of reservation and, I hope, with a generous measure of

TABLE 3.2 Factor Analyses of Repeated Measurements and Difference Scores of Four State Anxiety and Four Trait Anxiety Marker Variables

Variable	Occasion 1		Occasion 2		Differences
	Trait	state	Trait	state	State
1. State Anxiety	−.07	.75	.05	.63	.78
2. State Anxiety	−.11	.76	−.05	.69	.78
3. State Anxiety	.21	.53	−.01	.72	.57
4. State Anxiety	.09	.60	.01	.62	.55
5. Trait Anxiety	.65	.12	.66	.06	.15
6. Trait Anxiety	.80	−.01	.71	.07	.15
7. Trait Anxiety	.71	.20	.79	.13	.10
8. Trait Anxiety	.70	.18	.75	.19	.16

Note. After Nesselroade and Cable, 1974.

constructiveness. I will conclude that the promise of differential research in personality will be rendered more attainable if we attend more closely to the choice of grist to be processed in the individual differences mill.

To begin, with respect to individual differences approaches to drawing developmental inferences, there is a limitation that needs to be recognized. On the one hand, individual differences measurements, to the extent that they reflect underlying change processes, are like the past perfect tense in that they signify action begun in the past and ended in the past or just ended. Scores on attributes, once obtained and recorded for individuals, have, in an important sense, stopped the action even though the causal processes may continue to effect change after the point of measurement. Those scores, which represent the individual as he or she is to that point in time, essentially catch the individual in a "freeze frame" situation. Thus what we can learn from the scores and their interrelationships about how the scores come about is in reference to action to that point in time. We can compare means, compute correlations, and even do behavior genetic analyses on the scores, but whatever we do to them, they don't inform directly about the individual as he or she continues to exist and change after measurement.

To go beyond obtained scores (or even a sequence of measurements) to consideration of the future (what the individual might become after the last measurement) leads us to using differences (e.g., age differences) to infer the course of changes (e.g., age changes). Differences, however, might or might not provide valid inferences concerning changes. One can study individual differences and be content with inferences that are incomplete with respect to development and change, or one can try to draw inferences to future events using a basis that in many cases is suspect. In a sense, then, an individual differences study is analogous to an archeological "dig" except that when the researcher retreats to his laboratory, his precious artifacts are test scores instead of bones, teeth, and pottery shards.

In regard to the study of personality, broadly defined, one can recognize different lines of research stemming from the individual differences tradition. In this section, we will examine two of them. The first, which is exemplified by work in the areas of human abilities and broad personality traits such as extraversion and anxiety (Wiggins, 1968), is focused on the more or less stable attributes that are valued as predictors of a variety of performance measures and other behavioral criteria. This we will refer to as traditional individual differences work. The second approach, which has been discussed to some extent, involves two kinds of applications: (1) the study of individual differences (and similarities) in intraindividual changes, and (2) the study of similarities and differences between individuals in the organization of intraindividual changes. An example of the first is the analysis of group data reflecting longitudinal information (e.g., growth curves or other developmental trajectories). The second is exemplified by the P-technique factor analysis mentioned above, in which organization is inferred from patterns of covariation of changes over time. Thus in contrast to traditional individual differences foci, the *organization of changes within persons* becomes the focus of individual differences strategies. Let us consider each of the individual differences approaches in more detail.

The Traditional Individual Differences Approach and Prediction

From Binet on, students of behavior have sought explicit ways to index individuals with scores—scores that remained valid over unspecified intervals of time and that could be used as input into prediction schemes. These prediction algorithms are expected to yield as outputs other characterizing indexes of those individuals. As long as the algorithm holds and the input scores accurately represent the individual, one can make differential predictions about people, provided people differ on the characteristics used for input. There are several ways in which prediction can break down. For example, one might have an invalid algorithm (which includes the use or irrelevant input), the outcome measure may be unreliable, or individuals might not be sufficiently differentiated from one another on the inputs to provide differential outputs.

There is another reason why prediction schemes as outlined above might fail—one that is of central concern for the present discussion. *Individuals' scores on predictor attributes might change during the interval between assessment of those predictors and execution of the behavior one intends to predict.* If the changes in predictor attributes are sufficiently differential, then the individual differences information in the original assessments is no longer valid input to the prediction algorithm. Differential predictions are still yielded, but for the individuals as they were when the predictor measurements were made, not as they are when the criterion behavior is occurring.

No wonder such a high premium was placed on the concept of stable, trait-like attributes during the highly formative years of our science! But developmentalists want to focus on changes, and therein lies the difficulty.

In large part, then, it seems that the desire of psychologists to develop prediction schemes has driven the study of many psychological phenomena. The individual differences approach, at least when stable individual differences are used, is highly compatíble with the goal of prediction. Work in the human abilities area exemplifies this general level of research. Lamiell (1981) pointed out, however, that personality researchers have relied heavily on individual differences approaches, even when they were not appropriate or were not applied to appropriate phenomena in light of the question one sought to answer. My premise is that for developmentalists there are more appropriate data to which the individual differences approach can be applied.

Interindividual Differences in Intraindividual Change

Summarizing points covered earlier, there is a considerable amount of evidence favoring acknowledging but distinguishing between more or less stable and more or less changeable attributes of the organism, that is, the complementarity of constancy and change conceptions. Both are required to represent the richness of the individual's personality and behavioral characteristics. Two lines of evidence that challenge the application of traditional individual differences methods have been raised. One, exemplified by the concept of change or developmental trajectory, emphasizes individual differences in changes as opposed to individual differences in more or less static properties of the organism. The second, exemplified by the trait-state distinction, forces us to come to grips with the idea that not all individual differences that are manifest at a particular time are reflective of stable individual differences.

Intraindividual change is the focus of theorizing about age-related phenomena and the target of longitudinal research designs. It has been parceled up more or less unambiguously into age and time of measurement effects in sequential research designs (Baltes, 1968; Schaie, 1965). In brief, it is the centerpiece of developmental research. It seems appropriate, then, to study variability associated with intraindividual change by focusing on similarities and differences among individuals in intraindividual change patterns. Some aspects of this distinction are illustrated in Figure 3.9. The trajectories of persons A and B show differences in periodicity of intraindividual fluctuations but similarity in overall shape or trajectory. Comparisons of the trajectories of persons A and C highlight similarity in periodicity and difference in overall shape. Trajectories of persons B and C differ both in periodicity and shape.

Parallels of this kind of representation are found in the learning curve analysis literature in discussions by, for example, Tucker (1958, 1966). Tucker proposed the disentangling of interindividual differences in performance on a

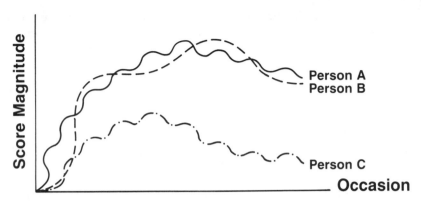

FIGURE 3.9 Differences and similarities in intraindividual changes.

learning task from generalized forms of the learning function. By methods analogous to principal components analysis, one decomposes the successive trial scores of individuals into (1) intraindividual change patterns (one or more learning curves that applied in greater or lesser degree to the recovery of each individual's learning curve) and (2) interindividual differences (and similarities) in those change patterns (the greater or lesser degree to which a given generalized curve was involved in reproducing an individual's performance curve). McCall, Appelbaum, and Hogarty (1973), for example, used this general approach to determine trajectories of IQ development in children. In a somewhat similar vein, Rogosa and Willett (1985) have articulated the study of change in a variety of behavioral variables in terms of interindividual differences in intraindividual changes, and Meredith and Tisak (1984) and McArdle (1988) have discussed elaborate models for studying growth and change from a similar perspective. Thus there are numerous examples of the individual differences approach being applied to patterns of change in a manner analogous to the traditional analysis of individual differences in scores on various attributes.

In the study of developmental phenomena, changes over the life-span, which developmentalists (e.g., Baltes, 1987) have argued can be multidirectional and multidimensional and which are argued to be temporally and culturally embedded, demand differential representations of individual's lives while recognizing generalized trends or patterns of changes. The individual differences methods now emerging for analyzing growth and change seem to offer much promise for meeting the developmentalist's objectives. The two general approaches discussed in the present chapter have involved what Cattell (1952, 1966) referred to as P-technique and T-technique in the context of the covariation chart and the data box. The two kinds of data are identified in Figure 3.10. The classification mode that both data sets have in common is the occasions mode, the one that gives developmental research its character.

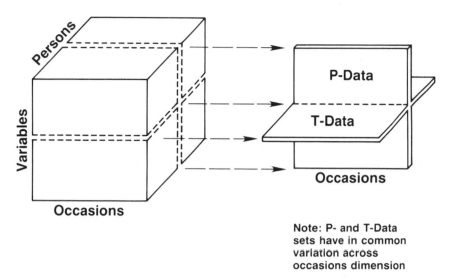

Note: P- and T-Data
sets have in common
variation across
occasions dimension

FIGURE 3.10 P- and T-data in relation to the data box.

The application of individual differences strategies (e.g., MRSRM designs and P-technique factor analysis) to individual level data representing intraindividual change over generous selections of occasions/situations is a promising adjunct to the study of personality and its development. In addition to opening up a richer representation of content for study by exposing the organization of change at the individual level, it can help to sweep aside idiosyncrasies at the measurement level that may not be important at deeper levels of organization. Once a level of individual representation appropriate to one's objectives is obtained, the analysis of similarities and differences in those individual representations can be conducted using the powerful analytic tools that are being more and more commonly used.

Summary

Traditional individual differences approaches have emphasized the study of relatively stable scores. For the developmentalist, it is important to identify and understand changes in phenomena. Hence the application of individual differences thinking to intraindividual change phenomena offers a general, promising approach to understanding how developmental phenomena are organized and occur.

In this chapter, I have tried to argue for striking a balance between two kinds of individual differences that are measured at a given occasion of measurement: (1) relatively constant or stable ones and (2) intraindividual change and interindividual differences therein. Approaching the analysis of individual differences from a change orientation doesn't preclude finding stability (providing measuring instruments are reliable). Beginning with a stability orientation (and insensitive measures) can militate against finding changes, however.

FUTURE DEVELOPMENTS

Where can we expect concerns with change and stability in adult development to take us from here? What kind of methodological agenda is implied if we are to realize further the promise of a life-span orientation to the study of adult personality development? It is always risky to look ahead but certainly permissible in the present context. What might we expect in the way of conceptual and mathematical models in the coming years?

From a design point of view, it seems desirable to pay closer attention to the theoretical demands that developmental questions place on data. If questions call for data that comprehensively represent occasions and variables, for example, then researchers will not be able to take much comfort in studies that sport great numbers of persons unless they also meet the variables and occasions needs prescribed by the questions. Selection on all modes of data and its effects on inferences will become a more and more salient design consideration, I believe. Thus, for example, intensive measurement of small Ns may become a more widely accepted research design serving the broader goal of nomothetic regularity.

From a measurement point of view, there will probably be a more general acceptance of multivariate approaches and a heightened awareness of the need for measures that are appropriately sensitive to changes. We know that differential changes, as manifested by low test-retest correlations, do not necessarily imply that a phenomenon of interest has been poorly measured. One does not know the extent to which past findings of stability in attributes might have been due in part to the use of items and instruments that were selected because they did not show much change. Through researchers attending more closely to concerns with change, measurement lore may well begin to outgrow the legacy of its close association with the study of human abilities during its formative years.

Finally, from a modeling perspective, there is much about which to be optimistic, provided one is also patient. In a paper entitled "An Essay on the Importance of Being Nonlinear," West (1985) identified five stages of progression in understanding in terms of models that are used to represent pertinent phenomena in a given discipline. The five stages are

1. Detailed verbal descriptions culminating in general concepts that synthesize observations into a few fundamental principles.
2. The quantification of Stage 1 concepts and their subsequent rendering into static linear (mathematical) relationships.

3. The generalization of the relationships in Stage 2 into a linear dynamic description from which the relaxation of the process toward the Stage 2 relations can be determined.
4. A fundamental shift in perspective to reexamine the representation of Stage 1 ideas to include the concept of dynamic steady states. Such states require a nonlinear representation and may have little or no direct relation to Stage 3 concepts.
5. The faithful mathematical transcription of Stage 1 understanding into a fully dynamic nonlinear theory whose "solutions" approach the dynamic steady states in Stage 4 with increasing time.

Obviously, personality research, with or without a developmental orientation, has not progressed very far in West's scheme. To return to the opening metaphor, however, West's stages 3, 4, and 5 create a vague and admittedly distant shadow on the horizon for bold sailors to steer toward. Perhaps the wrestling of developmentalists with concepts of change and stability will help to stir the breeze in a favorable direction.

ACKNOWLEDGMENT

The writer thanks Donald Ford for a valuable early consultation on the organization and content of this manuscript and Paul Baltes, Jeff Burr, Richard Lerner, Robert Plomin, Bruce Pugesek, Chip Scialfa, and Alex von Eye for helpful comments and suggestions leading to the final version. Joy Barger and Tarrie Ofstrosky did the technical preparation of the manuscript. Their assistance is acknowledged with pleasure. The author gratefully acknowledges the support of the Max Planck Institute for Human Development and Education, West Berlin, the MacArthur Foundation Research Program on Developmental Aging, and the National Institute on Aging postdoctoral training grant 1 T32 AG00110.

REFERENCES

Allison, P. D. (1984). *Event history analysis: Regression for longitudinal events data.* Beverly Hills, CA: Sage.

Allport, G. W. (1937). *Personality.* New York: Holt.

Allport, G. W. (1950). *The nature of personality: Selected papers.* Cambridge, MA: Addison-Wesley.

Baer, D. M. (1973). The control of developmental process: Why wait? In J. R. Nesselroade & H. W. Reese (Eds.), *Life-span developmental psychology: Methodological issues* (pp. 185–193). New York: Academic Press.

Baltes, M. M. (1986, November). *Selective optimization with compensation: The dynamics between independence and dependence.* Paper presented at the 39th annual meeting of the Gerontological Society of America, Chicago, IL.

Baltes, P. B. (1968). Longitudinal and cross-sectional sequences in the study of age and generation effects. *Human Development, 11,* 145–171.

Baltes, P. B. (1987). Theoretical propositions of life-span developmental psychology: On the dynamics between growth and decline. *Developmental Psychology, 23,* 611–626.

Baltes, P. B., & Nesselroade, J. R. (1970). Multivariate longitudinal and cross-sectional sequences for analyzing ontogenetic and generational change: A methodological note. *Developmental Psychology, 2,* 163–168.

Baltes, P. B., & Nesselroade, J. R. (1973). The development of analysis of individual differences on multiple measures. In J. R. Nesselroade & H. W. Reese (Eds.), *Life-span developmental psychology: Methodological issues* (pp. 219–251). New York: Academic Press.

Baltes, P. B., & Reese, H. W. (1984). The life-span perspective in developmental psychology. In M. H. Bornstein & M. E. Lamb (Eds.), *Developmental psychology: An advanced textbook* (pp. 493–531). Hillsdale, NJ: Lawrence Erlbaum Associates.

Baltes, P. B., Reese, H. W., & Nesselroade, J. R. (1977). *Life-span developmental psychology: Introduction to research methods.* Monterey, CA: Brooks/Cole.

Baltes, P. B., & Schaie, K. W. (1976). On the plasticity of intelligence in adulthood and old age: Where Horn and Donaldson fail. *American Psychologist, 31,* 720–725.

Bandura, A. (1982). The psychology of chance encounters and life paths. *American Psychologist, 37,* 747–755.

Bentler, P. M. (1980). Multivariate analysis with latent variables: Causal modeling. *Annual Review of Psychology, 31,* 419–456.

Bereiter, C. (1963). Some persisting dilemmas in the measurement of change. In C. W. Harris (Ed.), *Problems in measuring change* (pp. 3–20). Madison, WI: University of Wisconsin Press.

Block, J. (1977). Advancing the psychology of personality: Paradigmatic shift or improving the quality of research. In D. Magnusson & N. S. Endler (Eds.), *Personality at the crossroads: Current issues in interactional psychology* (pp. 37–63). Hillsdale, NJ: Lawrence Erlbaum Associates.

Block, J. (1981). Some enduring and consequential structures of personality. In A. I. Rabin, J. Aronoff, A. Barclay, & R. Zucker (Eds.), *Further explorations in personality* (pp. 27–43). New York: Wiley.

Brim, O. G., Jr., & Kagan, J. (Eds.). (1980). *Constancy and change in human development.* Cambridge, MA: Harvard University Press.

Brunswick, E. (1956). *Perception and the representative design of psychological experiments.* Berkeley, CA: University of California Press.

Cairns, R. B. (1986). Phenomena lost: Issues in the study of development. In J. Valsiner (Ed.), *The individual subject and scientific psychology* (pp. 97–111). New York: Plenum Press.

Campbell, D. T., & Stanley, J. C. (1966). *Experimental and quasi-experimental designs for research.* Chicago: Rand McNally.

Cardinet, J., Tourneur, Y., & Allal, L. (1981). Extension of generalizability theory and its applications in educational measurement. *Journal of Educational Measurement, 18,* 183-204.

Caspi, A. (1987). Personality in the life course. *Journal of Personality and Social Psychology, 53,* 1203-1213.

Cattell, R. B. (1952). *Factor analysis.* New York: Harper & Row.

Cattell, R. B. (1963). The structuring of change by P- and incremental-R techniques. In C. W. Harris (Ed.), *Problems in measuring change* (pp. 167-198). Madison, WI: University of Wisconsin Press.

Cattell, R. B. (1966). The data box: Its ordering of total resources in terms of possible relational systems. In R. B. Cattell (Ed.), *Handbook of multivariate experimental psychology* (pp. 67-128). Chicago: Rand McNally.

Cattell, R. B., Cattell, A. K. S., & Rhymer, R. M. (1947). P-technique demonstrated in determining psycho-physical source traits in a normal individual. *Psychometrika, 12,* 267-288.

Cattell, R. B., & Scheier, I. H. (1961). *The meaning and measurement of neuroticism and anxiety.* New York: Ronald Press.

Cook, T. D., & Campbell, D. T. (1979). *Quasi-experimentation: Design and analysis issues for field settings.* Chicago: Rand McNally.

Corneal, S. E., & Nesselroade, J. R. (1988). *A stepchild's experience across two households: An investigation of emotional response patterns by P-technique factor analysis.* Unpublished manuscript, Department of Individual and Family Studies, Pennsylvania State University.

Costa, P. T., Jr., & McCrae, R. R. (1980). Still stable after all these years: Personality as a key to some issues in adulthood and old age. In P. B. Baltes & O. G. Brim, Jr. (Eds.), *Life-span development and behavior* (Vol. 3, pp. 66-102). New York: Academic Press.

Cronbach, L. J. (1957). The two disciplines of scientific psychology. *American Psychologist, 12,* 671-684.

Cronbach, L. J., & Furby, L. (1970). How we should measure "change"—Or should we? *Psychological Bulletin, 74,* 68-80.

Cronbach, L. J., Gleser, G. C., Nanda, H., & Rajaratnam, N. (1972). *The dependability of behavioral measures.* New York: Wiley.

Cunningham, W. R., & Birren, J. E. (1980). Age changes in the factor structure of intellectual abilities in adulthood and old age. *Educational and Psychological Measurement, 40,* 271-290.

Elder, G. H., Jr. (1985). Perspectives on the life course. In G. H. Elder, Jr. (Ed.), *Life course dynamics: Trajectories and transitions 1968-1980* (pp. 23-49). Ithaca, NY: Cornell University Press.

Elder, G. H., Jr., & Liker, J. K. (1982). Hard times in women's lives: Historical influences across forty years. *American Journal of Sociology, 88,* 241-269.

Epstein, S. (1979). The stability of behavior: I. On predicting most of the people much of the time. *Journal of Personality and Social Psychology, 37,* 1097-1126.

Epstein, S., & O'Brien, E. J. (1985). The person-situation debate in historical and current perspectives. *Psychological Bulletin, 98,* 513-537.

Erikson, E. H. (1959). Identity and the life cycle. *Psychological Issues Monograph I.* New York: International University Press.

Eysenck, H. J. (1983). Cicero and the state-trait theory of anxiety: Another case of delayed recognition. *American Psychologist, 38,* 114.

Featherman, D. L., & Lerner, R. M. (1985). Ontogenesis and sociogenesis: Problematics for theory and research about development and socialization across the life span. *American Sociological Review, 50,* 659–676.

Fitzgerald, J. M., Nesselroade, J. R., & Baltes, P. B. (1973). Emergence of adult intellectual structure: Prior to or during adolescence? *Developmental Psychology, 9,* 114–119.

Ford, D. H. (1987). *Humans as self-constructing living systems: A developmental perspective on behavior and personality.* Hillsdale, NJ: Lawrence Erlbaum Associates.

Ford, M. E., & Ford, D. H. (Eds.). (1987). *Humans as self-constructing living systems: Putting the framework to work.* Hillsdale, NJ: Lawrence Erlbaum Associates.

Hertzog, C., & Schaie, K. W. (1986). Stability and change in adult intellectual development: 1. Analysis of longitudinal covariance structures. *Psychology and Aging, 1,* 159–171.

Hooker, K. A., Nesselroade, D. W., Nesselroade, J. R., & Lerner, R. M. (1987). The structure of intraindividual temperament in the context of mother-child dyads: P-technique factor analysis of short term change. *Developmental Psychology, 23,* 332–346.

Horn, J. L. (1966). Short period fluctuations in intelligence. *Final Report* (NSG-518). University of Denver, Denver, CO.

Hultsch, D. F., & Hickey, T. (1978). External validity in the study of human development: Theoretical and methodological issues. *Human Development, 21,* 76–91.

Humphreys, L. G. (1962). The organization of human abilities. *American Psychologist, 17,* 475–483.

Lamiell, J. T. (1981). Toward an idiothetic psychology of personality. *American Psychologist, 36,* 276–289.

Lebo, M. A., & Nesselroade, J. R. (1978). Intraindividual differences dimensions of mood change during pregnancy identified in five P-technique factor analyses. *Journal of Research in Personality, 12,* 205–224.

Lerner, R. M. (1984). *On the nature of human plasticity.* New York: Cambridge University Press.

Lerner, R. M. (1988). Personality development: A life-span perspective. In E. M. Hetherington, R. M. Lerner, & R. M. Perlmutter (Eds.), *Child development in lifespan perspective* (pp. 21–46). Hillsdale, NJ: Lawrence Erlbaum Associates.

Leventhal, H., & Tomarken, A. J. (1986). Emotion: Today's problem. In M. R. Rosenzweig & L. W. Porter (Eds.), *Annual review of psychology* (pp. 565–610). Palo Alto, CA: Annual Reviews, Inc.

Luborsky, L., & Mintz, J. (1972). The contribution of P-technique to personality, psychotherapy, and psychosomatic research. In R. M. Dreger (Ed.), *Multivariate personality research: Contributions to the understanding of personality in honor of Raymond B. Cattell* (pp. 387–410. Baton Rouge, LA: Claitor's Publishing Division.

McArdle, J. J. (1988). Dynamic but structural equation modeling of repeated measures data. In J. R. Nesselroade & R. B. Cattell (Eds.), *Handbook of multivariate statistical psychology* (2nd ed., pp. 561–614). New York: Plenum Press.

McCall, R. B. (1977). Challenges to a science of developmental psychology. *Child Development, 48,* 333-344.

McCall, R. B., Appelbaum, M. I., & Hogarty, P. (1973). Developmental changes in mental performance. *Monographs of the Society for Research in Child Development, 38* (3, Serial No. 150).

McClearn, G. E., Pedersen, N. L., Plomin, R., Nesselroade, J. R., & Friberg, L. (1988). *SATSA: Effects of rearing environment on behavior in later life.* Unpublished manuscript.

Meredith, W., & Tisak, J. (1984, June). "Tuckerizing" curves. Paper presented at the annual meeting of the Psychometric Society, Santa Barbara, CA.

Miller, D. T., & Turnbull, W. (1986). Expectancies and interpersonal processes. In M. R. Rosenzweig & L. W. Porter (Eds.), *Annual review of psychology* (pp. 233-256). Palo Alto, CA: Annual Reviews, Inc.

Mischel, W. (1979). On the interface of cognition and personality: Beyond the person-situation debate. *American Psychologist, 34,* 740-754.

Mischel, W., & Peake, P. (1982). Beyond déjà-vu in the search for cross situational consistency. *Psychological Review, 89,* 730-755.

Molenaar, P. C. M. (1985). A dynamic factor model for the analysis of multivariate time series. *Psychometrika, 50,* 181-202.

Mortimer, J. T., Finch, M. D., & Kumka, D. (1982). Persistence and change in development: The multidimensional self-concept. In P. B. Baltes & O. G. Brim, Jr. (Eds.), *Life-span development and behavior* (Vol. 4, pp. 263-313). New York: Academic Press.

Nesselroade, J. R. (1970). Application of multivariate strategies to problems of measuring and structuring long term change. In L. R. Gaulet & P. B. Baltes (Eds.), *Life-span developmental psychology: Research and theory* (pp. 193-207). New York: Academic Press.

Nesselroade, J. R. (1983). Temporal selection and factorial invariance in the study of change and development. In P. B. Baltes & O. G. Brim, Jr. (Eds.), *Life-span development and behavior* (Vol. 5, pp. 60-87). New York: Academic Press.

Nesselroade, J. R. (1986). Selection and generalization in investigations of interrelationships among variables: Some commentary on aging research. *Educational Gerontology, 12,* 395-402.

Nesselroade, J. R. (1987). Some implications of the trait-state distinction for the study of development across the life-span: The case of personality research. In P. B. Baltes, D. L. Featherman, & R. M. Lerner (Eds.), *Life-span development and behavior* (Vol. 8, pp. 163-189). Hillsdale, NJ: Lawrence Erlbaum Associates.

Nesselroade, J. R. (1988). Sampling and generalizability: Adult development and aging research issues examined within the general methodological framework of selection. In K. W. Schaie, R. T. Campbell, W. Meredith, & S. C. Rawlings (Eds.), *Methodological issues in aging research* (pp. 13-42). New York: Springer.

Nesselroade, J. R., & Bartsch, T. W. (1977). Multivariate experimental perspectives on the construct validity of the trait-state distinction. In R. B. Cattell & R. M. Dreger (Eds.), *Handbook of modern personality theory* (pp. 221-238) New York: Hemisphere.

Nesselroade, J. R., & Cable, D. G. (1974). "Sometimes it's okay to factor difference scores"—the separation of trait and state anxiety. *Multivariate Behavioral Research*, *9*, 273-290.

Nesselroade, J. R., & Cattell, R. B. (Eds.). (1988). *Handbook of multivariate experimental psychology* (2nd ed.). New York: Plenum Press.

Nesselroade, J. R., & Ford, D. H. (1985). P-technique comes of age: Multivariate, replicated, single-subject designs for research on older adults. *Research on Aging*, *7*, 46-80.

Nesselroade, J. R., & Ford, D. H. (1987). Methodological considerations in modeling living systems. In M. E. Ford & D. H. Ford (Eds.), *Humans as self-constructing living systems: Putting the framework to work* (pp. 47-79). Hillsdale, NJ: Lawrence Erlbaum Associates.

Nesselroade, J. R., & Labouvie, E. W. (1985). Research design. In J. E. Birren & K. W. Schaie (Eds.), *Handbook of the psychology of aging* (2nd ed., pp. 35-60). New York: Van Nostrand Reinhold.

Nesselroade, J. R., Mitteness, L., & Thompson, L. K. (1984). Short-term changes in anxiety, fatigue, and other psychological states in older adulthood. *Research on Aging*, *6*, 3-23.

Nesselroade, J. R., Pruchno, R., & Jacobs, A. (1986). Reliability and stability in the measurement of psychological states: An illustration with anxiety measures. *Psychologische Beitraege*, *28*, 255-264.

Nesselroade, J. R., Schaie, K. W., & Baltes, P. B. (1972). Ontogenetic and generational components of structural and quantitative change in adult behavior. *Journal of Gerontology*, *27*, 222-228.

Nunnally, J. C. (1967). *Psychometric theory*. New York: McGraw-Hill.

Office of Strategic Services Assessment Staff. (1948). *Assessment of men*. New York: Rinehart.

Plomin, R. (1986). *Development, genetics, and psychology*. Hillsdale, NJ: Lawrence Erlbaum Associates.

Roberts, M. L., & Nesselroade, J. R. (1986). State variability in locus of control measures: P-technique factor analyses of short-term change. *Journal of Research in Personality*, *20*, 529-545.

Rogosa, D., Brandt, D., & Zimowski, M. (1982). A growth curve approach to the measurement of change. *Psychological Bulletin*, *92*, 726-748.

Rogosa, D. R., & Willett, J. B. (1985). Understanding correlates of change by modeling individual differences in growth. *Psychometrika*, *50*, 203-228.

Rowe, J. W., & Kahn, R. L. (1987). Human aging: Usual and successful. *Science*, *237*, 143-149.

Schaie, K. W. (1965). A general model for the study of developmental problems. *Psychological Bulletin*, *64*, 92-107.

Schaie, K. W. (1983). The Seattle longitudinal study: A twenty-one year exploration of psychometric intelligence in adulthood. In K. W. Schaie (Ed.), *Longitudinal studies of adults psychological development* (pp. 64-135). New York: Guilford Press.

Singer, J. L., & Kolligian, J., Jr. (1987). Personality: Developments in the study of private experience. In M. R. Rosenzweig & L. W. Porter (Eds.), *Annual review of psychology* (pp. 533-574). Palo Alto, CA: Annual Reviews, Inc.

Speilberger, C. D., Lushene, R. E., & McAdoo, W. G. (1969). *The state-trait anxiety inventory (STAI) test manual, form* X. Palo Alto, CA: Consulting Psychologists Press.

Speilberger, C. D., Lushene, R. E., & McAdoo, W. G. (1977). Theory and measurement of anxiety states. In R. B. Cattell & R. M. Dreger (Eds.), *Handbook of modern personality theory* (pp. 239–253) Washington, DC: Hemisphere.

Troll, L. E. (1982). *Continuations: Adult development and aging.* Monterey, CA: Brooks/Cole.

Tucker, L. R. (1958). Determination of parameters of a functional relation by factor analysis. *Psychometrika, 23,* 19–23.

Tucker, L. R. (1966). Learning theory and multivariate experiment: Illustration by determination of generalized learning curves. In R. B. Cattell (Ed.), *Handbook of multivariate experimental psychology.* Chicago: Rand McNally.

Tuma, N. B., & Hannan, M. T. (1984). *Social dynamics: Models and methods.* New York: John Wiley.

von Eye, A. (1982). Statistical and methodological problems of prevention research in psychology [original in German]. In J. Brandstadter & A. von Eye (Eds.), *Psychologische Praevention* (pp. 305–439). Bern: Huber.

West, B. J. (1985). An essay on the importance of being nonlinear. *Lecture Notes in Biomathematics* (No. 62). Berlin: Springer.

Wiggins, J. S. (1968). Personality structure. *Annual Review of Psychology, 19,* 293–350.

Wohlwill, J. F. (1973). *The study of behavioral development.* New York: Academic Press.

Wohlwill, J. F. (1989). Relations between method and theory in development research: A partial-isomorphism view. In P. VanGeert (Ed.), *Annals of theoretical psychology* (Vol. 6, in press). New York: Plenum Press.

Zevon, M. A., & Tellegen, A. (1982). The structure of mood change: An idiographic/nomothetic analysis. *Journal of Personality and Social Psychology, 43,* 111–122.

Zuckerman, M., & Lubin, B. (1965). *Manual for the multiple affect adjective check list.* San Diego, CA: Educational and Industrial Testing Services.

4

Psyche Embedded:
A Place for Body,
Relationships, and Culture
in Personality Theory

Carol Gilligan, Lyn Mikel Brown,
and Annie G. Rogers

A NOTE BY THE FIRST AUTHOR

The word "personality" has its roots in the Latin *per*, meaning through, and *sonare*, meaning to sound, and for a long time, as long as I can remember, I have listened to the sounds of things, as a way of knowing what has happening or what was going on. As a student in college, I learned from extraordinarily gifted teachers how to listen to the sounds of voices in written texts; I also studied perception with the Gestalt psychologist Hans Wallach, whose demonstrations of illusion I found riveting: that things could seem so clearly to be one way (the moon larger on the horizon, the lights moving in the visual display) and yet it was possible to gain evidence, to demonstrate and in that sense to know that they were not as they appeared. In retrospect, it seems a short step—although in fact it was many years—to my current interest in the questions about language and theory, in ways of speaking and seeing, which are at the center of this present work.

Thanks to Mark Tappan for his helpful comments on an earlier version of this manuscript. The research reported in this paper was supported by grants from the Cleveland Foundation and the Geraldine Rockefeller Dodge Foundation.

At a certain point in my life, long after I finished my graduate training, in the historical moment of the early 1970s, after I had been married for some years and involved in raising three children, I noticed what at first seemed incomprehensible: that psychologists studying persona and lives, or adolescence and adulthood, or identity and morality, had for the most part studied only boys and men. And I noticed that I had not noticed this, that speaking as a psychologist, I had in essence learned to disembody myself and also separate myself from relationships and from culture, or perhaps, more correctly, had learned to see and to speak about relationships and culture from the standpoint of the Western tradition as it has been created over the centuries largely by men. As I began to do research on people's experiences of identity crisis and moral conflict, and began in that context to listen to the ways people talk about morality and about themselves and about relationships in their lives, I heard in women's conceptions of self and morality a different voice from the voices which have been amplified by psychological theory. Since then, I have devoted my work to the conundrum of sex differences, to the themes of voice and vision, and to taking soundings into development, as described in this Murray Lecture.

I especially welcomed the invitation to participate in the Murray Lecture series because I was a student of Murray at Harvard (hence the memory of the whale pin on his lapel) and also because his explorations of personality *in* nature, *in* society, and *in* culture seemed so germane to the intention of the joint work represented in this paper: the effort to embed Psyche in body, relationships, and culture. In combining three voices and visions, the "we" of this paper is an orchestration. I chose to write jointly with Lyn Mikel Brown and Annie Rogers because in trying to develop a new language and describe a new way of thinking, it seemed necessary to work in concert—in part to check out with one another the veracity of what we seemed to be hearing and seeing and in part to encourage, in the polyphony of our working conversations, the move from different voices to a musical language and from different perspectives to a new method of reading.

CONUNDRUM

In the quiet of this beginning, we raise the question: What language, what words will we choose in speaking about Psyche—currently known as "the self," the modern heir to the soul, the sense of an I, the sense of a center of feeling, of consciousness, of being in life, of appearing, of taking part, of standing in human condition, of living in connection with others by virtue of having a common sense, or perhaps sensibility, or perhaps a common spirit—a breath, a wind, what once might have been called the hands of a living god? If we may start by clearing the table—of the books, the Xeroxes, the homework, the laboratory apparatus—and spreading a clean cloth, or, if you prefer a dramatic rather than a domestic image, by clearing the stage, then enter Psyche, the soul embodied. Let us ask again in this modern time the age-old question about the relation of soul to body and extend this question to place psyche in the world of relationships and ask about the effects of living with others in time and in place, in culture, in memory, in history, in civilization. For a moment, let us imagine high drama: Let us abduct Psyche from the seraglio of contemporary psychology—and take her, and wash her, and start again. But wait—by embodying Psyche, we have engendered her. How can sex be a difference that makes no difference in personality? Yet to talk about sex differences means to embed Psyche in body, in relationship, and in culture.

We will speak, then, of Psyche as in a body, and therefore in historical time and cultural space. In doing so, however, we speak in language that itself is a legacy of culture, whose medium, words, enters into the body (through the porches of the ears, as Hamlet's father said) and becomes etched in memory and thus part of psyche or soul. How will we then speak about Psyche embedded in these ways?

In his reading of the Hebrew Bible, Robert Alter (1981) sees the art of narrative as necessary to its vision. Only through a narrative art could the ancient Hebrew writers have arrived at a way of seeing people as living reflectively (before God), in the changing medium of time, "incessantly and perplexingly in relationship with others" (p. 22). Placed in time and in relationship, personality or character becomes indeterminate, open to change or reversal. And meaning similarly becomes indeterminate, subject always to revision, to the possibility of seeing anew. This complex moral and psychological realism is, Alter claims, inseparable from a narrative art.

Perhaps this same impulse toward narrative led Henry Murray to reach for *Moby Dick*, to wear always on his lapel an image of a whale, artfully crafted, an icon of his intention to create a theory of personality that would encompass the complex moral and psychological realism of a novel—an exploration of personality *in* nature, *in* society, and *in* culture (the title of one of his books; Kluckhohn & Murray, 1967). Perhaps the same intention led Freud in the fledgling days of his science to write, apologizing profusely, case histories that read like short stories. In this way Freud was able to convey the complexity and the logic of the realm of the psyche, which he felt himself suddenly to be entering, relying on the medium of words, stripping away layers of meaning, proceeding layer by layer. "We liked to compare it with the technique of excavating a buried city," he said, writing of his work with Fraulien Elisabeth von R. (1895, p. 132). Perhaps the narrative art of Freud's early clinical writing also enabled him to render the connection between himself and his patients, to record how he was moved, was affected or touched by his patients; "If we put greater misfortune on one side and entertain a girl's feelings, we cannot refrain," he writes, "from deep human sympathy with Fraulein Elisabeth" (p. 144). Words, the medium of the treatment, created a channel for feelings.

Yet this narrative art, with its implicit vision of life lived in relationship and in time, yielded in Freud's case, as in Murray's, to an impulse that was deemed "scientific"—an impulse announced by Freud in terms of a decision to "scientifically sift" his language. In the name of science, Psyche was disembedded, disembodied, and rendered an "object." Let us begin with a puzzle—in reverse form, a syllogism:

If sex is a difference that makes little or no difference in personality, then Psyche is encapsulated, walled off from body, from relationships, and from culture. Conversely, if Psyche is embodied and also in relationship and in culture, then, since human bodies are characterized by sexual dimorphism, since human cultures are largely male creations and disproportionately represent men's lives, since sex is a difference that makes a difference in terms of social and economic status and perspectives, and since human relationships typically follow different patterns for male and female children, we would expect to find sex differences writ large in personality theory, and the differences in the lives of women and men illuminated in terms of psychological development. That this is not the case presents a problem. Relying for the moment only on logic, we find the claim of no sex differences to be theoretically incoherent, implying a separation of Psyche from body, relationships, and culture that, psychologically speaking, makes no sense. Looking around us, we see in this separation a gap between psychological theory and people's experience.

In the move away from a narrative art to a science that rejects narrative art, psychology has lost an awareness of voice and vision, and with it the recognition that a story can be told from more than one angle and a situation seen in different lights. In the absence of voice and vision, the ability to render differences fades into the stark alternatives of a universal standpoint—the presumption of a God's-eye position—or the abandonment to riotous relativism—the claim to have no perspective or terms. We propose to solve our conundrum—to embed Psyche and to speak about difference—by recovering voice and vision as concepts that link Psyche with body, with relationship, and with culture.

We are continuing to clear the table, wiping away for a moment the lines of distinction between body, relationship, and culture in order to reveal how relationships are themselves "cultures" and how bodies are full of holes and signs. Thus Psyche embedded lives in a constant state of exchange with the world, taking in through the permeable membranes of the senses—the portholes of the eyes, the porches of the ears—images and sounds and making them over into colors and textures, orchestrations, rendering them through a cultural reading into symbols and signs. To embed Psyche in this way implies a change in the language of psychology, and a shift perhaps in its fundamental motivation—away from control and toward reception, a relinquishing of the age-old hopes for certainty or justification and a settling instead for understanding, for a better way of reading or making sense, and also a giving up of the wish for autonomy and objectivity: the belief that one can know the truth by oneself and in this sense can be self-governing. Evelyn Keller (1985) suggests in her recent *Reflections on Gender and Science* that we consider a change in the root metaphors of science—the metaphors used in defining knowledge (see also Keller & Grontkowski, 1983). Specifically, she argues for a shift away from the privileging of sight and vision—the reliance on the "mind's eye" or the "natural light" of reason—because of the way in which visual images encourage atemporality, objectification, and a split between subject and object, body and mind. Metaphors of voice and hearing, in contrast, do not carry the same implications of separation and control but instead draw attention to human connection—to the relationship between speaker and listener, to the possibility of different languages, and thus to the potential for misunderstanding and mistranslation as well as to the ability of people to see and to speak about themselves and the world in more than one way. In short, by suggesting a change in the language and the metaphors of psychology, we imply the need for a metaphysical shift: a change in stance, a new voice, a different perspective, a change of heart. What does it mean, in the context of the present moment in the late twentieth century in Western culture, to risk, for ourselves as we risk for Psyche, the innocence of inquiry, "the pain of being born" (Nussbaum, 1986b, p. 257)?

STRUGGLING TO FIND A WAY TO TALK ABOUT DIFFERENCES

Once Psyche is embedded—embodied and placed in history, in personal and cultural space and time, then as psychologists we face the question, how will we talk about differences, including the question, what differences will we choose to talk about, and from what vantage point and in whose terms? Traditionally, personality psychologists, the Aristotelians of the profession, have talked about differences in terms of character—character traits or personality styles. Developmental psychologists, more Platonic, have talked about differences in terms of stages, mapped across the universal plain, the field of human development. Both of these discourses have recently been disrupted by a series of interpretive questions: What is the point of view from which a psychologist observes the field that he or she is describing? Who is observing whom and from what vantage point? Who is speaking about whom and in whose terms?

  Into this panoply of interpretive questions, the question of sex difference enters—at once so innocent and so deeply disruptive because the two-ness of sex challenges the framework within which differences are typically discussed. Neither one nor many, the male/female division calls attention to the limitations of the Platonic legacy—the assumption that behind the world of appearance there is one true reality, one ideal type or pure form—and also challenges the antithesis of this position: the assumption that the opposite of the one is the many, that the alternative to a unified truth is a relentless relativism, an unmanageable diversity. Inevitably, the quest for the one pure form founders on the question: what is the pure form of the human body? Is it male or female? Similarly, the search for an objective stance or a disinterested position runs aground when it comes to discussing sex differences: Who, other than Tiresias, could possibly claim neutrality? One reason the sex difference question is so disturbing may be that it exposes these limitations in current ways of thinking about differences and calls for a reformulation.

As psychologists, we are aware of the pitfalls of our professional discourse: the tendency to make false claims of universality by speaking as if all mothers could be represented by "the mother" or all children by "the child." We also are familiar with the tendency to give lip service to relationships and culture and then to speak about psychic life as if it took place outside of space and time. As women, however, we are sensitized to difference—aware of how easily difference becomes deviation and deviation turns into sin. As women, we know how readily psychological language can cloak moral judgment, allowing statements of value to pass for scientific norms. No one has written more powerfully about the slide from difference to deviance than Toni Morrison (1970) in *The Bluest Eye*, nor captured with the economy of naming a character "Pecola" the relationship within a norm driven culture between peculiarity and sin. No one, perhaps, has seen so deeply or written so scathingly about the psychological costs of justifying a norm that renders one deviant by definition—helplessly and inescapably deficient. Morrison's novel, written with the double clarity of difference in race and gender, points to the problems that women face in entering a psychology that is not only norm driven but also normed largely on samples of men.

We begin by entering history and picking up from our vantage point in the present moment a trail of evidence in the writings of other women who have entered philosophy and psychology in the last half century and struggled to find new ways of speaking: Susanne Langer, Hannah Arendt, Jane Loevinger, Jean Baker Miller, and, most recently, Martha Nussbaum. In their attempts to reframe basic questions about the human condition, the good life, and the psychological endeavor, we find a chain of thinking that leads from a sense of an impasse to a sense of an opening.

The first link in the chain is a disturbance about methods. Susanne Langer, writing in 1951, noted a "great key change" in philosophy, a change in the questions that followed from the recognition that human understanding is essentially transformational: It proceeds by way of signs and symbols. In this basic notion of symbolization, Langer saw an opening—a way of freeing psychology as well as philosophy from "the deadlocked paradoxes of mind and body, reason and impulse, autonomy and law" (Langer, 1951, p. 25). The wellspring of this transformation lay in the arts, which held the potential of releasing psychology from the grip of a "militant methodology"—a methodology based on a kind of idolatry, a worship of gods of the physical sciences, the "idols of the laboratory" (Langer, 1967) that could not unlock the secrets of the human psyche or soul.

Langer's dismay over psychologists' methods was echoed by Hannah Arendt's (1958) distress over the way in which the laws of statistics acted to flatten or remove difference and thus eroded the human condition, which Arendt saw us one of plurality. Arendt's alarm over the modern tendency toward "the rule by nobody," which does not necessarily signify no rule but may, under certain conditions, turn out to be one of the cruelest and most tyrannical forms of government, was heightened by her suspicion that the rule by nobody breeds and depends on the modern behavioral sciences, specifically on the statistical methods that reduce the plurality of human life to a single, potentially tyrannical, composite norm. In the desire to normalize people and to equate difference with deviance from the norm, Arendt saw a witting or unwitting prelude to rendering the behavior of humans (en masse) predictable and therefore subject to control.

The unfortunate truth about modern social science, as Arendt saw it in the late 1950s, was that the effort to predict behavior statistically, using large numbers of subjects to infer laws and norms, cultivated as intolerance of difference. In essence, modern social science, entering the human condition, affects that condition adversely by creating conglomerate norms and encouraging conformity to such norms in the name of science or progress. That individuals in psychological case histories are named like characters in Kafka's novels—by a single initial or a first name and initial, K. or at most, Joseph K.—serves to illustrate Arendt's point. In a century where Arendt found the overriding moral problem to be one of thoughtlessness or mindless conformity—the obedience to authority that Stanley Milgram documented in his unsettling laboratory experiments (Milgram, 1974)—the behavioral sciences seemed to be contributing to as well as documenting the phenomenon.

In this light, we read with particular interest a common emphasis on openness and vulnerability in the otherwise very different work of Jane Loevinger, Martha Nussbaum, and Jean Baker Miller. To Loevinger (1957, 1979) openness is the mark of good science, a science built on methods that are open to new evidence and also not encumbered or shrouded by a mystifying language. To Nussbaum (1986a), openness and vulnerability connote what is quintessentially human: the fact of mortality, the ability to be fatally wounded. The fragility—the special beauty—of human excellence or goodness has its roots in this soil and therefore, as rendered in the Greek poetic tradition, "is something whose very nature it is to be in need, a growing thing in the world that could not be made invulnerable and keep its own particular fineness" (p. 2). Yet if it is true that "a lot about us is messy, needy, uncontrolled, rooted in the dirt and standing helplessly in the rain, it is also true that there is something about us that is pure and purely active, something that we could think of as divine, immortal, intelligible, unitary, indissoluble, ever self-consistent and invariable" (p. 2). In fact, it is precisely this tension between two ways of thinking about human goodness that defines the parameters of the moral life.

Looking back through Kant, Nussbaum theorizes, philosophers have lost sight of the wisdom present in the odes of Pindar and the Greek tragedies. In part this forgetting may stem from the fact that those people who have been most involved with human fragility and neediness, with helplessness, with mess, need, dirt, and lack of control, have been women—those who have been most occupied with taking care of growing things. Looking back through Kant and the major contemporary Western philosophers—all male and mostly not involved in taking care of living things, it is easy for us to understand the oversight Nussbaum traces, as well as her own perception of the problem, as in part a reflection of sex differences, though she herself does not cast it in these terms.

Jean Baker Miller (1976), however, identifies the qualities of openness and vulnerability with women, in whose situation she finds "a crucial key to understanding the psychological order." Miller's question is centrally about differences: What do people do to people who are different from them, and why? Noting that the encounter with difference can become the occasion for cruelty and tyranny, she also sees the engagement of difference as essential to human growth. The psychological order, in Miller's analysis, is an order both of inequality (domination/subordination) and of connection (symbolized by the family, the crucible, the milieu in which the human psyche is formed). Miller notes that women not only have carried for both sexes the activities of caring for those others who are needy, dependent, and helpless but also have carried in themselves the qualities of fragility and vulnerability, which Nussbaum links with goodness and Miller considers a sign of psychological strength.

Thus the fragility or vulnerability attendant upon remaining open to the world, which Loevinger sees in the good scientist and Miller in women and Nussbaum in the good person—a person worthy of praise—defines a common moral voice or vision that links the writing of these women to our present endeavor. The shift in perspective and in method also highlights the concepts of moral voice and vision that offer a way of placing body, relationships, and culture at the center of personality theory.

To summarize: to take the fact of sex difference seriously and to embed Psyche in body means to give up the Platonic legacy of one pure form, along with its nemesis of endless relativism. At the same time, the embodiment of Psyche calls attention to vulnerability—to the ability of people to be wounded by others and also to wound others and themselves—and thus to the hope for protection, the wish for morality, the wish that people would or the belief that they should act justly and take care. To embed Psyche in relationship means to leave behind the image of perfection and the search for self-sufficiency and control. And finally, to embed Psyche in relationships and culture means to open psychology to moral scrutiny—to observe what voices are amplified and what voices are muted or silenced, as well as to identify values currently masquerading as psychological norms.

THE SENSE OF AN OPENING: VOICES AND VISIONS

Our sense of an opening follows from the creation of a method of working: a guide to reading for self and moral voice that may best be compared to a process of ear training—somewhat along the lines of *A Young Person's Guide to the Orchestra* (Britten, 1946) or like learning to distinguish the oboe from the clarinet in Prokofiev's *Peter and the Wolf*. We use these analogies both to convey the precedents for what we are attempting and also the very basic intention of our endeavor: to provide a way for a reader to tune his or her ear to the voice of a person telling a story about moral conflict and to listen for the voices of justice and care. The entire procedure can be compared to gaining entry into the world of another by following the story that person tells—what constitutes moral conflict or creates uncertainty or marks a turning point or choice in that person's world; then listening for self—for the I who narrates and appears as the protagonist in a moral drama—and for the languages of justice and care, which mark vulnerabilities people feel in relationships—concerns about oppression and concerns about abandonment and strategies for protecting oneself and other people. To mix the metaphor, narratives of moral conflict provide snapshots of people acting in the world of relationships, a world where people are vulnerable, where they can wound themselves and others, where something of value is at stake—a world well marked by language and culture. Listening for self challenges the reader to hear the voice of another person speaking; it also creates an avenue of connection between reader and speaker, an avenue widened by the commonality of moral language and human concerns.

We begin with a narrative, told by a particular person in a particular place and time, specifically a person asked by a researcher to speak about an experience of moral conflict, and thus to speak about vulnerability: about being wrong, being hurt, being uncertain, being wounded—intentionally, unintentionally, by other people or by acts and events beyond human control. In reading these narratives, we assume no neutral, God's-eye position. What then becomes our claim for the integrity or validity or usefulness to others of our interpretations?

We have sprinkled metaphors of voice and vision throughout our written and spoken reports to draw attention to our interest in ways of seeing and ways of speaking. Our Reading Guide specifies four readings as a way of putting into action our research finding that people have more than one way to tell a story and can see a situation through different lenses and in different lights.

Over the years of listening to moral conflicts, we have discovered that such stories typically have the unity and perspective of good drama, moving from crisis to denouement. But we also have found that these stories about moral conflict often pertain to what people deem vitally important, so that they tend to engage the attention of listener and speaker and are often remembered by both over the 1-year interval that tends to punctuate our longitudinal research. As moral language marks experiences of vulnerability in a world of relationship and is itself the legacy of a culture, it provides a way of listening to Psyche embedded and thus a new way of exploring empirically the place of body, relationship, and culture in personality psychology. Here then is our method, our way of reading, for which we provide a "Reader's Guide."[1]

Reading for Self and Moral Voice

Our Reader's Guide (Brown et al., 1987) is an interpretive method. As such it contrasts with coding manuals that are designed to teach coders to match key words or phrases or target sentences to a predetermined set of categories (see, e.g., Colby & Kohlberg, 1987). Instead, it is designed to teach people to hear moral voice and spot moral orientation.[2] Using our guide, a reader reads for self and moral voice. Listening for moral voice, the reader hears stories people tell about themselves and others, stories often built on a tension between conflicting commitments people make or between responses that seem incompatible. They may search for inclusive solutions to such conflicts, for creative solutions that remove the dilemma, or they may seek a rule or a principle that clarifies what they should do, or they may experience tragic conflict: a sense that however they turn, something of value will be lost irreparably. In designing our method, we sought to hold and represent the sense of tension that people often convey, and also to record the complexity of the narratives in order to capture the situational, the personal, and the cultural dimensions of

[1]The Reader's Guide grew out of a 3-year collaboration that included the following people: Lyn Mikel Brown, Dianne Argyris, Jane Attanucci, Betty Bardige, Carol Gilligan, Kay Johnston, Barb Miller, Richard Osborne, Janie Ward, Grant Wiggins, and David Wilcox.
[2]It is important to mention the work of Nona Lyons (1982), who developed an earlier coding system designed to identify moral orientation. Her method was the first attempt to systematically represent care and justice as distinct moral perspectives, and we owe her work a great debt. Our Reader's Guide was constructed in part to remedy certain conceptual problems we found with Lyons's method and other methods that represent justice and care as bipolar dimensions or opposing categories within a single world view (see Colby & Kohlberg, 1987; Walker, de Vries, & Trevethan, 1987). We found especially troubling the opposition between self and other and the linking of this opposition to the contrast between justice and care. Our Reader's Guide differs from Lyons's effort in complex ways, and a detailed discussion is beyond the scope of this paper. However, we are preparing such a discussion as part of the introduction to the Reader's Guide.

psychic life, including language and voice, perspectives and visions, and the relationship between the reader's and the narrator's ways of seeing and speaking. Justice and care are voices tracked as they weave in and out of a narrative. In this sense they are not "coding" categories but rather channels of connection, markers of a common social landscape, the longitude and latitude of oppression and abandonment, along which people map powerful feelings, thoughts, hopes, and fears.

We have chosen to speak about *reading* for self and moral voice to highlight the interpretive nature of our work. In describing a way of reading, we try to teach not only a way of listening, a way of attending, but also a way of responding. To move away from the framing of moral questions in terms of the contrast between a unitary view of moral truth and endless moral relativism, we have shifted the focus of attention from abstract moral truths to the observable world of social relationships where people can describe something that happened which they thought was unfair or situations in which someone did not listen. We define two desirable visions of relationship (a vision of justice and a vision of care) and map the social and moral world by the sounds of two voices. Our two-voice method records conflict and tension, as well as harmony and resolution. And because we have two visions, we never lose sight of the fact of perspective. Thus we have worked to develop a method that highlights the interpretive nature of the reading process, and we have tried to operationalize a way of listening, a way of attending to self and moral voice that takes into account both our stance as researchers and the stance of the person speaking within the text.

Our method grew out of our effort to create and teach to others a theoretical framework that could encompass two voices and visions that we heard recurring in the data of our research and also across generations and cultures: the voices of justice and care, the visions of equality and attachment or connection between people[3] (see Gilligan, 1977, 1982, 1986; Gilligan & Wiggins, 1987).

Listening for Justice and Care

Here are adolescents talking about morality. First, the voices of teenagers speaking about care, that is, not hurting, paying attention, taking action, creating and sustaining connection:

---

[3]We have struggled with a language to describe the complexity of the moral vision of caring in relationship, since many relational terms carry negative valences; for example, "attachment" is often heard as overly emotional, nonintellectual, and is used to mean enmeshment or fusion with another; "connection" seems to us slightly better but loses some of the emotional overtones of "attachment." As a result, we have often used both together, since either one alone seems inadequate. This heightens our awareness of the need for a richer and more specific language to describe the experiences of relationship.

WHAT MAKES SOMETHING A MORAL PROBLEM?
When it hurts someone. When something is done that hurts someone.

WHAT DO YOU MEAN BY MORALS?
Morals are what you believe in, and I believe that someone I care about, I don't want to let something happen. If I know that there's even a remote possibility of something happening, I should take action when you can, or when anyone can.

WHAT DOES MORALITY MEAN TO YOU?
A good feeling, a feeling good.

HOW DO YOU GET THAT?
Just by making friends and letting them know you are there and showing them that you're kind.

WHAT MAKES THAT A MORAL PROBLEM FOR YOU?
The simple act of "doing it" is not a moral issue, but it's what can result, a child can result and that's moral I think.

WHAT WOULD MAKE SOMETHING A MORAL PROBLEM?
If it hurt the person or it endangered your house or something like that, then it would be wrong or whatever. If it would help other people or help somebody, then it would probably be better than the thing that was wrong.

Now, here are teenagers speaking in terms of justice, that is, treating others fairly, maintaining standards of reciprocity and respect, anchoring oneself to a standard like Odysseus tying himself to the mast:

WHAT DOES MORALITY MEAN TO YOU?
Sticking to what you believe in and not letting your environment, like this, or things that happen, affect it in a large way. . . . Your morals are the things you believe in, not just religion. They're life's rules and stuff. I think it's very important to have morals. It keeps you going. If you don't have morals you can be moved in the wind too easily.

WHAT DOES MORALITY MEAN TO YOU?
When I think of moral I think of a defined right and defined wrong, and there is no way of falling in between. . . . Morality tells me my values. This had nothing to do with my values. It just had to do with my life, my friendship with somebody.

WHAT MAKES THAT MORAL?
I have my standards and that's what's important, not how everyone's going to look at me.

WHAT MAKES THAT A MORAL PROBLEM FOR YOU?
It wouldn't be fair to my parents or myself, so I just didn't do it [drink]. . . . It's important to me to maintain a good reputation in a way. . . . It is kind of repayment, you know; I am getting a lot out of this and they spend a lot of money and it is one of the few things they ask me, not to get in trouble, just to study your hardest. . . . I think that's perfectly fair. I mean, if they ask a lot of things, then that's not fair, but those are pretty simple requests for what they give me. . . .

WHAT WAS AT STAKE FOR YOU IN THIS DILEMMA?
What is at stake is proving whether my judgment in that case was correct or incorrect, I think.

WHAT WOULD BE MORAL?
I mean, you can argue with someone as long as you are not being malicious to their character, like their views. I mean, everyone has a right to their own views. It's sort of like freedom of speech. . . . You are allowed to speak your own thoughts because it is not actually being malicious, you're just telling other people what you feel; they don't necessarily have to feel what you feel.

Remember the care voice?

[I considered] just what was best for everyone involved . . . because I didn't want to upset anyone, or I didn't want anyone to get hurt.

I don't think anybody is self-sufficient, and no woman is an island.

In these voices we hear different visions of relationship—two visions of a world in which people treat each other well. Here is a 12-year-old boy conveying a vision of relationships guided by justice: "The fair thing would be to listen to him. Take in his idea as a possible thing to do. Then if they see some valid reason for not doing it, to tell him in a just, mannerly way, instead of saying something that shoots the whole thing down."

His vision of justice incorporates the act of listening, with an eye to respect toward the other, that is, not "saying something that shoots the whole thing down" but presenting reasons in a "just, mannerly way." This same 12-year-old conveys a vision of relationships guided by care:

. . . A lot of times I've noticed that if you're with a bunch of friends and your other friends keep putting down the other friend, he starts to feel really unwanted. You know, like his ideas really don't count for anything. And he's just with you, to be with you, like another . . . heart. And so, I think you really have to show that person that you care what their thoughts are. Or else they're just going to feel low.

His vision of care involves attention to the feelings of the other and the meaning and experience of relationship between friends—"He's . . . with you, to be with you, like another . . . heart." Responsibility to this experience of relationship requires that "you really have to show that person that you care what their thoughts are"; that is, it requires a responsiveness to the other and his feelings.

From these visions one can extract two moral injunctions: that one should treat others "in a just, mannerly way" and that one should care about "what their feelings and thoughts are."

These two visions of relationship recur in narratives of moral conflict and ground our method of analysis and interpretation. Our Reader's Guide is designed to track moral voice and to locate self in relation to these voices and visions—are these voices claimed or unclaimed? Are these visions owned or disowned? To demonstrate how our method works, we will first present an overview of our interpretive procedures and then go through a narrative, showing you how we tune our ears to the voice of the speaker and pay close attention to the themes of justice and care in the story told.

Interpretive Procedures

As readers (or interpreters) using our Guide, we first locate a narrative of real-life moral conflict in a larger interview text and then prepare to read the story at least *four* different times, taking four soundings. During each reading we listen for a different voice or approach the narrative from a different standpoint.

The first time we read to get a sense of the story told by the narrator. Like a literary critic or a psychoanalyst, we look for clues to meaning in verbal patterns or psychic processes: recurrent words and images, central metaphors, emotional resonances, as well as shifts in meaning, inconsistencies in style, revisions and absences in the text as well as shifts in narrative position—the use of first, second, and third person voice. The first time we read, then, our attention will be focused on the narrator's story as he or she tells it. The goal is simply to understand the context, the drama (the who, what, when, where, and why of the story); to listen, to attempt to "hear" as clearly as possible the narrator's tale.

In the second reading, we listen for "self," by which we mean the narrator, the speaking voice, the "I," the person who is telling this story and also the person who appears as an actor in this story, the protagonist in this drama of moral conflict and choice. In the third and fourth readings we listen for moral voice: in the third reading we listen for care and in the fourth reading for justice.

We have sometimes talked of each reading as looking through a different interpretive lens; each lens brings into focus different aspects of the narrative. To switch metaphors, each reading amplifies a different voice. A given statement may have different meanings depending on the lens, and a meaning may become apparent by using one lens that is hidden from view by using another. We use different graphics to represent passages on the interview text gleaned from each reading; capital letters represent self, underlined passages concern care, and boldface letters represent justice. To mix metaphors, we have found that this visual technique of representation attunes the reader at once to the specific languages or voices of the narrator without losing sight of the larger story or the way these voices are orchestrated to convey the conflict.

We have assumed in developing our Reader's Guide that a story of conflict told by another can be heard and understood by a careful reader. In our open-ended interview format we have partially assured the coherence of the story by training interviewers to ask the narrator clarifying and activating questions in addition to standard interview questions about the construction of the moral dilemma or drama, the resolution of the problem, and the evaluation of the action or choice (see Appendix 1 for a copy of our moral conflict and choice interview questions).

Because we assume common concerns and a common language, we believe in the possibility of understanding the narrator's story. After all, all people, by virtue of being human, are vulnerable to oppression and abandonment and therefore have access to experiences that underlie concerns about justice and injustice, care and carelessness. We also believe in the importance of these experiences in structuring psyche. Our method of tracking moral voice embeds psyche in relationships because moral language itself is embedded in relationship and culture, inscribed into the soul.

A Guided Reading: The Case of Tanya

To illustrate the Reading Guide, we turn to Tanya, a 12-year-old in one of our studies, a member of the seventh grade. What can we learn about Tanya by asking her to tell us about a time when she experienced moral conflict, when she had to make a decision and she was not sure what she should do?[4] One of the things we have learned from our studies is that children, as well as adolescents and adults, will respond to this question and tell stories in which they appear as the protagonist in a moral drama. Let's begin with the first reading; asked to speak about an experience of moral conflict, what does Tanya speak of?

The First Reading: Reading for Plot

When we were at camp [2 years ago], I went to camp with my sister and my cousin, and he was really young, he was, like, maybe 7, and he got really, really homesick. It was overnight. And he was like, always crying at night and stuff. And we had this camp guide who was really tough and I was really afraid of him . . . And he said, "Nobody is allowed to use the phone," and so my cousin really wanted to call his parents, [Yah] and it was kind of up to me to go ask the guy if he could. So, either like I got bawled out by this guy and asked, or I didn't do anything about it, and he was my cousin, so I had to help him, so I went and asked the guy if he could use the phone and he started giving me this lecture about how there shouldn't be homesickness in the camp. And I said, "Sorry, but he's only 7." [Yah] And he was really young and so he finally got to use the phone, so he used the phone. And then we had a camp

---

[4]The full text of Tanya's interview, with readers' "Worksheets" and case analysis for self and moral voice are presented in Appendixes 2 and 3.

meeting, and um, and the guy started saying, "Any kid here who gets homesick shouldn't be here," and he didn't say my cousin's name, but like, he was like, almost in tears.

In the first reading one reads for the plot. The goal is to understand the narrative; what is the story that is being told? What are the conflicts described and, more generally, what is the landscape of this psychological and social world, as indicated by the relationships mentioned, the use of moral language, repeated words and themes, seeming contradictions, and key images and metaphors?

Tanya's story is about her cousin's homesickness, the intrasigence of a camp director, and her decision, despite her fear, to help her cousin call his parents. The conflict was, she says succinctly, "me saving myself or saving him." She decided to help her cousin because "nothing bad was going to happen to me"— the camp director might intimidate her and hurt her feelings but he "can't beat me up or anything." She realized that "it was worth letting [her cousin] talk to his parents . . . he was . . . screaming [and having] nightmares . . . He wasn't being able to have any fun and he paid for it . . . he was like almost homesick, you know. That's why I guess they call it homesick." The camp director, she thinks, "was really callous." Looking back, Tanya says that it's obvious that her decision was right—at least for her. "It might not be for you or somebody else, but it's helping out my cousin and that camp director, it was a rule, but people are more important than rules." Besides, she notes, the camp director was contradicting himself; they say "We're here to help our kids, to make them have fun." Her cousin, she observes, "wasn't having fun, he was just contradicting the whole slogan." Tanya considers the story she has told to be about a moral problem because "I could have gotten out of it easily, you know, and it wasn't my feeling, my cousin's, but he was like really close . . . I wasn't feeling what he was feeling, but I did have a little empathy, but not that much. So, either I could have gotten out of it and said, "I'm not going up to that camp director, you go up yourself" to my cousin, but he was like very miserable and I almost felt like he did in a way, so, I did go up because I felt miserable having him feel miserable."

Listening to this narrative of moral conflict, we note that Tanya states the problem on several levels—as a conflict between saving herself and saving her cousin, as a conflict between people and rules, as a conflict between doing nothing and doing something in a situation where she sees the possibility of doing something to help. The relationships involved are Tanya's relationship with her cousin, with herself, with the camp director, and with her friends, as well as the cousin's relationship with his parents. A possible contradiction in the story is between Tanya's sense that the right thing was obvious and that she did the right thing, and her sense of moral conflict.

The Second Reading: Reading for Self

In the second reading, we read for "self," tuning our ears to the voice of the person telling the story in the interview text. Here is Tanya, speaking about herself:

> I went to camp . . . I was really afraid . . . it was kind of up to me . . . either I got bawled out and asked, or I didn't do anything about it . . . I had to help him . . . So I went and asked . . . [I considered] what was right and wrong . . . I said, "This guy can intimidate me, but he can't beat me up" . . . [I realized] . . . I have to do this . . . I mean . . . I'm sure, I was sure . . . he was my cousin and we've always been kind of close . . . I either helped him out or, like I helped myself, or I did what was for him, or I couldn't go for myself because I didn't want to be like, I was really afraid . . . it was me saving myself or saving him . . . I mean . . . nothing bad was going to happen to me. So I realized . . . so I guess he did kind of realize . . . I mean . . . so I don't . . . it's kind of like a victory . . . I'm sure, I don't know what it was . . . It's obvious [that] it is [right] for me . . . I felt it . . . I could have gotten out of it easily . . . it wasn't my feeling . . . I wasn't feeling what he was feeling . . . I did have a little empathy, but not that much . . . I could have gotten out of it . . . I could have said, "I'm not going up to that camp director" . . . I almost felt like [my cousin] did in a way . . . I did go up because I felt miserable having him feel miserable.

In this second reading Tanya's voice carries the sound of a clear, confident, candid, psychologically astute and shrewd 12-year-old, concerned about her cousin and also about herself, indignant at the camp director's lack of concern, sure of her perceptions and judgments, stubborn, determined, and capable of making intriguing observations ("either you feel it all the way or you just recognize it," referring to the difference between her response to her cousin's homesickness and that of her friends) and also capable of making what would seem, given most descriptions of child development, an astonishing distinction for a 12-year-old: between empathy—feeling another person's feelings—and responding to another person's feeling with feelings of one's own.

This second reading, designed to attune one's ear to the voice of the person speaking, is key to a shift in stance with respect to analyzing or interpreting the interview text, a shift marked by the change in language from coding, which implies fitting a person into a preexisting set of categories, to reading, which implies opening one's eyes and ears to the words of another, taking in his or her story. The exercise of directing my attention to the way the person speaks about herself is designed to highlight or amplify the terms in which she sees and presents herself. Through this method or in this way, I come into relationship with her, by paying attention to her way of seeing and speaking. Put simply, I listen to her voice and attend to her vision and thus make some space between her way of speaking and seeing and my own. In the process, I, the reader, become engaged with or involved with her, the speaker, and as I listen for the way in which she speaks about herself, I am likely to experience myself coming into relation with her, so that I begin to know her terms and to respond to what she is saying emotionally as well as intellectually. As her words about herself enter my psyche, a process of connection begins between her feelings and thoughts and my feelings and thoughts in response to hers, so that she affects me, the researcher, and I begin to learn from her—about her, about myself, and about the world we share in common, here specifically the world of relationships and its geography of moral concern. Once I allow the voice of another to enter into my psyche, I can no longer claim a detached position. I am affected by her, and her words may lead me to think about a variety of things and to feel sad, or happy, or jealous, or angry, or bored, or frustrated, or comforted, or hopeful. But by allowing her words to enter my psyche, I gain the sense of an entry, an opening, a way into her story in her terms. Thus relationship or connection, rather than blurring perspective or diminishing judgment, signifies an opening of self to other, creating a channel for information, an avenue to knowledge. Evelyn Keller (1983), in her biography of the geneticist Barbara McClintock, records McClintock's description of her research as depending on her gaining a "feeling for the organism" so that she and the corn she was studying became "friends." Reading for self, we seek to establish this kind of relationship with the people whom we study. Listening to the way in which they speak about themselves, we find that we develop a feeling for them.

In the third and fourth readings for moral voice, this connection between reader and speaker is forged on the common ground of moral concern about justice and care.

The Third Reading: Reading for Care

Here is Tanya speaking about care:

> He was really young, he was like maybe 7, and he got really, really homesick. It was overnight. And he was like, always crying at night and stuff . . . and so my cousin really wanted to call his parents, . . . and he was my cousin, so I had to help him . . . And I said "Sorry, but he's only 7" . . . he was like, almost in tears . . . the right thing was to go because it was my cousin's good, you know. And he wasn't going to die or anything, but, you know, he's afraid to go to camp now, because he's like 9 now and he doesn't want to go back . . . This guy can intimidate me, but he can't beat me up or anything . . . I'll realize that that's just the way he is, but I have to do this . . . [to] help [my cousin] out . . . the conflict was that he was my cousin and we've always been kind of close . . . it was me saving myself or saving him . . . nothing bad was going to happen to me . . . he felt a lot better . . . my cousin was screaming, has nightmares, and it was really bad . . . my cousin lives 7 minutes away from us, so I lived with my cousin but I would never see the [camp director] again . . . [What was at stake was] kind of like the ego, you know, and nothing physically and nothing that anybody else would see, it's just like my feelings being hurt and I hate being yelled at

... but my cousin ... he was like feeling really, really low ... really bad ... it's either, like you feel it, like all the way or you just, like, recognize it, you know ... it's helping out my cousin and that camp director, you know, it was a rule, but people are more important than rules ... he was just a little kid ... my cousin wasn't having fun ... He was ... really close, but I wasn't feeling what he was feeling, but I did have a little empathy ... he was ... very miserable and I almost felt like he did in a way, so I did go up because I felt miserable having him feel miserable.

Listening for care draws attention to a contradiction in Tanya's thinking: It was a moral problem, she says, because it wasn't her feelings, it was her cousin's feelings that she was risking her own feelings for in going up to the camp director. And yet, she says, she was miserable because he was miserable. Moral language does not capture Tanya's description of relationship insofar as it implies acting either for another or for oneself. In Tanya's relational orientation, her attentiveness to the feelings of her cousin and her wish to respond to his need are tied in with her own feelings because her cousin's unhappiness affects her. But his feelings are not the same as her feelings, as she states clearly; he is not she. Tanya's care voice draws the reader's attention to her knowledge of human relationships and psychological processes, knowledge that suggests close and careful observations. We notice her fine distinctions, first between feeling another person's problem "all the way" as opposed to "just recognizing it," and second between empathizing with another versus responding to his feelings with feelings of one's own. These distinctions, made by a 12-year-old child, are compelling, reminiscent of the careful drawings of the naturalist in their attention to detail and to accurate representation. Like the exquisite botanical drawings of the late nineteenth century, Tanya's recording of people's thoughts and feelings leaves us as readers with the impression of her as someone who watches closely and listens carefully to the human world around her. The care voice that runs through her description of moral conflict speaks of relationships in terms of attachment and detachment—her connection with her cousin, the camp director's "callousness" or apparent lack of concern. Care narratives draw attention to the vulnerability of people to carelessness, to the capacity of people to be wounded by indifference, detachment, and disconnection, as well as to the experience of being abandoned or not listened to or not seen. Consequently care narratives address the complexities of creating and sustaining human connection, finding the threads that will attach people to themselves and to others, enabling and enhancing perception and response, such as Tanya describes in relation to her cousin.

But what about justice?

The Fourth Reading: Reading for Justice

The fourth reading, for justice, highlights Tanya's concerns about fairness. It was unfair, she implies, that her cousin "wasn't [having] any fun and he paid for it"—meaning the camp, where the director had said "we're here to help our kids, to make them have fun." She also recognizes the disparity in power between the camp director and her cousin:

> The way I saw it by that time was like this guy is a big bully and he can have anything the way he wants it. So . . . I guess it was kind of big giving in for him [to let my cousin use the phone] . . . He goes . . . on his reputation, you know, that was a rule and he couldn't break it, but he said yes, but he started giving us this lecture . . . But I did something for him, my cousin, and it's kind of like a victory, it's like you won over this guy so be happy.

Put in justice terms, it was unfair for someone not to be happy at camp and not to be able to do anything about it, especially since he had paid to have fun at camp. It also was oppressive for a camp director to place his concern with reputation over the misery of a /-year-old and to take advantage of the fact that the 7-year-old was under his direction while he "could have anything the way he wants it."

Tanya also alludes to the protective power of justice when she says that the camp director could intimidate her and hurt her feelings, but he "can't beat me up or anything."

Summary: Interpretation

Thus this 12-year-old is cognizant of the clais of both care and justice, of the vulnerability of people both to abandonment and to oppression, and of the intensity of feelings that lie behind the wish for justice (or at least for fairness) and for love (or at least for care). Taking action that turns out to be effective in securing a response to her cousin's distress, she tells a story that, when told in justice terms, renders her the victor over the callous camp director. But she also knows that the camp director "had another point of view," that he "probably [thought] kids always get homesick and what difference does it make, he's not going to die." In the end Tanya relies on a system of justice that will hold the camp director accountable and that she feels will prevent him from beating her up, which would leave evidence, something that someone else could see. To protect herself and her cousin from psychological violence, where what was at stake was "the ego, you know, and nothing physically and nothing that anybody else would see . . . like my feelings being hurt," Tanya draws on an ethic of care to support her capacity to care, and guided by this ethic she finds an inclusive solution to the dilemma—people are more important than rules, she says, and in the end her cousin felt better, she no longer felt miserable, and the camp director, albeit at her cousin's expense, salvaged his reputation by giving a lecture.

With these four guided readings of an interview text of only six pages—

Tanya's story of moral conflict told in response to the interviewer's question and then further elaborations of that story in answer to the interviewer's further questions and requests for clarification—we have arrived at a fairly complex portrayal of 12-year-old Tanya. By tuning our ear to her voice, we open our inquiry to her perceptions; by listening for the ways in which she speaks about justice and about care, we see how she walks across the terrain of human relationships that we are studying.

Reading first with one interpretive lens and then another, listening first for one voice and then another, we hear and convey the way in which a situation can be seen differently from different perspectives and a story told from more than one angle, or in different terms by Tanya and also by ourselves. The independence of justice and care perspectives was tested in a study that found that these two moral voices and visions are neither positively nor negatively correlated—neither polar opposites nor mirror images nor versions of each other (Rogers, 1987, 1988a). Drawing on this evidence that justice and care are simply different voices and visions, we struggle with the question of how to describe the relationship between them—how to talk about this difference. In our Reader's Guide, our procedures for hearing moral voice and spotting moral orientation reflect our recognition that the same words in an interview text can be used as evidence for justice and as evidence for care, depending on the lens through which one is reading. A case in point is Tanya's statement "He was my cousin, so I had to help him" or "Sorry, he's only 7." Reading for care, one could understand these statements to reflect her attentiveness and her re- sponse to her cousin's distress. One also could cite them as evidence of the necessity for response that she feels and of her belief in her ability to do something to help her cousin. Tanya's care narrative is premised on her ability to talk to the director and her belief that he will listen to her—a belief in her efficacy as a person who is able and willing to care for another, which may be why she remembers and tells this story.

Yet reading for justice, a reader may see in these same statements of Tanya's evidence for a felt sense of obligation or duty contingent upon occupying the role of cousin (a good cousin takes care of her cousin) or upon being an older child. The fact that Tanya is Indian suggests that this may be a cultural norm of family responsibility and obligation.

Care and justice themes may be interwoven throughout the narrative, or both may be woven into a single statement. And judgments can be made, both within the narrative or by the reader, about different renditions of justice and care.[5] So that, for example, one can see "bad justice" in the rigid or blind

---

[5] It is important to note, however, that we distinguish between the narrator's actual words and the reader's interpretations of those words. The Worksheets presented in Appendix 3 are designed to make apparent the interpretive stance of the reader and to encourage the reader to leave a detailed "trail of evidence" for his or her interpretive summaries of each case.

adherence to moral principles or rules and "good justice" in the attentiveness to differential power and the potential for oppression that it creates. And one can see "bad care" in the strategies of exclusion that often are valorized in the name of care—the sacrifice of self or of other—just as one can see "good care" in the search for inclusive solutions that are responsive to everyone involved.

Finally, the Reader's Guide, in tuning the reader's ear to the voice of the speaking self—the "I" in the interview text—and by amplifying moral voice and vision, draws attention to a danger that inheres both in psychological development and in psychological theories, namely, the danger of losing voice or vision, of striving for safety, clarity, or justification at the expense of voice or vision and thus of oversimplifying or reducing the experience of conflict, removing the possibility of tragedy or genuine dilemma. As our Reader's Guide asks the reader to listen for the voice of the person speaking, as a prerequisite to learning something from her or him, so too it calls attention to the orchestration of moral voices within the narrative of conflict as a facet of human personality or character, which is endlessly varied and thus endlessly interesting.

Traditionally, the value of openness in science has been taken to mean the opening of theory to new and discrepant empirical data—an openness we see exemplified in the work of Jane Loevinger. In our own approach, we think about the openness or the opening of the theorist to the empirical world of creating a way for the voices of others to enter into the researcher's psyche. In creating a method to facilitate this entrance, we hope to encourage new soundings and new insight.

Our belief in the possibility of different perspectives on moral problems and in the potential for conflict among them, that is, for the experience of real dilemma, has been central to the development of our method. In fact, we believe that tension between differing moral voices and conflict between opposing visions are part of a good human life. With Martha Nussbaum (1986a), we believe that "a conflict-free life would be lacking in value and beauty next to a life in which it is possible for conflict to arise" (p. 81). Like Nussbaum, we define two positions or ways of thinking about a good human life. We embrace, then, both the possibility of creative resolutions to moral conflict, that is, the possibility of finding inclusive solutions, and the possibility of tragedy, of situations where something of value is lost, no matter what.

Fifteen-year-old Rachael, asked to speak about what was a powerful learning experience for her, talks not about school but about her family and the lesson she learned about "people and their relationships and . . . life." What she saw in this lesson was "the power of love."

> My grandfather had Alzheimer's, and they lived very close to us, and I'd see him just about every day, except during the summer and stuff, and watching the general progression of his illness and the different effects on people, like my mother.

IT WAS HER FATHER?
It was her father. And I think I have learned the most about people and their
relationships and about, you know, about life, too, from that experience. It was a very
powerful experience.

CAN YOU TALK A LITTLE BIT MORE ABOUT HOW IT AFFECTED YOU IN
TERMS OF TEACHING YOU ABOUT LIFE?
Again, it made me appreciate a lot more about not only a life but the ability to—of
thought, and I don't know, it is still a really strange experience that somebody you
know, they are still there, but they're just not the person you know, and it really
taught me about what's inside, how you can have the shell there, but it's just not the
person you think it is, and it is also interesting to me to see—I mean, my mom, I
don't think she ever came to the conclusion that her father was less than perfect and
so when she finally, here her father, a person that she had looked up to all these years
and thought was godlike and here, you know, practically like a baby. It was strange,
her reactions.

IT MUST HAVE BEEN SO HARD FOR YOU.
It was. It's hard for my grandmother too, and I am amazed that she could live with it
as long as she did, because how much she put up with it all. She—in a way I think she
was too stubborn a lot of the times. She just wouldn't give in and have anyone help
her. But it certainly shows the power of love.

We have tried to create a method, specifically a way of reading, that holds
"the power of love," as reflected here by Rachel's judgment of her grandmother as "too stubborn a lot of the times," by her realization that "she could
live with it as long as she did," by her recognition of what her grandmother put
up with, and by the strangeness to Rachael of her mother's reactions. Chance
has given her grandfather a physically debilitating and emotionally painful
terminal illness, which affects everyone around him. Fifteen-year-old Rachael
observes the vulnerability, the fragility, of life, and also human goodness and
strength. She witnesses the powerlessness of her grandfather's transformation,
how hard this is for three generations of women, the shifting of appearances,
the disjunction between inside and outside, and the shift in her mother's
perceptions of her father from perfection to "practically like a baby." To
represent this multilayered nature of physic life, to record this story and its
developmental implications, requires a language that is polyphonic.

SOUNDINGS: INTO DEVELOPMENT

Soundings has many meanings: measuring the depth or examining the bottom
of a body of water, making or giving forth sound, and sound that is resonant,
sonorous. In all these senses of the word, we are taking soundings into the
development of Psyche. We are consciously arranging these soundings in
musical terms because by drawing on the language of music rather than the

musical terms because by drawing on the language of music rather than the visual arts, the idea of development enters time. Psyche can be represented as in relationship with others and herself, relationships that exist in the medium of time and change. The unity of self can then be compared to the unity of a musical composition where meaning at any one moment is indeterminate, since it can only be apprehended in time. Then one can speak about themes that develop, change key, recur, drop out; of discrete movements characterized by changes in rhythm and tempo, of harmonic sequences that change the sound of individual notes and intervals; of leitmotifs that convey character and dramatize the ways in which people affect or move one another. In addition, a shift from a visual imagery, which depicts Psyche as fixed, still, stopped in time, and from positional metaphors to a musical language makes it possible to think about differences in terms other than those of invidious comparison.

If we imagine a child as visually positioned in relation to others (smaller and immature in relation to a standard of what we call human), we can talk about the child's progression toward an ideal of equality or to a position of domination. But if we imagine a child engaged in responsive relationships, we can also talk about the transformations or changes in his or her experiences of those relationships, the changing qualities of human connection over time, and the different tonalities that tend to characterize particular relationships. For example, mother-daughter relationships or relationships between fathers and daughters characteristically differ in tone from relationships between mothers and sons and fathers and sons and extend differently through time. During the period of adolescence, for instance, the harmonic pattern and the discordant notes of these various relationships tend to differ, so that one would rarely mistake one for the other. Similarly, the rhythms of male and female sexuality are not the same, and sexual relationships have different implications for males and females in adolescence, so that boys and girls, when speaking of sexuality, all tell a story recognizably sexual, but tell it in different terms.

As we listen to people speaking and imagine different ways of speaking, which in turn imply different ways of seeing, feeling, and thinking, male and female development may be characterized in terms of a particular way of arranging themes that pertain to the experience of one's body and relationships with others and to living within a family and a culture.

In a variety of school and after-school settings, we have listened to girls and boys who have been interviewed annually over a period of years (Gilligan, Johnston, & Miller, 1988; Gilligan, Ward, & Taylor, 1988). We have asked them to describe themselves, to talk about important relationships in their lives, including their relationships with their parents and friends; to describe experiences of conflict and choice; to discuss their lives in school, how they learn, and their hopes and expectations for the future.

Metaphors of Voice and Vision:
Themes of Connection and Separation

Themes familiar from traditional accounts of adolescent psychology appeared in these teenagers' descriptions, connected to a visual imagery of self and other denoting separation, individuation, and concerns about autonomy and freedom. This psychological framework is aligned with the American tradition, with its emphasis on individual rights and independence from others, and fostered by formal education. Within this framework, femininity is either idealized (associated with altruistic self-sacrifice) or appears as suspect, disturbing. Girls reflecting back on their childhoods from this perspective speak of growing apart from their parents and of their wish to lead their own lives, a wish often coupled with the wish that their mothers would do the same. "I have grown," Becky explains, "I have kind of grown apart from my parents. I don't think we have become less close; it's just that now I am beginning to see more, you know, me myself, not me and Mom and Dad. In the past," she says, in a passage filled with the visual images,

> I really had no notion of myself, of just me and not me in relation to my friends or me in relation to my parents or anything. I see myself . . . I see, I feel a lot less scared about myself, because when you associate yourself so much with others that you can't kind of separate yourself from a group, you feel there are times when you feel all alone and you have to think, Wow! I remember, this is really strange, but at moments kind of being stricken with fright. I would look into the mirror and say: "This is me, X. These are my hands, and I am all alone, and I am not glued to any other person."

The following year, when as a senior in high school Becky talked about her mother, a visual language continued to mark her discourse of separation.

> I see her as a middle-aged woman with her own life and her own problems, very separate from mine. And it is fascinating to me to see her as a person, a real, whole, complete person who makes bad judgments and who yells when she is upset and who really doesn't function rationally all the time. So she is important to me. She doesn't really influence me anymore, but she is important to me.

This quintessentially adolescent description is so in line with the language and imagery of contemporary psychology, with its emphasis on separation and on the adolescent deflation of idealized images of parents, the perception of parents as "real people," that it is surprising when Becky, after speaking about the similarity between herself and her mother ("My mother and I are basically caring people and outgoing people. I see a lot of her in me, but it doesn't scare me; it used to terrify me, because I used to think, Oh God, I am going to end up like her"), suddenly observes, "I don't think anybody is self-sufficient, and no woman is an island."

With this statement, the talk of separation, with its imagery of seeing and of mirrors, suddenly yields to a different language for describing connection and closeness with others, a language of talking, of listening, of being with, of being touched. "I can't imagine going through a rough time," Becky says, "without somebody there to talk to or somebody to be with or hold my hand."

When we privilege visual metaphors of separation and signify what we mean by development in a positional language, Becky's unexpected statement may appear as a "regression" to a less separate, less independent, less developed position. Or we might simply gloss over her words. But if we think of our language and how it shapes her understanding of her experience, of our interpretation as one that obscures or recognizes her meanings, then we may feel compelled to wonder about the meaning of development, the very words we have used to describe her development.

Ten years ago (Gilligan, 1977) the specification of a voice that differed from the voices that have guided and been amplified by developmental psychologists immediately raised questions about development, which were linked to questions about women. Listening to women's conceptions of self and morality drew attention to a different voice and also to the extent to which developmental theories had been drawn from studies of men. Variations in women's ways of speaking about morality and about themselves suggested patterns—distinctions between different women and also changes in a woman's thinking in the face of crisis and over time. These changes could be framed in terms of the vocabulary commonly used by developmental psychologists—that is, in terms of stages, positions, levels, and the transitions between them. Women's concerns about their own survival in the face of what they perceived to be abandonment by others, their concerns about their appearance or "goodness" in the eyes of others, and their concerns about truth—specifically truths about relationships and about violence—suggested a pattern of increasingly sophisticated thinking about the nature of relationships. This pattern more or less conformed to the progression from an egocentric, through a normative or conventional, to an autonomous or reflective or critical position—the progression that most developmental theorists have traced.

The two transitions in this process—from "selfishness" to responsibility and from "goodness" to truth—however, seemed reparative, repairing a loss or correcting an error or undoing an exclusion of others or of self. While women labeled their exclusion of others as "selfish" and as cause for being considered "bad women," they tended—following the norms or conventions of feminine virtue—to label their exclusion of themselves as "good." Yet the "selfless" position that has been valorized within Western culture and associated with idealized images of mothers seemed so painful for women and was often accompanied by signs of psychological distress—symptoms of eating disorders and depression (Jack, 1987; Steiner-Adair, 1986). The fact that women were, in convention terms, "doing good and feeling bad," as Jean Baker Miller (1976) put it, began to focus a number of questions about women's activities and cultural values and also about problems of inclusion and exclusion on a societal and cultural as well as on a personal scale. Asked to speak about conflicts and choices, women spoke about problems of inclusion and exclusion in a way that suggested a growing understanding of the logic of relationships and also an awareness of problems in relationship, having to do with the inclusion and the exclusion of women within a larger framework of relationships—in the family, in the society, and in the transgenerational cultural world. Women's concerns about inclusion and exclusion were not simply interpersonal concerns, and the representation of women's relational concerns as "interpersonal" or "conventional" seemed to contribute to women's confusion, to augment the problems of growing up female within a tradition where "human" often meant male.

Attention to this confusion—to the tension between psychological theories of human development and the experience and situation of women—suggested that what had been represented as steps in a developmental progression might be better conceived as an interplay of voices, creating a "contrapuntal theme, woven into the cycle of life and recurring in varying forms of people's judgments, fantasies and thoughts" (Gilligan, 1982, p. 1). This interplay of voices seemed particularly intense in the lives of both women and men at times of crisis and change. Thus insights gained by studying women's conceptions of self, relationship, and morality, taken together with the recurrent problems psychologists had encountered in understanding or interpreting women's experience, raised the question as to whether there was a need for new language—a shift from a visual imagery of stages, steps, positions, and levels to a musical language of counterpoint and theme.

Development: An etymology

By studying the origin and historical meanings of words, we turn now to questions about development like etymologists. This may seem at first like an esoteric choice, but to know the history of words is to recover the full meaning of their present form and sense. For worn and altered within a particular discipline, words may take on peculiarly narrow meanings.

In order to understand the many possible meanings of the word "develop," to wash our language of the layers of theory collected upon it, and to restore root meanings of ideas, we turn to the *Oxford English Dictionary* (Murray, Bradley, Craigie, & Onions, 1978; OED hereafter). The oldest meanings of the word "develop" are "apart" (*dis*) and "to wrap" (*voloper*) from the Latin and French. In Italy in the 14th century *suiluppara* meant "to unwrap, disentangle, to rid free." In modern Italian this word means "to enwrap, to bundle, to roll up, to entangle." The OED gives four major meanings to the word "develop": (1) to unfold, unroll, to flatten out a curved surface, to cut out of its enfolding cover; (2) to lay open by removal of that which enfolds, to unveil, to unfold (as a tale, the meaning of a thing); to disclose, to reveal; (3) to unfold more fully, bring out all that is potentially contained in; and (4) to change a mathematical function, to expand into the form of a series, (a) to cause to grow, (b) said of a series and sharing progression from a simple or lower to a higher or more complex type.

Developmental psychologists have taken on the fourth meaning and elaborated this notion into stages of cognitive, moral, social, and emotional growth. We are now recovering the first three meanings of development, particularly the third meaning: to unfold more fully, to bring out all that is potentially contained within. Among the uses of this meaning cited by the OED is the musical use of a melody or theme developed by frequent changes of key, or harmony. . . . A fragment of melody is said to be developed when its outline is altered and expanded so as to create new interest." (vol. 3, p. 280). Of course, all these meanings do not exclude the meaning of development as growth or expansion, with the connotation that what develops becomes gradually fuller, larger, and better. When this meaning is put in context beside other meanings of development and stripped of the notion of linear progress that currently undergirds hierarchical stage models of development, it too can become a new way to comprehend the process of development. The infant, who is exquisitely responsive, experiences attachment differently from the adult. The mother or father or caretaker who serves as the interpreter and nurturer of the infant's new attachment becomes attached to the infant in the process of that care, but the attachment is not the same. The young child who fails to control an impulse and breaks a rule is not the same as the teenager who breaks a law to protest the making of nuclear arms, knowing and accepting the consequences he or she risks to do this. Development implies a telos—and the telos is a fuller and, in some ways, more adequate way to understand the world and live one's life. But to organize this growth into stages and to call some stages higher, or more complex, misses the point. Development is fraught with vulnerabilities; it entails both losses and gains, and it is open to the world beyond the individual's personal control, including changes in relationships critical to growth.

Models of Development: Development as a Double Fugue

What model, or models, of development capture this kind of complexity? Lacking a language and unable to speak clearly within the constraints of the language of current developmental theory, we turn back to the OED. The meaning of development in its musical sense, of altering or expanding a basic melody, of picking up different voices and a recurrent contrapuntal theme, suggests the musical form of the fugue, or of the double fugue.[6] The OED tells

---

[6]Dianne Argyris suggested the idea of a fugue to Annie Rogers in a discussion about development.

us that the fugue was described by Stainer and Barret in 1880 as "a polyphonic composition on one or more short subjects or themes, which are harmonized according to the laws of counterpoint, and introduced from time to time with various contrapuntal devices" (vol. 4, p. 585). Webster (1970) describes a fugue as "a musical form or composition design for a definite number of instruments or voices in which a subject is announced in one voice and then developed contrapuntally by each of the other voices." A double fugue is the common term for a fugue on two subjects or themes, in which the two begin together. This musical form is sensitive to development in its many meanings and in a plurality of voices.

An additional note, from Samuel Pepys' *Diary*, cited in the OED, clarifies the fine fit of the fugue as a musical form with the notion of listening to many voices. Pepys wrote, "The sense of the words being lost by not being heard [is corrected] especially as they set them with Fuges of words, one after another." The fugue then offers a way to listen to many voices, as themes, and variations on themes, and to correct for not listening to particular voices. Fugue also comes from the Latin word *fuga*, "flight," and in modern psychiatry means a temporary flight from conscious experience, or a state of amnesia. During the process of development, human beings compose a fugue and are sometimes seemingly subject to fugue states. In other words, we might ask what becomes lost, forgotten, or silenced as development occurs, and in what contexts do certain kinds of losses occur?

The Plainsong of Justice and Care

Let us look more closely at the key terms of musical notation. The theme, the OED says, "in music [is] the principle melody, plainsong, or canto fermo in a contrapuntal piece; also a simple tune on which variations are constructed." A themester is one who labors at a theme, or one can be themeless, without a theme, and then a theme-maker furnishes a theme or subject. This language of labor and loss is sensitive to the active, constructive nature of development. We are all, fundamentally, themesters.

Listening to themes allows us to hear differences in voices. For example, the plainsong of care—its themes of connection and response to others—beginning with great clarity and simplicity, can be heard clearly in the words of 13-year-old girls and boys who wrote responses to sentence stems on the Washington University Sentence Completion Test, Loevinger's measure of ego development:

> The thing I like about myself is—I can make good friends.
> When people are helpless—I try to help them.
> A good father—is caring and he has fun with you.
> My conscience bothers me if—I have hurt someone's feelings.

And the plainsong of justice—its themes of fairness, respect for rights, and independence—can be heard just as clearly in their responses:

My conscience bothers me if—I am unfair or betray a friend.
When a child will not join in group activities—the poor kid has a right to be alone!
The thing I like about myself is—I do things my own way.

The Counterpoint of Justice and Care

Using the musical form of the fugue, a composer develops one or more short subjects or themes, "harmonized according to the laws of counterpoint." Webster (1970, p. 324) defines counterpoint as "a melody accompanying another melody . . . the art of adding a related, but independent melody . . . [with] fixed rules of harmony, to make a harmonic whole, . . . a thing set up in contrast or interaction with another." Themes within the basic melody of the care voice may be enriched by adding themes of the justice voice, in counterpoint, through discernable rules of English grammar, that is, conjunctions, independent and dependent clauses, and the like. Such an example written by a teenage girl is "My mother and I—love and confide in one another but I am also quite independent." Or themes within either voice alone may become resonant and become rich in tone as they are contrapuntally placed together in a single sentence. A teenage boy writes, "A good father—gives his children a set of rules to live by and plays an important role in raising them."

The form of the fugue, understood in this way, reflects the very process of development. Loevinger and her colleagues discern high ego levels partially by examining how ideas are contrasted and combined, and we mark the orchestration of justice and care voices as a sign of moral maturity.

But the words "counterpoint" and "contrapuntal" have older meanings. Counterpoint, the OED says, comes from the French word *contrepointe*, "against," or "meeting of points." This is not the imagery of opposition and war, however, but of the process of quilting. The term meant "to quilt, or quilt stabbed or stitched through." A counterpoint-maker is a quilt-maker. And contrapuntal meant "a back-stitch in sewing, elaborating a quilt or tapestry," and only later "the harmonic treatment of melodies as a counterpoint in a musical composition." So the terms "counterpoint" and "contrapuntal" meant to elaborate a design, in a quilt, a tapestry, and, later, a musical composition.

What does the elaboration, the fine counterpoint of justice and care voices, sound like? In what ways does it differ when the plainsong is justice and care is developed contrapuntally, or when the basic melody is care and justice is developed contrapuntally? When we listen carefully to male and female voices, what does the fugue of development sound like played, as it were, as a double fugue? What are the contrapuntal devices of language that, when used by a speaker or writer to wrap themes and variations on themes together, result in a rich harmony?

At 16, the clear plainsong of justice and care is not so easy to discern in sentence completions. Instead, the variations on themes suggest a more complex fugue of voices. To listen to boys and girls at this age requires more effort. It is necessary to attune one's ear to contrapuntal variations within and across the voices of justice and care.

Within care, this sounds like

> My mother and I—get along well though we sometimes run into tension.

Attention to the quality of relationship leads to a description of tension in relationship, which contains an implicit acknowledgment of difference, lending new meaning to "getting along."

Across justice and care, this variation sounds like

> My conscience bothers me if—I did not follow through on something I promised or said something mean about someone else.

Two themes are introduced, a commitment to keeping promises and a concern with not hurting others. These themes are joined by the word "or," laying out alternative causes of regret.

A Method for Identifying Content Themes of Justice and Care

Sentence stems are a well established way to take soundings of psychic processes. The method of reading sentence stems for moral voice (Rogers, 1988b) makes it possible to consider the relationship between our analysis of moral voice and our exploration of development in terms of a musical notation and a standard measure of development. This method also brings together the musical meanings of development with the positional stages of Loevinger's theory of ego development.[7]

By attending closely to the language of the writer and by observing his or her grammatical constructions as a manifestation of Psyche and a source of developmental understanding, one can hear changes in the way themes of justice and care sound at different times, for different individuals.

[7]The method alluded to here is described in detail in *Two Developmental Voices: A Method for Identifying a Fugue of Justice and Care Themes in Sentence Completions* (Rogers, 1988b). In brief, sentence stem responses to items of the Washington University Sentence Completion Test are coded for ego development using empirical scoring manuals constructed by Loevinger (Loevinger & Wessler, 1970; Loevinger, Wessler, & Redmore, 1970) and then read for 16 different content themes of moral voice. Character sketches, written for each individual, are based on ego development stage descriptions as well as themes of moral voice.

Putting the themes back together, like chords, for an entire set of written responses to sentence stems makes it possible to describe what one hears as a fugue of voices. Joining the themes of voice to the meaning of development as a process of laying open, unfolding, or revealing (a tale, the meaning of something) allows us to write character sketches of people. Loevinger and her colleagues originally wrote character descriptions of the people they studied by asking what sort of person would have written the test protocol they were examining. Similarly, we listen closely to sentence completions, looking for sets of themes, repetitions, overlaps, logical gaps, inconsistencies, erasures, and changes in tone to guide our sketches of the character or personality of the writer.

What do our sentence stem soundings into development, listening for themes of moral voice, add to the understanding of character and development?

The Case of Tanya

Remember 12-year-old Tanya, who spoke about responding to her younger cousin's distress at camp? She is a participant in a current longitudinal study of girls' development. In addition to being interviewed, she also filled out the Washington University Sentence Completion Test. Her ego development level is Conscientious-conventional.

What this tells us about Tanya is that, according to Loevinger's theory (1976), she is in the transition between the Conformist and the Conscientious stages, a time in development marked by a heightened consciousness of oneself and one's feelings. As Loevinger's theory would predict, Tanya sees multiple possibilities and alternatives in situations. She is able to think about what is appropriate and to talk about exceptions and contingencies, as she clearly does in the case of her cousin. She has a conception of striving, or goals, purposes, and expectations. She is aware of differences in feelings and can express concern for others with this awareness.

After reading Tanya's responses for themes of moral voice, what can we add to this picture? When she speaks in the voice of care, Tanya talks in plain, uncompromising terms about what she believes in, a form of care rooted in listening to and caring for herself—she believes that she can count on herself, that she knows and follows her own desires, that she knows what is right, and that she values the capacity to speak up. In the following statements we hear the tone of a 12-year-old girl who can speak directly of her own needs and wants, of what she knows without a doubt, and even of what she shouldn't know.

> The thing I like about myself is—that I can usually count on myself for doing the things I want to do.

A girl has a right to—be whatever she wants to be.
A girl feels good when—she knows she did something right.
A woman should always—speak up for what she feels.
My conscience bothers me if—I know something I shouldn't know.

When Tanya talks about relationships, she is sensitive to differences in perception and to differences in human beings that can't be collapsed into general norms. These ideas underlie a capacity to know others in their own terms, one characteristic of the care voice.

My mother and I—look the same, but never feel the same way about things.
A good mother—will never be, all mothers are different and have different qualities.

This child is capable of reaching out to others in a gracious, nonthreatening way, and of expressing empathy in a way that reveals the interdependence of her happiness with her mother's well-being. She also describes her own vulnerability to loss, her own longing to matter to others.

When a child will not join in group activities—no special attention should be given
    but she should be nicely questioned and urged on.
If my mother—relaxed and had a good time I would be happy. I have empathy for her.
When they avoided me—I felt left out.
Sometimes she wished that—she could mean more to other people.

In her statements about men and women, we hear themes of justice (her concerns with a potential for oppression and with equality), and we see a disparity between Tanya's ideals of equality and her perceptions of women's inferior status. The tone of her remarks (only in these statements) becomes argumentative and somewhat defensive.

A wife should—have as much power as the husband and she should be working.
For a woman a career is—the same thing as it is for a man.
Women are lucky because—they can prove many things.
The worst thing about being a woman—is being spit on by men.

The fugue of voices we hear in Tanya's responses is the clear plainsong of care and a quieter plainsong of justice, with very little conscious contrast or conflict between the themes of these two voices.[8]

[8]The plainsong of justice and care themes we discern in Tanya's sentence stem responses echoes the clarity and candidness of her statements about care and justice in our analysis of her interview narrative using the Reader's Guide. Preliminary evidence of the validity of the moral voices of justice and care on Washington University Sentence Completion Test responses and the real-life conflict and choice interview (Rogers, 1988b) point to promising directions for validating developmental themes of moral voice revealed by these two different measures.

The Case of Laura

If we turn now to another girl, Laura, a 16-year-old and a sophomore in high school, we find that, according to Loevinger's theory of ego development, she is more advanced in ego development than Tanya; her fugue of voices also sounds different. Laura's ego level is the Conscientious stage. This implies that she can describe inner states and individual differences in vivid terms, that she is capable of articulating long-term goals and ideals, that she can think not only in terms of interpersonal differences but also in terms of how people affect one another. Laura spontaneously refers to psychological development in herself, something that, Loevinger observes, almost never occurs at previous levels. Listen to her sentence completions:

> The thing I like about myself is—that I can apply myself to any situation, and with effort, succeed.
> What gets me into trouble is—when I don't plan ahead, and act impulsively too often in a given time.
> If I can't get what I want—I sometimes have a fit, but I'm going to try to outgrow that soon.

These capacities, however, come into conflict with what Laura expects of herself as a girl growing into a woman in Western culture. How she defines herself seems conflicted and difficult. As if to say that to achieve her goals and to know how to trust are incompatible, she erases one part of her response.

> Women are lucky because—they have a lot of choices open to them and people don't expect as much from them, so it's easier to be impressive.
> Men are lucky because—they are given expectations to achieve so are often given more encouragement.
> My main problem is—losing interest and becoming an underachiever.
> I am—happiest when [I have achieved my goals—erased] I know I can trust people.

Laura speaks in terms of themes of care as she describes her relationships with her parents—her capacity to disagree with her mother (though she seems to doubt herself) and her appreciation of her father's attention and willingness to accept her as she is.

> My mother and I—don't always agree, but she is usually right, and I love her.
> My father—comes to my field hockey and lacrosse games and he's always really proud of me when I do something well, and if I don't do anything well he just smiles and doesn't worry about it.

Laura's understanding of relationships includes ideas that people should be able to be themselves, that honesty and trust are necessary, that love feels good, and that one should be able to set limits in relationships. Yet for all of this clarity, she seems unable to trust others, to find people who are trustworthy, and feels dishonest in her relationships.

> I feel sorry—for anyone who is intimidated and can't be themselves.
> A girl has a right to—ask people to back-off and expect them to do so.
> I just can't stand people—who are back-biting or two-faced.
> A woman feels good when—she is loved.
> Sometimes she wished that—he could be honest and trust her.
> Usually she felt that sex—was alright if it was with the right person and she could really trust him with anything. That is very, very rare, though.
> My conscience bothers me if—I feel dishonest with others and I feel this way often.

Her confusion seems compounded by the themes of her moral vision. The ability of women, wives and mothers, to care is linked with notions of selfless love and self-sacrifice and to cultural prescriptions for how women should behave.

> A wife should—take care of her husband (they usually don't know much about cooking etc.).
> A husband has a right to—expect his wife to be willing to listen and understand.
> A good mother—is there for her children and husband regardless of all other things.

The fugue of voices we hear in Laura's responses is the counterpoint of themes of both care and justice, sung now and then in a clear way, but more often in a confused and wavering voice.[9]

Soundings: Through Character, into Development

These character sketches are soundings into development that reveal not only the emerging psychological strengths of adolescents but also the conflicts that girls face coming of age in a culture whose conventions are not the same for women and men. The close analysis of themes is a method for unwrapping the complexities of development by listening closely to language; this allows us to differentiate the clear voice from the wavering voice, to mark passages of certainty and passages of confusion, and to note how and when it becomes difficult to speak. Though Laura at 16 is more sophisticated in her thinking and at a more advanced level in Loevinger's scale of ego development than 12-year-old Tanya, something is different by mid-adolescence. From listening to her responses to the above sentence stems, it appears that Laura does not have Tanya's clear way of speaking nor Tanya's knowledge of relationships, a

---

[9]Both Tanya's and Laura's entire Washington University Sentence Completion Tests are contained in Appendix 4.

knowledge that does not exclude herself. And these differences are not captured by a linear model of development. At 16, Laura faces a major conflict in becoming at once an adult and a woman in Western culture, the deeply knotted dilemma of how to listen both to herself and to the tradition, how to care for herself and also for others. Girls' and women's solution to this dilemma has often been either to deny difference in the name of equality, or to deny self in the name of morality, as if psyche were not affected in significant ways by gender. This dilemma is frequently so difficult for adolescent girls and adult women that it can confound belief in their own perception and experience, leading to equivocation and contradiction, such as we started to see in Laura's sentence stems.

The sense of an opening that came with working out a method for listening to self and moral voice in complex interview narratives has become a slightly wider opening: soundings into development. Listening to a fugue of voices that can be traced over time and tied to the development of self, these two openings, we have found, feed back into the stream of personality theory. The shift to a musical language gives us a way out of the deadlocked paradox of self and relationship that continues to plague the fields of personality theory and developmental psychology—that one can only experience self in the context of relationships with others and one can only experience relationship if one distinguishes other from self. Because music is a language of movement and time—notes are heard in relation to other notes and become part of themes, leitmotifs, melodies—a musical notation gives us a way to capture people speaking in relationship, living in body and culture.

ENDING WITH CONVERSATION

Any description of psychology, personality, or development involves choices about how to speak and where to stand. As three women, we have chosen to focus on problems of language, to speak about the problem of sex differences, to draw on the voices of other women, to listen with particular attention to girls during adolescence, to talk together about these questions. Among ourselves, we talk about the fact that both the strength and the limitation of our method are tied to its medium: words. Our approach relies on people's ability—our own and that of the people we study—to articulate thoughts and feelings in patterns of speech and silence. Although we have talked with adolescents from a variety of backgrounds and heard about a variety of experiences, our method is new, our research is always in process, and our approach requires a good deal more use and verification.

Among ourselves, we have tried in writing this paper and in representing our method to avoid technical language and mechanistic images; we have taken our metaphors often from physical senses (voice and vision) and from art—

especially from music—in an attempt to represent the dailiness of human experience and the complexity of psychic life. We have tried to show how the language we use affects what we are aware of by contrasting two moral voices that direct attention to different aspects of relationship. Our choice of language itself represents our sense of an opening to different voices and to other aspects of experience beyond those we have chosen to represent.

Together, we speak of the fact that we have posed questions in this paper that we have not fully answered. In the beginning of the section entitled "The Sense of an Opening" we stated, "We assume no God's-eye perspective." By this we mean that by virtue of being human, we begin with an acknowledgement of relationship—with the children, adolescents, and adults we interview, with the texts and tests we interpret, with the methods we create to make such interpretations, and with the insights gleaned from such methods, which in turn become part of a store of knowledge about ourselves, our own histories, and a source of new questions. Disclaiming a neutral or objective perspective, we live, as it were, glued to our own shadows. Listening for self in our own narratives about psychology, we chide ourselves when we slip into abstractions or "ex cathedra'" judgments. Listening for moral voice in our own narratives, we discover channels of connection between ourselves and others—places where differences run deep and also places where light filters through to the bottom. And then we ask ourselves: What claims can we make for the integrity or validity or usefulness to others of our way of listening and seeing, of our interpretations, of what we have learned and what we have created?

Between the endless fascination of stories and the eternal discussion of interpretations, we have sought to place a method that is at once systematic and attentive to the stories of those whom we study and to their interpretations—the way they see and speak about what they feel and think and see and hear and do. Our assumptions about the commonality of moral concerns allow us to listen not only for what is spoken but also for what is unspoken or silent. By tracking the voice of the speaking self, we listen for where that voice falters, sings, argues, reaches out, appears, and disappears. Our belief that a good human life is polyphonic becomes the basis for making judgments: that the absence of moral voice, like the absence of self, marks a locus of concern.

In sum, we draw distinctions between justice and care as moral voices to capture differences, but our concept of moral voice cuts across familiar dichotomies of thinking and feeling, egoism and altruism, self and other, theoretical and practical reasoning, which we have seen as limiting the representation of both women and men. Just as our practice of listening for self draws us into relationship with the people we listen to, our separate reading for the voices of justice and care draws our attention to shifts in world view. This way of reading highlights the dominant world view within the field of personality and developmental psychology and captures our own sense of changing position and shifting ground.

We find ourselves struggling to describe what we experience as a changed way of doing research, and thus we need to consider again the meaning of such terms as reliability and validity as marks of good science. As we revise our Reader's Guide, we grapple with how to talk about "reliable readers" and "valid interpretations" (see Brown, Tappan, Gilligan, Miller, & Argyris, in press).

By talking about two voices, we are constantly aware of voice, but we remind ourselves that we speak within and stand within the voices and perspectives we describe. We speak about justice and care, drawing on our own experiences and thinking also about where we stand in relation to issues of justice and of care within a larger societal and cultural world. Admittedly, we stand more firmly in the care perspective and perhaps speak more urgently about exclusion. Valuing openness, we have tried to create a method that is open to a plurality of voices—to 4 plus n readings—so that others using our method may record differences whose complexity, truth, and significance elude us or lie beyond the scope of our present research.

We try to remain attentive to missing voices and think about what our methods do not capture, to remember other channels or pathways into the study of morality and self, to think about our own limitations as readers. In analyzing justice and care themes in Loevinger's sentence completions, we have become interested in the relationship between our interpretive methods of reading and standard methods of specifying development.

Most of all, these days, we talk about development. From our studies of moral narratives, we have learned a great deal about psyche—about vulnerability, about relationship, and about culture—but to speak of development we must talk about patterns and commonalities and imbue observed psychic changes with direction and value. How we will handle this tension in our own work is of utmost importance to us.

Bringing our work into the setting of the Henry Murray lectures in personality, we have come to open a conversation with our colleagues. We have made a radical proposal: that to deal better with differences, we need a change in language. Otherwise, we cannot see how to solve the problem raised by our conundrum: How can sex be a difference that makes no difference for personality and development?

Our choice of a musical language opens a pathway to speak about differences that avoids the pitfalls and presumptions of invidious comparison. We have consciously chosen a language that represents psychological research as an activity of relationship and have sought to demonstrate the ways our method of inquiry—our interview questions and Reader's Guide—makes it possible to render the complexity of psychic experience. By multiple readings we weave the concepts of voice and vision into the very fabric of our research. By multiple readings we also call attention to voice and vision. Thus we have the sense of gaining a window into psychic life through which we can observe or, to return to voice metaphors, listen to Psyche speaking about herself/himself and about the experience of living in relationship with others, speaking in a moral language that encodes and conveys not only the experience of relationships but also a cultural legacy. In this transhistorical dialogue of moral discourse, people have recorded across place and time the human experiences of being wounded and being vulnerable, the human wish for protection and for comfort, the various strategies people create or glean for protecting themselves and others, and the fate of such efforts. The challenge and the potential in our method lies in its capacity for bringing together systematic inquiry with a narrative art that embeds Psyche in relationship and time. In our data we hear the kinds of stories that clinicians hear—stories of conflict, of anguish, sometimes stories of wounding, sometimes of recovery, sometimes of discovery; stories of loss, caring, strength; stories of illusion and disillusion, stories of resistance and capitulation, of heroism and courage—in short, narratives that have to do with the ways people think and feel about themselves living in a common social world, a world in which people may experience conflict and also may choose to wound or not to wound, to protect or to destroy something or someone of great value. To join such stories with a method of systematic inquiry holds the potential that Murray may have envisioned of joining a narrative art with the psychological study of human lives.

In writing this paper, we have deliberately focused much of our discussion on girls. It is still hard to listen to girls and women within the traditions of Western culture, even in the late twentieth century. Bringing girls' voices into this paper, we have performed in some sense an act of trespassing. The territory into which we trespass is familiar to us as psychologists; we know the language and terrain of our discipline. But as women we are also strangers in a strange land, paradoxically able to pass for natives. With this double vision, we walk sometimes steadily, sometimes unsteadily, a path we have made in an effort to convey what we hear in listening to girls and women and to bring these voices into the language spoken by psychologists. To the extent that we are able to do this, we make a clearing for a new conversation.

REFERENCES

Alter, R. (1981). *The art of biblical narrative*. New York: Basic Books.
Arendt, H. (1958). *The human condition*. Chicago: University of Chicago Press.
Britten, B. (1946). *Young person's guide to the orchestra*. Op. 34, Bernstein, L., New York Philharmonic, Col. 3-CBS D3S-785.
Brown, L., Argyris, D., Attanucci, J., Bardige, B., Gilligan, C., Johnston, K., Miller, B., Osborne, R., Ward, J., Wiggins, G., & Wilcox, D. (1987). *A guide to reading narratives of moral conflict and choice for self and moral voice* (Monograph

No. 2). Cambridge, MA: The Center for the Study of Gender, Education, and Human Development, Harvard University.

Brown, L., Tappan, M., Gilligan, C., Miller, B., & Argyris, D. (in press). Reading for self and moral voice: A method for interpreting narratives of real-life moral conflict and choice. In M. Packer & R. Addison (Eds.), *Interpretive investigations: Contributions to psychological research.* Albany, NY: SUNY Press.

Colby, A., & Kohlberg, L. (1987). *The measurement of moral judgment.* New York: Cambridge University Press.

Freud, S. (1895). Fraulein Elisabeth von R. In J. Breuer & S. Freud, *Studies on hysteria.* New York: Basic Books.

Gilligan, C. (1977). In a different voice: Women's conceptions of self and of morality. *Harvard Educational Review, 47,* 481–517.

Gilligan, C. (1982). *In a different voice: Psychological theory and women's development.* Cambridge, MA: Harvard University Press.

Gilligan, C. (1986). Remapping the moral domain: New images of self in relationship. In T. Heller, M. Sosna, & D. Wellbery (Eds.), *Reconstructing individualism: Autonomy, individualism, and the self in Western thought.* Stanford, CA: Stanford University Press.

Gilligan, C., Ward, J., & Taylor, J. (Eds.). (1988). *Mapping the moral domain: A contribution of women's thinking to psychology and education.* Cambridge, MA: Harvard University Press.

Gilligan, C., Johnston, D. K., & Miller, B. (1988). *Moral voice, adolescent development, and secondary education: A study of the Green River School* (Monograph No. 3). Cambridge, MA: Report of the Project on Adolescence, The Center for the Study of Gender, Education, and Human Development, Harvard University.

Gilligan, C., & Wiggins, G. (1987). The origins of morality in early childhood relationships. In J. Kagan & S. Lamb (Eds.), *The emergence of morality in young children.* Chicago: The University of Chicago Press.

Jack, D. (1987). Silencing the self: The power of social imperatives in female depression. In R. Formanek & A. Gurian (Eds.), *Women and depression: A lifespan perspective* (pp. 41–45). New York: Springer.

Keller, E. (1983). *A feeling for the organism.* New York: W. H. Freeman.

Keller, E. (1985). *Reflections on gender and science.* New Haven, CT: Yale University Press.

Keller, E., & Grontkowski, C. (1983). The mind's eye. In S. Harding & M. Hintikka (Eds.), *Discovering reality* (pp. 207–224). Boston: D. Reidel.

Kluckhohn, C., & Murray, H. (1967). *Personality in nature, society, and culture.* New York: Alfred A. Knopf.

Langer, S. (1951). Philosophy in a new key. Cambridge, MA: Harvard University Press.

Langer, S. (1967). *Mind: An essay on human feeling.* Baltimore: Johns Hopkins University Press.

Loevinger, J. (1957). Objective tests as instruments of psychological theory. *Psychological Reports, 3,* 635–694.

Loevinger, J. (1976). *Ego development: Conceptions and theories.* San Francisco: Jossey-Bass.

Loevinger, J. (1979). Theory and data in the measurement of ego development. In J. Loevinger, *Scientific ways in the study of ego development* (pp. 1-24). Worcester, MA: Clark University Press.

Loevinger, J., & Wessler, R. (1970). *Measuring ego development I: Construction and use of a sentence completion test.* San Francisco: Jossey-Bass.

Loevinger, J., Wessler, R., & Redmore, C. (1970). *Measuring ego development II: Scoring manual for women and girls.* San Fancisco: Jossey-Bass.

Lyons, N. (1982). *Conceptions of self and morality and modes of moral choice: Identifying justice and care in judgments of actual moral dilemmas.* Unpublished doctoral dissertation, Harvard University.

Milgram, S. (1974). *Obedience to authority: An experimental view.* New York: Harper & Row.

Miller, J. (1976). *Toward a new psychology of women.* Boston: Beacon Press.

Morrison, T. (1970). *The bluest eye.* New York: Washington Square Press.

Murray, J., Bradley, H., Craigie, W., & Onions, C. (Eds.). (1978). *The Oxford English Dictionary* (4th ed.). Oxford: Claredon Press.

Nussbaum, M. (1986a). *The fragility of goodness.* Cambridge, England: Cambridge University Press.

Nussbaum, M. (1986b). Love and the individual: Romantic rightness and Platonic aspiration. In T. Heller, M. Sosna, & D. Wellbery (Eds.), *Reconstructing individualism: Autonomy, individualism, and the self in Western thought.* Stanford, CA: Stanford University Press.

Rogers, A. (1987). *Gender differences in moral thinking: A validity study of two moral orientations.* Unpublished doctoral dissertation, Washington University.

Rogers, A. (1988a). *The question of gender differences: A validity study of two moral orientations.* Manuscript submitted for publication.

Rogers, A. (1988b). *Two developmental voices: A method for identifying a fugue of justice and care themes in sentence completions.* Unpublished manuscript, Harvard University.

Steiner-Adair, C. (1986). The body-politic: Normal female adolescent development and the development of eating disorders. *Journal of the American Academy of Psychoanalysis, 14,* 95-114.

Walker, L., de Vries, B., & Trevethan, S. (1987). Moral stages and moral orientations in real-life and hypothetical dilemmas. *Child Development, 58,* 842-858.

Appendix 1

Real-Life Moral Conflict and Choice Interview

All people have had the experience of being in a situation where they had to make a decision but weren't sure of what they should do. Would you describe a situation when you faced a moral conflict and you had to make a decision but weren't sure what you should do?

1. What was the situation? (Be sure you get a full elaboration of the story).
2. What was the conflict for you in that situation? Why was it a conflict?
3. In thinking about what to do, what did you consider? Why? Anything else you considered?
4. What did you decide to do? What happened?
5. Do you think it was the right thing to do? Why/why not?
6. What was at stake for you in this dilemma? What was at stake for others? In general, what was at stake?
7. How did you feel about it? How did you feel about it for the other(s) involved?
8. Is there another way to see the problem (other than the way you described it)?
9. When you think back over the conflict you described, do you think you learned anything from it?
10. Do you consider the situation you described a moral problem? Why/why not?
11. What does morality mean to you? What makes something a moral problem for you?

Note to Interviewers: Questions should follow references to judgments about the situation. Follow any references to feelings that are mentioned, for example, Why did you feel mad or angry? Also follow moral language, that is, should, ought. Questions should focus on in whose terms judgments are made. Try to understand the terms of the self and the self's perspective on the terms of the other.

Appendix 2

Interview-Narrative #217-1 (Tanya)

I: Can you tell me a situation where you faced a moral conflict, you had to make a decision, but you weren't sure what was the right thing to do?

R: I guess that's kind of one, the one I just told you.

I: With your friend?

R: Who's getting out of line, yah. But also when we were at camp, I went to camp with my sister and my cousin, and he was really young, he was like maybe 7, and he got really, really homesick. It was overnight. And he was like, always crying at night and stuff. And we had this camp guide who was really tough and I was really afraid of him, it was like 2 years ago and I was really afraid of him. And he said, "Nobody is allowed to use the phone," and so my cousin really wanted to call his parents, (Yah) and it was kind of up to me to go ask the guy if he could. So, either like I got bawled out by this guy and asked, or I didn't do anything about it, and he was my cousin, so I had to help him, so I went and asked the guy if he could use the phone and he started giving me this lecture about how there shouldn't be homesickness in the camp. And I said, "Sorry, but he's only 7." (Yah!) And he was really young and so he finally got to use the phone, so he used the phone. And then we had a camp meeting, and um, and the guy started saying, "Any kid here who gets homesick shouldn't be here," and he didn't say my cousin's name, but like, he was like, almost in tears.

I: Oh, and your cousin was there when he said that? Oh, that wasn't very nice.

R: Yah. It was really mean.

I: When you were in this situation, you knew the camp counselor had this policy that you couldn't call, but you also knew that you wanted to help your cousin out. What kinds of things did you consider in thinking about what to do?

R: Well, mostly that, first of all, what was right and wrong. (Um, hum) And the right thing was to go because it was my cousin's good, you know. (Um, hum) And he wasn't going to die or anything, but, you know, he's afraid to go to camp now, because he's like 9 now (Yah) and he doesn't want to go back, (Hmm) and so I, like I said, "This guy can intimidate me, but he can't beat me up or anything." (Yah) I'll realize that that's just the way he is, but I have to do this, so. I mean, he might be . . . he might say no, but it can't hurt asking.

I: Ah, ha. So, can you think of what was the conflict for you when you were trying to decide between, um, between the two options?

R: Just to either keep on my cousin for the week, you know, just help him out, (Um, hum) or have him, like the thing he wanted to do was go home, (Yah) but, I'm sure, I was sure he wouldn't be able to do that, so if he just talked to his mom, he did feel better, (Okay) but the conflict was the he was my cousin and we've always been kind of close, and I either helped him out or, like I helped myself or I did what was for him, or I couldn't go for myself, because I didn't want to be like, I was really afraid of that guy, and it was me saving myself or saving him. So I mean, nothing bad was going to happen to me. So I realized that it was worth letting him talk to his parents.

I: Do you think this was the right thing to do?

R: Yah.

I: Why?

R: Why? Because he felt a lot better and even though the guy was, was like giving us a lecture and getting really mean, he was, he was like, he let us use the phone, so I guess he did kind of realize, cause, my cousin was screaming, has nightmares, and it was really bad, he was with his friends, so he let him use the phone, but still, I mean I would never see the guy again, you know, if I didn't go back to the camp, but I lived, like my cousin lives 7 minutes away from us, so I lived with my cousin but I would never see that guy again.

I: I see, okay. So that factored into it, that you were going to see your cousin over and over and over.

R: Yah, so . . .

I: Okay. What was at stake for you in the dilemma?

R: Kind of like the ego, you know, and nothing physically and nothing that anybody else would see, it's just like my feelings being hurt and I hate being yelled at, so . . .

I: Ah, okay. All right, um, and then what was at stake for the other people involved?

R: The camp director, nothing, but my cousin, just kind a like, to be able to feel better, you know, (Um, hum) he was like feeling really, really low. He wasn't being able to have any fun and he paid for it, so he had to do something and he was just like really bad. He was like almost homesick, you know. That's why I guess they call it homesick, but.

I: Right. Well now, why do you think there was nothing at stake for the camp director?

R: Because, I'm sure there was, but the way I saw it by that time was like this guy is a big bully and he can have anything the way he wants it. So I don't, I guess it was kind of big giving in for him, you know. (Ah, huh) And I guess that kind of showed he was thinking, I know he was now, so I was really surprised, letting him use the phone, but he goes, see his like reputation, you know, that was a rule and he couldn't break it, but he said yes, but he started giving us this lecture.

I: All right, okay. So how did you feel about it?

R: How did I feel? (Um, hum) I felt good, but I felt really bad when the camp director went out and said that in the meeting, (Yah) I was just like, but I did something for him, my cousin, and it's kind of like a victory, you know, it's like you won over this guy so be happy.

I: Oh, okay. Even if he did act like a creep the next day or whatever?

R: Yah.

I: Do you think there is another way to see the problem, from anybody else's perspective?

R: Yah, I'm sure, I don't know what it was, but the camp director had another point of view. He was probably, like, "Kids always get homesick and what difference does it make, he's not going to die," you know, but he wasn't that kid, (Yah) and so he had a totally different point of view from my cousin and I. (Um, hm) And then like my friends probably, they knew about it, and they were like, "I understand but it's not, why does he cry all the time," you know. (Yah) It's like, either you feel it, like all the way or you just, like, recognize it, you know?

I: Sure, sure. It sounds like the camp director wasn't doing either of those two.

R: I know, he was really callous.

I: Yah. Okay, so when you think back over the conflict that you just described, do you think you learned anything from it?

R: It's obvious that I was right.

I: It's obvious that you were right?

R: Yah. The decision was right, you know.

I: Now, why is it obvious?

R: It's obvious because, no it isn't, but it is for me. It might not be for you or somebody else, but it's helping out my cousin and that camp director, you know, it was a rule, but people are more important than rules, you know. So he was just a little kid, you know, and they were trying out things, and the camp director, they were saying, "We're here to help our kids, to make them have fun," but my cousin wasn't having fun, he was just contradicting the whole slogan, (Yah) you know, (Right . . .) so it wasn't for that, and it was just like, I guess if you did ask somebody they would say, "That is right," but then you say the answer, and "I don't know . . . the reason, you know."

I: But you felt it was right?

R: Yah, I felt it was right.

I: Do you consider this situation you described a moral problem?

R: What's that?

I: I don't want to define it, because then you have my definition. But, um, oh, okay, let me try this one: What does morality mean to you? When you hear that word, what does that mean?

R: Morality? Probably it has to do with the person . . . Oh! We did this in English the other day.

I: (Laughs) So I hear.

R: Morality, it's like the difference between right and wrong, you know, and it's when the person like chooses the right thing, it's like, in the long run, or, um, even in that little experience or that little incident, but, um, it's just like what's deep down what you think is going to be right, and what's going to help you out or help the other person out, and then the conflict is what is a decision, but it's like not going to do anything, it's just gonna maybe make things, life, easier.

I: Okay, well, then I would like to ask you, what is a moral problem for you? What do you think makes a moral problem?

R: Maybe when, you know, it has something to do with people or your friends, or just even a dog or something, and it's going to be easier, I mean, it's like if you're lazy, it's easier to take the wrong one, so it's like a decision.

I: Okay. Do you think the situation, the story with your cousin and the camp director, would that be considered a moral problem for you?

R: Yeah, because I could have gotten out of it easily, you know, and it wasn't my feeling, my cousin's, but he was like really close, but I wasn't feeling what he was feeling, but I did have a little empathy, but not that much. So, either I could have gotten out of it and said, "I'm not going up to that camp director, you go up yourself," to my cousin, but he was like very miserable and I almost felt like he did in a way, so I did go up because I felt miserable having him feel miserable.

I: Right. I bet.

Coded Interview-Narrative #217-1 (Tanya): Italics = care; boldface = justice; all caps = self responses.

I: Can you tell me a situation where you faced a moral conflict, you had to make a decision, but you weren't sure what was the right thing to do?

R: I guess that's kind of one, the one I just told you.

I: With your friend?

R: Who's getting out of line, yah. But also when we were at camp, I WENT TO CAMP with my sister and my cousin, and *he was really young, he was like maybe 7, and he got really, really homesick. It was overnight.* And *he was like, always crying at night and stuff.* And we had this camp guide who was really tough and I WAS REALLY AFRAID of him, it was like 2 years ago and I was really afraid of him. **And he said, "Nobody is allowed to use the phone,"** *and so my cousin really wanted to call his parents,* (Yah) and it was kind of up to me to go ask the guy if he could. So, EITHER LIKE I GOT BAWLED OUT BY THIS GUY AND ASKED, OR I DIDN'T DO ANYTHING ABOUT IT, **and he was my cousin, so I HAD TO HELP HIM,** SO I WENT AND ASKED the guy if he could use the phone and **he started giving me this lecture about how there shouldn't be homesickness in the camp.** *AND I SAID, "SORRY, BUT HE'S ONLY 7."* (Yah!) *And he was really young* and so he finally got to use the phone, so he used the phone. And then we had a camp meeting, and um, and the guy started saying **"Any kid here who gets homesick shouldn't be here,"** and he didn't say my cousin's name, but like, *he was like, almost in tears.*

I: Oh, and your cousin was there when he said that? Oh, that wasn't very nice.

R: Yah. It was really mean.

I: When you were in this situation, you knew the camp counselor had this policy that you couldn't call, but you also knew that you wanted to help your cousin out. What kinds of things did you consider in thinking about what to do?

R: Well, mostly that, first of all, WHAT WAS RIGHT AND WRONG. (Um, hum) **And the right thing was to go because it was my cousin's good, you know.** (Um, hum) *And he wasn't going to die or anything, but, you know, he's afraid to go to camp now, because he's like 9 now* (Yah) *and he doesn't want to go back,* (Hmm) and SO I, LIKE I SAID, "THIS GUY CAN INTIMI-DATE ME, BUT HE CAN'T BEAT ME UP OR ANYTHING." (Yah) I'LL REALIZE THAT THAT'S JUST THE WAY HE IS, BUT **I HAVE TO DO THIS,** so. I mean, he might be . . . he might say no, but it can't hurt asking.

I: Ah, ha. So, can you think of what was the conflict for you when you were trying to decide between, um, between the two options?

R: Just to either KEEP ON MY COUSIN for the week, you know, JUST HELP HIM OUT, (Um, hum) or have him, like the thing he wanted to do was go home, (Yah) but, I'M SURE, I WAS SURE he wouldn't be able to do that, so if he just talked to his mom, *he did feel better*, (Okay) but *the conflict was that HE WAS MY COUSIN AND WE'VE ALWAYS BEEN KIND OF CLOSE, AND I EITHER HELP HELPED HIM OUT OR, LIKE I HELPED MYSELF OR I DID WHAT WAS FOR HIM, OR I COULDN'T GO FOR MYSELF*, BECAUSE I DIDN'T WANT TO BE LIKE, *I WAS REALLY AFRAID* of that guy, and *IT WAS ME SAVING MYSELF OR SAVING HIM.* So I MEAN, *NOTHING BAD WAS GOING TO HAPPEN TO ME.* SO I REALIZED that it was worth letting him talk to his parents.

I: Do you think this was the right thing to do?

R: Yah.

I: Why?

R: Why? *Because he felt a lot better* and even though the guy was, was like giving us a lecture and getting really mean, he was, he was like, he let us use the phone, so I GUESS HE DID KIND OF REALIZE, *cause, my cousin was screaming, has nightmares, and it was really bad,* he was with his friends, so he let him use the phone, but still, I MEAN I would never see the guy again, you know, if I didn't go back to the camp, *but I lived, like my cousin lives 7 minutes away from us, so I lived with my cousin but I would never see that guy again.*

I: I see, okay. So that factored into it, that you were going to see your cousin over and over and over.

R: Yah, so . . .

I: Okay. What was at stake for you in the dilemma?

R: *Kind of like the ego,* you know, *and nothing physically and nothing that anybody else would see, IT'S JUST LIKE MY FEELINGS BEING HURT AND I HATE BEING YELLED AT,* SO . . .

I: Ah, okay. All right, um, and then what was at stake for the other people involved?

R: The camp director, nothing, *but my cousin,* just kind of like, *to be able to feel better,* you know, (Um, hum) *he was like feeling really, really low.* **He wasn't being able to have any fun and he paid for it, so he had to do something** and *he was just like really bad. He was like almost homesick,* you know. That's why I guess they call it homesick, but.

I: Right. Well now, why do you think there was nothing at stake for the camp director?

R: Because, I'm sure there was, BUT THE WAY I SAW IT by that time was like **this guy is a big bully and he can have anything the way he wants it.** SO I DON'T, **I GUESS it was kind of big giving in for him,** you know. (Ah, huh)

And I GUESS that kind of showed he was thinking, I KNOW he was now, SO I
WAS REALLY SURPRISED, letting him use the phone, but he goes, **see his
like reputation, you know, that was a rule and he couldn't break it**, but he
said yes, *but* he started giving us this lecture.

I: All right, okay. So how did you feel about it?

R: How did I feel? (Um, hum) I FELT GOOD, BUT I FELT REALLY BAD
when the camp director went out and said that in the meeting, (Yah) I WAS
JUST LIKE, but *I DID SOMETHING for him, my cousin*, and **IT'S KIND OF
LIKE A VICTORY**, YOU KNOW, *IT'S LIKE YOU WON OVER THIS
GUY SO BE HAPPY*.

I: Oh, okay. Even if he did act like a creep the next day or whatever?

R: Yah.

I: Do you think there is another way to see the problem, from anybody else's
perspective?

R: Yah, I'M SURE, I DON'T NOW WHAT IT WAS, but the camp director
had another point of view. **He was probably, like, "Kids always get homesick
and what difference does it make, he's not going to die,"** you know, *but he
wasn't that kid*, (Yah) and so he had a totally different point of view from my
cousin and I. (Um, hm) And then like my friends probably, they knew about it,
and they were like, "I understand but it's not, why does he cry all the time," you
know. (Yah) *It's like, either you feel it, like all the way or you just, like,
recognize it, you know?*

I: Sure, sure. It sounds like the camp director wasn't doing either of those
two.

R: I know, he was really callous.

I: Yah. Okay, so when you think back over the conflict that you just
described, do you think you learned anything from it?

R: It's obvious that I was right.

I: It's obvious that you were right?

R: Yah. The decision was right, you know.

I: Now, why is it obvious?

R: IT'S OBVIOUS BECAUSE, no it isn't, BUT IT IS FOR ME. It might not
be for you or somebody else, but *it's helping out my cousin and that camp
director*, you know, *it was a rule, but people are more important than rules*, you
know. So he was just a little kid, you know, and they were trying out things,
and the camp director, **they were saying, "We're here to help our kids, to
make them have fun,"** but my cousin wasn't having fun, he was just contradicting the whole slogan, (Yah) you know, (Right . . .) so it wasn't for that,
and it was just like, I guess if you did ask somebody they would say, "That is

right," but then you say the answer, and "I don't know . . . the reason, you know."

I: But you felt it was right?

R: Yah, I FELT IT WAS RIGHT.

I: Do you consider this situation you described a moral problem?

R: What's that?

I: I don't want to define it, because then you have my definition. But, um, oh, okay, let me try this one: What does morality mean to you? When you hear that word, what does that mean?

R: Morality? Probably it has to do with the person . . . Oh! We did this in English the other day.

I: (Laughs) So I hear.

R: Morality, it's like the difference between right and wrong, you know, and it's when the person like chooses the right thing, it's like, in the long run, or, um, even in that little experience or that little incident, but, um, it's just like what's deep down what you think is going to be right, and *what's going to help you out or help the other person out*, and then the conflict is what is a decision, but it's like not going to do anything, it's just gonna maybe make things, life, easier.

I: Okay, well, then I would like to ask you, what is a moral problem for you? What do you think makes a moral problem?

R: Maybe when, you know, it has something to do with people or your friends, or just even a dog or something, and it's going to be easier, I mean, it's like if you're lazy, it's easier to take the wrong one, so it's like a decision.

I: Okay. Do you think the situation, the story with your cousin and the camp director, would that be considered a moral problem for you?

R: Yeah, because I COULD HAVE GOTTEN OUT OF IT EASILY, you know, and IT WASN'T MY FEELING, my cousin's, but *he was like really close, but I WASN'T FEELING WHAT HE WAS FEELING, but I DID HAVE A LITTLE EMPATHY, BUT NOT THAT MUCH. So, either I COULD HAVE GOTTEN OUT OF IT AND SAID*, "I'm not going up to that camp director, you go up yourself," to my cousin, *but he was like very miserable and I ALMOST FELT LIKE HE DID IN A WAY, SO I DID GO UP BECAUSE I FELT MISERABLE HAVING HIM FEEL MISERABLE.*

I: Right. I bet.

Appendix 3

After reading (and underlining) for self, care, and justice, the reader is asked to fill in the following summary Worksheets. While the Reader's Guide explains the interpretive procedure, the Worksheets provide a place for the reader to document relevant pieces of text and to make observations and interpretive remarks. The Worksheets, then, are designed to highlight the critical move from the narrator's actual words to a reader's interpretations or summary of them with respect to moral voice. Since they require the reader to substantiate his or her interpretation of the text with quotes from the interview, these Worksheets stand between the Reading Guide (and the reader) and the interview text. They leave a trial of evidence for a reader's interpretation that can be followed by another reader.

In attempting to move from a reading of a particular interview narrative of moral conflict and choice, such as Tanya's, to an extensive summary of the reading recorded on the summary Worksheets, to a final representation of the way in which self and moral voice are manifest and articulated in the narrative, we have developed a typology that we have called narrative Types (see Brown et al., in press). These categorical types distinguish between narratives with respect to the ways in which the moral voices of justice and care are represented. In sum, the overall Narrative Type that summarizes a particular narrative of moral conflict and choice is actually composed of three separate but related dimensions of self and moral voice: Presence, Predominance, and Alignment.

These Narrative Types provide a simplified tool for data analysis. They allow us to represent, in the form of a categorical typology, some of the aspects of narratives of moral conflict and choice relevant to self and the two moral voices, justice and care. As such they allow us to compare groups of narratives—comparisons that would be unwieldy at best, using only the summary Worksheets obtained from a reader's use of the Reader's Guide. We want to stress, however, that these Types are by no means the only way to move from the Worksheets to a representation of the data captured by the reader. Dianne

Argyris, a coauthor of the Reader's Guide, is now working with descriptive summaries of the cases, rather than with the Narrative Typologies.) But they do provide a useful way to generate and explore interesting hypotheses regarding the ways in which self and moral voice are manifest in narratives of moral conflict and choice.

WORKSHEETS

I. First Reading—Understanding the Story

A. *Briefly Note All Conflicts* in the section of the interview entitled "Moral Conflict and choice" (please cite page numbers where found).

(p. 13) "I guess that's kind of one, the one I just told you." [May want to refer to previous section to pick up this conflict with her friend "getting out of line." She does not elaborate here.]

(pp. 13-16) ". . . I went to camp with my sister and my cousin, and he was really young . . . and he got really homesick . . . And we had this camp guide who was really tough and I was really afraid of him . . . And he said, "Nobody is allowed to use the phone" . . . my cousin really wanted to call his parents . . . and it was kind of up to me to ask the guy if he could. So either like I got bawled out by this guy and asked, or I didn't do anything about it . . . but the conflict was that he was my cousin and we've always been kind of close, and I either helped him out or like I helped myself . . . it was me saving myself or saving him . . .

B. *Please Make Notes Here on the First Reading*—e.g., relationships, general moral language, repeated words and themes, contradictions, and key images and metaphors.

Relationships—with her cousin, with the camp director, with herself, with her friends. She mentions in the beginning of the story that her sister was also at camp, but does not mention her again. It's unclear where the sister stood in relation to all that happened; from the narrative it appears she was not involved though we don't know why (e.g., was she also younger and therefore not as able to help?)

Repeated themes—She says three times "I was really afraid" of counselor (p. 13).

Contradictions—She notes a contradiction in the camp directors' belief that "we're here to help our kids, to make them have fun," when her cousin was obviously "contradicting the whole slogan."

Possible contradiction in her narrative—her sense that the right thing to do was obvious for her, and her experience of this as a moral conflict. "I felt good but I felt really bad" (p. 14).

Moral language—[Note that they discussed morality "in English the other day."] Morality is "what's deep down what you think is going to be right, and what's going to help you out or help the other person out . . ." She considers the story to be a story about morality because "I could have gotten out of it easily . . . it wasn't my feeling, my cousins, but he was like really close . . . so either I could have gotten out of it easily . . . but he was very miserable and I almost felt like he did in a way, so I did go up because I felt miserable having him feel miserable" (p. 16).

II. Second Reading—Self

A. *Self and the Narrative of Action*

What actions does self take in the conflict?

Summary/Interpretation

1. Choosing self—Does the narrator see or describe a choice? What is the choice? How is the choice made?

(p. 13) I was really afraid . . . it was kind of up to me . . . either . . . I got bawled out . . . and asked or I didn't do anything about it . . . I had to tell him . . . So I went and asked . . .

She seems to have made the choice by herself (though she talked with her friends, it's not clear how they were involved in her choice), clearly at some personal risk; later she talks about "the ego," her fear of being yelled at. Was her sister involved?

2. What is self describing him/herself as saying and/or doing?
(p. 13) I had to tell him . . . so I went and asked . . .

A sense of certainty, urgency.

I said, "This guy can intimidate me but he can't beat me up."

She seems aware and sure of the boundaries to the camp director's potential aggression toward her.

(p. 16) I did go up because I felt miserable having him feel miserable.

Experience of interdependence with cousin and his distress seemed to motivate action on her part.

3. What is self thinking or considering or feeling?

(p. 13) I was really afraid . . . it was kind of up to me . . . either I got bawled out and asked or I didn't do anything about it. I considered what was right and wrong . . .

Fear for herself vs. sense of responsibility to act; she says she was really afraid twice; fear of being "bawled out."

(pp. 13–14) He was my cousin and we've always been kind of close . . . I either helped him out or, like I helped myself . . . it was me saving myself or saving him . . .

Focus on their close relationship, conflict between responding to his distress or to her fear of the consequences.

(p. 14) . . . nothing bad was going to happen to me . . .

Ref. to the fact that counselor "can't beat me up."

(p. 15) I guess it was kind of like a victory.

(p. 16) . . . it wasn't my feeling . . . I wasn't feeling what he was feeling . . . I did have a little empathy . . . I almost felt like my cousin did in a way . . . I did go up because I felt miserable having him feel miserable.

She seems to be distinguishing her cousin's feelings from her own, while trying to explain her feelings of empathy for him . . . and her felt need to respond to his misery. She distinguishes relational fusion from interdependence.

B. *Self in Relationship*

1. What is organizing frame for the relationship(s) described in the conflict?

Summary/Interpretation

With her cousin—(p. 13) It was kind of up to me to go ask the guy if he could (use the phone) . . . he was my cousin, so I had to help him . . . he was really young . . . it was my cousin's good . . . we've always been kind of close . . . (p. 14) my cousin lives 7 minutes away from us . . . (p. 16) I almost felt like he did in a way . . .

She describes her feelings of attachment to her cousin, and her felt need to respond seems connected to these descriptions. Yet she also observes his vulnerability and distress, connected to his young age, and may feel responsible for him, both because she is older and witnesses this (and therefore has more power than he does to act) and because she is a relative and may feel it is her role or her duty to act on his behalf (Not clear whether she was given special responsibility for her cousin by her/his family?)

With the camp counselor—(p. 13) I was really afraid of him . . . so either I got bawled out by this guy and asked . . . he started giving me this lecture . . . I said sorry, but he's only 7 . . . this guy can intimidate me, but he can't beat me up or anything . . . (p. 14) I would never see that guy again . . . this guy is a big bully and he can have anything the way he wants it . . . it was a big giving in for him . . . (p. 15) was like a victory . . . like you won over this guy so be happy.

Her fear of him, his relative position and power, point to a relationship of inequality. This makes her experience of victory over him sensible. And makes her act of speaking up ("I said sorry, but he's only 7") seem quite brave. She is aware that there are limits to what he can do (as a camp counselor); this awareness seems to allow her to speak up . . . and to react to her cousin's distress.

With herself—(p. 13) So, like I said, this guy can intimidate me, but he can't beat me up or anything . . . (p. 14) it was me saving myself or saving him . . . kind of like the ego . . . nothing that anybody else would see . . . my feelings being hurt and I hate being yelled at . . . (p. 15) it's like you won over this guy so be happy.

She seems to be letting us in on a series of internal dialogues . . . Her way of sorting through the issues in this conflict that represent different parts of herself—fear, potential embarrassment, damage to her ego, final sense of victory. This dialogue sets up the conflict in a way that represents her in relation to herself and includes concern for her self (selves?) as a central factor in the choices she makes.

C. What Is at Stake for Self?

1. (p. 14) I was really afraid of him . . . it was me saving myself or saving him . . . kind of like the ego . . . nothing physically and nothing that anybody else would see, it's just like my feelings being hurt and I hate being yelled at . . .

Her own fear of a bruised ego, of being yelled at, having hurt feelings in conflict with her cousin's distress . . . she's clear that she was not at risk for physical abuse.

III. Third Reading—Care

A. *Is the Care Orientation Articulated?*   Yes

1. How would you characterize care?   Summary/Interpretation

(p. 13) . . . he was really young . . . he got really homesick . . . he was almost in tears . . .   Attention to cousin's distress.

. . . he was my cousin, so I had to help him . . . the right thing was to go because he was my cousin . . . he was my cousin and we've always been kind of close . . . (p. 14) Cousin lives 7 minutes away from us, so I would live with my cousin, but I would never see that guy again . . . he (cousin) was like really close . . .   Description of close relationship with cousin, which will be maintained beyond this situation.

(p. 14) . . . so I realized it was worth letting him talk to his parents . . . what's going to help you out will help the other person out (re: def. of morality, p. 16) . . . he was like very miserable and I almost felt like he did in a way, so I . . . did go up because I was miserable having him feel miserable.   Response to need of the cousin based on relationship with him and the impact of that relationship on her (interdependence).

(p. 13) . . . I said "Sorry, but he's only 7" (p. 15) . . . people are more important than rules . . . but my cousin wasn't having fun, he was just contradicting the whole slogan.   Consideration of cousin and particular circumstances, over the rule as a whole.

Understanding of counselor's view— (p. 13) I'll realize that's the way he is, but I have to do this . . . (p. 14) I guess it was kind of big giving in for him . . .   Attention to and understanding of perspective of others as concerns relevant to outcome of conflict, including attention to her own as one of many possible views.

Awareness of impact of her own view
on situation—(p. 13) This guy can
intimidate me . . . I was afraid . . . my
feelings being hurt . . .
Awareness of cousin's view (p. 13)
. . . he was really homesick.

B. *If Care Is Not (Clearly Articulated?)*

(p. 14) . . . it was me saving myself or
saving him . . .

How does care of self fit in here? Her
assurance that she cannot be physically hurt or that "nothing bad was
going to happen to me" seems at odds
with this dichotomy . . . here she
makes it sound as though choosing
her cousin is self-sacrificial?

C. *Does Self Align with Care? How Do You Know?*

Appears so—awareness of her own needs and the extent to which she could
be harmed (what's at stake was the ego) mitigates the few phrases in which
she sounds self-sacrificial. Deciding her fears and hurt feelings were not as
important as her cousin's distress, she responds to her cousin, She focuses on
their closeness and distinguishes between feeling what he was feeling and
feeling empathy. She believes that people in general, and her cousin in this
situation in particular, are more important than rules, at least those that are
enforced without exception or attention to particularities of the situation.

IV. Fourth Reading—Justice

A. *Is the Justice Orientation Articulated?*

Yes

1. How would you characterize justice?

Summary/Interpretation

Re: counselor—(p. 14) . . . His reputation (was at stake) . . . that was a
rule and he couldn't break it . . .
(p. 15) He was probably, like kids
always get homesick and what difference does it make . . .

Reference to an understanding of
rules (but rejects their enforcement
without attention to the particular
case).

(p. 15) . . . people are more important than rules . . . camp directors say we're here to help our kids, to make them have fun, but my cousin wasn't having fun, he was just contradicting the whole slogan.

Understanding the spirit of the law vs. the letter of the law . . . counselor was not paying attention to the exception in cousin's case.

(p. 14) . . . He wasn't being able to have any fun and be paid for it, so he had to do something . . .

Not to let the cousin call would be unfair, since cousin was not getting what he was due for his money, what the camp promised.

B. *If Justice Is Not (Clearly) Articulated in This Conflict?*

1. What would constitute justice in this conflict?

(p. 13) . . . this guy can intimidate me, but he can't beat me up or anything . . .

She seems aware that the system (or convention) will protect her from physical abuse . . .

(p. 15) . . . but I did something for him, my cousin, and it's kind of like a victory . . . you won over this guy so be happy . . .

Framing the outcome as a victory makes most sense in the context of a struggle between what she perceived as unfair about the counselor's actions and her (and her cousin's) less powerful position with respect to him.

(p. 13) . . . and he was my cousin, so I had to help him . . .

Not clear if she experienced a sense of duty to care for him, or was given responsibility for him?

C. *Does Self Align with Justice? How Do You Know?*

No . . . though she does allude to protection from a system that would limit the actions of the counselor, she seems most attentive to her own fears and her cousin's distress and pits this against a definition of justice that is blind to particular circumstances, that is, blind to the spirit of the law.

V. Interpretive Summary—Self in Relation to Justice and Care

Both care and justice are present; at times certain phrases can be understood from either perspective, depending on the lens. (E.g., "He was my cousin and so I had to help him" can refer to their closeness or to the fact that she was responsible due to her role as older relative. Also, "I said, 'sorry he's only 7'" can refer to her empathy for his distress at such a young age or her anger at the counselor's advantage in power and oppressive treatment.)

She rejects a form of justice that places importance of reputation or rules for the sake of rules (i.e., that do not consider exceptions) over persons in need . . . She focuses *predominantly* on care concerns—the relationship with her cousin, her own fears and needs, and her cousin's distress.

Appendix 4

Tanya's Sentence Completion Test (Girl's Form 2-77a)

1. If I had more money—I would be no more happier, but I would be more content to spend when I do.
2. A wife should—have as much power as the husband and she should be working.
3. When a child will not join in group activities—no special attention should be given but she should nicely be questioned and urged on.
4. My mother and I—look the same, but never feel the same way about things.
5. The thing I like about myself is—I can usually count on myself for doing the things I want to do.
6. Being with other people—I enjoy very much, but when I'm wrong I need to concentrate.
7. If my mother—relaxed and had a good time I would be happy. I have empathy for her.
8. Education—is on almost the top of my list when I think of the future.
9. What gets me into trouble is—when I do bad in school or don't do what I'm told to do.
10. A good mother—will never be, all mothers are different and have different qualities.
11. I feel sorry—for anyone who can't get to where they want to go.
12. The worst thing about being a woman—is being spit on by men.
13. Women are lucky because—they can prove many things.
14. At times she worried about—letting people down.
15. She felt proud that she—had gotten where she was so far.
16. Rules are—do things right.
17. When she thought of her mother, she—fell silent with a grin on her face.
18. When I get mad—all I want is to be left alone.
19. When they avoided me—I felt left out.

20. Raising a family—is probably one of the toughest jobs there is.
21. I am—sitting at a table.
22. A girl has a right to—be whatever she wants to be.
23. I just can't stand people who—don't take things seriously when they should.
24. My father—is the perfect example of what and how I want to be when I grow up.
25. If I can't get what I want—I try to forget about it and think about the things I already have.
26. A girl feels good when—she knows she did something right.
27. My main problem is—that I worry with my imagination.
28. Crime and delinquency could be halted if—the world halted.
29. Sometimes she wished that—she could mean more to other people.
30. When I am criticized—I take it personally and always think about it, but try to fix it.
31. For a woman a career is—the same thing it is for a man.
32. When people are helpless—they are in the ditch of morality.
33. When my mother spanked me, I—spanked her back.
34. Men are lucky because—they don't get pregnant.
35. My conscience bothers me if—I know something I shouldn't know.
36. A woman should always—speak up for what she feels.
37. A good father—is my father.

Note. Item 37 is added to the 36 items of this form of the test.

Laura's Sentence Completion Test (Women's Form 81)

1. When a child will not join in group activities—his friends should go see what is wrong.
2. Raising a family—is really important and shouldn't be under-rated.
3. When I am criticized—I should try to accept what I am told, but I usually don't too well.
4. A man's job—can be done by a woman if she chooses.
5. Being with other people—is usually more fun than being alone, but not necessarily more fun than being with just a few.
6. The thing I like about myself is—that I can apply myself to any situation, and with effort, succeed.
7. My mother and I—don't always agree, but she is usually right, and I love her.
8. What gets me into trouble is—when I don't plan ahead, and act impulsively too often in a given time.
9. Education—is necessary to survive in the world.
10. When people are helpless—you should try to help them if you can in any way.

11. Women are lucky because—they have a lot of choices open to them and people don't expect as much from them so it's easier to be impressive.
12. A good father—takes time to [erased—come to] spend with his children when he is home.
13. A girl has a right to—ask people to back-off and expect them to do so.
14. When they talked about sex, I—was convinced to become a nun.
15. A wife should—take care of her husband (they usually don't know much about cooking etc.).
16. I feel sorry—for anyone who is intimidated and can't be themselves.
17. A man feels good when—he knows who his friends are and has good friends.
18. Rules are—important, but should be always able to modify to fit the situation.
19. Crime and delinquency could be halted if—education and morality could be put into culture of poorer educated.
20. Men are lucky because—they are given expectations to achieve so are often given more encouragement.
21. I just can't stand people who—are back-biting or two-faced.
22. At times she worried about—what she would do after college.
23. I am—happiest when [erased—I have achieved my goals] I know I can trust people.
24. A woman feels good when—she is loved.
25. My main problem is—losing interest and becoming "an underachiever."
26. A husband has a right to—expect his wife to be willing to listen and understand.
27. The worst thing about being a woman is—[no response]
28. A good mother—is there for her children and her husband regardless of all other things.
29. When I am with a man—I don't think I can generalize about this—everyone is different.
30. Sometimes she wished that—he could be honest and trust her.
31. My father—comes to my field hockey and lacrosse games and he's always really proud of me when I do something well, and if I don't do anything well he just smiles and doesn't worry about it.
32. If I can't get whet I want—I sometimes have a fit, but I'm going to try to outgrow that soon.
33. Usually she felt that sex—was alright if it was with the right person and she really could trust him with anything. That is very, very rare, though.
34. For a woman a career is—good if she can handle it plus everything else.
35. My conscience bothers me if—I feel dishonest with others and I feel this way often.
36. A woman should always—be able to smile, if you can't keep things in perspective, you are in trouble.

5

Unity and Purpose in Human Lives: The Emergence of Identity as a Life Story

Dan P. McAdams

INTRODUCTION

Again and again, personality psychologists have turned to Henry Murray's (1938) *Explorations in Personality* to justify what they do. Psychologists who study personality dispositions such as traits (Epstein, 1984; Wiggins & Broughton, 1985) and motives (McClelland, 1981) point to Murray's conviction that personality is comprised, in part, of underlying and stable factors, such as psychogenic needs and complexes, that make for longitudinal and cross-situational consistency in behavior. Their intellectual antagonists—those who argue for the primacy of situational factors in the determination of human behavior (Mischel, 1984; Moos, 1976)—also invoke Murray, for Murray was one of the first personality psychologists to recognize the importance of the environmental context in shaping human behavior and experience, captured in his concept of the "press." Those who call themselves "interactionists," eschewing the late trait versus situation debate, find sustenance in Murray's emphasis on the interaction of need and press and in such interactional concepts as "thema" and "serial," first suggested in *Explorations* (Endler, 1981). Psychologists who adopt biographical approaches to personality (McAdams & Ochberg, 1988) and who seek the understanding of the whole person through the intensive study of the individual case (Runyan, 1982) are likely to view their own work as part of the legacy of Murray's "personological tradition."

I was a graduate student at Harvard in the mid-1970s when I first learned of Henry Murray, *Explorations*, and the personological tradition. I learned of Murray from my conversations with David McClelland, who emphasized Murray's motivational emphasis in the study of lives, and from George Goethals's inspiring lectures in his "Psychology of the Human Life-Span," where the focus was more on biography and the structure of lives as integrated, story-like wholes. Though Murray had long since retired by the time I reached Harvard, his legacy flourished in a heady folklore about the man and his times—stories about the heyday of the Harvard Psychological Clinic shortly before and after World War II and of the great pioneers in personology, such as Robert White, Silvan Tomkins, Erik Homburger Erikson, Nevitt Sanford, and Donald MacKinnon. I identified strongly with this tradition, reading everything I could get my hands on by and about Murray, his intellectual mission at Harvard, and the halcyon days of the 1930s leading up to the publication of *Explorations*.

By the time I finally met Henry Murray in person, he had already assumed larger-than-life proportions in my own life story—my own sacred mythology of the self, that story providing *my* life with a sense of unity and purpose. For me as a graduate student, he was the greatest intellectual hero, a messianic figure whose writings promised to save me from what I saw as the desultory world of states, traits, samples, signs, situations, and cutting scores in personality psychology. Personology was something of a holy mission for me, and *Explorations* was its canonical text. Though my grandiosity has been tempered since my years at Harvard, and my vision has broadened to encompass many different traditions in personality psychology, Murray and personology continue to be important parts of my own story making, the construction of my own professional and personal identity. And I continue to look to *Explorations* for intellectual sustenance and intrigue. For example, in recent years I have puzzled over the meaning of one of Murray's most disarmingly pithy statements, buried in this fourth "primary proposition" of personality, on page 39 of *Explorations* (1938). It reads: "The history of the organism *is* the organism."

What does this statement mean?

Murray's remark can be read on many different levels and from many different perspectives. From a methodological perspective, the statement may be viewed as an appeal for the use of biographical and autobiographical techniques in personality research. Indeed, the next sentence in *Explorations* (1938) reads: "This proposition calls for biographical studies" (p. 39). Like Dollard (1935), Frenkel (1936), Allport (1937), and certain other social scientists of the day, Murray (1938) favored biographical methods in the study of human behavior. College men who participated as subjects in Murray's studies at the Harvard Psychological Clinic in the 1930s were asked to prepare autobiographies that served as springboards for subsequent interviewing and testing (White, 1981). In examining how persons made sense of their own biographical histories, Murray joined a small group of methodological mavericks, for the ascending view in the 1930s and 1940s was that the science of psychology would advance most quickly through experimental and highly quantitative, *not* biographical and qualitative, methods of investigation. With a few notable exceptions (e.g., Erikson, 1958; White, 1966), biographical explorations of lives declined markedly after World War II and through the early 1970s. Recent years, however, have witnessed a resurgence of interest in biographical and life history methodologies, both in psychology (e.g., Anderson, 1981; Howe, 1982; Levinson, 1981; McAdams, 1988a; Rosenwald, 1988) and in other social sciences (e.g., Bertaux, 1981; Runyan, 1988).

A second interpretation of Murray's remark underscores his *developmental* conception of the person. Murray's (1938) commitment to a life-span, developmental view of personality is evident in the sentences immediately preceding the statement with which I am concerned:

> The organism consists of an infinitely complex series of temporally related activities extending from birth to death. Because of the meaningful connection of sequences the life cycle of a single individual should be taken as a unit, the *long unit* for psychology. It is feasible to study the organism during one episode of its existence, but it should be recognized that this is but an arbitrarily selected part of the whole. The history of the organism *is* the organism. (p. 39)

At a time when experimental psychologists scrutinized single episodes of molecular behavior in order to assess basic laws of learning and performance that might apply to all organisms of all ages, Murray stressed that any single episode of human behavior must be understood in its developmental context. The "long unit" of analysis for the personologist was to be the single developing organism—an integrated totality changing over time. Though Murray set forth few explicitly developmental propositions for personality, his emphasis on the dynamic wholeness of lives from birth to death foreshadowed the rise of life-span developmental psychology in the 1970s and 1980s (Baltes, Reese, & Lipsitt, 1980; Datan, Rodeheaver, & Hughes, 1987). For Murray, behavior was embedded in "an infinitely complex series of temporally related activities" and events. Simple, linear relations in which Event A causes Event B are likely to be rare amidst such complexity, signaling the need for complex, bidirectional models of human behavior and development, as we see in the currently popular "transactional" models of development (Sameroff, 1982) and various "systems" approaches (Haley, 1980; Schwartz, 1987).

A third and more radical interpretation of Murray's statement is to take him literally. The history of the organism *is*, in some fundamental sense, the organism. *A person is a history.* Yet as personologists should know better than anybody, a person is *many things*. Exactly what particular "thing" we wish to identify with "person" depends largely on the perspective we assume via-à-vis the person. Thus a person cannot *be* a history and nothing else: From one sociological perspective, for instance, the person may be an "actor" playing roles and putting on performances (Goffman, 1959; Hogan, 1987); from the standpoint of the Kohutian analyst, on the other hand, the person may be the locus of an intrapsychic self, unconsciously forged through early object relations and the dynamics of the family (Kohut, 1977).

But what is the person from the standpoint of the person? How does a person define him- or herself as a person? It is from this subjective standpoint, I believe, that the person can be said to be a *history*—a subjectively composed and construed life story that integrates one's past, present, and future. The main thesis of my life story model of identity is that a person defines him- or herself by constructing an autobiographical *story* of the self, complete with setting, scene, character, plot, and theme (McAdams, 1985b, 1987). The story is the person's *identity* (Erikson, 1959). The story provides the person with a sense of unity and purpose in life—a sense that one is a whole being moving forward in a particular direction. From the standpoint of personal identity, therefore, the person is both historian and history—a storyteller who creates the self in the telling (Cohler, 1982; McAdams, 1988b; Sartre, 1964). As Cohler writes, "Lives are organized in the same manner as other narratives, including historical interpretations, and are understandable according to the same socially shared definition of a sensible or followable presentation" (p. 207). It is this rather literal interpretation of Murray's statement that I wish to pursue in this chapter, with the goal of outlining for the first time a life-span perspective for the emergence of identity as a life story. Let us then explore how the person composes and, indeed, *becomes* a history over the course of the human life cycle.

THE ORIGINS OF STORY

Narrative Tone: The Attachment Bond in Infancy

Mink (1978) writes that the story is a "primary and irreducible form of human comprehension" (p. 132). In all known human societies, we are born to *become* tellers of stories. But we certainly cannot tell them, nor comprehend them, at birth. Stories bind together events in time, organizing reality in terms of connected past, present, and future—beginnings, middles, and endings. As far as we can tell, the newborn has little if any sense of the temporal order of things, of narrative beginnings, middles, and endings (Piaget, 1954). Further, most stories are conveyed through language, though there exist other effective modes of storytelling, like pantomime. And stories require the use of what Piaget has called the "semiotic function"—the ability to use one thing (like a word, gesture, image) to stand for another. In their timeless, prelinguistic, and presemiotic condition, infants cannot express and comprehend stories. Yet I would submit that the infant's experience of the world may influence the development of a general orientation or attitude toward story that will become manifest later on. I call this *narrative tone.*

Erikson (1963) and others (Bowlby, 1969; Mahler, Pine, & Bergman, 1975) have argued that the psychosocial centerpiece of the first year of life is the developing bond of love between the caregiver and the infant. The development of caregiver-infant attachment organizes experiences of trust and mistrust, security and anxiety in the first year of life. The lifelong legacy of attachment is a pervasive and unconscious attitude about people, the world, and the self (Shaver & Rubenstein, 1980; Sroufe, 1979). Erikson calls this attitude *hope.* Hope is the enduring legacy of the person's "prehistoric" existence—that developmental epoch before one becomes both historian and history:

> Hope is verified by a combination of experiences in the individual's "prehistoric" era, the time before speech and verbal memory. Both psychoanalysis and genetic psychology consider central in that period of growth the secure apperception of an "object." The psychologists mean by this the ability to perceive the *enduring quality* of the *thing world* while psychoanalysts speak loosely of a first love-object, i.e., the experience of the care-taking person as a *coherent being,* who reciprocates one's physical and emotional needs in expectable ways and therefore deserves to be endowed with trust, and whose face is recognized as it recognizes. These two kinds of object are the first knowledge, the first verification, and thus the basis of hope. . . .
>
> *Hope is the enduring belief in the attainability of fervent wishes, in spite of the dark urges and rages which mark the beginning of existence.* Hope is the ontogenetic basis of faith, and is nourished by the adult faith which pervades patterns of care. (Erikson, 1963, pp. 116–118, italics in the original)

Before he or she is able to articulate "fervent wishes" in language, the infant emerges from the first year of the life in the family with an unconscious and "enduring belief" concerning the extent to which wishes or intentions are "attainable." According to Bruner (1986), the essence of a story is that it "deals with the vicissitudes of *intention*" (p. 17). To the extent, therefore, that the bond of love between infant and caregiver provides an enduring belief in the attainability of human intentions, Erikson's hope is fundamentally a perspective *on narrative* as well. A hopeful, optimistic narrative tone or attitude suggests that human beings are capable of attaining their "fervent wishes," that human intentions may be realized over time. It suggests that the world is predictable and understandable, that things can work out in the long run, that stories have happy endings, as they often do in *comedy* and *romance* (Frye, 1957). A relatively hopeless, pessimistic narrative tone or attitude suggests that human beings do not get what they wish for, that human intentions are repeatedly foiled over time. From a more pessimistic perspective, the world is capricious and unpredictable, narratives take unforeseen turns, things rarely work out over time, and stories have unhappy endings, as they often do in *tragedy* and *irony* (Frye).

The research by Ainsworth, Stroufe, and many other developmental psychologists distinguishes between patterns of secure and insecure attachment during the first year of life (Ainsworth, Blehar, Waters, & Wall, 1978; Main, 1981; Sroufe, 1979). Securely attached 1-year-olds (called "B-babies") find comfort and confidence in the presence of their primary attachment objects, usually mother and father. When the attachment object is on the scene, the B-baby will explore the environment in a vigorous and independent manner, periodically checking back with the caregiver to "refuel" with security. When separated from the caregiver, the B-baby may cry and show considerable distress. But reunion is usually a joyous event, as if the infant is willing to "forgive and forget" the separation and revel in the re-found security of the moment. Insecurely attached infants, on the other hand, express a great deal of avoidance ("A-babies") and/or resistance ("C-babies") in the presence of their attachment objects, especially when reunited after brief separations. They appear more tentative, less trusting in their explorations of the environment, even in the presence of the caregiver. Short-term longitudinal studies have yielded a number of important findings regarding differences between securely and insecurely attached infants as they develop through nursery school. In general, children who were securely attached at age 1 tend to show more pretend play and exploratory behavior at age 2 (Hazen & Durrett, 1982; Matas, Arend, & Sroufe, 1978; Slade, 1987) and are rated by their teachers as more socially competent, by their peers as more popular, and by observers as more dominant and initiating in nursery school and kindergarten (LaFreniere & Sroufe, 1985), compared to children who were insecurely attached as infants.

The major thrust of the attachment research is that security begets *competence*. In very simple terms, B-babies grow up to behave, as children, in more competent ways than do A-babies and C-babies. From an Eriksonian perspective, an abundance of infantile trust reaps a childhood harvest of autonomy, initiative, and industry. Moving from a consideration of "adaptive" behavior to one of personal narrative, however, may require a more subtle theoretical analysis. The quality of the early bond of love between caregiver and infant, in conjunction with other as yet unspecified early experiences, may predispose the individual to imbue narrative—stories of all kinds, including those constructed about the self—with a general and characteristic quality or tone, ranging from optimistic and trustful to pessimistic and mistrustful. This distinction between a positive and a negative narrative tone, however, does *not* map neatly onto other more familiar distinctions concerning competent behavior and general adaptation. In adulthood, a "comic" life story may be no more or less "adaptive" than a "tragic" or "ironic" one. Rather, people differ markedly in the characteristic ways in which they approach story over the course of human life, the ways in which they are likely to comprehend the vicissitudes of human intentions in time, linking beginnings, middles, and endings. And they construct different sorts of narratives about themselves. If identity is a life story, then the origins of the narrative may reside in "prehistoric" experiences centered on trust and hope. The histories we make and become have a characteristic intonation that may be based, in part, on the quality of our earliest experiences of relating to the attachment object.

Early Childhood Images

A turning point in my daughter's life was the day she saw *Snow White*. It was almost a year ago; she was 3 years old. The original Walt Disney version of the fairy tale was playing at a local theater, so I took the opportunity to escort Ruth Megan to her first full-length movie. I worried that she might not be able to sit still through the 90-minute performance, so we positioned ourselves near the aisle in case we had to make an expeditious getaway. My worries were absurd. For 90 minutes she hardly moved a muscle, her eyes frozen open, riveted to the screen even through the ending credits.

Since that day, my family has lived with Snow White and the Seven Dwarfs. All seven of the dwarfs ride with us in the car to nursery school—Grumpy, Happy, Doc, Bashful, Sleepy, Sneezy, and Dopey. The Wicked Queen, the Peddler Woman (who is the Queen in disguise), the Queen's Huntsman, and the Handsome Prince frequently show up for dinner. When she first met a classmate named William, Ruth told him that she lived in a little cottage (like the Dwarfs') tucked far away in the woods. (Incredulous, William told her she was crazy, and then reported that he would be traveling to nursery school next week in his flying car.) When William comes over for lunch these days, Ruth pretends that she is the Wicked Queen and he is the Queen's Huntsman, and the two of them terrorize her little sister, Amanda, who is 1½ and cast in the pitiful role of Snow White. They steal her stuffed animals and threaten to lock her up, even kill her, (William's idea, I am sure); they hide poisoned apples under her pillow. On other days, Ruth herself is Snow White, organizing regular birthday parties for Grumpy, her favorite dwarf, taping pink crepe paper all over the dining room, making birthday cakes out of sugar, pepper, oregano, and water.

My daughter is obsessed with the story of Snow White! Yet it is not so much the integrated story—from beginning to end—that so fascinates her. Rather, it is various pieces of the story, easily divorced from their coherent narrative context, that she appropriates into her daily life of fantasy, play, and fun. One day she is the Wicked Queen. The next day she is Bashful. Her identification with each of these characters is ephemeral and idiosyncratic. Recently she was

Grumpy, rescuing three of the "Little Ponies" who were stranded on a cliff. Yet in *Snow White*, Grumpy never rescues anybody. And there are no ponies in the movie—they originate from a popular television show.

Although Ruth seems to recognize that stories have a certain canonical form, she does not insist that her own renditions conform to the canon. Her make-believe world is inconsistent, illogical, and very fluid. It is populated by a rich and ever-expanding repertoire of *images*. It is the images in stories—not the stories themselves—that Ruth zeroes in on. This is not to say that she cannot follow a story's plot or that she fails to appreciate the dramatic building of tension in narrative, the climax, and the denouement. Ruth has a pretty good sense of the whole story, from beginning to end, of Snow White and the Seven Dwarfs. But it is not the whole story that captures her imagination, for it is too big and complex, too systematic and progressive, to find its way *in toto* into her daily world of imagination and play. Instead, Ruth dwells on the images, reworking them daily into her own fantastical plots.

The 4-year-old's approach to narrative reflects the *preoperational* level of cognitive development characteristic of this age (Inhelder & Piaget, 1958). According to Piaget, preoperational thinking is fluid and magical, unrestrained by the dictates of logical operations. The child represents the world with symbols and images, but she does not insist that these semiotic representations remain true to logic or context. Snow White can be both dead and alive at the same time, walking around while she doesn't move a muscle. And she can do things that are completely unrelated to her original identity in the fairy tale, like organize birthday parties or accompany the Scarecrow, Tin Man, and Cowardly Lion to the Land of Oz. These logical and contextual inconsistencies do not bother most 4-year-olds, for what appeals most to them in narrative is their *egocentric* appropriation of image, not the coherent narrative itself. This kind of fantasy-based egocentrism is a hallmark of preoperational thought.

From the standpoint of narrative, therefore, the nursery school child busily acquires a stockpile of rich, emotionally laden images for idiosyncratic story building (Fowler, 1981). The major sources for these images are the family, peers, schools and churches, books, and especially the media. While children assimilate images from these sources, they also employ their fertile imaginations to generate their own images, often elaborating on stock characters, scenes, and narrative tidbits to which they are exposed in their favorite stories. By the time we reach kindergarten, each of us has already developed a unique treasure trove of culturally grounded images, providing the raw material for the personal construction of narrative. Over time each of us adds to the stockpile, assimilating and generating images from a myriad of public and private encounters with narrative. And we repeatedly rework and reappropriate these earliest images over the life-span, retrieving again and again the prehistory of the child as we make history in adulthood.

Human Intentions and the Organization of Motives

Most children have a good working definition of story by the time they are 5 or 6 years of age (Applebee, 1978). For instance, a first-grader implicitly knows that stories have connected beginnings, middles, and endings, that there is usually a main character, that the character does something that pushes the plot forward, and so on (Stein & Policastro, 1984). The first-grader can distinguish between "story" and other forms of discourse. If you read her an instructions manual for grooming her Barbie doll or a description of the planet Mars, she is likely to consider such a presentation to be a "bad" story or a "*non*story"—different from "Snow White and the Seven Dwarfs" in some basic way, though she may not be able to articulate the difference clearly. Stories that violate implicit narrative conventions—for instance, those that have no endings or those in which an initiating event is followed by an unrelated series of events—are seen as odd and confusing. A number of studies have shown that elementary school children (as well as adults) more easily remember stories that have a conventional form than those that are missing essential story elements or in which elements are mixed up. When recalling stories originally presented in unconventional form, children (and adults) also appear to invoke standard story *schemas*, frequently converting in recall a poorly formed story to good form by rearranging elements that are mixed up and/or inventing new elements as substitutes for those that were missing in the original story (Mandler, 1984).

Elementary school children, therefore, are able to organize the "vicissitudes of human intention" (Bruner, 1986) into coherent narratives with beginnings, middles, and endings. As accounts of human intentions, stories tell what characters are *striving* to do, what they *want* and how they go about trying to get what they want over time. There is no story without intention. Further, *there may be no intention without story.* The story is the most natural vehicle for transporting the meaning and the course of human intentions. Until children understand what a story is, they may be unable to comprehend the world and themselves in terms of human intentions organized in time. This does not mean, however, that even infants do not "intend" to do things. Indeed, Piaget (1952) has traced the origins of intentionality back to the primary circular reactions of ages 1 to 4 months, when the infant intentionally repeats an "interesting" behavior that first occurs by chance. But infants and very young children do not conceptualize intentions as springing from internal wants and desires that they "have" and upon which they may act over time in order to achieve a desired end state (Kegan, 1982). They are not able to sustain the kind of distance in consciousness that suggests that I (a subject, a character) *have* (possess, own) an intention (an object), that the intention exists "inside of" me, as something upon which I may or may not *act*. Narrative action is guided by intentions, as characters choose to pursue certain goal states over time. Goal-directed activity ends when the goal is achieved or when the achievement is irrevocably blocked, or when the character's intentions change.

In this regard, it is intriguing to note that the most popular, albeit controversial, methods of assessing individual differences in human *motivation* in personality psychology have, since the time of Freud, relied on stories (McAdams, in press-a; McClelland, 1985). In *The Interpretation of Dreams*, Freud (1900/1953) outlined a method for discerning the dreamer's unconscious motives, lurking beneath and between the manifest lines of the remembered dream story. Murray's (1943; Morgan & Murray, 1935) Thematic Apperception Test (TAT) was designed to elicit conscious narrative fantasies that could be mined for motivational themes. The vast research literature inspired by McClelland's and Atkinson's adaptation of Murray's TAT documents the success of measuring individual differences in motives by analyzing the intentions of characters in imaginative stories (Atkinson, 1958; McClelland, 1961, 1985; McClelland, Atkinson, Clark, & Lowell, 1953; Stewart, 1982; Winter, 1973). In McClelland's (1985) view, a motive is a recurrent preference or readiness for a particular quality of experience, which emergizes, directs, and selects behavior. Motives speak to what people want in life, what they are trying to do, what they consciously and unconsciously *intend*, wish, or desire to have and to be. Motives are most sensitively assessed, McClelland maintains, by discerning the intentions of characters in imaginative narrative responses, such as a person's dreams and TAT stories or in a culture's myths, legends, and folk tales.

Therefore stories organize human motives. And reciprocally, motives organize stories. Those internal forces that energize, direct, and select human behavior are given expression and meaning in narrative. A person with a strong achievement motive tends to compose imaginative TAT stories in which characters strive to perform in better and more efficient ways, in which they confront and attempt to overcome obstacles to better performance, in which their attempts result in good feelings when they are successful and bad feelings when they fail (McClelland et al., 1953). Stories like these are loaded with achievement *themes*—recurrent content motifs about characters who intend over time to "do better." A particular human motive confers upon a story a characteristic thematic quality. The thematic quality is captured in the various systems of content analysis designed by researchers who have sought to measure individual differences in motives concerning achievement (McClelland et al.), affiliation (Atkinson, Heyns, & Veroff, 1954), intimacy (McAdams, 1980), and power (Veroff, 1957; Winter, 1973).

Two superordinate dimensions with respect to which various content themes in stories can be ordered are what Bakan (1966) calls *agency* and *communion*. Agency denotes themes of separation of the individual from and mastery of the individual over the environment, subsuming such concepts as achievement, power, control, and isolation. Communion denotes themes of union of the individual with the environment and surrendering individuality to a larger whole of which the individual is a part, subsuming concepts of intimacy, love, cooperation, and merger. In most general terms, many of the greatest stories in Western cultures concern agency and communion, tales in which characters strive for glory and love, separation and closeness, mastery and merger. Bakan's distinction recaptures what the ancient Greek philosopher Empedocles (Russell, 1945/1972) understood to be the two great forces of the cosmos: strife (agency) and love (communion). And it recasts a fundamental dualism in human motivation that has been variously described as that between the death (aggressive) and life (erotic) instincts (Freud, 1920/1955), the need for autonomy and the need for surrender (Angyal, 1941), fear of life (which motivates a person to separate from others) and fear of death (which motivates a person to unite with others) (Becker, 1973; Rank, 1936/1978), the striving for superiority and social interest (Adler, 1927), the "psychologics" of independence and inclusion (Kegan, 1982), the evolutionarily adaptive tendencies toward status and acceptance (Hogan, Jones, & Creek, 1985), and the "psychological magnification" of excitement/interest and joy/enjoyment (Tomkins, 1987).

With respect to the assessment of human motives through content analysis of stories, such as imaginative TAT stories, the two motives that best parallel Bakan's distinction of agency and communion are the *power* and the *intimacy* motives, respectively (McAdams, 1984a; in press-b). The power motive is a recurrent preference or readiness for experiences of feeling strong and having an impact on the world. The intimacy motive is a recurrent preference or readiness for experiences of feeling close to and in communion with others, engaging in warm, friendly, and mutual interaction. People high in power motivation have a recurrent desire to influence and master their environments as strong and forceful agents. People high in intimacy motivation have a recurrent desire to share themselves with others in a trusting, communal way. Both motives are conceived as relatively stable individual-difference variables of personality that function to energize, direct, and select behavior in certain situations (McClelland, 1985).

A substantial body of research shows that individual differences in power and intimacy motivation, assessed through content analysis of TAT stories, are consistently related to important and theoretically predictable differences in behavior among college students and older adults. Power motivation has been positively related to activities reflecting patterns of self-assertiveness, instrumental attitudes toward others, concern for prestige and self-display, expansive risk taking, assuming positions of strong leadership in organizations, and (among males only) violent outbursts and sexual conquest (for reviews see McAdams, 1984a; McClelland, 1975, 1985; Winter, 1973; Winter & Carlson, 1988; Winter & Stewart, 1978). Intimacy motivation has been positively related to activities reflecting surrendering of control in relationships, reciprocal and noninstrumental interaction with others, concern for affective warmth and communal harmony in social encounters, more frequent displays of smiling, laughter, and eye contact in friendly conversations, and a special appreciation for the sincere self-disclosure and intensive listening characteristic of what Buber (1970) terms the "I-Thou" experience (for reviews see McAdams, 1982b, 1984a, 1989; McClelland, 1985).

Stories are readily compared and contrasted according to the extent to which characters seek power and intimacy, strength and closeness, agency and communion. These general thematic lines run through all sorts of narratives, from the most prosaic TAT stories to the most beloved fairy tales to the most complex life stories. Indeed, they are the two central thematic lines in which psychoanalysts have always considered to be *the* primordial story of childhood—Oedipus the king. And they run strong and deep in many life stories composed by adolescents and adults as their own identities. By the age of 6 we understand the canons of a well formed story. We are now able, therefore, to couch the vicissitudes of human intentions in narrative terms. Our own emerging motivational tendencies organize and are organized by our favorite stories, both those we hear and those we create. Our recurrent desires for strength and closeness find expression in stories. And largely through the stories we hear and create, we gather together our motivational resources and eventually consolidate our various wants, desires, and intentions within broad motivational dispositions, such as the power and the intimacy motives.

THE EMERGENCE OF A NARRATIVE SELF

From Tale to Myth

There are at least two good reasons that fairy tales often begin with the words "Once upon a time," and both relate directly to the fact that fairy tales are for children. First, this opening line clearly establishes a fantasy setting—a time and space of make-believe—that encourages the child to engage the text in an imaginative way. Bettelheim (1976) argues that only when children know that a tale is completely fantastical and make-believe can they feel *safe* enough to project themselves into the story and thereby experience vicariously the trials and eventual triumphs of the heroes and heroines. The heroic actions of Little Red Riding Hood or Jack (and the Beanstalk) portray conflicts and fears that are very salient in the unconscious lives of the 4- and 5-year-old children who are so fascinated by these tales. These conflicts and fears, according to Bettelheim, typically concern power and love, the two fundamental dynamics of the Oedipus complex. By identifying with the protagonist in the fairy tale, the child indirectly and safely experiences the dramatic struggles of the wicked wolf and the little girl, the ferocious ogre and the little boy and, like the protagonist, emerges victorious (lives happily ever after) in the end. In exceedingly subtle ways, fairy tales speak encouragement to the child whose confidence has been shaken by the dramatic Oedipal tragedy he or she is experiencing on the unconscious level. Fairy tales thereby promote psychological growth and integration for the young child, who lives an analogous story of power and love unconsciously.

A second reason that fairy tales begin with the words "Once upon a time" is that it is necessary that these stories, like the children who listen to them, have no *historical* referent. Fairy tales are "prehistoric" and "nonhistoric." They exist outside history both because they are purely fictional (whereas history deals partly with fact) and because they are timeless and spaceless—they could have taken place at any time and in any place. To the extent we know anything about time or space in fairy tales, we may say that the events occurred "long ago" and in a "faraway place." Though adolescents and adults may define themselves by composing their own life stories, simultaneously becoming historians and the histories they create, the child has virtually no historical perspective on the self. Not only does he have little understanding of the particular historical moment in which he lives, but he also fails to comprehend his own life in historical terms—as having a past, present, and future that are coherently linked. Fairy tales enchant the prehistoric child, for he might as well have lived "once upon a time" as in this particular time and place. At the same time, *they gently nudge him in the direction of history*. Fairy tales take the child on a journey about "growing up," moving from the infantile present to a more "mature" future in which Cinderella marries the prince and Little Red Riding Hood escapes the wolf (Bettelheim, 1976). Thus while they beckon the prehistoric child with a world that is timeless and spaceless, fairy tales also presage history in subtle and mild ways, reminding the child that he or she is headed toward a future and that things are going to change.

As children move through elementary school and toward adolescence, they become exposed to a greater variety of prose narratives, eventually encompassing fairy and folk *tales* as well as *legends* and *myths*. Whereas tales are make-believe and nonhistorical, legends and myths are generally assumed to bear some relation to history, and they are believed to embody *truth* (Bascom, 1965). Indeed, the third and fourth grader who has reached Piaget's stage of *concrete operations* is much more concerned than the younger child with what is *true* in the concrete world of reality. He greatly values, therefore, stories that have truth. A legend is usually a secular story about the recent past involving real human beings, such as legends of Davy Crockett, George Washington, and Babe Ruth. The narrative is thought to embody some degree of truth, though apocryphal elements may be acknowledged. Thus George Washington may have never chopped down a cherry tree and then admitted the transgression to his father, but the legend illustrates the "truth" about George Washington: He was an honest man.

A myth, on the other hand, is a sacred story about the distant past involving nonhuman beings, such as gods, spirits, and larger-than-life figures like Oedipus. More than legends, myths are viewed as containing ultimate truth, often of a literal nature (Campbell, 1962; Charme, 1984). Myths like the Genesis creation story and the story of Noah and the flood explain how the world came to be and why the world is like it is. In Christian families, most children (and many adults) believe that these stories are literally true, that they relate actual historical events set in a particular time and place. Other Christian adults find various kinds of figurative truths in these stories, sometimes arguing that their symbolic interpretations reveal "deeper" or more "profound" truths than literal interpretations. Regardless of their parents' religious persuasions, most middle-class children in Western societies are exposed to a large number of myths from both Judeo-Christian and Hellenic sources. Children consider these stories to be different from fairy tales, more realistic and linked to ultimate history, ultimate beginnings, middles, and endings.

Myths are different in another way too. As Bettelheim has pointed out, myths often embody a *moral* dimension, whereas fairy tales deal mostly with more basic issues of survival. Little Red Riding Hood learns that she should not talk to strange wolves—not because it is morally wrong to do so but because she will get eaten. Adam and Eve, on the other hand, learn that disobeying God is wrong—they have sinned. Likewise, Oedipus learns the awful truth of his own immoral actions, as unwitting as they are. From Bettelheim's psychoanalytic perspective, myths typically deal with post-Oedipal, superego demands, suggesting that they are developmentally more "sophisticated" than fairy tales, which are predominantly Oedipal and pre-Oedipal. Fairy tales are for young children; myths are the stuff of late childhood and early adolescence. The moral dimension of myths, furthermore, imparts a serious and somewhat pessimistic quality to these prose narratives. Mythic heroes usually suffer, and they rarely live happily ever after.

As older children come to appreciate legend and myth, they begin to expect that stories should be imbued with moral meaning, that they should tell us about not only what is but also what should be. Adolescents, however, begin to see that different stories may have different, even conflicting, moral meanings. While Christ's parable of the prodigal son urges the person to accept lovingly even the most flagrant sinner, the story of Noah shows that sinners should be destroyed. How does one reconcile these inconsistencies? How does the adolescent deal with conflicts concerning what is good and what is true in different stories?

The answer, according to Fowler (1981), is that in our teenage years, we begin to distrust stories. We endeavor to step away from narrative—in a sense, to embrace more systematic and abstract formats for expressing truth and goodness. What we seek is *ideology*—an internally consistent and logical system of beliefs and values. In their concrete contextuality, myths and other stories cannot directly provide the abstract answers the adolescent wants. Yet while the adolescent looks beyond story in the search for ideology, the consolidation of an internally consistent and logical system of beliefs and values paves the way for an eventual *return* to story and the coming emergence of a new narrative conception of the self.

Formal Operations and the Ideological Setting

On the relation of ideology to identity, Erikson (1958) writes:

> We will call what young people in their teens and early 20s look for in religion and other dogmatic systems *ideology*. At the most it is a militant system with uniformed members and uniform goals; at the least it is a "way of life," or what the Germans call a *Weltanschaung*, a world view which is consonant with existing theory, available knowledge, and common sense, and yet is significantly more: an utopian outlook, a cosmic mood, or a doctrinal logic, all shared as self-evident beyond any need for demonstration. (p. 41)

In religion and other "dogmatic systems," writes Erikson, the adolescent looks for sweeping answers concerning questions about what is, what might be, and what should be. It is in adolescence that the person is first likely to ask questions of ultimate concern, to wonder in the abstract "What is true?" "What is good?" and "What is the purpose of life?" These philosophical puzzlements are encompassed by a larger question that is both personal and ultimate: "Who am I?" Ideology and identity, therefore, are two sides of the same coin, in Erikson's view. In order to define who they are, adolescents seek an abstract system of beliefs and values—an ideology—that will put the self into context. This *ideological setting* for identity (McAdams, 1985b, 1987) grounds the life story within a particular ontological, epistemological, ethical, and religious "time and space." Yet one's personal ideology is no more synonymous with one's identity than is the setting of a story synonymous with the story itself. Rather, the ideological setting tells the adolescent "when and where" the story takes place, outlining the ultimate parameters of the universe within which the person believes his or her life is lived. As Fowler (1981) puts it, our view "of the ultimate environment determines the ways we arrange the scenery and grasp the plot in our lives' plays" (p. 29).

Erikson (1963) writes, "It is the ideological outlook of a society that speaks most clearly to the adolescent who is eager to be affirmed by his peers, and is ready to be confirmed by rituals, creeds, and programs which at the same time define what is evil, uncanny, and inimical" (p. 263). Fairy tales, legends, and myths do not explicitly articulate an ideology that satisfies the adolescent's desire to know what he or she should *believe*. In a sense, stories are simultaneously too much and too little for the adolescent. They contain and suggest much that may seem superfluous—concrete details, conflicting motives, complicated plots, contradictory messages. This is all irrelevant in the eyes of the person who wants a single logical and coherent system of belief. And stories contain precious little that can be easily taken out of the concrete narrative context and generalized, in an abstract manner, to all of life. More satisfying to the adolescent mind may be such systematic explications of belief as *theories* and *creeds*, which lay it all out, once and for all. Religious creeds, for example, tell the "believer" what is true for every concrete situation and for all time. Listen to the sweeping and unambiguous language of the Apostle's Creed, memorized by many Christians when they are "confirmed" as teenagers in the Catholic church and in many mainline Protestant denominations and recited in Sunday services as an affirmation of communal belief:

I believe in God, the Father almighty,
   creator of heaven and earth.

I believe in Jesus Christ, his only Son, our Lord.
   He was conceived by the power of the Holy Spirit
     and born of the virgin Mary.
   He suffered under Pontius Pilate,
     was crucified, died, and was buried.
   He descended into hell.
   On the third day he rose again.
   He ascended into heaven,
     and is seated at the right hand of the Father.
   He will come again to judge the living and the dead.

I believe in the Holy Spirit,
   the holy Catholic Church,
   the communion of saints,
   the forgiveness of sins,
   the resurrection of the body,
   and the life everlasting. Amen.

                               (*The Lutheran Book of Worship*, 1978, p. 65)

    The Apostle's Creed is not a story. Rather, it is a list of what every individual who abides by this religious orientation is supposed to believe to be true. Within it are briefly enumerated such Christian doctrines as the creation of the world, the virgin birth, the forgiveness of sins, the resurrection of Christ, and the Trinity. In many denominations of Christianity, teenagers learn various rationales for each of these doctrines, explained point by point through careful analyses of scriptural references that are sometimes called "proof texts." Like the proofs that high school students learn in their geometry classes, these pedagogical exercises draw on the adolescent's new-found ability to conceptualize what is and what might be abstract, formal terms.

The adolescent's rejection of story in favor of ideology—captured in creeds, proofs, and other abstract formulations—reflects what Piaget describes as the move from concrete to *formal operational* thinking (Inhelder & Piaget, 1958). Before adolescence, the individual's thinking is bound to the concrete and immediate world. The 9-year-old may be a master in cognitively classifying and ordering his or her physical environment—a naive Aristotle preoccupied with the inductive systematization of the concrete. But the 16-year-old can step away, in a cognitive sense, from his or her operations on the world and perform operations on these operations, engage in analyses of prior analyses, think about thinking. The adolescent's mind expands to consider even his or her own thought processes, taking thought itself as an objective of reflection. Inductive classification of the concrete is supplemented by hypothetico-deduction in the realm of the formal or abstract. For the first time, the individual is cognitively able to entertain those philosophical issues that require concerted and systematic abstraction and consideration of the hypothetical. Formal operations, therefore, provides the cognitive underpinnings for the common adolescent preoccupation with hypothetical "ideals"—the ideal society, religion, family, world, self (Elkind, 1981). This consideration of ideals, furthermore, may catalyze a thoroughgoing examination of previously unquestioned beliefs and values from childhood. As the adolescent notes the striking contrast between perfect ideals and imperfect reality, he or she may endeavor to formulate a new, more personalized creed by which to live and to make sense of the world as it is and as it should be.

The development of ideology in adolescence is both a private and an interpersonal endeavor, a product of introspection (Kohlberg & Gilligan, 1971; Perry, 1970) and social influence (Damon & Colby, 1987) that is negotiated within a specific cultural context (Shweder & Much, 1987). The consolidation of an ideological setting may follow many different pathways in adolescence. At one extreme are adolescents who remain relatively concrete in their approach to questions of ultimate concern. Their beliefs are vague and unstable, and they show little inclination to organize belief within a systematic framework. They resemble what Kohlberg (1981) has described in the context of moral development as the "preconventional" thinker. Their ideology is tacit, for the most part, and exceedingly *diffuse* (McAdams, 1985b). Other adolescents accept various conventional systems of belief, more or less adopting some combination of the standard formulations offered by society concerning what is good and what is true. To the extent that these adolescents accept conventional dogma without seriously questioning its validity for their lives, they exhibit what Erikson (1959) has termed ideological *foreclosure*. Those adolescents who *do* take issue with conventional beliefs may explore a wide variety of ideological alternatives, rejecting various forms of the status quo and entering what Erikson has called a period of ideological *moratorium*. They may emerge from adolescence with a more personalized and complex ideological position, blending aspects of conventional viewpoints with the products of their own ideological explorations, fashioning what Kohlberg would term a "postconventional" formulation that animates their understanding of moral, ethical, religious, and political issues (Marcia, 1980; McAdams, Booth, & Selvik, 1981).

By the end of adolescence or shortly thereafter, the person has consolidated an ideological setting for his or her identity story (McAdams, 1985b). The ideological setting situates the action of the person's evolving life story within a particular locus of belief and value—a locus shaped by society's conventions regarding the good and the true and the individual's struggles to find meaning within or outside of conventions. There are many different ways to map the ideological terrain of a given life story. A very simple and useful approach, however, is suggested by Gilligan (1982) and Forsyth (1980, 1985). Gilligan distinguishes between an ideology of justice and individual rights on the one hand and an ideology of care and social responsibilities on the other. The two approaches to ideology mirror Bakan's aforementioned distinction between agency and communion—two general thematic lines in narrative. An ideology of justice and rights suggests an agentic ideological setting in which individuals are viewed as autonomous agents who, in their ultimate individuality, are likely now and again to clash. Justice sorts out what is fair when independent agents, each granted basic individual rights, come together and clash. Gilligan's second approach—what she has called the "different voice" in moral psychology— suggests a communal ideological setting in which individuals are viewed as interdependent parts of larger networks. One's duties to specific others within the network must be evaluated according to standards of care and compassion. Gilligan maintains that men are more likely to couch ideology in the agentic terms of justice and rights, whereas women tend to view moral issues in more communal terms, emphasizing care and responsibilities. Research support for this proposed sex difference, however, is mixed (Brabeck, 1983; Ford & Lowery, 1986).

As Figure 5.1 shows, Gilligan's justice and care orientations may be viewed as two general types of ideological settings within a two-dimensional space organized according to the orthogonal axes of agency and communion. Gilligan's ideology of justice is high on agency and low on communion; her ideology of care is high on communion and low on agency. A third type of ideological setting mixes justice and care, a concern for the individual's abstract rights and the contextual responsibilities of interpersonal communities. Such a perspective bears some resemblance to what Forsyth (1985) has termed a "situationist" perspective of "ethical ideologies." In Forsyth's terms, situationists are highly relativistic and idealistic. They carefully evaluate a situation in order to determine what the fairest and most compassionate response should be. They are concerned both about the individual's pan-situational rights and the spe-

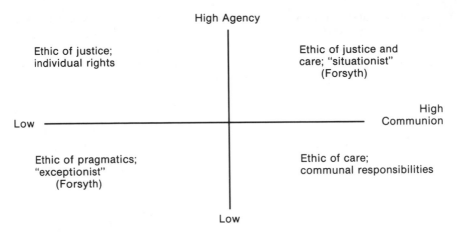

FIGURE 5.1 Four types of ideological settings.

cific interpersonal responsibilities inherent in the situation. A fourth type of ideological setting, low on agency and communion, is labeled by Forsyth as the "exceptionist" position. An ideological setting that is neither strongly agentic nor communal may suggest that exceptions are the rule in issues of ultimate and ethical concern. Principles of justice and care give way to pragmatics. As Forsyth (1980) puts it, "Exceptionists believe that absolute moral principles are important, but that one must apply these rules pragmatically" (p. 177). What is true and what is good are evaluated in terms of what works.

The validity of this fourfold taxonomy of ideological settings is unknown. While Gilligan's and Forsyth's distinctions may capture important differences in people's moral and ethical orientations, they have not been extended to other key dimensions of personal ideology, such as politics and religion. Future research should investigate the extent to which individuals view their religious beliefs, for instance, in individualistic and agentic terms versus interdependent and communal terms.

The Past and the Future

To borrow a felicitous phrase from William Wordsworth, identity enables us to "bind our days together anew" (Langbaum, 1982). In late adolescence and young adulthood, we confront the unprecedented problem of binding together our lives in time. We seek to understand the present in terms of the past and future, the past in terms of the present and future, and the future in terms of the past and present. If we are to attain the status of "adult," writes Erikson, then we must recast our own lives as history:

To be adult means, among other things, to see one's own life in continuous perspective, both in retrospect and prospect. By accepting some definition as to who he is, usually on the basis of a function in an economy, a place in the sequence of generations, and a status in the structure of society, the adult is able to selectively reconstruct his past in such a way that, step for step, it seems to have planned him, or better he seems to have planned it. In this sense, psychologically we *do* choose our parents, our family history, and the history of our kings, heroes, and gods. By making them our own, we maneuver ourselves into the inner position of proprietors, of creators. (Erikson, 1958, pp. 111–112)

Adolescents and adults reconstruct their own pasts, Erikson contends, so that it appears to them that the past has been "planned" by them. Life is put into a historical context. Adolescents and adults create their own histories to justify their present stance in the world, and in so doing they *do* choose their parents, their kings and queens, their heroes and heroines, and their gods. They write histories—dramatic narrative accounts of the past—complete with the heroes and villains who are the protagonists of the story. This narrative integration specifies setting, scene, character, plot, and theme.

The emergence of a historical perspective is grounded in adolescent cognitive development. The advent of formal operations presents the adolescent with a new, abstract problem: How am I the *same* person from one situation to the next? How am I *continuous* over time? How am I a *whole* and *unitary* person moving forward in space and time with *purpose*? The concrete thinker of childhood may experience many "different selves," writes Breger (1974), but "is not bothered by inconsistencies between them, by his [or her] lack of unity or wholeness" (p. 330). Identity is an abstraction that cannot be appreciated by the child: "The idea of a unitary or whole self in which past memories of who one was, present experiences of who one is, and future expectations of who one will be, is the sort of abstraction that the child simply does not think about" (p. 330)

Beyond cognitive development, biology plays its part in the emergence of identity and history as paramount concerns in adolescence. Erikson argues that the awakening of genital sexuality at puberty ushers in a qualitatively new psychosexual chapter in life, one that must be integrated with what has come before. Biologically, adolescents find themselves the sometimes mystified inhabitants of suddenly adult-like bodies whose sexual urgings are difficult to understand fully and even more difficult to ignore. The adolescent is compelled from within, therefore, to formulate new understandings of his or her bodily, sexual, and social selves. Puberty may mark a turning point in the adolescent's self-perceived developmental course, as childhood comes to represent, in the adolescent's mind, a distant and bygone era.

According to Erikson, society "collaborates" with the promptings from within the individual to push identity and history onto center stage in adolescence. Paralleling cognitive, biological, and psychosexual changes are the shifts in society's expectations about what the individual, who was a child but is now almost an adult, should be doing, thinking, and feeling. Erikson (1959) writes, "It is of great relevance to the young individual's identity formation that he be responded to, and be given adult status as a person whose gradual growth and transformation makes sense to those who begin to make sense to him" (p. 111). In general, modern Western societies "expect" their adolescents to bind together their days anew by examining occupational, interpersonal, and ideological offerings of society and eventually by making a commitment to a personalized niche in the adult world. As Erikson (1959) describes it,

> the period can be viewed as a psychosocial moratorium during which the individual through free role experimentation may find a niche in some section of his society, a niche which is firmly defined and yet seems to be uniquely made for him. In finding it the young adult gains an assured sense of inner continuity and social sameness which will bridge what he was as a child and what he is about to become, and will reconcile his conception of himself and his community's recognition of him. (p. 111)

Expressing the same psychosocial sentiment in more explicitly narrative terms, Bruner (1960) writes, "The mythologically instructed community provides its members with a library of scripts" against which the individual may judge his or her own "internal drama" (p. 281). "Life, then, produces myth, and finally imitates it" (p. 283).

The idea that adolescence and young adulthood usher in a historical perspective in the human life cycle is reinforced by a number of other theorists. Cohler (1982) describes a process that can be "observed during adolescence and young adulthood, when persons 'remodel' their histories in a manner analogous to that in which a nation much later rewrites its history in order to create successive legends about the past relevant to that later point in history" (p. 218). Hankiss (1981) describes the same process as a "mythological rearranging" of life undertaken by each individual in late adolescence and young adulthood. Hankiss writes, "Everyone builds his or her own theory about the history and the course of his or her life by attempting to classify his or her particular successes and fortunes, gifts and choices, and favourable and unfavourable elements of his or her fate according to a coherent, explanatory principle and to incorporate them within an *historical unit*" (p. 203). Similarly, Kohli (1981) asks the question, how does the individual "thematize" his or her own life history? According to Kohli, the answer is not simply a matter of listing past accomplishments and predicting future ones. Instead, one's life is thematized within a "structured self-image." Kohli writes, "Life histories are thus not a collection of all events of the individual's life course, but rather 'structured self images.' This comes close to some notions of identity" (p. 65).

From a philosophical standpoint, Sartre (1964) argued that men and women living in modern Western societies are challenged to construct their own life stories that embody individual truth amidst a world that appears to hold no universal truths (Charme, 1984; McAdams, 1988b). According to Sartre, "The essential form of the self is that of a retrospective story that creates order out of the chaos of experience" (Charme, p. 2). Ideally, the story should be *mythic*, embodying narrative answers to psychological, sociological, metaphysical, and cosmological concerns that have traditionally been addressed in the great myths of culture. In the wake of science's demythologizing of the cosmos, Sartre advocates a remythologizing of the self. The person's mythically rendered life history, therefore, serves to *sacralize* the self and *valorize* life, a point reinforced by Feinstein (1979) in his discussion of *personal mythologies*. A person's own mythic history provides life with a sense of unity and purpose.

From a Sartrean perspective, the person's past is reconstructed within the current demands of the myth. Beginning in adolescence, we *choose* in the *present* to remember the past in a certain way. In the making of history, there is no objective bedrock of the past from which to fashion the myth. The past is malleable, changing, ever synthesized and resynthesized by present life choices. Yet it is not infinitely malleable, and certain more-or-less validated facts must be woven into a story that attempts to be both coherent and true. History and identity are both "made" and "found out," in Sartre's view. Imagination and discovery work together and nourish each other.

In reconstructing the past, adolescents and adults underscore special *scenes* that stand out in bold print. These critical incidents may complicate the plot structure, move the plot forward, or change the direction of the plot. I term these *nuclear episodes*. Nuclear episodes are concrete and circumscribed events from the past that the historian deems to be especially important.

As key incidents in an evolving identity saga, nuclear episodes can be broadly classified into two general types: episodes of *continuity* and episodes of *change*. In an episode of continuity, a specific incident in the story affirms what the story maker sees as an identity "truth." For instance, a person whose identity is viewed to be a history of caregiving may highlight a particular scene from the past in which he or she provided care under extraordinary conditions. The incident encapsules in a narrative nutshell what the person sees as an essential thread of continuity in his or her life story. In this case, the episode may serve as "proof from my past" that "I am what I am." Other episodes of continuity may connect the present with the past via an implicit narrative line which suggests that the past nuclear episode serves as an explanation for or a foreshadowing of some aspect of one's present life situation. The nuclear episode may function as an "origin myth," detailing the genesis of a particular value or value system, perceived personality trait, or any other characterological attribution made by the individual about the self.

Nuclear episodes of change, on the other hand, mark perceived turning points in history, sometimes signaling the end of one epoch and the beginning of another. Episodes of change may be positive or negative in affective tone, and indeed some of the clearest cases are reported as life story low points. The individual may speak of "bottoming out" or "turning the corner" in the cases of moving from a deteriorating life situation to an improving one. In some cases, the language suggests the reverse: "a turn for the worse," "a loss of innocence," "a fall from grace."

The content of nuclear episodes can be further characterized in terms of the thematic lines of agency and communion. Agentic nuclear episodes highlight the exercise of physical, psychological, or spiritual *strength*; the exertion of *impact* upon other people and one's environment; vigorous physical *action* or movement; and heightened *status* or prestige. Communal nuclear episodes highlight mutual sharing and *communication*; feelings of heightened *love* and *liking*; *sympathy* or empathy for others; and tender interpersonal *touch*. Studies examining the content of such nuclear episodes as "peak experiences," "significant religious experiences," and "important positive childhood experiences" show that college students high in power motivation, assessed on the TAT, relate critical life story scenes laden with agentic content themes; students high in intimacy motivation emphasize communal themes in their nuclear episodes (McAdams, 1982a, 1985b; McAdams et al., 1981).

If history is given form by the present, it is also shaped by expectations about the future. The emerging historical perspective of adolescence includes the realization that the future must make sense in terms of the past and present. The adolescent's first imaginal renditions of the future, however, may not look extremely sensible. Elkind (1981) writes of the *personal fable* of adolescence—a fantastical story about the self and the future that some teenagers construct and tell. The personal fable usually underscores the adolescent's perceived uniqueness—"nobody has ever done what I have done," "nobody has ever experienced what I have experienced," "nobody can truly understand me"—and the fantasy that he or she will one day attain stupendous greatness. Elkind views these unrealistic narratives as cognitive "mistakes" or egocentrisms, inevitable results of not quite knowing how to rein in the power of formal-operational thought. He suggests that the personal fable fades with experience and maturity. From a narrative standpoint on identity, however, the personal fable may be seen as a first and very rough draft of identity. It is eventually edited, rewritten, reworked, and made more realistic as the young person becomes more knowledgable about the opportunities and limitations of defining the self in his or her particular society. As we formulate more mature life stories in early and later adulthood, we realize that other people have their own stories—both similar to and different from ours—and that we live within a historical and social matrix with its own narrative parameters.

THE REFINEMENT OF NARRATIVE CHARACTER

A Case

A 38-year-old divorced social worker, Roberta K., participated as one of 50 men and women who were interviewed and given a number of psychological tests in an intensive study of adults' life stories (McAdams, 1985b). Let us briefly consider the story she constructed to define who she is, who she has been, and who she may be in the future.

Roberta has traveled the world over. Her life story reads like a romantic adventure, reminiscent of heroic epics like the *Odyssey*. In her life story, she is often cast in the guise of the restless heroine who encounters one dramatic challenge after another. She is constantly moving, ever seeking new places, new experiences, and new people. In describing her philosophy of life, Roberta states, "Life is a journey. It is the journey that matters, not the arrival. I will not stop running; I refuse until I'm in a wheelchair." The nuclear episodes from her past are virtually always set in exotic, faraway places like Mexico and the Orient. There are illicit love affairs, experiments with drugs, tempestuous relations with lovers and friends, strange foods, strange customs, and captivating conversations. Her life story is populated by forceful people who have an *impact* on one another and on their worlds. The most important people in her life tend to reflect the character traits that she most values in herself: They are ambitious, adventurous, restless, cosmopolitan, dramatic, and sophisticated.

Roberta is a forceful "agent" who makes big things happen. Like the ancient Greek god Hermes, she is always on the move, restless, changing, affecting others and being affected in dramatic ways. Her central image of herself is that of "the swift traveler." The origins of this image of self can be seen in Roberta's mythological reconstruction of her elementary school years. Attending a Catholic school, Roberta found herself repeatedly "moving against" the nuns who were her teachers. Though she was not generally considered a troublemaker, she drove the nuns daffy with her incessant questions, her endless insistence that they always tell her "why" things were the way they were. Although her teachers complained that Roberta was a bit of a pain, Roberta's mother encouraged her further, taking secret delight in her daughter's ability to ruffle the feathers of the status quo. One of Roberta's aunts, too, consistently supported her adventures. The aunt is one of Roberta's greatest heroines in life because "she always believed in trying new things."

Roberta left for Mexico shortly after high school graduation. In retrospect, she sees this move as an example of "running away." It is by no means the last example. Although she has held the same job for the past 8 years, Roberta continues to travel, regularly visiting Latin America where she has some very dear friends. In Roberta's life story, physical travel mirrors the psychological and spiritual journey she perceives. In her eyes, she is ever expanding, ever growing, and ever changing. If you stay in one place, she maintains, you get bored and you get dumb. Movement—both physical and psychological—brings with it excitement and a worldly wisdom that cannot be found in books. It is very important to Roberta that she see herself as a worldly and sophisticated woman who, in many senses of the phrase, has "been around the world." She scoffs at those who never move and never change, who "stay home" in a physical and psychological sense, afraid to explore the world. In Roberta's view, these people are stagnant and naive.

Yet Roberta has been naive herself, and she tends to "stay home" more than one might think. This links up with a second, though somewhat subsidiary, image of self in this life story: Roberta, the "naive idealist." Roberta tells of her early years, before the nuns, when she was always "the good little girl," and of a later period as a young adult when she naively "wanted to save the world." She sees these chapters in her life story as necessary stages in her own growth, through which she needed to develop in order to attain the sophistication she now believes she has found. Another necessary "stage" was her marriage. In her late 20s she married a man she met in Latin America, but the marriage seems to have been a failure from the start. As Roberta tells it, she was still too naive and unsophisticated—she had not "been around" enough—to know what she wanted in an intimate and sexual relationship. Though she and her husband were very compatible in bed, they fought constantly everywhere else, and neither ever fully understood the other. Shortly after they divorced, Roberta's mother died, and her younger brother developed a serious kidney ailment that required major hospitalization. This was the low point in her life story.

But Roberta rebounded with gusto. She began to date older men whom she felt she could respect. She resumed her travels to distant lands. She found a job as a social worker that provided her with a good deal of authority in her work as well as the fulfillment that comes with "doing my bit for mankind." She began caring for her ailing father. It is as if she has continued to enact the role of the naive yet compassionate idealist in her relationship with her father while emplotting the more dominant image of self—the swift traveler—in her literal travelings and through the psychological journey she perceives. Thus the two dominant images of self in her life story—seeming antagonists that they are—have achieved a kind of tentative reconciliation.

In sum, Roberta has constructed a highly agentic, powerful life story to define who she is, casting herself in the two main character roles of swift traveler and naive idealist. It is not surprising that her TAT protocols suggest a strong power motive. Roberta is no ruthless Machiavellian, however. She does not exploit people. But her life story is organized according to power, even though she can be and often is a very caring and intimate person. Roberta lives for change and adventure. She values freedom and strength—key virtues in her own highly agentic ideological setting. The two central images of self in her life story—the swift traveler and the naive idealist—are organized along the thematic line of agency/power. One is seen as highly powerful (moving, growing, sophisticated); the other is lacking in power (staying home, naive, doing my bit for mankind).

Characters in Narrative

William James (1892) believed that defining the adult self—what he called the "empirical me"—involved choosing the appropriate *character* that a person might play in life. He wrote:

> With most objects of desire, physical nature restricts our choice to but one of many represented goods, and even so it is here. I am often confronted by the necessity of standing by one of my empirical selves and relinquishing the rest. Not that I would not, if I could, be both handsome and fat and well dressed, and a great lady-killer, as well as a philosopher; a philanthropist, statesmen, warrior, and African explorer, as well as a "tone-poet" and saint. But the thing is simply impossible. The millionaire's work would run counter to the saint's; the bon-vivant and the philanthropist would trip each other up; the philosopher and the lady-killer could not well keep house in the same tenement of clay. Such different *characters* may conceivably at the outset of life be alike possible to a man. But to make any one of them actual, the rest must more or less be suppressed. So the seeker of his truest, strongest, deepest self must review the list carefully, and pick out the one on which to stake his salvation. All other selves thereupon become unreal, but the fortunes of this self are real. Its failures are real failures, its triumphs real triumphs, carrying shame and gladness with them. This is as strong an example as there is of that selective industry of the mind. . . . Our thought, incessantly deciding, among many things of a kind, which ones for it shall be realities, here chooses one of many *possible selves* or *characters*, and forthwith reckons it no shame to fail in any of those not adopted expressly as its own. (James, 1892/1963, p. 174, italics added)

In Roberta's life story, the swift traveler and the naive idealist may be seen as the two central *characters* whose "failures" and "triumphs," in James's words, carry "shame and gladness." Neither of these two characters corresponds completely to Roberta herself, nor even to her identity per se. Indeed, Roberta is many things, one of which is her identity. Her identity is her life story. The main characters in her life story are the swift traveler and the naive idealist, internal "empirical me's" that function as protagonists in narrative. Yet contrary to James's suggestion that the adult surveys the "list" of stock characters in life and "stakes his salvation" on one of them, Roberta's evolving identity proves more dynamic than a simple character choice. To make identity is to create story, and as the story develops different characters emerge to play their roles. Characters may be consciously chosen, or they may emerge unwittingly in the course of the narrative. Over time, adults *articulate* and *refine* the central characters in their identities.

I use the term *imago* to refer to the main characters in a person's life story. An imago is *a personified and idealized image of the self* that functions as a protagonist in a life story (McAdams, 1984b, 1985a, 1985b). Imagoes are larger and more encompassing than situationally specific roles and rather integrate numerous roles to suggest a "synchronic sameness" in identity—that the person is indeed the same person from one situation to the next, acting and experiencing as a particular kind of character across many different contexts. For example, an adult may see him- or herself as the sophisticated and intellectual professor, the rough-around-the-edges working boy or girl from the wrong side of town, the consummate caregiver always available to those in need, the corporate executive playing out the American dream, the worldly traveler in search of the new and the exotic, the athlete, the sage, the soldier, the teacher, the clown, or the peacemaker. Each of these might qualify as an imago. Imagoes exist as highly personalized and carefully crafted parts of the self, and they may be highlighted as heroes (or villains) in certain chapters of the life story, expressed through a particular subset of the adult's values and interests, and often embodied in external role models and other significant people in the adult's life. A person's life story may contain one imago or many, though the presence of two conflicting images of self, as in the case of Roberta, seems to be common (McAdams, 1985a, 1985b).

To a large extent, society prescribes standard imago forms. Over much of the life-span, the person acquaints him- or herself with a panoply of social roles, tacitly or explicitly evaluating each with respect to its suitability for the self. The process may begin with the images young children discern in their earliest favorite stories. MacIntyre (1984) writes:

A central thesis then begins to emerge: man is in his action and practice, as well as in his fictions, essentially a story-telling animal. He is not essentially, but becomes through his history, a teller of stories that aspire to truth. But the key question for men is not about their own authorship; I can only answer the question "What am I to do?" if I can answer the prior question "Of what story or stories do I find myself a part?" We enter human society, that is, with one or more imputed characters—roles into which we have been drafted—and we have to learn what they are in order to be able to understand how others respond to us and how our responses to them are apt to be construed. It is through hearing stories about wicked stepmothers, lost children, good but misguided kings, wolves that suckle twin boys, youngest sons who waste their inheritance on riotous living and go into exile to live with the swine, that children learn or mislearn both what a child and what a parent is, what the cast of characters may be in the drama into which they have been born and what the ways of the world are. Deprive children of stories and you leave them unscripted, anxious stutterers in their actions as in their words. Hence there is no way to give us an understanding of any society, including our own, except through the stock of stories which constitute its initial dramatic resources. Mythology, in its original sense, is at the heart of things. (p. 216)

In adolescence and adulthood, the person examines more carefully and more self-consciously the cast of characters his or her society offers as narrative resources for personal identity. Different societies offer different sorts of characters. Indeed, different echelons of a particular society may offer strikingly different images of what it means to be an adult and what a person can achieve during his or her adult years. Over time, furthermore, a society's stock characters change. Writes MacIntyre (1984): "What is specific to each culture is in large and central part what is specific to its stock of *characters*. So the culture of Victorian England was partially defined by the *characters* of the Public School Headmaster, the Explorer and the Engineer; and that of Wilhelmine Germany was similarly defined by such *characters* as those of the Prussian Officer, the Professor and the Social Democrat" (p. 28).

In their acclaimed analysis of contemporary American society, the authors of *Habits of the Heart* (Bellah, Madsen, Sullivan, Swidler, & Tipton, 1985) argue that a particular society and its members are given form and content by the "representative characters" that society provides:

> A representative character is a kind of symbol. It is a way by which we can bring together in one concentrated image the way people in a given social environment organize and give meaning and direction to their lives. In fact, a representative character is more than a collection of individual traits or personalities. It is rather a public image that helps define, for a given group of people, just what kinds of personality traits it is good and legitimate to develop. A representative character provides an ideal, a point of reference and focus, that gives living expression to a vision of life, as in our society today sports figures legitimate the strivings of youth and the scientist represents objective competence. (p. 39)

In the view of Bellah et al. (1985), two representative characters of traditional American society in the nineteenth and early twentieth centuries were the "Independent Citizen" and the "Entrepreneur." In recent years, they suggest, two new characters have risen to the fore to personify the traits contemporary Americans value the most: the "Manager" and the "Therapist." Both characters reflect middle-class Americans' preoccupation with attaining a satisfying and relatively autonomous style of life and becoming effective organizers of their worlds and their selves. The Manager organizes the human and nonhuman resources available to the organization that employs him or her so as to improve the organization's position in the marketplace. "His role is to persuade, inspire, manipulate, cajole, and intimidate those he manages so that his organization measures up to criteria of effectiveness shaped ultimately by the market" (p. 45). The Therapist, like the Manager, "is a specialist in mobilizing resources for effective action, only here the resources are largely internal to the individual and the measure of effectiveness is the elusive criterion of personal satisfaction" (p. 47). In contemporary middle-class America, "the goal of living is to achieve some combination of occupation and 'lifestyle' that is economically possible and psychically tolerable, that 'works.' The therapist, like the manager, takes the ends as they are given; the focus is upon the effectiveness of the means" (p. 47).

Bellah and MacIntyre suggest that particular societies at particular points in their histories present their members with representative characters around which they may construct personal identities. The person's own story making, therefore, always reflects the prevalent stories and the main characters in those stories that a culture affirms. In addition to these culturally representative characters, however, I would submit that there exists a second and more enduring panoply of character types that goes back at least to the ancient Greeks and that continues to provide many Westerners with personified resources for the making of identity. As Jung (1961) has suggested, certain stock character types may have a timeless quality, grounded as they are in the basic patterns of life that many disparate societies have traditionally shared. These include such characters as "the caregiver," "the warrior," "the sage," and "the healer."

In Figure 5.2, I have portrayed my own rather fanciful and highly provisional taxonomy of character types—a tentative classification system for imagoes, organized according to the thematic lines of agency and communion (McAdams, 1985b). I have given the imago types names derived from the mythology of ancient Greece. The gods and goddesses of the ancient Green pantheon represent, on one level at least, projected personifications of what the Greeks understood, and perhaps what many Westerners have traditionally understood, to be fundamental human propensities and strivings. Larger and more powerful than mortals, the Greek deities made love and war, experienced rage, envy, and joy, and performed acts of heroism and ignominy in ways that were remarkably human. Each of the major deities, furthermore, personified a distinctive set of personality traits that were repeatedly manifested in the myths and legends in which his or her behavior may be observed.

My research on imagoes has examined carefully the life stories of approximately 75 adult men and women, ranging in age from about 35 to 50 years (McAdams, 1984a, 1985a, 1985b). Lengthy life story interviews have been coded to identify at least one dominant imago resembling one of the types in Figure 5.2. The results of the codings have been related to other personality variables obtained from independent measures, such as power and intimacy motivation, assessed on the TAT.

The findings show that those adults who score high on power motivation and low on intimacy motivation, assessed on the TAT, tend to construct life stories in which at least one of the protagonists, or imagoes, is represented in

Class 2: (High Agency and High Communion)

1. *The Healer* (Apollo):
   prophet, artist, protector, organizer, legislator.

2. *The Counselor* (Athene):
   arbiter, therapist, teacher, guide, peacemaker.

3. *The Humanist* (Prometheus):
   defender of the weak, revolutionary, evangelist.

Class 1: (High Agency)

1. *The Ruler* (Zeus):
   judge, conqueror, seducer, creator, sage, celebrity.

2. *The Swift Traveller* (Hermes):
   explorer, adventurer, trickster, rabble-rouser, persuader, gambler, entrepreneur.

3. *The Warrior* (Ares):
   fighter, soldier, policeman.

Class 3: (High Communion)

1. *The Caregiver* (Demeter):
   altruist, martyr.

2. *The Loyal Friend* (Hera):
   spouse, helpmate, chum, confidante, sibling, assistant.

3. *The Lover* (Aphrodite):
   charmer, enchanter.

Class 4: (Low Agency and Low Communion)

1. *The Homemaker* (Hestia):
   domestic, ritualist.

2. *The Wage-Earner* (Hephaestus):
   craftsman, laborer.

3. *The Escapist* (Dionysius):
   pleasure-seeker, hedonist, player, epicure, child.

FIGURE 5.2 A taxonomy of imagoes.

Box 1 of Figure 5.2, designating highly agentic imagoes: Hermes, the swift traveler (as in the case of Roberta); Ares, the warrior; or the many faceted Zeus, ruler, sage, and celebrity. By contrast, men and women scoring high in intimacy motivation and low in power motivation tend to emphasize the communal imagoes in Box 3: Demeter, the caregiver; Hera, the loyal friend; or Aphrodite, the lover. Some adults score relatively high on both power and intimacy motivation. Their life stories tend to be populated by the protagonists in Box 2, who are both highly agentic and highly communal: Apollo, the healer, artist, and organizer; Athene, the counselor, teacher, and peacemaker; or Prometheus, the defender of the underdog, rebel, and humanist. Finally, a significant number of adults score low on both power and intimacy motivation. Their life stories tend to accentuate the exploits of those relatively nonagentic and noncommunal deities in Box 4: Hestia, the keeper of Olympus, whose duties revolve around daily rituals and ceremonies; Hephaestus, the craftsman and wage earner; and Dionysius, the escapist, who flees from Hestia's domestic scene and Hephaestus's world of work to sing, dance, play, and drink.

The Nature of the Imago

In his analysis of the identity formation of George Bernard Shaw, Erikson (1959) identified three major characters in Shaw's self-defining life story: Shaw, "the snob"; Shaw, "the noisemaker"; and Shaw, "the diabolical one." Each of these internalized identity structures is associated with characteristic roles, recurrent behavioral scripts, and consistent attitudes, hopes, fears, and goals in Shaw's life. Each, moreover, appears to be "born" in a specific biographical episode from Shaw's childhood. More encompassing than the mere "roles" that Shaw plays in daily living, these characters cut across a host of identity domains while integrating essential information about the self to be found in Shaw's past, his present situation as a middle-aged adult writing his autobiography, and his expectations for the future. According to Erikson, the young Shaw's maturation in adulthood is signified by an integration of the three images of the self within a larger, superordinate character, deemed Shaw, "the actor." The emergence of the actor imago created "for myself a fantastic personality fit and apt for dealing with men, and adaptable for the various parts I had to play as author, journalist, orator, politician, committee man, man of the world, and so forth" (quoted in Erikson, 1959, p. 109).

The concept of the imago as a personified and idealized image of the self bears some resemblance to a number of related concepts in the diverse literatures of clinical psychoanalysis and object relations theory (Fairbairn, 1952; Freud, 1923/1961; Jacobson, 1964; Jung, 1943; Sullivan, 1953), academic personality and social psychology (Cantor & Mischel, 1979; Markus, 1984; Martindale, 1980; Rogers, 1981), sociology (Bellah et al., 1985), and moral philosophy (MacIntyre, 1984). Like Jung's (1943) archetypes and Sullivan's (1953) personifications, imagoes are idealization—not flesh-and-blood persons—that are nonetheless emotionally charged. Each imago exists as a personified "me," taking center stage during certain scenes in "my" life story and playing a minimal role during others. Like Freud's (1923/1961) "ego ideal" and Jacobson's (1964) "wished-for self-image," an imago is partly formed through identification with loved (and hated) people in the person's life, though many other forces and factors shape the content of an imago. And like Steiner's (1974) "scripts" and "counterscripts," as well as a number of other conceptualizations (Jung, Sullivan, Fairbairn), imagoes appear to be arranged in pairs of dialectical opposites, as in the case of Roberta's "swift traveler" and "naive idealist." The synthesis of opposing imagoes over time is a hallmark of the mature adult self (McAdams, 1985b), a process that may bear some relation to Jung's (1943) concept of "individuation."

From a more cognitive standpoint, imagoes may be viewed as superordinate "self-schemata" (Markus & Sentis, 1982). Imagoes organize and evaluate self information, simplifying complex and contradictory information about the self and filling in gaps when self-relevant information is missing. Their structure is not unlike that of a "prototype," a fuzzy set of exemplary and peripheral features and attributes organized within a personified characterization of self (Cantor & Mischel, 1979; Rogers, 1981). Like Martindale's (1980) concept of "subselves" and Markus's (1984) concept of "possible selves," imagoes may specify recurrent behavioral plans or action scripts. Idealized and personified images of the self provide the adult with a repertoire of plans and scripts that can be activated in behavior in the service of important personality dispositions, such as the power and intimacy motives. Imagoes therefore give cognitive form to basic human motives—such as the agentic desire to be strong and the communal desire to be close—by personifying them and thereby specifying what the person should do, how he or she should act, in order to fulfill these motives over time (McAdams, 1985b).

As far as identity is concerned, therefore, one of the major tasks of early and middle adulthood is the articulation, refinement, and integration of imagoes. Having established an ideological setting and developed a historical perspective for identity in late adolescence and early adulthood, the adult now faces the narrative challenge of characterization. What are the main characters in my life story? How were they born? How will they develop? How will they flourish and fail? How do they relate to each other? What kind of story are they trying to tell? Watkins (1986) conceives of the adult self as a grand chorus of internalized characters who engage in "imaginal dialogues" with one another. She argues that the adult who seeks psychological maturity must engender and promote the "animation," "articulation," and "specification" of each of the many characters within the self (pp. 114–116). Unity and purpose in adult life comes from playing out in their fullest manifestation the central characters of one's life story. These characters may conflict with one another, revealing major rifts and contradictions within the self. But the contradictions must be played out if unity and purpose are to be attained. Unity and purpose in life are the by-products of a life story that recognizes the many discordant facets of the self, giving all characters their voice and their due. Walt Whitman's (1959) "Song of Myself" affirms the bold and expansive nature of mature adult identity:

> I cannot understand the mystery but
> I am always conscious of myself as two.
> Do I contradict myself?

> Very well then I contradict myself,
> I am large, I contain multitudes.

Yet how are these characters to be played out? Who writes their scripts? The articulation and refinement of narrative character in adulthood is a consummately psychosocial affair. The individual and society collaborate every step of the way. The collaboration may not always be a happy one, but the individual adult cannot even hope to compose a mature narrative of the self— one that provides life with unity and purpose—in the absence of a social and cultural context. Indeed, the prospect of the adult creating characterizations of the self completely out of blue is nonsensical, for the social world provides the person with the main resources for story construction and identity making from early childhood onward. In stories and in lives, we cannot transcend our resources. The social environment presents the person with a complex myriad of opportunities and constraints—a framework of things, people, ideas, institutions, traditions, and relationships that strongly determines the outlines of the person's own life story. At the same time, the person transforms and appropriates these resources to fit a narrative that makes sense to him or her, a narrative that affirms in what ways he or she is different from and similar to other adults in the same social environment (Baumeister, 1986).

The refinement of narrative character involves the full expression of various imagoes as main characters in the life story. For instance, the life story of Roberta is enhanced by the full expression of both the swift traveler and the naive idealist. The full expression of each character brings out both strengths and weaknesses of each. Thus the naive idealist—for all its timidity and ignorance—is the narrative vehicle through which Roberta makes strong commitments to family and work, "doing her bit for mankind," as she puts it. And the swift traveler—for all its strength and dynamism—seems uncomfortably restless at times, as if it is running "away" from the past as much as it is running "toward" the future. While Roberta clearly favors the swift traveler, she is relatively successful in giving both characters their due. Many other adults, on the other hand, work to suppress those characters in their life stories that they find less than ideal, often projecting them onto other people or denying the validity of the characters by belittling them, ignoring them, or treating them as if they were "aliens" within.

The refinement of narrative character also involves the integration of disparate imagoes. As the adult engenders the full expression of various imagoes, he or she also works to reconcile conflict among imagoes without undermining the integrity of the characters in the story. As Jung (1943), Levinson (1981), and others have suggested, reconciliation of opposite imagoes of the self is a cardinal attribute of the maturity of self in adulthood. Many psychologists have argued that such a reconciliation is not generally possible until midlife.

Among 50 life stories I collected from adults aged 35 to 50 years (McAdams, 1985a), I identified 12 that seemed to reveal significant integration of discordant imagoes. It is difficult, however, to generalize about these life stories. In each case the integration of characters was accomplished in a different way. One woman, for instance, integrated the imago of the "loyal friend" (Hera) with an image of the self as a strong and masterful agent through her occupational role as a psychotherapist. In providing psychological services to others, she was able to fulfill a strong need to be a friend to those who were less fortunate than she while mastering an intellectually challenging field of inquiry. A professor integrated an imago of "the teacher" (Athene) with that of "the student" in going back to school to get an MBA while continuing his teaching at the university. He maintained that only when he had a mentor or teacher in his life could he be an effective teacher as well. For this man, life essentially involved the transmission of knowledge down through a great chain of teachers and students. One is constantly learning while teaching.

A good example of the integration of imagoes is the life story of Jessica (McAdams, 1985a, pp. 207–208). Jessica is 35 years old, white, Protestant, and middle class. Early in her life story interview, she reports that she has "always" been preoccupied with where she "stood in the world." In her mythological reconstruction of the past, the preoccupation stems from her ethnic lineage: half German (her mother) and half Sicilian (her father). Even in childhood she was very concerned with where she stood in relation to this essential duality in her life. Was she the more rational and orderly German or the passionate and impetuous Sicilian? In adulthood, the duality translates into a conflict between Jessica, "the artist" (the hot-blooded Sicilian), and Jessica, "the realist" (the rational German). The artist transforms reality through imagination, but the realist is better able to get along in the day-to-day world because of her more pragmatic and systematic mode of operation. The artist is corporeal: She uses her body (hands) to form physical matter into something beautiful. The realist is more cognitive: She uses her mind to manipulate abstractions in order to solve problems. The two imagoes in Jessica's story contradict each other and often come into conflict.

After failing to make a decent living as a professional artist, Jessica has moved into the business world and is currently working toward an MBA. She is very happy about the switch. In her work she now relies on her German rationality—her ability to use her mind in a systematic and effective manner. Yet the artist imago has blossomed anew in an attitude toward her own life as a kind of artistic endeavor in itself. Jessica is herself the creation and creator. She works on her own personal development the way the artist works on a masterpiece. She sees herself as continually changing—forever an unfinished work of art. At present the artist and the realist appear reconciled—in balance. "Humans need to search for balance in their lives," states Jessica. Jessica believes that her preoccupation with the question of where she stands in the world has urged her to identify the conflicting parts of her self and to attempt to integrate them—to refine the main characters in her life story. She insists, however, that integration is an ephemeral thing, here in one chapter and gone in the next. The truth of the matter is, in her words, that "conflict is inevitable, and we have to accept it."

THE TELEOLOGICAL TRANSFORMATION OF NARRATIVE

Endings and Midlife

In contemporary American society, midlife or middle age is roughly considered to last from about age 40 to age 65. As Cohler (1982) points out, "This is a socially determined definition of midlife based on shared definitions of the timetable for the life course as a whole" (p. 223). Many Americans expect to live well into their late 70s and 80s. The midlife chunk of time is seen as comprising that long period of life following early adulthood and preceding retirement and/or becoming a "senior citizen." Biological change may play a role in demarcating the midlife period, but for the most part this epoch in the history of the human organism is defined by the person's subjective assessment of timing and the passage of social milestones. All human societies provide normative benchmarks to guide this assessment.

As the adult enters midlife, he or she comes to realize that the life course is likely to be about half over and that there is now less time ahead in the future than behind in the past. Such a realization may lead to an increased concern with one's own mortality (Marshall, 1975; Sill, 1980), or what Neugarten and Datan (1972) call the "personalization of death." Experiences of loss become more salient—loss of others through death of parents and friends and through separation from children who have moved away, loss of vitality through changes in athletic and reproductive capacities, and loss of hopes and aspirations through the inevitable instrumental and interpersonal disappointments that accompany adult life (Jacques, 1965; Kernberg, 1980; Levinson, 1981).

Psychologists have observed a number of behavioral and attitudinal trends in midlife that may, on one level or another, be viewed as responses to one's growing concerns about mortality. The middle years may bring an increase in the use of reminiscences in daily life (Livson & Peskin, 1980; Lowenthal, Thurnher, & Chiriboga, et al., 1975), an enhanced appreciation for the internal world of thoughts and feelings, and somewhat less interest in establishing new interpersonal and instrumental engagements (Neugarten, 1979). According to Jung (1961), it is not until midlife that men are able to accept and integrate a hitherto suppressed femininity (the anima). With the end of active parenting at midlife, Gutmann (1980) argues, women are likely to become more instrumental and executive in their approach to life, eschewing the dependent and self-effacing ways of their youth. Midlife men, on the other hand, are more likely to abandon the vigorous and aggressive manner of young adulthood in favor of more passive and contemplative roles. Jacques (1965) has suggested that midlife may mark significant changes in the adult's efforts to be creative. Before midlife, an artist's creative productions are more likely to emerge in a spontaneous and "hot-from-the-fire" manner, whereas after midlife creativity is more deliberate and "sculpted." The work of the younger artist may be highly optimistic and idealistic, laden with themes of pure desire and glorious romance. With the increasing concern over mortality at midlife, however, the idealism may give way to a more contemplative pessimism and a "recognition and acceptance that inherent goodness is accompanied by hate and destructive force within" (Jacques, p. 505). Creative products speak a more philosophical and sober language after midlife—a result, says Jacques, of the artist's own confrontation with the prospect of death.

All of these changes can make their way into the life story, transforming the past, the present, and expectations for the future and rewriting the narrative to accommodate the growing realization that the End is nearer than one would like it to be. Therefore the life story of a middle-aged man or woman is likely to be more philosophical, ironic, and sculpted than the hot-from-the-fire narrative produced in early adulthood. The story is likely to place greater emphasis on themes of loss and separation and to incorporate a greater variety of self-relevant material suggestive of contrasexual and other previously suppressed or unarticulated aspects of the self. These developments should enhance the refinement of narrative character, enrich the understanding of one's past, and point the narrative toward an envisioned *ending* in the future.

As Sartre (1964) points out, the ending of a story shapes all that comes before it. A good story leaves the reader with the impression that the scenes, the characters, and the plot were all developed by the author to lead up to a particular and appropriate ending. If identity is an integrative life narrative providing the person with a sense of unity and purpose in life, then it is probably in midlife that the adult becomes especially concerned about how the story is going to end. One's sense of wholeness and direction in life is teleologically anchored. If I am to know who I am as an adult, then I must conceptualize my life in terms of a *telos*—an end point that justifies my life strivings. I must formulate a clear vision of what I am going to do in the future in order to bring the narrative to a good completion. "Living happily ever after" is not enough; fairy tales provide poor models for the teleological transformation of narrative in the middle adult years.

Further complicating the adult's search for an appropriate ending to his or her life story is the fact that he or she generally does not want the story to end. If not the greatest fear that every man or woman faces, the fear of one's own death certainly ranks toward the top, and some have even suggested that it is *the* ultimate and primal fear from which all other fears derive (e.g., Becker, 1973). What is needed, therefore, is a satisfying ending for a life story that implies, at the same time, that the story does not *really* End! The ending of a life story should defy the mortality of the person, suggesting an immortality of the self extending through subsequent generations. It is in midlife that the making of identity through narrative is likely to focus on the problem of mortality and the End. During this time in the human life cycle, the adult may be preoccupied with fashioning and then incorporating into identity what I have termed a *generativity script* (Albrecht, De St. Aubin, & McAdams, 1988; McAdams, 1985a; McAdams, Ruetzel, & Foley, 1986).

The Generativity Script

It is a mistake to separate neatly, as does Erikson's (1963) theory of psychosocial stages, the concepts of identity and generativity. According to Erikson's eight-stage theory, the person first resolves the psychosocial issue of "identity versus role confusion" in late adolescence and young adulthood (Stage 5 in Erikson's scheme) and then proceeds sequentially through Stage 6 ("intimacy vs. isolation") and Stage 7 ("generativity vs. stagnation") during the early and middle adult years. The central assumption is that a person must first know who he or she is (identity) before he or she can commit the self to others in long-term interpersonal relationships (intimacy). The establishment of mature intimacy then paves the way for generativity, conceived as establishing, promoting, and guiding the next generation. According to the most clichéd renditions of Erikson's theory, the person first finds a niche in the occupational world (identity), then gets married (intimacy), and finally builds a family and raises children (generativity).

However, Erikson's own writings, especially his biographical case studies (Erikson, 1958, 1969, 1976, 1980), suggest that things are often more complicated and that adulthood may not lend itself well to a neat demarcation of stages. Indeed, I would suggest that identity is far too big an issue in the human life cycle to be confined to a discrete stage at the end of adolescence and the beginning of adulthood. Instead, identity *first* becomes a central concern at this time in the life cycle, with the emergence of formal operational thinking and the development of a historical perspective on the self. The adolescent or young adult may be preoccupied with certain facets of identity—especially the consolidation of an ideological setting to ground the emerging life story. But once these facets are resolved, new ones arise, such as the refinement of narrative characters and the composition of a generativity script. The problem of identity does not go away after early adulthood. Identity is a stubborn and a jealous god. Once the individual becomes a historian of the self, the history and the history making expand to encompass as much as they can. Generativity therefore becomes part of identity. In order to know who I am, I must have some inkling of what I have done and what I am going to do in the future in order to be generative. My generativity script for the future must make sense in terms of an established framework of belief and value (ideological setting), my idealized and personified images of self (imagoes), and the landmark events from my past (nuclear episodes).

The generativity script is the adult's plan or outline specifying what he or she hopes to *do* in order to leave a legacy of the self to the next generation. In Kotre's (1984) terms, generativity involves "the desire to invest one's substance in forms of life and work that will outlive the self" (p. 10). Through generativity, the adult attains a kind of immortality through a legacy that is generated and then offered to subsequent generations. The scope of one's generativity script may be narrow or broad. As an example of an extraordinarily broad script for generativity, Erikson (1969) describes Mahatma Gandhi's generative commitment to an entire nation:

> From the moment in January of 1915 when Gandhi set foot on a pier reserved for important arrivals in Bombay, he behaved like a man who knew the nature and the extent of India's calamity and that of his own fundamental mission. A mature man of middle age has not only made up his mind as to what, in the various compartments of his life, he does and does not *care for*, he is also firm in his vision of what he *will* and *can* take *care of*. He takes as his baseline what he irreducibly is and reaches out for what only he can, and therefore, must *do*. (p. 255, italics in the original)

Gandhi's generativity script provided his own life with unity and purpose while uniting his fellow Indians to move forward with a larger purpose of their own. In Gandhi's monumental life story, therefore, we see a coming together of what Erikson (1975) calls "life history" and "the historical moment." Not only was Gandhi his own history, but the object of his generative mission, India itself, became part of that history as well, as he became part of the larger history of an emerging nation. Gandhi's generative efforts defy that most vexing and absorbing problem for the middle-aged man or woman: the problem of immortality. Indeed, Gandhi's legacy lives on, long after his life was ended by an assassin's attack.

Very few adults, however, fashion a generativity script as encompassing as that which comes out of Gandhi's life story. Yet many behave in highly generative ways. Kotre (1984) identifies four general ways in which adults may be generative. Through biological generativity, the adult conceives, gives birth to, and nurses the infant. In parental generativity, the adult raises a child, providing nurturance and discipline. In technical generativity, the adult develops a skill that is passed down to others. The generative object in this case is the apprentice who learns the skill. In cultural generativity, the adult creates, renovates, or conserves some aspect of culture that ultimately survives as a system of symbols. The generative object is the culture itself.

In generativity, the adult promotes and guides the next generation through such creative behaviors as parenting, teaching, leading, and making and doing things that benefit a community as a whole. The generative adult commits him- or herself to the continuation and even the improvement of society as a whole, through the next generation. The generative adult nurtures, supports, guides, teaches, leads, and promotes the next *generation* while *generating* life products and producing outcomes that aim to benefit the social system and promote its continuity from one generation to the next.

A key prerequisite for generative action, Erikson suggests, is a "belief in the species." In speculating on the antecedents of adult *failure* in generativity, Erikson (1963) writes, "The reasons are often to be found in early childhood impressions; in excessive self-love based on a too strenuously self-made personality; and finally (and here we return to the beginnings) in the lack of some faith, some 'belief in the species,' which would make a child appear to be a welcome trust of the community" (p. 267). In other words, healthy generativity is founded on a basic belief or faith in the goodness and/or worthwhileness of human life— human life in the past, the present, and as evaluated for the future. To believe in the (human) species is to place hope and trust in the advancement or betterment of human life in the future, even in the face, perhaps, of compelling evidence of human destructiveness and deprivation. The most generative adults should hold a strong belief in human progress, a fundamental faith in humankind, and hope for the future (Van de Water & McAdams, 1988).

Mature generativity involves a creative blend of both agency and communion—the two fundamental thematic lines of narrative. As such, generativity incorporates two very different human activities. The first involves the making of a life *product*. The product may be tangible or intangible, living or inanimate. Thus a generative product may be child, a career, a book, the family business, a legacy of hard work, an idea, a piece of advice, or any of a multitude of phenomena that an adult may create as an expression of the self. This first process is a highly agentic and self-expansive, even narcissistic, affair. The individual fashions someone or something in his or her own image. The product is viewed as a statement of the self, an expansion of the agent's sphere of influence.

The second process, on the other hand, involves giving the product up, offering it to the environment (others, the next generation, posterity) as a *gift* that lives on. This second step is highly communal, involving "the participation of the individual in some larger organism of which the individual is a part" (Bakan, 1966, p. 15). Generativity assumes, in the words of Becker (1973), "that the things [and the ideas and the people] that man creates in society are of lasting worth and meaning, that they outlive or outshine death and decay, that man and his products count" (p. 5). Becker adds, "If you are going to be a hero, then you must give a gift" (p. 173). Becker's concept of "heroism" resembles closely Erikson's concept of generativity (McAdams, 1985a). In both, the adult attains a kind of immortality through generated gifts.

Consistent with this dual-process view of generativity are the results of a study of generativity scripts in the life stories of 50 midlife men and women (McAdams et al., 1986). Each adult was asked to describe his or her overall dream or vision for the future. The accounts were coded for the degree to which the individual emphasized generative action in future years. All participants, furthermore, were administered the TAT before the interview. Those adults who scored high on *both* power and intimacy motivations, as assessed via the TAT, described the most generative plans for the future. In other words, those men and women with the strongest needs to feel strong and to feel close—to be a forceful agent and to merge with others in communities of care—showed the highest levels of generativity as expressed in their hopes and dreams for the future.

In sum, the generative man or woman must first fashion a legacy of the self (a highly powerful, agentic act) and then offer it up to others as a gift (an act of self-surrender and communion). This kind of synthesis of agency and communion provides a person's life story with a telos with respect to which the entire narrative must be reconciled. The telos rounds out the story, providing an envisioned "ending" that gives birth to new beginnings. The life story that contains a vital generativity script generates new stories that outlive the storyteller him- or herself, assuring the continuity of the story—the continuity of identity—into the next generation, and perhaps beyond.

Integrity and Later Adulthood

The life story may be revised and rewritten through the adult years. Throughout middle age, the adult is likely to work on the refinement of narrative character and the composition of a generativity script. Certain "on-time" and normative transitions in the life cycle—such as the birth of children in young adulthood, one's 40th birthday, children's leaving home in middle adulthood, retirement—may occasion extensive revision of the narrative, as the adult subjectively apprehends a move from one life chapter to another (Cohler & Boxer, 1984). Unexpected transitions, especially those involving separation, loss, failure, sickness, or death, may precipitate more jarring transformations of identity. Even chance events—both positive and negative—can have a major impact, making it extremely difficult for the personologist, and even the person him- or herself, to predict how a life story will change over time and how things will eventually "turn out" (Cohler, 1982; Goethals, 1980).

In later adulthood, writes Erikson, the person looks back on what has been and either accepts (integrity) or rejects (despair) the one and only life he or she has lived:

Only in him who in some way has taken care of things and people and has adapted himself to the triumphs and disappointments adherent to being, the originator of others or the generator of products and ideas—only in him may gradually ripen the fruit of these seven stages. I know no better word for it than ego integrity. Lacking a clear definition, I shall point to a few constituents of this state of mind. It is the ego's accrued assurance of its proclivity for order and meaning. It is a post-narcissistic love of the human ego—not of the self—as an experience which conveys some world order and spiritual sense, no matter how dearly paid for. It is the acceptance of one's one and only life cycle as something that had to be and that, by necessity, permitted no substitutions: it thus means a new, a different love of one's parents. It is a comradeship with the ordering ways of distant times and different pursuits, as expressed in the simple products and sayings of such times and pursuits. Although aware of the relativity of all the various life styles which have given meaning to human striving, the possessor of integrity is ready to defend the dignity of his own life style against all physical and economic threats. For he knows that an individual life is the accidental coincidence of but one life cycle with but one segment of history; and that for him all human integrity stands or falls with the one style of integrity of which he partakes. (1963, p. 268)

Erikson's passage suggests that in the later years of life the person's history-making endeavors come to an end, and he or she begins to *review* the history that has been made. From adolescence onward, the person "looks back" on life, while looking ahead as well, to provide a historical perspective on the self. In the later years of adulthood, however, the person looks back on the process of looking back, reviews and critiques the one and only life history that has now been produced. What Erikson describes as a "post-narcissistic" approach to life may mean, on one level at least, the attainment of a certain kind of distance on one's own history and the process of making it. Ego integrity involves the eventual *acceptance* of that history—as "something that had to be and that, by necessity, permitted no substitutions." As such, integrity stands in marked contrast to generativity. While in generativity the adult seeks to generate a gift to offer to the next generation, integrity challenges him or her to accept what has been given, to receive, graciously, "one's one and only life-cycle" as if it were a gift.

On the other hand, the later years of adulthood may involve more in the way of active history making than Erikson implies. Butler (1975) describes the *life review* in old age as a concerted reflection upon one's past in order to "settle accounts" before one dies. While my life story model of identity suggests that people continually "settle accounts" from adolescence onward, Butler's proposition suggests a *final* settling that may be especially intensive. Butler's concept of life review can, in fact, be interpreted in a number of different ways. On the one hand, it may simply be seen as one last attempt to make sense of the past in light of what is to come, no different in kind than the many attempts that have preceded it, going back as far as adolescence. Because it is perceived as a "last" attempt, however, it may lead to an extensive revision of the past and a much clearer articulation of the linkages between past, present, and future than has been achieved before.

On the other hand, the life review of old age may be viewed as a conscious explication of what has hitherto developed on a partly conscious and unconscious level. In other words, Butler's life review may make explicit the tacit history that the individual has been creating all along. In this sense, the aged person finally comes to understand his or her identity on a conscious and explicit level, though he or she has been articulating it unconsciously for many years before. From yet another perspective, Butler's life review may be virtually the same as Erikson's notion of integrity—an *acceptance* of the past for what it "had to be." In this sense, the older adult's remembrance of things past may be closer to a review of history than a remaking of it, a metahistorical perspective that attempts to make sense of the process of forging unity and purpose in life through story. Up until old age, the adult operates both as historian and history, the agent and the object of his or her own story making. In the later years of adulthood, however, he or she may step away from the history and the process of being a historian. The history that has been made and the process that has made it may become the objects of conscious reflection and review.

The later years present other ambiguities for the personologist who views the individual from a life story perspective. In contemporary middle-class society, for example, many adults live well into their 80s and beyond. Those who have been employed often retire around the age of 65 or 70. Their children have usually left home long ago. In that one's occupational and parental roles are prime outlets for the expression of one's generativity script, the years of retirement may be seen as a "post-generative" period in some, if not many, lives. Though many adults in their 70s and 80s continue to be generative by being grandparents and making other contributions to the next generations, others (finances and health willing) disengage themselves from virtually all generative pursuits and devote themselves to relaxation and fun. How is such a period of the life-span to be incorporated into a person's life story? Is it seen as a return to childhood? A reward for hard work? An escape? How does the older person connect this most recent epoch to those historical periods preceding it?

Perhaps this last query begs the question. Some adults may *not* feel the need to connect this postgenerative stage to what has come before. They may view it, instead, as a stepping out of history, a movement away from rendering life meaningful through narrative, even a return to a "prehistoric" period in life in which the person lives from day to day, savoring the present for its own sake. While some might view such a development in the life cycle as a regression to childhood, others might argue that it represents something of an enlightenment in old age—a transcendence of history, an embrace of what some have called the "eternal moment."

CONCLUSION

In Figure 5.3, I have summarized some of the main features of the life story model of identity in the context of the human life cycle. Although a person begins to seek unity and purpose in life by constructing a self-defining life story in adolescence and young adulthood, the origins of the story and the story-making process reside in the caregiver-attachment bond of infancy. The quality

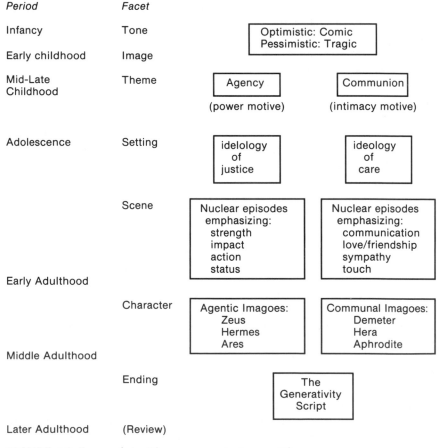

FIGURE 5.3 Facets of the life story over the human life-span.

of attachment may be instrumental in predisposing the person to approach narrative from either an optimistic (comic or romantic) or pessimistic (tragic or ironic) orientation, imbuing narrative with a general *tone* or flavor ranging from highly positive to highly negative. The preoperational child is immersed in the *images* of story, incorporating and inventing emotionally charged pictures, symbols, and patterns that become the raw stuff of future story making. Later, in elementary school, the child comes to organize human intentions within story, providing the groundwork for the development and consolidation of basic human motives, such as the power and the intimacy motives. Motivational tendencies are revealed through recurrent goal-oriented *themes* in the stories that children (and adults) tell and create. Roughly paralleling the power and the intimacy motives, the two superordinate thematic lines of narrative are what Bakan has termed agency and communion.

With the advent of formal operational thinking, the adolescent adopts a historical perspective on life, seeking to integrate his or her own past, present, and future into a coherent and self-defining life story. The thematic content of the story can be characterized in terms of the extent to which the adolescent and adult emphasizes themes of agency and/or communion in the text. One of the first challenges of story-making—identity formation—in adolescence is the consolidation of an *ideological setting* for the story. The ideological setting is a backdrop of belief and value that situates the action of the narrative in a particular ontological, epistemological, ethical, and religious context. Like stories as a whole, ideological settings may be characterized in terms of the extent to which they underscore human agency (freedom, individual rights, and principles of justice) and/or human communion (equality, community responsibilities, and principles of care). With the emergence of a historical perspective on life, furthermore, the adolescent begins to rearrange and remythologize his or her own past, highlighting certain key events or *scenes* that mark self-continuity and self-change. I call these scenes *nuclear episodes*, and they too may be viewed from the standpoint of agency and communion.

In early and middle adulthood, men and women articulate their identities further by refining narrative *character*. The *imago* is a personified and idealized image of the self that functions as a main character in a person's life story. A particular life story is likely to contain more than one imago, suggesting that the person is represented within his or her own story in a variety of guises, some of which may conflict. Imagoes may be highly agentic, highly communal, high on both agency and communion, or low on both, as characterized in my provisional taxonomy of imagoes derived from the mythology of ancient Greece. The individual's refinement of narrative character is strongly influenced by the kind of character roles offered by his or her society and by the important interpersonal relationships he or she establishes over the life-span.

As the person moves from early to middle adulthood, he or she focuses increasingly on the composition of a *generativity script* for the life story. The generativity script is a plan or outline for the future that specifies what the adult will do in order to leave a legacy of the self to the next generation and thereby promote the conservation or advancement of a social community or society as a whole. Mature generativity blends agency and communion, as the adult must first create a product as a powerful extension of the self and then offer the product to the environment as a self-surrendering gift, an expression of care and commitment to a social world that is larger than the self. In later adulthood, the person may review the life story he or she has made, as well as the process of making the story itself, and either accept it as something that is good and "had to be" (Erikson's ego integrity) or reject it as a squandered opportunity that cannot be regained (Erikson's despair). The last years of adulthood may be occasioned by a movement away from story making, a transcendence of personal history to be replaced by a savoring of the "here and now."

The life story model of identity provides a framework for conceptualizing the development of the whole person, from birth to death. In the spirit of Henry Murray's explorations in personality and the personological tradition that was his generative gift, the life story model provides a promising new way to address how the single person is like all other persons, like some other persons, and like no other person (Murray & Kluckhohn, 1953). The key to the approach can be found in the pages of *Explorations in Personality* (Murray, 1938) when Murray writes, "The history of the organism *is* the organism." I take this statement to be both figuratively and literally true. The life story model of identity portrays the person as both history and historian, seeking unity and purpose in life by making, telling, and living a self-defining history. The history is a story of the self's past, present, and future—a mythically structured fable of the creation and the development of the self, believed to embody truth. Weinstein (1981) expresses well the gist of a life story approach to the study of persons and lives:

> How does one transform the grittiness of the world into the fable of life? Far from being an aesthetic afterthought, the creation of form is at the very heart of both life and art. The shaping impulse is coextensive with life itself; not so much jars, but our very *identity*, must be made. And there is considerable drama in such efforts.

REFERENCES

Adler, A. (1927). *The practice and theory of individual psychology*. New York: Harcourt Brace Jovanovich.

Ainsworth, M. D. S., Blehar, M. C., Waters, E., & Wall, S. (1978). *Patterns of attachment: A psychological study of the strange situation*. Hillsdale, NJ: Lawrence Erlbaum Associates.

Albrecht, R., De St. Aubin, E., & McAdams, D. P. (1988). *Themes of generativity in adults' life stories*. Paper presented at meeting of American Psychological Association, Atlanta, GA.

Allport, G. W. (1937). *Personality: A psychological interpretation*. New York: Holt.

Anderson, J. W. (1981). Psychobiographical methodology: The case of William James. In L. Wheeler (Ed.), *Review of personality and social psychology* (Vol. 2, pp. 245–272). Beverly Hills, CA: Sage.

Angyal, A. (1941). *Foundations for a science of personality*. New York: Viking Press.

Applebee, A. N. (1978). *The child's concept of story*. Chicago: University of Chicago Press.

Atkinson, J. W. (Ed.). (1958). *Motives in fantasy, action, and society*. Princeton, NJ: D. Van Nostrand Co.

Atkinson, J. W., Heyns, R. W., & Veroff, J. (1954). The effect of experimental arousal of the affiliation motive on thematic apperception. *Journal of Abnormal and Social Psychology, 49*, 405–410.

Bakan, D. (1966). *The duality of human existence: Isolation and communion in Western man*. Boston: Beacon Press.

Baltes, P. B., Reese, H. W., & Lipsitt, L. P. (1980). Life-span developmental psychology. *Annual Review of Psychology, 31*, 65–110.

Bascom, W. (1965). The forms of folklore: Prose narratives. *Journal of American Folklore, 78*, 3–20.

Baumeister, R. (1986). *Identity: Cultural change and the struggle for self*. New York: Oxford University Press.

Becker, E. (1973). *The denial of death*. New York: Free Press.

Bellah, R. N., Madsen, R., Sullivan, W. M., Swidler, A., & Tipton, S. M. (1985). *Habits of the heart: Individualism and commitment in American life*. Berkeley, CA: University of California Press.

Bertaux, D. (Ed.). (1981). *Biography and society: The life history approach in the social sciences*. Beverly Hills, CA: Sage.

Bettelheim, B. (1976). *The uses of enchantment: The meaning and importance of fairy tales*. New York: Alfred A. Knopf.

Bowlby, J. (1969). *Attachment and loss: Vol. 1. Attachment*. New York: Basic Books.

Brabeck, M. (1983). Moral judgment: Theory and research on differences between males and females. *Developmental Review, 3*, 274–291.

Breger, L. (1974). *From instinct to identity: The development of personality*. Englewood Cliffs, NJ: Prentice-Hall.

Bruner, J. S. (1960). Myth and identity. In H. A. Murray (Ed.), *Myth and mythmaking* (pp. 276–287). New York: George Braziller.

Bruner, J. S. (1986). *Actual minds, possible worlds*. Cambridge, MA: Harvard University Press.

Buber, M. (1970). *I and thou*. New York: Charles Scribner's Sons.

Butler, R. N. (1975). *Why survive? Being old in America*. New York: Harper & Row.

Campbell, J. (1962). *The masks of God: Oriental mythology*. New York: Viking Press.

Cantor, N., & Mischel, W. (1979). Prototypes in person perception. In L. Berkowitz (Ed.), *Advances in experimental social psychology* (Vol. 12, pp. 3–52). New York: Academic Press.

Charme, S. L. (1984). *Meaning and myth in the study of lives: A Sartrean perspective.* Philadelphia: University of Pennsylvania Press.

Cohler, B. J. (1982). Personal narrative and the life course. In P. Baltes & O. G. Brim, Jr. (Eds.), *Life-span development and behavior* (Vol. 4, pp. 205–241). New York: Academic Press.

Cohler, B. J., & Boxer, A. M. (1984). Personal adjustment, well being, and life events. In C. Z. Malatesta & C. E. Izard (Eds.), *Emotion in adult development* (pp. 85–100). Beverly Hills, CA: Sage.

Damon, W., & Colby, A. (1987). Social influence and moral change. In W. M. Kurtines & J. L. Gewirtz (Eds.), *Moral development through social interaction* (pp. 3–19). New York: Wiley.

Datan, N., Rodeheaver, D., & Hughes, F. (1987). Adult development and aging. *Annual Review of Psychology, 38,* 153–180.

Dollard, J. (1935). *Criteria for the life history.* New Haven, CT: Yale University Press.

Elkind, D. (1981). *Children and adolescents: Interpretive essays on Jean Piaget* (3rd ed.). New York: Oxford University Press.

Endler, N. S. (1981). Persons, situations, and their interactions. In A. I. Rabin, J. Aronoff, A. M. Barclay, & R. A. Zucker (Eds.), *Further explorations in personality* (pp. 114–151). New York: Wiley.

Epstein, S. (1984). The stability of behavior across time and situations. In R. A. Zucker, J. Aronoff, & A. I. Rabin (Eds.), *Personality and the prediction of behavior* (pp. 209–268). Orlando, FL: Academic Press.

Erikson, E. H. (1958). *Young man Luther: A study in psychoanalysis and history.* New York: W. W. Norton.

Erikson, E. H. (1959). Identity and the life cycle: Selected papers. *Psychological Issues, 1,* 5–165.

Erikson, E. H. (1963). *Childhood and society.* (2nd ed.). New York: W. W. Norton.

Erikson, E. H. (1969). *Gandhi's truth: On the origins of militant nonviolence.* New York: W. W. Norton.

Erikson, E. H. (1975). *Life history and the historical moment.* New York: W. W. Norton.

Erikson, E. H. (1976). Reflections on Dr. Borg's life cycle. In E. H. Erikson (Ed.), *Adulthood* (pp. 1–31). New York: W. W. Norton.

Erikson, E. H. (1980). Themes of adulthood in the Freud-Jung correspondence. In N. J. Smelser & E. H. Erikson (Eds.), *Themes of work and love in adulthood* (pp. 43–74). Cambridge, MA: Harvard University Press.

Fairbairn, W. R. D. (1952). *Psychoanalytic studies of the personality: An object relations theory of personality.* London: Routledge & Kegan Paul.

Feinstein, A. D. (1979). Personal mythology as a paradigm for a holistic public psychology. *American Journal of Orthopsychiatry, 49,* 198–217.

Ford, C. F., & Lowery, C. R. (1986). Gender differences in moral reasoning: A comparison of the use of justice and care orientations. *Journal of Personality and Social Psychology, 50,* 777–783.

Forsyth, D. R. (1980). A taxonomy of ethical ideologies. *Journal of Personality and Social Psychology, 39,* 175–184.

Forsyth, D. R. (1985). Individual differences in information processing during moral judgment. *Journal of Personality and Social Psychology, 49,* 264-272.

Fowler, J. W. (1981). *Stages of faith: The psychology of human development and the quest for meaning.* New York: Harper & Row.

Frenkel, E. (1936). Studies in biographical psychology. *Character and Personality, 5,* 1-35.

Freud, S. (1953). *The interpretation of dreams.* In J. Strachey (Ed.), *The standard edition of the complete psychological works of Sigmund Freud* (Vols. 4-5). London: Hogarth Press. (Original work published 1900).

Freud, S. (1955). Beyond the pleasure principle. In J. Strachey (Ed.), *The standard edition of the complete psychological works of Sigmund Freud* (Vol. 19). London: Hogarth Press.

Frye, N. (1957). *The anatomy of criticism.* Princeton, NJ: Princeton University Press.

Gilligan, C. (1982). *In a different voice.* Cambridge, MA: Harvard University Press.

Goethals, G. W. (1980). *Agency and chance in the human life cycle: A clinical case.* Paper presented at the Grand Rounds of McLean Hospital, Belmont, MA

Goffman, E. (1959). *The presentation of self in everyday life.* New York: Doubleday.

Gutmann, D. L. (1980). The postparental years: Clinical problems and developmental possibilities. In W. H. Norman & T. J. Scaramella (Eds.), *Mid-life: Developmental and clinical issues* (pp. 38-52). New York: Bruner/Mazel.

Haley, J. (1980). *Leaving home.* New York: McGraw-Hill.

Hankiss, A. (1981). Ontologies of the self: On the mythological rearranging of one's life history. In D. Bertaux (Ed.), *Biography and society: The life history approach in the social sciences* (pp. 203-209). Beverly Hills, CA: Sage.

Hazen, N. L., & Durrett, M. E. (1982). Relationship of security of attachment to exploration and cognitive mapping abilities in 2-year-olds. *Developmental Psychology, 18,* 751-759.

Hogan, R. (1987). Personality psychology: Back to basics. In J. Aronoff, A. I. Rabin & R. A. Zucker (Eds.), *The emergence of personality* (pp. 79-104). New York: Springer.

Hogan, R., Jones, W., & Cheek, J. (1985). Socioanalytic theory: An alternative to armadillo psychology. In B. R. Schlenker (Ed.), *The self and social life* (pp. 175-198). New York: McGraw-Hill.

Howe, M. J. A. (1982). Biographical evidence and the development of outstanding individuals. *American Psychologist, 37,* 1071-1081.

Inhelder, B., & Piaget, J. (1958). *The growth of logical thinking from childhood to adolescence.* New York: Basic Books.

Jacobson, E. (1964). *The self and object world.* New York: International Universities Press.

Jacques, E. (1965). Death and the midlife crisis. *International Journal of Psycho-Analysis, 46,* 502-514.

James, W. (1963). *Psychology: A briefer course.* New York: Fawcett. (Original work published 1892)

Jung, C. G. (1943). The psychology of the unconscious. In *Collected works* (Vol. 7). Princeton, NJ: Princeton University Press.

Jung, C. G. (1961). *Memories, dreams, reflections*. New York: Random House.

Kegan, R. (1982). *The evolving self: Problem and process in human development*. Cambridge, MA: Harvard University Press.

Kernberg, O. (1980). *Internal world and external reality*. New York: Jason Aronson.

Kohlberg, L. (1981). *The philosophy of moral development: Moral stages and the idea of justice: Vol. 1. Essays on moral development*. New York: Harper & Row.

Kohlberg, L., & Gilligan, C. (1971). The adolescent as a philosopher: The discovery of the self in a post-conventional world. *Daedalus*, Fall, 1051–1086.

Kohli, M. (1981). Biography: Account, text, method. In D. Bertaux (Ed.), *Biography and society: The life history approach in the social sciences* (pp. 61–75). Beverly Hills, CA: Sage.

Kohut, H. (1977). *The restoration of the self*. New York: International Universities Press.

Kotre, J. (1984). *Outliving the self: Generativity and the interpretation of lives*. Baltimore, MD: Johns Hopkins University Press.

LaFreniere, P. J., & Sroufe, L. A. (1985). Profiles of peer competence in the preschool: Interrelations between measures, influence of social ecology, and relation to attachment history. *Developmental Psychology, 21*, 56–69.

Langbaum, R. (1982). *The mysteries of identity: A theme in modern literature*. Chicago: University of Chicago Press.

Levinson, D. J. (1981). Exploration in biography: Evolution of the individual life structure in adulthood. In A. I. Rabin, J. Aronoff, A. M. Barclay, & R. A. Zucker (Eds.), *Further explorations in personality* (pp. 44–79). New York: Wiley.

Livson, N., & Peskin, H. (1980). Perspectives on adolescence from longitudinal research. In J. Adelson (Ed.), *Handbook of adolescent psychology* (pp. 47–98). New York: Wiley.

Lowenthal, M. F., Thurnher, M., Chiriboga, D., et al. (1975). *Four stages of life: A comparative study of men and women facing transitions*. San Francisco: Jossey-Bass.

The Lutheran book of worship. Minneapolis, MN: Augsburg Publishing House, 1978.

MacIntyre, I. (1984). *Beyond virtue*. Notre Dame, IN: University of Notre Dame Press.

Mahler, M. S., Pine, F., & Bergman, A. (1975). *The psychological birth of the human infant*. New York: Basic Books.

Main, M. (1981). *Avoidance in the service of attachment: A working paper*. In K. Immelmann, G. Barlow, L. Petrinovich, and M. Main (Eds.) *Behavioral development: Bielefeld interdisciplinary project*. New York: Cambridge University Press.

Mandler, J. M. (1984). *Stories, scripts, and scenes: Aspects of schema theory*. Hillsdale, NJ: Lawrence Erlbaum Associates.

Marcia, J. E. (1980). Identity in adolescence. In J. Adelson (Ed.), *Handbook of adolescent psychology* (pp. 159–187). New York: Wiley.

Markus, H. (1984). *Possible selves*. Paper presented at the Boston University Symposium for the Interdisciplinary Study of Personality, Boston, MA.

Markus, H., & Sentis, K. (1982). The self in social information processing. In J. Suls (Ed.), *Psychological perspectives on the self* (Vol. 1, pp. 41–70). Hillsdale, NJ: Lawrence Erlbaum Associates.

Marshall, V. (1975). Age and awareness of finitude in developmental gerontology. *Omega, 6,* 113-129.

Martindale, C. (1980). Subselves: The internal representation of situational and personal dispositions. In L. Wheeler (Ed.), *Review of personality and social psychology* (Vol. 1, pp. 193-218). Beverly Hills, CA: Sage.

Matas, L., Arend, R., & Sroufe, L. A. (1978). Continuity of adaptation in the second year: The relationship between quality of attachment and later competence. *Child Development, 49,* 547-556.

McAdams, D. P. (1980). A thematic coding system for the intimacy motive. *Journal of Research in Personality, 14,* 412-432.

McAdams, D. P. (1982a). Experiences of intimacy and power: Relationships between social motives and autobiographical memory. *Journal of Personality and Social Psychology, 42,* 292-302.

McAdams, D. P. (1982b). Intimacy motivation. In A. J. Stewart (Ed.), *Motivation and society: Essays in honor of David C. McClelland* (pp. 133-171). San Francisco: Jossey-Bass.

McAdams, D. P. (1984a). Human motives and personal relationships. In V. Derlega (Ed.), *Communication, intimacy, and close relationships* (pp. 41-70). New York: Academic Press.

McAdams, D. P. (1984b). Love, power, and images of the self. In C. Z. Malatesta & C. E. Izard (Eds.), *Emotion in adult development* (pp. 159-174). Beverly Hills, CA: Sage.

McAdams, D. P. (1985a). The "imago": A key narrative component of identity. In P. Shaver (Ed.), *Review of personality and social psychology: Vol. 6. Self, situations, and social behavior* (pp. 115-141). Beverly Hills, CA: Sage.

McAdams, D. P. (1985b). *Power, intimacy, and the life story: Personological inquiries into identity.* New York: Guilford Press.

McAdams, D. P. (1987). A life-story model of identity. In R. Hogan & W. Jones (Eds.), *Perspectives in personality* (Vol. 2, pp. 15-50). Greenwich, CT: JAI Press.

McAdams, D. P. (1988a). Biography, narrative, and lives: An introduction. *Journal of Personality, 56,* 1-18.

McAdams, D. P. (in press). Self and story. In A. J. Stewart, J. M. Healy, & D. J. Ozer (Eds.), *Perspectives in personality: Vol. 3. Approaches to understanding lives.* Greenwich, CT: JAI Press.

McAdams, D. P. (1989). *Intimacy: The need to be close.* New York: Doubleday.

McAdams, D. P. (in press-a). *The person: An introduction to personality psychology.* San Diego, CA: Harcourt Brace Jovanovich.

McAdams, D. P. (in press-b). Personal needs and personal relationships. In S. Duck (Ed.), *Handbook of personal relationships.* New York: John Wiley.

McAdams, D. P., Booth, L., & Selvik, R. (1981). Religious identity among students at a private college: Social motives, ego stage, and development. *Merrill-Palmer Quarterly, 27,* 219-239.

McAdams, D. P., & Ochberg, R. L. (Eds.). (1988). *Psychobiography and life narratives: A special issue of the Journal of Personality.* Durham, NC: Duke University Press.

McAdams, D. P., Ruetzel, K., & Foley, J. M. (1986). Complexity and generativity at mid-life: Relations among social motives, ego development, and adults' plans for the future. *Journal of Personality and Social Psychology, 50,* 800-807.

McClelland, D. C. (1961). *The achieving society*. Princeton, NJ: Van Nostrand.

McClelland, D. C. (1975). *Power: The inner experience*. New York: Irvington.

McClelland, D. C. (1981). Is personality consistent? In A. I. Rabin, J. Aronoff, A. M. Barclay, & R. A. Zucker (Eds.), *Further explorations in personality* (pp. 87–113). New York: John Wiley.

McClelland, D. C. (1985). *Human motivation*. New York: Cambridge University Press.

McClelland, D. C., Atkinson, J. W., Clark, R. A., & Lowell, E. L. (1953). *The achievement motive*. New York: Appleton-Century-Crofts.

Mink, L. O. (1978). Narrative form as a cognitive instrument. In R. H. Canary & H. Kozicki (Eds.), *The writing of history: Literary form and historical understanding* (pp. 129–149). Madison, WI: University of Wisconsin Press.

Mischel, W. (1984). On the predictability of behavior and the structure of personality. In R. A. Zucker, J. Aronoff, & A. I. Rabin (Eds.), *Personality and the prediction of behavior* (pp. 269–305). New York: Academic Press.

Moos, R. H. (1976). *Human adaptation: Coping with life crises*. Lexington, MA: D. C. Heath.

Morgan, C. D., & Murray, H. A. (1935). A method of investigating fantasies: The Thematic Apperception Test. *Archives of Neurology and Psychiatry, 34*, 289–306.

Murray, H. A. (1938). *Explorations in personality*. New York: Oxford University Press.

Murray, H. A. (1943). *The Thematic Apperception Test: Manual*. Cambridge, MA: Harvard University Press.

Murray, H. A., & Kluckhohn, C. (1953). *Personality in nature, society, and culture*. New York: Alfred A. Knopf.

Neugarten, B. (1979). Time, age, and the life cycle. *American Journal of Psychiatry, 136*, 887–894.

Neugarten, B., & Datan, N. (1974). The middle years. In S. Arieti (Ed.), *American handbook of psychiatry* (Vol. 1). New York: Basic Books.

Perry, W. C. (1970). *Forms of intellectual and ethical development in the college years*. New York: Holt, Rinehart and Winston.

Piaget, J. (1952). *The origins of intelligence in children*. New York: International Universities Press.

Piaget, J. (1954). *The construction of reality in the child*. New York: Basic Books.

Rank, O. (1978). *Truth and reality*. New York: W. W. Norton. (Original work published 1936)

Rogers, T. B. (1981). A model of the self as an aspect of the human information processing system. In N. Cantor & J. F. Kihlstrom (Eds.), *Personality, cognition, and social interaction* (pp. 193–214). Hillsdale, NJ: Lawrence Erlbaum Associates.

Rosenwald, G. C. (1988). A theory of multiple-case research. *Journal of Personality, 56*, 237–262.

Runyan, W. M. (1982). *Life histories and psychobiography: Explorations in theory and method*. New York: Oxford University Press.

Runyan, W. M. (1988). Progress in psychobiography. *Journal of Personality, 56*, 293–324.

Russell, B. (1972). *A history of Western philosophy*. New York: Simon & Schuster. (Original work published 1945)

Sameroff, A. J. (1982). Development and the dialectic: The need for a systems approach. In W. A. Collins (Ed.), *The concept of development* (pp. 83–104). Hillsdale, NJ: Lawrence Erlbaum Associates.

Sartre, J. P. (1964). *The words.* New York: George Braziller.

Schwartz, G. E. (1987). Personality and the unification of psychology and modern physics: A systems approach. In J. Aronoff, A. I. Rabin, & R. A. Zucker (Eds.), *The emergence of personality* (pp. 217–254). New York: Springer.

Shaver, P., & Rubenstein, C. (1980). Childhood attachment experience and adult loneliness. In L. Wheeler (Ed.), *Review of personality and social psychology* (Vol. 1, pp. 42–73). Beverly Hills, CA: Sage.

Shweder, R. A., & Much, N. C. (1987). Determinations of meaning: Discourse and moral socialization. In W. M. Kurtines & J. L. Gewirtz (Eds.), *Moral development through social interaction* (pp. 197–244). New York: John Wiley.

Sill, J. (1980). Disengagement reconsidered: Awareness of finitude. *Gerontologist, 20,* 457–462.

Slade, A. (1987). Quality of attachment and early symbolic play. *Developmental Psychology, 23,* 78 85.

Sroufe, L. A. (1979). The coherence of individual development: Early care, attachment and subsequent developmental issues. *American Psychologist, 34,* 834–841.

Stein, N. L., & Policastro, M. (1984). The concept of a story: Comparison of children's and teachers' viewpoints. In H. Mandl, N. L. Stein, & T. Trabasso (Eds.), *Learning and comprehension of text.* Hillsdale, NJ: Lawrence Erlbaum Associates.

Steiner, C. M. (1974). *Scripts people live.* New York: Grove Press.

Stewart, A. J. (Ed.). (1982). *Motivation and society: Essays in honor of David C. McClelland.* San Francisco: Jossey-Bass.

Sullivan, H. S. (1953). *The interpersonal theory of psychiatry.* New York: W. W. Norton.

Tomkins, S. S. (1987). Script theory. In J. Aronoff, A. I. Rabin, & R. A. Zucker (Eds.), *The emergence of personality* (pp. 147–216). New York: Springer.

Van de Water, D., & McAdams, D. P. (1988). *Generativity and Erikson's "belief in the species."* Manuscript under review.

Veroff, J. (1957). Development and validation of a projective measure of power motivation. *Journal of Abnormal and Social Psychology, 54,* 1–8.

Watkins, M. (1986). *Invisible guests: The development of imaginal dialogues.* Hillsdale, NJ: Analytic Press.

Weinstein, A. (1981). *Fictions of the self: 1550–1800.* Princeton, NJ: Princeton University Press.

White, R. A. (1966). *Lives in progress* (2nd ed.). New York: Holt, Rinehart & Winston.

White, R. A. (1981). Exploring personality the long way: The study of lives. In A. I. Rabin, J. Aronoff, A. M. Barclay, & R. A. Zucker (Eds.), *Further explorations in personality* (pp. 3–19). New York: John Wiley.

Whitman, W. (1959). *Leaves of grass.* New York: Viking Press.

Wiggins, J. S., & Broughton, R. (1985). The interpersonal circle: A structural model for the integration of personality research. In R. Hogan & W. Jones (Eds.), *Perspectives in personality* (Vol. 1, pp. 1–47). Greenwich, CT: JAI Press.

Winter, D. G. (1973). *The power motive.* New York: Free Press.

Winter, D. G., & Carlson, L. (1988). Using motive scores in the psychobiographical study of an individual: The case of Richard Nixon. *Journal of Personality, 56*, 73-101.

Winter, D. G., & Stewart, A. J. (1978). The power motive. In H. London & J. E. Exner, Jr. (Eds.), *Dimensions of personality* (pp. 391-447). New York: Wiley.

6

Studying Lives in a Changing Society: Sociological and Personological Explorations

Glen H. Elder and Avshalom Caspi

Shortly after World War II, Clyde Kluckhohn and Henry Murray (1948/1965) introduced a classic essay on personality formation with an observation that applies to the study of lives as well as to the human condition: "Every man is in certain respects (a) like all other men, (b) like some other men, (c) like no other man" (p. 53). The uniqueness of individual behavior reflects, in part, the diversity of the experienced social world. In the words of Kluckhohn and Murray (1948/1965), "There is uniqueness . . . in the number, kinds, and temporal order of critically determining situations . . . in the course of life." And, of course, there is also commonality based on the social order. Situational sequences, however, are not adequately described by either uniqueness or invariance.

Variation represents the central theme of this chapter. Environmental variations have behavioral consequences, and individual variations tell us something about how social change is likely to affect behavior and lives. Although a large number of studies have described the behavior patterns of individuals over the life-span (Brim & Kagan, 1980), they seldom give equal attention to social context (Bronfenbrenner, 1979). Moreover, most studies of social context and its influence are carried out as if it did not change. Missing from these formulations is the dynamic side of a changing social system. Indeed, studies that begin with the individual seldom do justice to the environment, and studies that begin with macroscopic trends or events often ignore the individual.

The challenge for any study of lives in a changing society is to keep both individual and environmental variations in the picture. Over the past decade, investigations of social and individual change have converged in a life course perspective that attends to their relationship (Elder, 1975). The life course refers to the social patterning of events and roles over the life-span, a process ever subject to the interaction of individual behavior with a changing society.

To highlight the challenge of linking lives and a changing environment, we begin this chapter with a review of preliminary studies of lives and changing times, examine the emergence of life course ideas and projects during the 1960s, and consider cohort analysis as a way of thinking about social change in lives. Next we explore the limitations of cohort studies for relating social change to lives and present a conceptual framework that permits the explication of historical effects. Actual examples of this framework appear in the Social Change Project, a program of work, launched by the senior author at the end of the 1960s, devoted to research on the relation between historical change and people's lives.

We describe the five key orienting principles that inform this work and then show their usefulness in studies of two macrohistorical changes, the Great Depression and World War II. The conclusion of this chapter brings us back to problems and promises in the multidisciplinary study of lives and to developments in theory and method for linking personality and the life course to the changing world in which people develop.

SOCIAL CHANGE, COHORTS, AND LIVES

The accelerating pace of city growth and industrial change in the early 1900s heightened the problematic features of lives. Seminal efforts to study these strains remain notable for the questions and issues they posed about the effects of a rapidly changing society. Fifty years later many of these issues, still unresolved, reappeared, but at a time when we had more understanding of the link between lives and the environment. The cohort approach, in particular, provided a way of thinking about this connection and actually studying it. We turn to some of these developments for background to our studies of the life course influences of the Depression and war.

Lives and Social Change: Preliminary Studies

In a landmark study of early social science, Thomas and Znaniecki (1918–1920) investigated the transition experience of Polish peasants as they left their rural homeland for major urban centers in Europe and the United States during the late nineteenth and early twentieth centuries. *The Polish Peasant in Europe and America* provides an ethnographic and historical account of village and country life in Poland and of the immigrants' settlement in their new urban environments.

The ambitious scope of this study called for a view of people's lives over time in a changing environment. Continuous life records, whether retrospective or prospective, offered such a view, and Thomas became an advocate of life history data and the longitudinal study. Writing in the mid-1920s, he urged that priority be given to the "longitudinal approach to life history" (Volkart, 1951, p. 593). Studies, he argued, should investigate "many types of life in different situations" and follow "groups of individuals into the future, getting a continuous record of experiences as they occur."

Little is known about the scientific reception of Thomas's proposal for longitudinal studies among students of human development at the time, though appropriate initiatives along this line were underway by the end of the 1920s. Lewis Terman's (1925, 1947) gifted children in California, first surveyed in 1922, were contacted once again in 1928. This step toward a longitudinal study was soon followed by others about 5 years apart up to the mid-1980s. Over 900 men and women completed forms in 1982. The various follow-ups did not ensure the development of life records with reasonably complete entries by year. Questions about work and earnings, for example, were not even asked for certain years. Moreover, the study almost succeeded in *not* collecting any systematic information on life experience through the Great Depression and World War II, two of the most encompassing social disruptions of this century. The 1950 follow-up was completely silent on World War II, much to the apparent disbelief of the nearly 500 men who served. Some insisted on communicating their sense of neglect on the edges of their questionnaire.

The many limitations of this oldest longitudinal study bring to mind the humorous reflections of James Morgan, the originator of the Michigan Panel Study of Income Dynamics: "If we had known we were going to live so long, we would have taken better care of ourselves" (Elder, 1985, p. 16). The same point can be made about longitudinal studies that were launched just before the Great Depression at the old Institute of Child Welfare (now called Human Development) at the University of California-Berkeley (Eichorn, Clausen, Haan, Honzik, & Mussen, 1981): Nancy Bayley's Berkeley Growth Study, Jean Macfarlane's Berkeley Guidance Study (both with birth years in 1928–1929, total sample greater than 250 cases), and the Oakland Adolescent or Growth Study directed by Harold Jones. Initially restricted in focus to development across the pre-adult years, all three samples have been followed up to later life and the 1980s.

Thomas knew about these longitudinal studies and actually refers to them in *The Child in America* (Thomas & Thomas, 1928). But unlike Thomas and his studies of immigrants, the principal investigators paid little if any attention to environmental change. A changing environment beyond the family did not inform their conceptual models. Children in the Oakland and Berkeley studies grew up in the Great Depression and were strongly influenced by World War II, yet neither of these historical events were considered relevant for developmental research. Despite this view, a number of processes in the socioeconomic environment of the 1930s and 1940s were included in the data collections of this period. However, they remained unused for the most part until the mid-1960s when social change became a salient issue in social science and politics.

Many forces and trends converged in the 1960s to focus attention on the interrelationship of social change and life patterns. Student unrest and racial strife posed questions that were not asked or pursued in prior decades, such as the diverse historical childhoods of young and old. Moreover, all members of the pioneering studies (e.g., Terman, Oakland Growth) were in their middle years at the time and consequently drew attention to aging in a rapidly changing society. In what sense were the Depression and war generations aging in different ways because of their historical experiences?

Along with these developments came a new wave of longitudinal studies, the refinement of techniques for analyzing life record data, and a rudimentary theory of the life course based on a sociological understanding of age (Elder, 1975; Riley, Johnson, & Foner, 1972). By the mid-1970s, developments in theory, data, and method clearly identified an emerging field of study linking social change to the life course. *Children of the Great Depression* (Elder, 1974) is part of this movement in the social sciences. Using longitudinal data from the Oakland Growth Study (birth years, 1920–1921), the study traced the effects of drastic income loss to the life experiences of adolescents and their adult careers.

The life course perspective of this chapter owes much to the analytical work of *Children of the Great Depression* (Elder, 1974). The senior author began this work, unknowingly, during his first assignment (1962–1965) as a research sociologist at the Institute of Human Development, University of California, Berkeley. Charged with the task of coding the data in the archive of the Oakland Growth Study, he soon faced the novel challenge of coding people and families that seemed to be changing constantly, owing in large part to the disruptions and hardships of the Great Depression. The archival data described both families and the Study child from the beginning to the end of the 1930s and then followed the Study child up to late adulthood. Instead of conceptualizing families and individuals at a point in time, the constancy of change required *ways* of representing them over time in a dynamic process. Eventually the life course became such a way and identified connections between social change and life patterns.

The ever-changing circumstances of the Oakland families were not, of course, a sufficient explanation for a study linking Depression hardship to people's lives. Some missing elements can be found in the life history of the senior author—from his exposure to the Great Depression as a young child in Cleveland to experiences in the mass mobilization of World War II, to a radical change in family residence from metropolis to the dairy country of Northwestern Pennsylvania at the beginning of high school. Drastic change and especially its effects on people have been issues of considerable interest to the senior author even since. The changefulness of the Depression years merely activated this sensitivity and eventually prompted a series of studies on social change and life experience.

This sensitivity also owes much to the influence of sociologists and behavioral scientists from the early Chicago school (up to 1935). Literally every one of the senior author's mentors was trained at the University of Chicago. Key figures in this great age of social science include Edward Sapir, John Dewey, George Herbert Mead, William I. Thomas (founder of the Chicago school of sociology), Everett Hughes, Herbert Blumer, Ernest Burgess, and Robert Park. Two mentors, Charles Bowerman and John Clausen, were trained at Chicago and studied under Ernest Burgess and Herbert Blumer. The distinctive features of the Chicago school strongly favor a contextual approach to lives and human development. They include an emphasis on empirical research, as against speculation; the insistence that people and groups be studied in their natural ecology; attention to the historical perspective—many of the classic works from the Chicago school are explicitly historical; a preference for multidisciplinary approaches and projects; and a problem orientation—Chicago-type studies were focused on the problems of community, institutions, and people, such as in mass migration, urban poverty, crime, and family disorder.

In view of these biographical connections to the Chicago school, it is not surprising to note that *Children of the Great Depression* and related work has important ties to *The Polish Peasant*. First, the Depression research investigated a type of problem that had much in common with the traditional experience of immigration from the Old World to the urban-industrial environment of large cities such as Chicago. *Children of the Great Depression* followed people and family units from the prosperous 1920s across the hard times of the 1930s. Some families lost heavily in the economic collapse, whereas others were largely spared this misfortune. In this natural experiment, such differences enabled a comparative design involving relatively nondeprived and deprived families.

The Polish Peasant's other contribution to *Children of the Great Depression* is conceptual. We see this in a dynamic view of group and individual experience across changing and historically specific times, one that does not lose sight of the larger setting and its social trends. The principal objective is to explicate the process by which change occurs in group structure and in the lives of members.

Well before work began on *The Polish Peasant*, Thomas outlined a model of crisis situations, one that assigned priority to the control of life situations in social experience (1909, pp. 13-26). Habitual patterns of behavior are maintained by situations in which the group or individual is able to produce outcomes that are in line with certain claims or expectations. Crises arise from a sharp disparity between claims and control, between expectations and the resources to achieve desired benefits. As a "disturbance of habit," crises heighten attentional capacities and the search for effective responses, possibly leading to a revision of the individual methods of control that give structure to life experience. Adaptations to the new situation and its demands represent efforts to restore control over one's life, but under terms of the new situation.

Three models illustrate different forms of the gap between claims and resources and call attention to different types of family and individual adaptation. First, aspirations may climb well above achievements or resources in a period of rapid economic growth. Following the severe economic depression of the early 1930s, economic aspirations rose sharply among Americans who were weary of doing without. The more their aspirations surpassed available resources, the greater the sense of frustration. Durkheim (1951, p. 248) refers to this dynamic as the "malady of unlimited aspiration." The more people have, the more they want, in an ever-escalating spiral.

In another scenario, claims remain fairly stable over time despite a sharp loss of income. This loss could occur through unemployment and failed businesses or through rampant inflation that diminishes the purchasing power of the dollar. In either case, available resources fall well below desires. Resource loss from unemployment calls for efforts to generate more income and to reduce expenditures. By comparison, an inflationary time provides less as a means of control. The dollar may continue to lose value in the face of efforts to produce higher earnings.

A third type of gap is illustrated by discontinuities between available resources before and after a crisis situation. Historically this is seen in the process of immigration experience. In migrating to America from the impoverished countryside of feudal nineteenth-century Poland, immigrants brought old skills from a rural society to an urban, industrial environment. The resulting discontinuity was experienced as a loss of mastery or control by new immigrants. Likewise, aspirations suited for the Polish countryside were inappropriate for urban America.

As elaborated from Thomas's early writings on crisis situations, this conceptualization proved especially useful in thinking about the consequences of family change for the individual in the hard pressed 1930s. Change in Depression families became a way to view the diverse experiences of children in the 1930s. But what about the long-term effects of the change? How should we think about this legacy? Satisfactory answers to such questions did not arise until studies of age in the 1960s began to bring temporality to families and individuals.

Familiar and even a bit worn at the time, the notion of an age-graded life course depicted a normative arrangement of social roles, events, and activities across the life-span. In twentieth-century America, childbearing typically followed marriage in the white population, and both events occurred early in the adult career. Left out of this sequence of average times is the concept of variation. Though most American women married around the age of 20 during the 1950s, some married much earlier, whereas others married as late as their 30s. The new study of age, relating people to social roles, brought fresh awareness of life course variation in social as well as historical space to the behavioral sciences (Elder, 1975; Riley et al., 1972).

This perspective assumes that the consequences of events and transitions across the life course vary according to their timing. There are cultural definitions of appropriate times for schooling, leaving home, marriage, and childbearing. As a rule, people are conscious of how the timing of their lives fits with cultural timetables and expectations. For example, a teenage birth is too early and brings undesirable or limited options. At the other extreme are late first births around the age of 40 in women's lives. These variations are complicated by the interlocking careers of people's lives, such as those of work, marriage, and parenthood. The scheduling of events and obligations entails the challenge of managing resources and pressures. A case in point is the economic squeeze of early childbearing, which reflects low-paying employment and the heavy demands of a young family.

Age through birth year also locates people in history, just as social age structures the life course. People are exposed to a range of experiences as they move through age-graded roles and accordingly share much of this world with other members of their cohort. Eras of accelerated change tend to pull the trajectories of age cohorts apart. An example of this effect comes from the records of American cohorts in the 1940s. Young men at the end of the 1930s were soon mobilized into the armed forces for the duration of World War II, and this experience frequently placed their lives on a different path in the postwar years. Only 6 years later, young men entered the postwar economy of peace and prosperity. Concerning the transition to adult status, Reuben Hill (1970, p. 322) observes that each cohort in times of rapid change "encounters at marriage a unique set of historical constraints and incentives which influence the timing of its crucial life decisions, making for marked generational dissimilarities in the life cycle career patterns."

The new study of age brought historical considerations and insights on age grading to the life course of people, but it neglected the "givens" of family ties. Kinship ties are established at birth as a lifetime network of mutual rights and obligations that link successive generations and the lives of their members.

Family patterns over the life-span generally evolve in a cycle of generational succession in which newborns are socialized to maturity, give birth to the next generation, grow old, and die. Within the life course of each generation, unexpected and involuntary events occur through life changes in related generations. Thus a young woman of 45 becomes a grandmother when her daughter has a first baby, and parents lose their status as son and daughter when their own parents die. As in the case of social age, the road map of kinship and the generations tells family members where they have been, are, and will be heading.

The life course of individual members of a family can be mapped by the three-dimensional space of family, historical, and life time (Figure 6.1). The historical meanings of birth year and passage through the age structure define life pathways on the grid of historical time and the life-span. Americans born in 1920, 1940, and 1960 span the same age grades, though along divergent paths that arise from the relation between age and events or roles. Historical times, such as depressions and wars, may alter the connection between family events and age, or change their temporal pattern—for example, among returning servicemen the completion of education may occur after their first marriage and full-time employment.

Another source of variation is the unstable pathway of family time. Figure 6.1 lists four generations on the family timetable, but the number and configu-

FIGURE 6.1 Life-course trajectories in three-dimensional space: life, family and historical time.

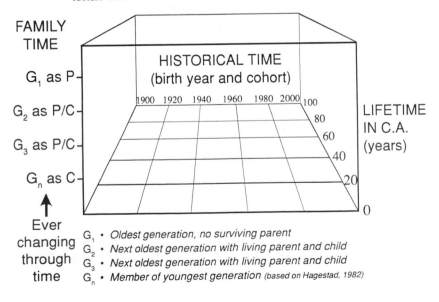

ration of the generations can vary sharply across a single life-span. Consider a person who was born in the late 1920s and became one of several great-grandchildren of a woman in her nineties. Three higher stations in the generational series are occupied: the parent, grandparent, and great-grandparent generations. This hierarchy continues up to the sixth year of the child's life when the great-grandmother dies. Only three stations remain on the generational ladder. By the time the child enters secondary school, both grandparents on the maternal and paternal side have died. The structure is now based on two generations, or the family circle of birth, maturation, reproduction, and death. In terms of Figure 6.1, G_1 and G_n make up the generational structure until the 1920s "child" has a child.

Adult behavior tends to vary according to whether adults have surviving parents and grandparents (Hagestad, 1982). For example, the emotional distance between parents and offspring increases when the former move to the last position of the generational line. Change in self or identity is another implication of generational turnover or the end of a generation. Change in one's family or generational position may also produce important consequences through conflict with age status. Accelerated childbearing across two generations is a good example of change that increases the disparity between two sources of status, age and kinship. A young mother becomes a very young grandmother.

Specific examples of such conflict come from Burton's study (1985) of three generational lineages among blacks in Los Angeles. Virtually all of the teenage mothers expected their own mothers to play a lead role in the care of their child. This expectation was never fulfilled in over four out of five cases. When mothers refused to become active grandmothers, the burden shifted to the shoulders of the great-grandmothers. One great-grandmother noted that she had no time for herself anymore. "I takes care of babies, grown children, and old people. I work too—I get so tired I don't know if I'll ever get to do something for myself."

Early and late events tell us much about life patterns and relations between the generations, but only age-related data on birth year locates people in precise historical times. Birth year information places people in history and thus according to major historical forces. When defined by birth year, membership in specific cohorts becomes a way of thinking about lives in a changing society.

Cohorts, History, and Models

One of the unique features of life course analysis involves its sensitivity to the interplay between lives and a changing society, as expressed in part through historically situated cohorts. Demographers have long used cohorts as a way of thinking about social change (back to the mid-1800s at least; Sundt, 1855/

1980), but we had to wait until Ryder's (1965) seminal essay to appreciate their full utility in linking special change to the life course. As each cohort encounters a historical event, whether war or peace, depression or prosperity, it "is distinctively marked by the career stage it occupies" (Ryder, p. 846).

With this life stage principle, Ryder (1965) provided a point of departure for greater understanding of the interaction between social change and life patterns. The implications of mass unemployment and war mobilization obviously vary among people of different ages, roles, and competencies, from children to young adults and the middle aged. Differences in life stage provide insight concerning the adaptive resources, options, and meanings that become potential elements in linking social change to life trajectories and personality. More will be said about the life stage principle when we consider the Depression and wartime studies.

Ryder (1965) made explicit the link between age and time and consequently led social scientists to a more sophisticated awareness of the connections between historical and individual time. By locating people in historical context, the analyst is drawn to the meaning of context for lives. Consider, for example, age differences in psychological functioning. If social change differentiates the life lines of adjacent cohorts, then age differences in behavior can be attributed to both history and maturation or aging. One of the better known examples of this ambiguity involves an assumed intellectual decline in old age, as measured across age groups (Baltes, Cornelius, & Nesselroade, 1979). Though conventional accounts of this decline focus on aging, one could also attribute the decline to educational and birthplace trends. As better educated and native-born people became more common in the general population, younger cohorts benefitted on tests of intellectual functioning.

Any comparison of cohorts involves at least three potential effects: cohort, period, and age. Cohort and period effects are historical in nature. Historical influence takes the form of a cohort effect when social change differentiates the life patterns of successive cohorts. Thus Americans who were born just before the 1930s were affected by Depression hardships more adversely than men and women who were 10 years younger (Elder, 1979). History also takes the form of a period effect when the influence of a social change or event is relatively uniform across successive cohorts. Secular trends in the scheduling of marriages and first births across the twentieth century are largely an expression of massive period effects. A third type of effect occurs through maturation or aging. In the mid-1960s, Schaie (1965; cf. 1984) proposed a general developmental model that addressed the task of estimating the three effects (cohort, period, and age) in relation to psychological functioning. Unfortunately, efforts to partition the variance according to these effects have not advanced our understanding of social change because of the ambiguous meaning of historical effects—cohort and period.

The ambiguous meaning of cohort effects presents no difficulty when historical change is not a key variable. For example, developmentalists may regard cohort variability as an error term and a source of ambiguous findings (Baltes et al., 1979). Social change and cohort are irrelevant for the issues at hand. In other cases, cohorts may be viewed as samples that permit a test of the generalization boundaries. The important question is whether the observed findings apply to different samples. These uses of the cohort variables are consistent with a longitudinal study of adolescent personality that Nesselroade and Baltes (1974) carried out in four cohorts, as defined by birth years in 1955, 1956, 1957, and 1958.

The central question concerned normative patterns in personality development, not historical influences, but the results showed large cohort differences between the first and last two cohorts. The authors made some effort to explain the puzzling findings, but the design is inappropriate for linking historical circumstances to behavior. Reese and McCluskey (1984) correctly note that it uses little more than speculation in explaining historical variations and that "speculation about probable causes without corroborating evidence is unlikely to be fruitful, unless it leads to theory-guided empirical questions" (p. 4).

A third view is centered more on social change through its account of cohort as a theoretical and process variable. Accordingly, "Cohort can be linked to a system of antecedent, process, and consequent events in ways that are useful for the description, explanation, and modification of developmental change" (Baltes et al., 1979, p. 80). Unfortunately, historical change is seldom part of this or any cohort model. Once proposed as a way of connecting social change and the life-span, cohort designs seem to have had the opposite effect, leading us away from historical considerations. Indeed, cohort-sequential studies generally symbolize the neglect of history as a developmentally relevant influence. Cohort-sequential research typically focuses on intercohort variation in development, not on historical forces that suggest rationales for expecting such variation.

A similar conclusion applies to cohort studies in sociology. The big story on marriage and marital instability trends across the twentieth century is the force of historical change, as recorded by period effects, but the meaning of these effects is unclear (Rodgers & Thornton, 1985). Likewise, a study of first births in America concludes that "period factors increase or decrease childbearing at all ages and for all subgroups within society" (Rindfuss, Morgan, & Swicegood, 1984, p. 368). But the range of potential influences under the "period" umbrella is so great that no conclusion can be drawn about specific effects. Period effects remain a black box, and the reason for such ill defined outcomes has much to do with motivating questions that ignore historical conditions. This neglect of history is not common to all cohort studies. For example, Hogan

(1981) has explored the transition to adulthood among American men in relation to the changing socioeconomic landscape of the twentieth century. But we have discovered very little about lives in a changing society from cohort studies.

Initially the concept of cohort seemed to offer a promising way of thinking about lives in a changing society. But the promise depends on originating research questions that actually *link* specific changes to the life course. These questions are rare. More often, questions assign environmental change to an error category or define multiple cohorts as a test of the generalization boundaries of specific findings. Even when history is substantively important, it may be operationalized as a period or cohort effect that provides no clue as to the precise nature of the influence. Finally, cohort analysis often restricts what we can learn about social change in lives by obscuring variations within successive cohorts. Members of a cohort are not uniformly exposed to depression or war, and experiential variations *within* specific cohorts represent a significant conceptual distinction.

Cohort Analysis: Outcomes and Event Designs

The summary observations offered above most readily fit a particular analytic model, an outcome design. As shown in Figure 6.2, an outcome design (Model A) surveys potential antecedent variables and weighs their relative influence in relation to a specific outcome. Even if some antecendents tap historical

FIGURE 6.2 Studying social change in the life course: two models.

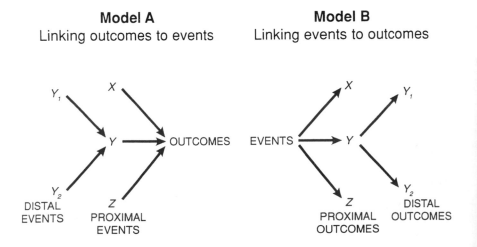

changes of great significance, the design does not focus on the process by which they find expression in lives. We end up with a partial assessment of a historical event.

Consider, for example, a study of the transition period from youth to adulthood. Antecedent and intervening variables enter the analysis in terms of their predictive or explanatory relevance for a host of timing variables, such as entry into parenthood. Variation in parental timing may be due, in part, to social changes of one kind or another, such as war mobilization during the early 1940s. The mobilization of men into the armed forces could accelerate or postpone the timing of parenthood. However, other factors are relevant, such as family income, parental personality, marital conflict, and school failure. History thus becomes a smaller part of the picture from analysis through interpretation.

Outcome models also slight the full range of an event's influence. Consider the recruitment of servicemen in World War II. Early recruitment (defined by age of recruit) has implications for autonomy, maturation, and events in the transition to adulthood, from education to work and marriage (Elder, 1986). Parenthood is only one of a number of outcomes. In at least two ways, then, an outcome model underplays the weight of social change in lives. First, historical events are only one set of influences and thus are not likely to be examined in depth. Second, the design fails to capture the full range of influences from a specific event. A single social change may have diverse and multiple effects.

Two cross-national studies of social change in lives provide examples of these points: (1) *The Civic Culture* by Almond and Verba (1963), based on a five-nation (United Kingdom, West Germany, Italy, Mexico, and United States) survey of political competence among men and women, and (2) the Inkeles and Smith (1974) study of individual modernity in samples of men from developing societies (Argentina, Chile, East Pakistan, India, Israel, and Nigeria).

With an age range of 40 years or more in each sample, Almond and Verba (1963) could have indexed exposure to major events and trends across the twentieth century—two world wars, a world depression, post-1945 affluence, an increase in education and urban living. Putting the wars and Depression aside, they focus on modernization and civic culture, with an emphasis on the self-confident citizen. This person is likely to "follow politics, to discuss politics, to be a more active partisan" (pp. 206–207). The self-confident citizen not only thinks "he can participate, he thinks that others ought to participate as well." Involvement in decision making within the family, school, and workplace, along with formal education, stand out as the primary developmental factors in the life histories of competent citizens. But what about the underlying historical forces and the causal sequence? These forces are largely unstudied, and so are their linkages to individual lives.

In *Becoming Modern*, Inkeles and Smith (1974) assign particular significance to schools, urban experience, factory work, and the mass media as sources of individual modernization. Qualities of individual modernity are geared to the requirements of a factory system. They include openness to new experience, readiness for social change, a range of opinions and attitudes, a well informed sense of efficacy, an orientation toward time and planning, trust, and personal ambition. The authors use age of worker to identify life stage, rather than historical location, and thus we never learn how the workers' lives relate to the major social changes of their time.

Inkeles and Smith (1974) suggest that schooling, urban residence, and factory work consistently enhance workers' modernity. For example, "Men of rural origin who stayed in the countryside to farm as their fathers had done were most likely to be frozen at the level of modernity that characterized them when they left school" (p. 285). Still largely unknown at the end of the study, however, is the process by which experiences fostered a modern outlook. Level of schooling does not tell us about the content of education, and duration of factory work leaves much about work experiences to the imagination. *Becoming Modern* provides a useful map of change influences for the next research step, an in-depth study of particular agents of historical change, such as the more successful factories.

These two studies establish an agenda for linking modernization with lives and personality. Using cross-sectional samples of the adult population, they view age status as an index of life stage rather than as an index of historical location and cohort membership. Each research design represents an outcome model that ignores other potential outcomes and, in particular, restricts the coverage of historical influences. Of course, these two studies could be viewed as the first phase of a multiphase project. The second phase begins with a social change and explicates its effects, transitory and enduring.

Explication of cohort and period effects guides the next step (Figure 6.2; Model B) by directing inquiry to a particular time, place, and event or condition. In the case of family events, such as marriages and births, estimates might direct inquiry to the 1930s and the postwar years. Beginning with an event, such as drastic income change, research would trace its effects through proximal and distal situations. By seeking to understand the consequences of a type of social change for the life course, an event design pursues the implications of change wherever they may lead. As shown in Model B (Figure 6.2), the consequences typically branch out across time, generating a number of outcomes. Proximal implications tend to emerge from an account of the change itself and then produce implications of their own for the life course.

This change in life experience is most clearly observed through primary environments, such as the family and peer group. *The Polish Peasant* (Thomas & Znaniecki, 1918-1920) followed this approach, as did *Children of the Great Depression* (Elder, 1974). For example, Thomas and Znaniecki show that emigration and resettlement of Polish immigrants in urban centers of the new world initiated a breakdown of traditional lifeways and a period of family disorganization in which family norms lost their effectiveness in regulating the behavior of members. These family dynamics, in turn, had consequences for individual behavior. Promiscuity and juvenile delinquency were common among the adolescent offspring of disorganized homes.

The event design relates history and social change to lives and personalities. By sketching the flow of influence from macrohistorical developments to the world of the individual, this formulation gives particular visibility to a sequence of downward causation across different levels of analysis. Thus government action in wartime affects the individual through locality groups such as the community, neighborhood, and family. Influences also flow in the other direction, most notably as the individual structures relationships and selects certain environments. Both causal directions illumine family and child experiences across periods of social change (Elder, Caspi, & Downey, 1986; Elder, Liker, & Cross, 1984).

The outcome perspective of Model A could serve as the initial step toward an explication of historical influences in Model B. But as a rule, research proceeds no further than Model A and its estimates of age, cohort, and period effects. The ambiguous meaning of such effects leaves room for speculation that can masquerade as empirical evidence. Speculation thus becomes a pseudofact with a life of its own. And as Robert Merton observes (1959, p. xv), pseudofacts "have a way of inducing pseudoproblems, which cannot be solved because matters are not as they purport to be."

Speculation and pseudofacts fare especially poorly in relation to the immense and compelling problems of a rapidly changing society. Our work is concerned with such rapid changes and especially with the children, born in the 1920s, who experienced at various times in their lives the historical sequence of a great depression, a world war, and a few years of peace and prosperity, followed by the Korean conflict. Their children grew up in the Vietnam era, facing the perils and dilemmas of this age.

To understand the imprint of changing times on the lives of these Americans, we must trace their effects through the primary worlds of family, work, and friends, since it is these environments that give specific meaning to new conditions. The Social Change Project illustrates this strategy with studies of Depression and wartime influences across the life course and generations.

CHANGING TIMES AND LIVES

Five conceptual issues define our thinking about the interaction between changing times and lives: control cycles, situational imperatives, the accentuation principle, the life stage distinction, and the concept of interdependent lives (Figure 6.3). The first three concepts refer to the correspondence between a changing environment and the life course. Using Murray's (1938) terminol-

FIGURE 6.3 Linking mechanisms.

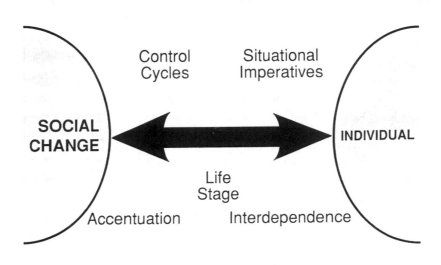

ogy, this correspondence refers to the press-need relationship in the fit between situation and person. The life stage distinction indicates where the
person is located within the life-span (older or younger) when major social
change occurs, and the concept of interdependence locates all lives in relation
to others who mediate the influence of social change.

Control Cycles

As elaborated from Thomas's early writings on crisis situations, social change
creates a disparity between claims and resources, goals and accomplishments,
and the corresponding loss of control prompts efforts to regain control. The
entire process resembles a *control cycle*. This cyclical process centers on the
connection between losing control and efforts to restore control over life
outcomes, a process documented by studies of reactance behavior.

Reactance feelings occur whenever one or more freedoms or expectations
are eliminated or threatened. Such feelings motivate efforts to regain or
preserve control. The Brehms (1982) refer to the substantial evidence for such
motivation and note that "it is the threat to control (which one already had)
that motivates an attempt to deal with the environment. And the attempts to
deal with the environment can be characterized as attempts to regain control"
(p. 375). Bandura (1987) stresses the motivating effects of setting higher
goals, achieving them, and setting even higher goals. The process entails the
production *and* reduction of discrepancies, disequilibration, and equilibration.

Four phases mark the relation between social change and control cycles:

1. The disparity between claims and resources may occur through increasing claims, declining resources, or a discontinuity between acquired and needed resources.
2. The experience of losing control over one's life situation evolves from the preceding disparity; the greater the disparity, the greater the sense of loss.
3. Enhanced by a sense of personal efficacy (see Bandura, 1987), efforts to restore control involve adjusting claims, resources, or both in terms of their relation. Equilibrium is achieved when claims match resources. Once claims are realized, they may be raised, thereby setting in motion another round of equilibrating initiatives. Residential change or migration can be viewed effectively from this vantage point (Priemus, 1986; Wolpert, 1966).
4. Potential alteration or recasting of the life course occurs through new lines of adaptation and their consequences. Women's employment is one example for hard pressed families, and career switching for more earnings is another.

The precipitating event for this process is one that substantially alters the balance between claims and resources. As the balance changes, the actor's control potential is threatened, and adaptive responses are called into play. Adaptive responses, of course, depend on current conditions, the structured situation in history. Responses to historical transitions and the loss of personal control entail choices among given options, and this constraint illustrates how a social institution (e.g., the economy) might shape the life course.

Situational Imperatives

One of the most important considerations in the dynamic of control cycles is the behavioral requirements or demands of the new situation. We refer to these demands as *situational imperatives*. In the 1930s, the imperatives of hard times for children were expressed in large part through households that became more labor intensive. Instead of the purchase of services and goods, family members had to produce more of these services and goods with their own labor. In this new world, young children had valued roles to play; they could contribute something to their family through an expanded range of chores and community tasks. In many respects, deprived families resembled an undermanned environment in which the work to be done exceeded the available labor. Such conditions favored an accelerated pace of movement toward adult status, a pace responsive to the "downward extension of adult-like obligations" in Depression times (Elder, 1974). What are the behavioral implications of this kind of environment? Barker (1968, p. 190) found inhabitants of undermanned settings to be involved in more challenging and consequential actions when compared to the occupants of overmanned environments; they are "busier, more versatile, and more orientated vis-a-vis the settings they inhabit, and more independent."

Another example of situational imperatives comes from a program of research on work and personality (Kohn, 1977; Kohn & Schooler, 1983). This research shows that the behavioral imperatives of work shape how men and women think and function. The most powerful imperative is occupational self-direction; the greater the self-direction, the more workers deal with substantively complex, nonroutinized tasks that entail minimal supervision. Job conditions that encourage self-direction are conducive to effective intellectual functioning and an open, flexible approach to others.

Both worker and situation must be part of a model in order to account for how aspects of the work setting and organization are linked to the personality of workers. Consider, for example, the degree of control a person exercises over the work process. In Kohn and Schooler's research, self-directed men seek control over their work, and such control reinforces a self-directed orientation. When this match fails to occur, the mismatch sets in motion a control cycle dynamic like that described earlier.

The Accentuation Principle

Adaptive responses are shaped by the requirements of the new situation, but they also depend on the social and psychological resources people bring to the newly changed situation. Individual and relational attributes, such as coping styles and the marital bond, affect adaptation to new circumstances. The *accentuation principle* refers to the increase in emphasis or salience of these already prominent characteristics during social transitions in the life course.

One of the earliest documented cases of accentuation comes from the pioneering research of Newcomb on women students of newly established Bennington College in rural Vermont, late 1930s (Newcomb, 1943). In the liberal environment of Bennington, entering students who were relatively independent of parental influences tended to shift their social and political attitudes more toward the college norm than other students.

Over 30 years later, Newcomb returned to this problem of personal change in a survey of the college student literature. With Feldman (1969), he concluded that the distinguishing attributes of entering college students were likely to be "reinforced and extended by the experience incurred in those selected settings." Though Newcomb's emphasis changed from a shift in attitudes to the reinforcement of initial views, both studies show the accentuation of dispositions through the interaction of life history and the demands of the new situation.

A similar account comes from Allport, Bruner, and Jandorf (1941) in a neglected study of personality under social catastrophe. Analyzing personal documents reporting the experiences of 90 individuals during the Nazi revolution, they argued that "very rarely does catastrophic . . . change produce catastrophic alterations in personality." On the contrary, the basic structure of personality persists despite the upset and upheaval in the total life space. Moreover, where change does take place, "it seems invariably to accentuate trends clearly present in the pre-crisis personality."

Transitions, historical and contemporary, frequently entail accentuation processes. A contemporary example appears in the literature on the transition of white and black children to the first grade. In a longitudinal sample of Baltimore children, Entwisle and Alexander (1988) document the unusual vulnerability of lower status black children to a downward academic spiral across this transition. In the higher-status group, black children did at least as well as white children in their school performance through first and second grade. However, the racial gap expanded markedly across this time period for the less advantaged children.

Black children did not do as well even though "the personal resources they brought with them—beginning test-scores, personal maturity level, and their home backgrounds, look similar to those of the white children." In an effort to explain this accentuation of the failure risk for disadvantaged black children, Entwisle and Alexander conclude that the primary influences appear to be more integral to the school environment than to the family. Teacher grading proved to be more negative for black than for white children, even though the children's original test scores were not different. More generally, they found that the evaluative contexts of school were much less supportive of black than of white children.

The accentuation of individual differences by historical transitions applies especially to stressful times. In the Great Depression, for example, severe economic hardship tended to make irritable and explosive men more explosive (Elder, Caspi, & Van Nguyen, 1986; Liker & Elder, 1983). This behavior undermined the quality of marriages and increased the arbitrary and punitive character of parental discipline. Corresponding outcomes on accentuation are reported by Patterson (1988) in samples of mothers and their children. On the other side of the equation are resources that moderate the adverse effects of family stress, such as nurturant marital relations and kin support. As we shall see later in this chapter, the selective accentuation of individual dispositions at points of stressful social transitions represents a powerful source of a well documented trend by age, that of increasing cohort heterogeneity up to old age.

The Life Stage Principle

A related principle derives from cohort research and addresses the *life-stage principle*: The influence of a historical event on the life course depends on the stage at which individuals experience the event. The life-stage principle offers a perspective on families and children that locates them within the life course and its age-graded tasks and experiences. It implies that the effects of social change should vary in type and relative influence across the life course and alerts the investigator to the complexity of interactions among historical, social, psychological, and biological factors.

Consider two families in 1930: Family A has two children born around 1920, and Family B has two children born in 1928 to 1930. On the basis of the life stage principle, we would expect the meaning and significance of Depression hardship to vary significantly between the two sets of children. The older children were 9 to 16 years old during the height of the Depression, too young to leave school and face a dismal employment situation and too old to be highly dependent on the family. By comparison, the younger children were 1 to 8 years old, ages when they were most dependent on their families in the midst of the economic crisis and thus at greatest risk of impaired development and life opportunities.

In addition to these differences, the historical experiences of offspring in these two families may have varied according to the ages of the parents. The parents in Family A were much older than those in Family B. Because an economic decline makes a difference in families through the lives of parents, this age difference has powerful implications for children.

Within the same family or household, siblings occupy different life stages at a point in history, no matter how small the variation may be, and differences of this kind are coupled with historical variation as well. In the past we thought of the chronology of siblings in terms of birth-order effects within the family. Now we recognize that children separated by a few years may grow up in very different times. Siblings only 5 years apart in 1940 were as different in history as the difference between combat experience on the island of Bougainville in the South Pacific and a class party at Berkeley High School.

Diverse life histories become the interweave of family and ties, softening the edges of cohort uniqueness. Through interdependent lives, the family serves as a meeting ground for members of different cohorts (Hagestad, 1982). With each person's actions a part of the social context of other members, any change in a member's life constitutes a change in the lives and context of other members.

Interdependent Lives

The concept of interdependent lives represents a central theme of family systems theories (Minuchin, 1985) and the life course approach. Systems approaches assume that the family is a social group, and its functioning as a whole is different from the sum of its parts. This arises because the properties of the family as a whole are derived from the properties of the relationships between individuals in the family and not just from the characteristics of the individuals as separate persons.

The expansion of analytic models from a dyadic unit (e.g., mother-child) to a family system (e.g., mother-father-child) provides knowledge of how interactions between two people influence and are influenced by a third person. The response of each person to the other is conditioned by his or her joint relationship to a third person. Thus changes within any individual or relationship may affect all other persons and relationships.

From a broader perspective, social change is expressed in lives through the experience of others, and the dynamics of interdependent represent a critical means by which macro events affect individual development (Elder, Caspi, & Burton, 1988). Consider, for example, the difference between growing up in the trying years of the Great Depression and in a society wholly mobilized for global war, 1940 to 1945. Here were literally two worlds of adolescence marked by the contrasting experience of significant others, including parents, grand parents, siblings, friends, and acquaintances. Hardship in the Great Depression influenced the lives of adolescents through the economic and job losses of their parents and also through its effects on relatives and neighbors. For example, the deprivations of relatives who were forced to double up often added to the strain of the times.

For young people during World War II, the distinctive features of adolescence included the military service of their fathers, brothers, and friends, the war-related employment of parents from sunup to sundown, and the mobilization of school children through the schools and churches for resource drives and civil defense. To understand these historical changes in the lives of adolescents, a study must regard this ever-changing social network as a linking process. All lives are lived interdependently, and this connectedness defines a medium through which historical change plays out its influence over time.

Control cycles, situational imperatives, processes of accentuation, life stage distinctions, and interdependent lives together provide an account of linkages between social change and life patterns. In the Social Change Project, this connection occurs through individuals, social relationships, and their interplay over time in situations with varying requirements. The dynamic evolves through families, a meeting ground for interdependent lives, and through other primary environments such as friendships. From this vantage point, the interaction between historical time and lifetime is a function of changes in the life course of all family members.

Children of Social History

With these issues in mind, our work examines the historical context of two birth cohorts who lived through the Great Depression and World War II: the

Oakland Growth sample of 167 members (birth dates, 1920–1921) and the
Berkeley Guidance sample of 214 members (birth dates, 1928–1929). Data
were collected on these cohorts across the 1930s on an annual basis and during
widely spaced follow-ups up to the 1980s. With pre-Depression birth dates
that differ by about 8 years, these cohorts appear to share the historical times
of the 1920s to the 1940s. In both cohorts, the Depression experience had
much to do with the sudden and prolonged misfortune of families. However,
Figure 6.4 shows prominent cohort variations in developmental stage at points
of prosperity, severe hardship, and war mobilization.

All members of the Oakland cohort were young children during the prosperity of the 1920s, a period of remarkable economic growth in California and
especially in the San Francisco Bay region. This stable childhood ensured a
measure of security and developmental continuity when they entered the
harsh, erratic regime of the Great Depression. They were too old by then to be
wholly dependent on the misfortunes of deprived households, and they avoided
the scars of widespread joblessness after high school by entering college and
the labor market as the country mobilized for war. Most of the men served
in the armed forces of World War II.

By contrast, members of the Berkeley cohort followed a timetable that
maximized their vulnerability to the historical upheavals of the time. They
encountered family hardships during the vulnerable years of early childhood
and the developmental problems of adolescence during a period of mass
mobilization in World War II. The Bay region became a war zone under the

FIGURE 6.4 Interaction of historical time and life stage.

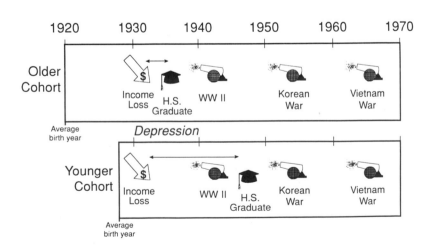

jurisdiction of the Fifth Army Command, and various signs of war mobilization exposed the young to an unsettled, if exhilarating, world. These include the mass transports of troops to Bay area ports and the Pacific theater, the large influx of war workers and their families, and round-the-clock activity of war industries and shipyards in the area. For members of the Berkeley cohort, deprivations of a childhood in the 1930s were soon followed by the disruptions and pressures of war.

A thorough understanding of the changing world of the Oakland and Berkeley cohorts must attend to both economic depression and war. But to take these times into account, we first had to make sense of the Depression years. An essential point of departure in studying the Depression experience is the wide variation in family loss. Some families lost heavily, while others managed to avoid meaningful losses altogether. Keeping this variation in mind, along with a 25% drop in cost of living, we identified two deprivational groups within the middle and working classes of 1929, using income loss (1929–1933) relative to the decline in cost of living (about 25% over this period). Families experienced heavy losses in assets only when the income loss exceeded 40% of their 1929 income. Accordingly, we defined deprived families in terms of losses about 34%; all other families were classified as nondeprived. This division proved to be equally well suited to the Berkeley cohort. By this criterion, 35% of the Berkeley families in the middle class were deprived, compared to 57% of the working-class families. Deprived families were more prevalent in both strata of the Oakland cohort (56% middle class vs. 69% working class), a difference that partially reflects the more business-oriented character of Oakland's economy.

From the early 1930s to the end of the decade, three modes of change distinguished the deprived families of Oakland and Berkeley from relatively nondeprived families: changes in family economy, family relationships, and level of social and psychological stress (Figure 6.5).

Drastic income loss shifted the household toward more labor-intensive operations by increasing (1) indebtedness as savings diminished, (2) curtailment and postponement of expenditures, (3) reliance on the earnings of women and older children, and (4) the substitution of family labor for money in acquiring goods and services. The labor-intensive household entailed a new system of behavioral imperatives (Elder, 1974; Elder, Van Nguyen, & Caspi, 1985).

Changes in family relationships, initiated by men's loss of earnings and jobs, represent the second mode of family change. Efforts to boost family support increased by the relative power of mothers, reduced the level and effectiveness of paternal control, and diminished the attractiveness of fathers as role models. Mothers became more central figures in the family, both in terms of affection and authority. The nature of family interdependence changed in response to the growing pressures of economic dislocation and loss.

FIGURE 6.5 Family patterns as linkages.

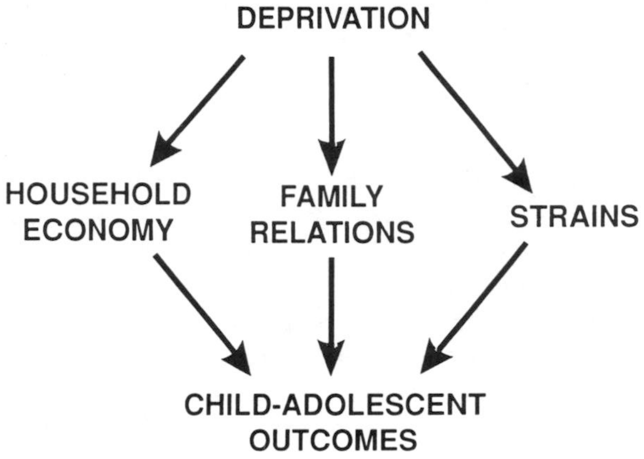

The third mode of change occurred through greater tensions, conflicts, and violence. Family deprivation increased men's behavioral impairment through heavy drinking, emotional depression, and health disabilities and the arbitrary and inconsistent discipline of children (Elder, Liker, & Cross, 1984; Elder, Liker, & Jaworski, 1984; Liker & Elder, 1983).

Although economic deprivation produced similar changes in the family environment of both cohorts (division of labor, altered family relationships, social strains), its developmental effects varied in ways that conform to differences in life stage relative to historical events. Historical conditions are variable at points in time and in how they are experienced by individuals of different ages. By encountering such times at different points in life, Oakland and Berkeley men and women have different stories to tell about their childhood and adolescence (Elder, 1979; Elder, Caspi, & Van Nguyen, 1986).

As young adolescents during the early 1930s, the Oakland males avoided the risk of being wholly dependent on a hard pressed family and of leaving school for the nether world of unemployment. As the economy worsened, their family hardships meant adult-like responsibilities. In deprived households, boys were more apt to aspire to grown-up status and to enter adult roles of marriage and work at an early age. Although self-image disturbances were characteristic of the economically deprived (an intense desire for social acceptance, emotional vulnerability, and self-consciousness), they showed little evidence of enduring disadvange or impairment from the Depression experience up to midlife.

Part of the reason centers on their unique family roles in economically deprived circumstances. The older Oakland boys were more likely to assume jobs outside the home in order to aid the financially troubled family. Family change of this sort enhanced their social and family independence and reduce their exposure to conflict and turmoil in the home.

By lowering adult-like responsibilities toward the adolescent years, the Great Depression accelerated the passage to adult roles. The same acceleration has been noted among contemporary children in one-parent households and in paid jobs. As Weiss (1979) has put it, children in these households "grow up faster." The contemporary work experience of teenage Americans may have adverse consequences, from premature affluence to less investment in schooling (Greenberg & Steinberg, 1986), but these effects do not appear in our data on the Oakland cohort.

A plausible reason for this difference involves the effect of hard times on families: The shift of households from capital to labor intensive made room for the valued contribution of children. These children had productive roles to perform. But in a more general sense, they were needed, and, in being needed, they had the chance and responsibility to make a real contribution to the welfare of others. Being needed gives rise to a sense of belonging and place, of being committed to something larger than the self. However onerous the task may be, there is gratification and even personal growth to be gained in being challenged by a real undertaking if it is not excessive or exploitative (Elder, 1974, p. 291).

But this is only part of the explanation. From a developmental standpoint, the wartime experience of this cohort was as consequential as their Depression experience. Nearly all of the Oakland men were in uniform by the time of the Normandy invasion in June 1944, and few were discharged before a completed term of 3 years. The military experience of Oakland men in World War II provided opportunities and initiatives for altering the substance and course of their later lives. Military service removed the Oakland men from the immediate influence and setting of home and community. In this sense, the transition represented a passage from family dependence to greater independence and autonomy. This family separation has noteworthy implications for men who came from mother-dominated and discordant families, as did a good many Oakland men from deprived households. The service also represented a moratorium relative to the age-graded life course, a legitimate time-out from the commitment pressures that Erikson (1959) describes in the concept of role diffusion.

However, the most critical implication of military service for the Oakland men involved the educational and vocational benefits of military service, both during the period of active duty and after returning to civilian life. The postwar benefits were most tangibly linked to the benefits of the Servicemen's Readjustment Act of 1944, the GI Bill (Olson, 1974). Estimates suggest that nearly half a million veterans took advantage of the GI Bill. Some of these men were members of the Oakland cohort (Figure 6.6). One can thus assume that wartime experiences and outcomes altered the Depression's legacy in the lives of Oakland males.

FIGURE 6.6 GI benefits by age at entry among Oakland veterans, in percentages.

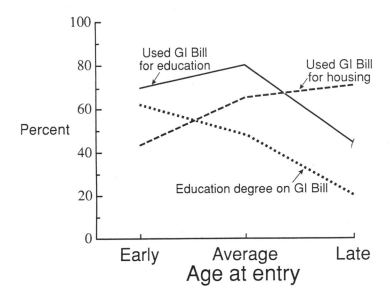

Adolescence carried very different meanings for females in the Oakland cohort who grew up deprived, and this may have much to do with the psychological vulnerability of early adolescent girls to environmental stress and to the self-esteem costs of social pressures in the larger social world of peers and school. During junior and senior high school, Oakland females from deprived families were socially disadvantaged relative to daughters of more affluent parents; the deprived were less well dressed in school than the nondeprived and more often felt excluded from the groups and social activities of age mates. The deprived girls were also more self-conscious and experienced more hurt feelings and mood swings.

The finding that girls appear to be more vulnerable than boys to environmental insult during the second decade of life has been previously detected in cross-sectional studies (e.g., Hetherington, 1981). Recent longitudinal studies similarly suggest that the transition into adolescence represents a time of psychological vulnerability for girls, and self-image disturbances appear to be more common among girls than boys during this period (Simmons & Blythe, 1987; Werner & Smith, 1982). Our findings suggest that family adaptations to drastic income loss may have compounded these stage-specific developmental difficulties for girls.

Indeed, the vulnerability of Oakland girls may be accounted for, in part, by their unique family experience in deprived households (Elder et al., 1985). In the scarcity economy of such households, the older Oakland girls were often called upon to assume major responsibilities as their mothers sought work. Family change of this sort meant greater exposure to discord and tension, especially from hard pressed fathers, and involved them in adult-like responsibilities that assigned priority to a domestic career of marriage and parenthood. Not surprisingly, in their life course and values, the deprived Oakland females resemble most the "ultra-domestic" climate of the postwar years. During adolescence, these girls were more inclined to favor marriage and family over a career when compared to girls who were spared family hardship, they tended to marry at an earlier age, and they more frequently dropped out of the labor force after marriage or before the birth of their first child. At midlife, family, children, and homemaking distinguished their priorities from those of the nondeprived, regardless of educational level or current social position.

These observations and findings apply only to adolescents in the Oakland cohort. Members of the Berkeley cohort encountered the same historical events, but at a different point in their lives. Seven to 8 years younger than their Oakland counterparts, the Berkeley children experienced the economic crisis when they were more dependent on family nurturance and more vulnerable to family instability, emotional strain, and conflict (Rutter, 1979). Family hardship came early in their lives and entailed a more prolonged deprivation experience, from the economic trough to the war years and departure from home. Thus in the Berkeley cohort, the causal link between economic deprivation in the early 1930s and adolescent behavior included a continuing pattern of socioeconomic instability, with its distorting influence on family life—the emotional strain of resource exhaustion, the loss of an effective, nurturant father, and marital discord.

Our findings show that the Berkeley boys who grew up in deprived households were less likely to be hopeful, self-directed, and confident about their future than youth who were spared such hardship. This dysphoric outlook is one element of a syndrome that emerged from personality ratings in adolescence—personal and social inadequacy, a passive mode of responding to life situations, feelings of victimization, withdrawal from adversity, and self-defeating behavior. In addition, boys from deprived families held lower aspirations during wartime adolescence than children from nondeprived families (no difference in IQ), and their scholastic performance turned sharply downward at this point, falling well below that of boys from nondeprived homes. Whereas deprivation among Oakland adolescents led to greater mobilization of effort and ambition for adult work and family security, the same historical conditions among the younger Berkeley boys fostered lowered expectations and achievements.

Moreover, whereas World War II may have functioned as a key turning point in the lives of the older Oakland males, the homefront experience of

Berkeley males provided an entirely different set of circumstances. They encountered World War II in the context of a family environment shaped by events of the depressed 1930s, and the return to better times through economic recovery during the later 1930s and war years did not always favor a more involved and effective role for deprived fathers in their lives. A good many of these fathers worked overtime in the late 1930s out of fear of job loss and economic need. In addition, labor shortages during World War II extended this pattern and drew mothers into the labor force. Perhaps even more than the Depression era, civilian mobilization reduced the effective home presence of both mothers and fathers for the Berkeley boys.

A different picture emerges among the Berkeley females. They were not less goal oriented, competent, or assertive than the nondeprived. Indeed, a deprived family environment actually offered greater family security for the younger Berkeley girls, a difference that reflects the warmth of mother-daughter relations under conditions of extreme hardship (Elder, Downey, & Cross, 1986). This female bond stands out as the strongest intergenerational tie among families in the Great Depression and represents a more general theme of family and kinship where male support is precarious or absent.

But if such bonds generally develop under economic hardship, why don't we find similar outcomes for the Oakland and Berkeley girls? In fact, there are similarities. In both cohorts, girls from deprived families were more likely to experience marital discord, a growing prominence of mothers as authority and affectional figures, and a more peripheral status among fathers.

The important difference involves the social-developmental status of the two groups of girls at the time of family hardship and the greater social involvement of the older girls with other girls and boys. Owing in large part to their families' precarious status, the Oakland girls were less equipped with clothes and a home life for social confidence and success. The younger Berkeley girls, however, were too young to face the competitive heterosexual pressures of secondary school.

Our findings suggest that the Berkeley girls fared substantially better than boys in relation to family stress. This corresponds with other research on sex differences in stress, coping, and development (Eme, 1979; Rutter, 1982). Various explanations have been offered for the consistent finding that during the first decade of life, boys are more vulnerable to environmental insult. In general, males are more vulnerable to a wide range of physical hazards, and it is possible that there is a parallel, biologically determined susceptibility to psychosocial stressors (Earls, 1987). It is also possible that boys' vulnerability to family stress may be a consequence of the greater extent of their exposure to discord (Hetherington, 1981) or of parents' different responses to problem behavior in boys than in girls (Maccoby & Jacklin, 1983; Snow, Jacklin, & Maccoby, 1983). Boys are more likely to react to family stress with disruptive behaviors, a type of reaction that is more likely to elicit a negative response from parents (Emery, 1982).

Moreover, assuming that control over the environment is more important for young boys than for girls, the environment of a discordant family in stressful times may be more disturbing for boys (Gunnar-Vongnechten, 1978). Block, Block, and Morrison (1981) have suggested, in addition, that the salience of the two parents may differ for boys and girls; for girls, the lesser salience of the father may attenuate the effects of family discord. This seems especially plausible in light of household changes in the Great Depression, since fathers' loss of earnings and resulting adaptation in family support increased the relative power of mothers concerning affection, authority, and completion of basic tasks and diminished the attractiveness of fathers as role models. At this point, however, we can draw no firm conclusions about the precise reasons for the heightened vulnerability of young boys to economic stress in the family, and the true picture likely reflects complex interactions among the processes enumerated above.

Collectively, these variations tell us much about the implications of life stage in the Depression experience. So also do situational imperatives and factors that accentuate or moderate the effect of family hardship, another theoretical principle. Consider the causal chain between heavy income loss and children's acting-out behavior (Elder, Caspi, & Van Nguyen, 1986). Children were most likely to be ill treated when fathers became more explosive, tense, and emotionally unstable. Families that suffered heavy losses became more discordant because of sharply rising financial tensions and the more volatile state of men. The more irritable and explosive men became under economic pressure, the more they tended to behave punitively and arbitrarily toward their offspring. Finally, such behavior by fathers increased the risk of children's negativism, tantrums, and irritability. This sequence was especially pronounced when fathers were unstable or irritable before their economic misfortune. Hard times made explosive men more explosive.

The strength of this sequence also increased when initial family relationships were hostile or weak, whether between father and child, mother and child, or the two parents. Consider a general model that defines the acting-out behavior of children as one result of a process in which fathers' emotional instability and family income loss increased their arbitrary behavior. The more arbitrary the behavior of fathers, the greater the likelihood of their children exhibiting problem behavior. The causal sequence is strongest when mothers ranked below average on affectional support for their children prior to the Depression. Children's vulnerability increased as maternal support decreased. By contrast, the presence of maternal support notably reduced the sustaining mechanisms for children's problem behavior during stressful times.

Overall, life stage distinctions proved to be essential for tracing out the short- and long-term effects of family hardship in the Great Depression. We located people according to their place in life and history as a first step toward relating events to actual families and lives. Any historical transition becomes a life transition for at least some people, and the control cycle principle provides some understanding of how social change promotes change in the life course. Families and individuals adapt to loss in ways that ensure greater control over life outcomes, and efforts to understand these adaptational efforts also draw attention to the behavioral implications of newly constructed situational imperatives. Moreover, the dynamics of change and adaptation were accentuated and moderated by personal and social factors in the hardship experience of the 1930s. For example, explosive men became more explosive under economic pressure, unravelling family ties and support. Finally, these various changes and adaptational efforts had to be considered in terms of a network of relationships within the family system.

But this is only part of the life story for men and women who were born in the 1920s. As they left the 1930s, the mobilization engines of World War II awaited them with roles and fates unknown. If the Depression experience turned people inward on a domestic problem, the early 1940s exposed them to the plight of a world at war. As we have already suggested, any complete account of Depression children had to move on to the full implications of their adolescence or young adulthood in a time of mass mobilization for war. The Oakland men and women were old enough to actually serve in the armed forces, whereas the war typically meant a home front adolescence for members of the Berkeley cohort. Nearly 90% of the Oakland men served in World War II, and approximately 70% of the Berkeley men served in the Korean conflict.

Initial efforts to probe the life course implications of wartime and military service produced some unexpected results. Surprisingly little work had examined the aftermath of wartime experience and military service in the lives of men and women. By comparison, studies of men in the service or immediately after discharge are quite common. The best known is the *American Soldier* series (Stouffer et al., 1949; Stouffer, Suchman, DeVinney, Star, & Williams, 1949). In addition, we found that little thought had been given to the conceptual relevance of war mobilization and military service for the life course. The only exception here concerns the experience of combat. These observations gain special significance in view of the nearly 20 million veterans from the 1940s and the Korean conflict who are now entering the later years of life. Nothing substantial is known about the enduring influence of an experience that many veterans regard as the most vivid, formative time of their adult life.

The complexity of wartime influences called for a strict scheduling of priorities in the research effort. For obvious reasons, we decided to begin with the male experience of war, military service, and military mobilization rather than with mobilization on the home front. Women in uniform were simply too scarce to permit analysis. An account of home front mobilization is planned in the near future and will pay special attention to the lives of both men and women.

MILITARY TIMES IN LIVES

Our studies of military times in the life course focus on three dimensions: the timing of mobilization, exposure to combat, and social relations (Figure 6.7). The timing of mobilization is an example of the life-stage principle at work. Members of a cohort who join up at different times in life are likely to experience different life courses. Combat resembles Depression hardship in being a traumatizing experience or event. Following the innovative approaches of Vietnam studies, we view combat as a multifaceted experience defined by variable exposure to death, gunfire, and firing. Social relations in wartime mediate the influence of combat on psychological well-being and social ties, just as families mediated the effects of Depression hardship in the 1930s.

War, Military Service, and Mobilization

Military mobilization severed many Depression youth from a past that meant hardship and restricted opportunity. In the transition to adulthood, "being mobilized" closed some options, created others, and postponed still others. For the most part, the military service broke with a past defined by hardship, frustration, and limited opportunity. Placed within this context, the military and its situational imperatives acquired special developmental significance in relation to the life course. In particular, mobilization promoted social independence, represented a legitimate time-out from the age-graded career, and broadened experiences.

The first feature of military experience entailed the "knifing-off" of past experience (Brotz & Wilson, 1946). Induction meant separation from the immediate influence of family and community, allowing a degree of social independence coupled with the establishment of new social ties. In particular, basic training fostered equality and comradeship among recruits by separating them from their pasts. It made prior identities irrelevant, required uniform dress and appearance, minimized privacy, and rewarded performance on the basis of group achievement. The irrelevance of a deprived background in this world produced a sense of being on one's own in obligation to mates. An Oakland veteran recalled his experience as "instant maturity." Similarly, an Oakland marine remembered entering this new world "sink or swim." Another spoke about "the unforgiving en-

FIGURE 6.7 War mobilization and military experience.

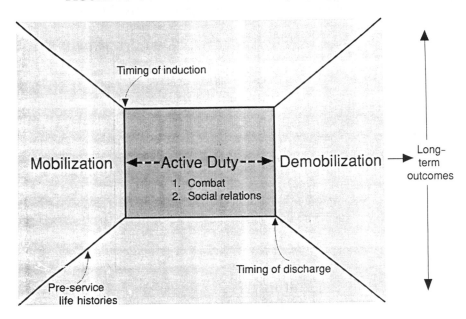

vironment" where the consequences of personal failure were felt by the entire unit.

A second feature of the military experience is the extent to which service time represents a clear-cut break from the age-graded career—a time-out or moratorium. Military duty provides a legitimate time-out from education, work, and family; it releases the recruit from the conventional expectations of an age-graded career. As a rule, presence in the service is not questioned, and neither is lack of career progress or work plans. The fact of military service provides adequate justification. Indeed, Stouffer and his associates (1949, vol. 2) noted that for many soldiers in World War II, "perhaps for a majority, the break caused by Army service [meant] a chance to evaluate where they had gotten and to reconsider where they were going" (p. 572).

For deprived youth who lacked self-direction and a sense of adequacy, military service offered developmental alternatives to the course charted by their families—separation from maternal control through involvement in a masculine culture, a legitimate time-out from work and educational pressures in a structured environment, and the opportunity to sort things out in activities that bolstered self-confidence, resolve, and goal setting. Some of these themes appear in the life reviews of veterans from deprived households, especially the "break" from a confused and painful family situation. One man recalled that he "finally realized what was happening and broke away, entered the Navy." Another described the time he joined the Army at 18 as the end of his mother's domination and the beginning of independence. Several men recalled the novel and rewarding experience of mastery on military tasks, of doing something well and on their own. Across this period, we see a contrast between descriptions of self before and after time in the military—from the implication of being "such a flop" in adolescence that "I couldn't do anything" to the claim that from "the day I went into the service, I was almost on my own . . . figured out my own situation and went on from there."

A third feature of mobilization entails a broadened range of perspective and social knowledge. Mobilization increases the scope of awareness of one-self and others and does so through an expanded range of interactional experiences, including new people and places, which promote greater tolerance of social diversity. Willard Waller (1940) once likened the process to "stirring soup; people are thrown together who have never seen one another before and will never see one another again" (p. 14). Out of this experience come greater awareness of self and others, an expanded range of interactional experiences with their behavior models and social support, and possibly a greater social tolerance of diversity. A veteran interviewed just after World War II in Havighurst's study (Havighurst, Baughman, Burgess, & Eaton, 1951, p. 188) spoke about the incredible diversity of his acquaintances in the service and their influence on his views. As he put it, the experience "sort of opens up your horizons. . . . You start thinking in broader terms than you did before."

Greater independence, a broader range of experience, and a time-out from career pressures do not exhaust features of war mobilization in World War II, but together they defined a pathway that offered a promising route to life opportunity and adult development for young men from the Depression decade.

Time of Mobilization

The timing of mobilization into the armed forces emerges as one of the most powerful determinants of service influences on the lives of men in both cohorts, Oakland and Berkeley (Elder, 1986, 1987). In both cases, the disadvantaged were more likely to be mobilized shortly after high school than other males. Three modes of disadvantage were most consequential: membership in an economically deprived family during the Great Depression, poor high school grades (although not lower IQ), and feelings of inadequacy in adolescence. All three factors predicted an early timing of military service and its route to greater opportunity. By midlife, however, the amount of social inequality among veterans before military service diminished to insignificance. In particular, the early entrants no longer appeared more disadvantaged than the later entrants in postwar America.

Early entry into military service functioned as a turning point in the life course, and it did so in two ways. One pathway involved situational changes that made the early entrants more ambitious, self-directed, and disciplined (Elder, 1986). Military service and its situational imperatives benefitted men from deprived circumstances by promoting independence, exposing recruits to new ideas and models, and providing a legitimate time-out or moratorium for those who were unsure of the course to follow in life. As a veteran of the Pacific theater explained, "A man's life can't help but expand when you go through things like that. You see things from a different perspective than you ever had before" (Havighurst et al., 1951, p. 172). Moreover, early entry tended to delay the timing of marriage and children, whereas later entry usually came after such events and in many cases actually disrupted family units. This disruption was expressed in a higher rate of marital dissolution among late entrants. Indeed, looking back on their military service from the 1980s, the late entrants stressed the disadvantages of their experience, especially in the maintenance of their family life and careers. Early entrants, by comparison, stressed the timeliness of their mobilization and the greater benefits than costs that they experienced over the years.

A second pathway involved the benefits of the GI Bill (Elder, 1987). Remembered now for its educational and housing benefits, the GI Bill was prompted by fear of the social and political danger of widespread unemployment among returning veterans. In many respects, the bill was a "child of 1944; it symbolized the mood of a country immersed in war, recalling the Depression, and worrying about the future" (Olson, 1974, p. 24).

At least in education, the GI Bill became a primary source of greater life opportunity for the California veterans in our studies. One man summed up his feelings this way: The GI Bill was *the* important influence "because it gave me an opportunity to go to college and to buy a home." The education portion of the GI Bill was designed for men in their early adult years—those who were most likely to want to complete an undergraduate education. Thus the usual structure of the life course made the bill and its benefits more attractive to the younger men who lacked the competing alternatives to higher education, such as marriage and a family or a full-time job. Indeed, this account describes well the actual correlation between age at entry and education benefits in both cohorts. Early entrants were far more likely than late entrants to rely on the GI Bill for support in completing an educational degree.

The degree of career change among men who entered the military at a young age corresponds to similar change on the psychological level. When surveyed in later life, the early entrants believed they had changed more since adolescence when compared to the beliefs of men who entered the service late (Elder, 1987). Objective evidence for this comes most directly from the Berkeley cohort. Using Q-sort ratings of personality in adolescence and at midlife, we find that developmental change toward greater self-direction and confidence is most characteristic of the early entrants in the cohort (Elder, 1986).

Overall, the central findings of this research on the timing of mobilization highlight the goodness-of-fit between the life course and historical change. Typically, military mobilization seeks young men not involved in families and career. However, manpower pressures, especially in World War II, prevented strict adherence to this standard. As the scope of recruitment included older men, personal disadvantages of the service multiplied through the incompatibility of simultaneous obligations — career, family, and military. Early entry, however, minimized such role conflicts and maximized the benefits of military service. From this perspective, military service was a timely developmental event for a large number of children who lived through the Great Depression.

Combat Experience

Military mobilization during World War II and the Korean conflict involved combat roles for only a minority of Oakland and Berkeley men. According to our multi-item measure, approximately a third of the veterans experienced heavy combat, and a similar proportion encountered light combat. Combat is unrelated to age at entry.

Stress disorders from combat were typically viewed as transient at the end of World War II. Psychiatric attention to these disorders declined accordingly over the postwar era, though a report in 1965 cites evidence "which demonstrates that many veterans have retained their original combat symptoms of startle reaction, recurrent nightmares, and irritability largely unchanged" (Archibald & Tuddenham, 1965, p. 475). Indeed, even after some 40 years, disturbing nightmares of war trauma have been documented in the lives of World War II veterans (van der Kolk, 1987). This legacy undoubtedly varies according to individual differences prior to combat, for example, on hardiness, stamina, or ego resilience. Indeed, studies of Vietnam veterans place considerable weight on such differences (Hendin & Haas, 1983).

Stress symptoms may persist in part through a life course dynamic in which initial symptomatology is sustained by the progressive accumulation of its interpersonal or social consequences. For example, a veteran's explosiveness and emotional distance may threaten his marriage and thereby reinforce a cycle of irritability and ill temper. With data from the 1985 survey, we find degree of combat experience to be highly correlated with reports of stress symptoms, traumatic memories, and guilt over survival (Elder & Clipp, 1989). Heavy combat veterans are most likely to report emotional and behavioral problems on leaving the service (over 50%), and those who did were more likely than other men to experience war-linked symptoms in later life.

Some 15 years after the end of World War II, a former Oakland marine with landings in the South Pacific spoke about the nightmares that tormented him for so long, the "hollering and screaming in the middle of the night." He observed that "I can close my eyes and feel the water under my arms. . . . the fear was awful. . . . it took every bit of energy I could summon, every bit of self-control, for me to get out of the landing boat." The terrifying nightmares and flashbacks ruled much of his life after demobilization.

> My father tried to wake me up from a nightmare, and I recall jumping out of bed and knocking him down. . . . the minute he touched me, I was up fighting. . . . another time at night he couldn't find me. . . . I was under the bed with my bayonet, scared to death. . . . I would also sit up in bed and count out loud, just as I did when I was using the tourniquet to keep me from bleeding to death. . . . my wife said it drove her crazy, just counting on and on. . . . we were married in 1948 so this stayed with me for a while.

He was still having frightening dreams of his battlefield experience in midlife.

Symptoms of post-traumatic stress are primarily concentrated among these heavy combat veterans, both immediately after the service and years later at midlife. But a large number had no record of these symptoms. Why not? Why did some men experience stress symptoms, while others avoided them altogether? One answer is found in late adolescence. Using ratings at this time, we compared veterans of combat who reported emotional problems on entry into civilian life with combat veterans who reported no problems of this kind. The measures were drawn from the California Q-sort and centered on self-adequacy and introspectiveness. Self-adequacy refers to the ability to achieve personal control, even in the midst of frontline chaos, whereas introspectiveness represents an orientation that amplifies stress (Hansell, Mechanic, & Brondolo, 1986), especially that involving the loss of comrades. On the whole, our findings show that men who expressed postservice symptoms of stress ranked much higher than other men in late adolescence on measures of self-inadequacy and introspectiveness (Elder & Clipp, 1989).

All of these findings refer to the pathology of traumatic combat experiences, yet successful coping with circumstances of this kind can actually build confidence and the resources for managing life's problems. Depending on conditions, a stressor may produce pathology, developmental growth, or a combination of these outcomes. Earlier we applied this dual perspective to severe family hardships in the 1930s, and the results clearly point to both outcomes. Wartime combat is more traumatic, of course, than the usual hardship experiences of the 1930s, but there is good reason to expect both consequences, even within the same person. For example, combat veterans in our samples speak of both managerial skill and an explosive temper as products of their experiences in World War II (Elder, 1987). An ex-marine exposed to the heaviest combat in the sample felt that it taught him the confidence and drive to overcome adversity. "All one needs is the willingness to survive, and the skill to cooperate with others, to be dependable and self-disciplined" (p. 253).

Is it possible that exposure to combat enhanced the ego resilience of at least some men? To explore this question, we drew upon a measure of ego resilience from the California Q-sort that refers to "resourceful adaptation to changing circumstances and environmental contingencies" (Block & Block, 1980, p. 48). With repeated measures in adolescence and again at age 40, we find that heavy combat veterans did indeed become significantly more resilient by midlife, when compared to other veterans (Elder & Clipp, 1989). Moreover, the least resilient men in adolescence were at greater risk of stress symptoms from combat than the more resilient (a ratio of five to one). Ego resilience, then, clearly moderated the stressful effects of wartime combat, just as an introspective orientation enhanced the risk of enduring stress reactions.

Both early entry into the service and exposure to combat experience, themselves unrelated, are linked to developmental change in personal functioning between adolescence and midlife. However, the mechanisms of change appear to differ in each case. Early mobilization caught the recruit at a timely point for developmental change, a time before the establishment of major career lines. By comparison, the postwar developmental gains observed among early combat veterans occurred largely among the men who were characterized as resilient in adolescence. These men were most able to adapt resourcefully to the stress of combat, thereby minimizing a legacy of health impairment.

Comradeship and Social Bonding

Neither time of mobilization nor men's exposure to combat tells us much about their military units and the influence of this shared experience on their lives. Yet we know that the war experience cannot be understood apart from the collective life of these units. Just as groups in combat mobilize social bonds and actions that provide support, the common loss of comrades can strengthen the ties that bind survivors, offering solace, understanding, and companionship across the years (Elder & Clipp, 1988). We explored the group's influence in two ways. The first approach centers on combat experience and ties to service mates that persist across the years. The second approach concerns the healing potential of social ties with service friends and with wives in the lives of combat veterans. The limited data for this inquiry come from the 1985 follow-up.

Development of comradeship in military units can be explained by group formation processes in basic training, by the dynamics of bonding in units with a strong command structure, and by group cohesion amid life-threatening circumstances. A marine veteran of Okinawa in the sample described his feelings when a buddy was shot. "All I could think of was how I could get him to the hospital . . . not that I was in danger of being killed. . . . it never occurred to me that way. We were a mutual survival society." Combat soldiers both fight and die for their comrades, not for abstract ideals or entities such as freedom, democracy, and one's country. A death among comrades thus ensures a measure of immortality as the fallen live on through the memories of survivors. In fact, men exposed to combat deaths in the Oakland and Berkeley cohorts were most likely to report enduring ties wth service mates as of 1985. These ties include the exchange of letters, cards, phone calls, and visits. Men with such ties were also likely to participate in occasional reunions of their primary military group.

The social bonds were instrumental in the healing process, if we are to judge from available data. Though memories of war trauma are strongly linked to the severity of combat experience, such memories were uncommon among veterans with service ties and an understanding wife. From the war years to the present, a number of men became less troubled by post-traumatic stress symptoms, a shift that appears to be linked to a supportive community of service mates and spouse.

A spouse of a combat veteran who had served on Iwo Jima stressed how important these mates and their periodic gatherings were to her husband's well-being. "The men are different in so many ways, but the war experience binds them together. . . . they become one as far as their emotions are concerned. They're one person, one thing, one thought." After returning to the battle sites on Iwo Jima with her husband, the veteran's wife noted a "difference in him. . . . he wasn't as uptight. Going back helped him to let go. . . . I don't think he holds any bitterness any longer in his soul."

Across the experience of combat, fallen comrades influence surviving mates through memories that bind one to another, and through memories and experiences that impair bonds of mutual obligation and loyalty. Comrades in battle have maximum responsibility for the welfare of mates and minimal ability to control this outcome. Nevertheless, a comrade's death amounts to failure to be dependable in the protector role. Survival guilt and an obligation to witness are likely outcomes. Four decades after the end of World War II, an Oakland veteran who replaced his senior officer spoke about how this event gave more weight and direction to his life. Ever since the war, "I have felt an added responsibility to lead a productive life."

Combat experience and social relations among comrades represent only two aspects of the experience of war and military mobilization, but together with time of entry their influence on the life course tells a story that has many similarities with the Depression's human consequences. In both cases, the effects of traumatic change or events vary by related social experiences, such as family supports and adaptations in the Great Depression and the loss of comrades in World War II. And in both cases, the time or life stage at which certain experiences occur determines their long-range implications. Both adverse and formative developments are linked to early exposure, as expressed in the lives of young boys in the 1930s and of young men in time of war. The fit of lives with a changing world is a matter of timing and timetables.

STUDYING HUMAN LIVES WITHIN AND ACROSS LEVELS: A CONCLUDING NOTE

Most studies of human lives in changing societies continue to follow one of two tracks, the individual or macroscopic level. The first approach includes case studies of individuals over a long segment of the life-span, as well as quantitative studies of behavioral continuity and change in the lives of people. Clues to behavioral change are provided by biological and maturational factors and by the proximal situation itself. For the most part, however, accounts of individual change and continuity remain fixed on this level of analysis. They rarely venture into the larger environment to examine the transformations that take place within it.

A similar conclusion applies to studies of the life course in aggregates or social structures. Explanations for life course change often draw upon a mix of cultural, demographic, and economic factors at the macro level, but they seldom relate patterns of individual behavior to large-scale structures and groups. In addition, studies of behavior settings are strangely out of step with the flow of human lives and life-span development. Developmentalists and personologists may be devoting more efforts to the study of people over time, but we see little evidence of this in the temporal study of environments.

One of the more persuasive examples of this neglect comes from the overworked and underdeveloped application of socioeconomic status or social class in developmental studies. Single measures of this aspect of the environment are commonly used even when the study children or adults are followed across annual data points over a number of years.

Moreover, correlations between social class and family or individual behavior are calculated without an explicit account of why social class matters. What is the mechanism by which an individual's class position influences his behavior and values? Over the past 25 years, Kohn and his colleagues (Kohn, 1977) have pursued questions of this sort, and their systematic efforts provide compelling answers and arguments for why the study of human lives in a changing society must relate the micro experience of lives and the macro level of institutions and structures. As Kohn makes clear, conditions of life influence how we think and believe, and both factors determine our choices regarding work, family, and education. Work influences personality, and personality influences work.

The flourishing area of life course studies owes much to the general recognition that any effort to make sense of development should consider how lives are formed by a rapidly changing society. Initially this recognition led to a methodological solution that simply provided a way to disentangle change within lives from change within society. Cohort-sequential designs and the estimation of cohort, period, and age effects are part of this methodological approach.

Research based on cohort-sequential designs provides estimates of social change as indexed by cohort or period measurements but generally leaves the meaning of these estimates open to speculation. What is meant by a significant cohort or period effect? The imprecise meaning of these effects typically refers to uncertainty regarding the more potent aspects of the environment. What environmental effects are grouped under a significant cohort or period effect? This uncertainty also leaves open the *mechanism* by which an environmental change alters the course and substance of human lives. An uncertain antecedent is necessarily coupled with an imprecise knowledge of the intervening processes. The only certainty is the outcome of interest.

An alternative approach to the interplay of social change and lives focuses directly on such connections. This is the approach of the Social Change Project as it has evolved over the past 20 years from initial studies of "children of the Great Depression" to investigations of war mobilization in human lives. The Depression studies traced the effect of drastic income loss through the family environment on the lives of Americans who were born in the 1920s. Research on war mobilization followed a similar explanatory mission: to assess and explain the multifaceted influence of war experience. By including a particular social change in the problem formulation, these studies have enlarged our understanding of the life course influences of dramatic social changes in twentieth-century America. Cohort studies have been much less successful in this respect because aspects of social change are typically not an explicit part of the original question.

The task of linking social change and lives is formidable because so little theory extends across levels. Theories may be readily available on the micro and macro level, but we have minimal theoretical guidance for the connection between them. How does the downward causation process work in linking macro events and environments to individual life experience? Five theoretical orientations have proven useful as linking mechanisms: the control cycle, the pressures of situational imperatives, the principle of accentuation, the notion of life stage, and interdependent lives.

The *control cycle* refers to a dynamic set in motion by a change in situation. Each change of situation entails some loss of control, which motivates efforts to regain control. Some transitions are an integral part of the normative life course, such as births, marriages, divorce, entry into and out of work. Other transitions stem from major historical change, such as the widespread hardship of the Depression era. Families in the Great Depression regained a measure of control over their situations through expenditure reductions and multiple earners. Older boys from these households soon experienced major life changes of their own through the increased demands and pressures of war mobilization. These include the loss of control so characteristic of heavy combat, the deaths of comrades, and the lifelong support of former service mates. Both historical periods contributed experiences that made the past potentially useful for managing stressful times across the life course. A combat veteran, for example, spoke movingly about how his war experience had given him the confidence to pull out of the valleys in life.

The control cycle dynamic varies according to the properties of the situation and the life history of experience and disposition that people bring to new environments. All situations have certain requirements for behavior. We have referred to these requirements as *situational imperatives*. For men who were mobilized for military service, basic training represented a loss of self-direction and individuality; the behavioral requirements shifted from self-direction to compliance and teamwork. For children in the Great Depression, deprived households exposed them to a more demanding set of expectations than households that avoided heavy losses. Both of these examples depict changes that magnified a loss of control and set in motion the dynamic of a control cycle.

Each change of situation interacts with the life history of experience and disposition. Certain dispositions and experiences can enhance the discontinuity of a new situation. Thus explosive personalities have a low threshold for losing control. Strong economic stress during the 1930s increased the explosiveness of men who were above average on this tendency before the Depression, and such behavior tended to increase the disorder of family life by undermining both parental and marital relations. We refer to this interaction between stress and disposition as an *accentuation process*. Initial dispositions are accentuated by stress. Another example of this process comes from the research on war experience and military service. The least resilient males before World War II were at considerable risk of enduring stress symptoms from exposure to intense combat. A brittle passivity accentuated the psychological costs of combat trauma.

Control cycles, situational imperatives, and accentuation refer to elements in the fit between a person and the situation, a lifelong preoccupation of Henry Murray. The fourth linking mechanism (*the life stage principle*) in our work places all of this within the life course of the individual by taking note of when the person comes to a new situation or circumstance. At what age did the individual experience the Great Depression and World War II? According to the life stage principle, the effect of social change varies according to the age of the person at the time. Age status is connected with competencies, social roles, and options that influence the meaning and adaptive possibilities of new situations. Thus the younger Berkeley boys were more vulnerable to family hardship than their older counterparts in the Oakland cohort, and they were more adversely influenced by economic deprivation. During World War II, the younger recruits to the military experienced more personal growth after adolescence than later entrants. By comparison, late entry typically meant greater life disruption and delay.

All of the linking processes described up to this point refer to the individual in a changing environment. The last mechanism places this actor within the social matrix of relationships (*interdependent lives*) and argues that social change has powerful consequences for the individual through the lives of related others. The family unit provides some of the best examples of these indirect effects. Severe economic hardship during the 1930s disrupted the family by undermining the effectiveness of each person. Thus fathers became more unstable under economic loss, and this instability weakened the marriage. In World War II, children were influenced by losses and other events in the family unit and by events that occurred to friends and even to the friends of friends.

In combination, the five mechanisms provide a way of thinking about the connection between lives and a changing society. Having established this connection, we still face the question of how or whether influences persist over the life-span. Under what conditions do the behavior patterns of a child persist into his or her adult years, and what is the legacy of war in men's and women's lives? We have just begun to explore these questions in research that extends across lives and the generations.

REFERENCES

Allport, G., Bruner, J. S., & Jandorf, E. M. (1941). Personality under social catastrophe: Ninety life histories of the Nazi revolution. *Character and Personality, 10,* 1–22.

Almond, G. A., & Verba, S. (1963). *The civic culture.* Princeton, NJ: Princeton University Press.

Archibald, H. C., & Tuddenham, R. D. (1965). Persistent stress reaction after combat. *Archives of General Psychiatry, 12,* 475–481.

Baltes, P. B., Cornelius, S. W., & Nesselroade, J. R. (1979). Cohort effects in developmental psychology. In J. R. Nesselroade & P. B. Baltes (Eds.), *Longitudinal research in the study of behavior and development* (pp. 1-39, 61-87). New York: Academic Press.

Bandura, A. (1987). Self-regulation of motivation and action through goal systems. In V. Hamilton, G. H. Bower, & N. H. Fryda (Eds.), *Cognition, motivation, and affect: A cognitive science view*. Dordrecht: Martinus Nijoff.

Barker, R. (1968). *Ecological psychology*. Stanford, CA: Stanford University Press.

Block, J., & Block, J. H. (1980). The role of ego-control and ego-resilience in the organization of behavior. In W. A. Collins (Ed.), *Minnesota symposia on child psychology* (Vol. 13, pp. 39-101). Hillsdale, NJ: Lawrence Erlbaum Associates.

Block, J. H., Block, J., & Morrison, A. (1981). Parental agreement-disagreement on child-rearing orientations and gender-related personality correlates in children. *Child Development, 52*, 965-974.

Brehm, S. S., & Brehm, J. W. (1982). *Psychological reactance: A theory of freedom and control*. New York: Academic Press.

Brim, O. G., Jr., & Kagan, J. (1980). *Constancy and change in human development*. Cambridge, MA: Harvard University Press.

Bronfenbrenner, U. (1979). *The ecology of human development*. Cambridge, MA: Harvard University Press.

Brotz, H., & Wilson, E. (1946). Characteristics of military society. *American Journal of Sociology, 51*, 371-375.

Burton, L. M. (1985). *Early and on-time grandmotherhood in multigenerational black families*. Unpublished doctoral dissertation, University of Southern California.

Durkheim, E. (1951). *Suicide*. New York: Free Press.

Earls, F. (1987). Sex differences in psychiatric disorders: Origins and developmental influences. *Psychiatric Development, 1*, 1-23.

Eichorn, D., Clausen, J. A., Hann, N., Honzik, M., & Mussen, P. (Eds.). (1981). *Present and past in middle life*. New York: Academic Press.

Elder, G. H., Jr. (1974). *Children of the Great Depression*. Chicago, IL: University of Chicago Press.

Elder, G. H., Jr. (1975). Age differentiation and the life course. *Annual Review of Sociology, 1*, 165-190.

Elder, G. H., Jr. (1979). Historical change in life patterns and personality. In P. B. Baltes & O. G. Brim, Jr. (Eds.), *Life-span development and behavior* (Vol. 2, pp. 117-159). New York: Academic Press.

Elder, G. H., Jr. (1985). Perspectives on the life course. In G. H. Elder, Jr. (Ed.), *Life course dynamics* (Chapter 1, pp. 23-49). Ithaca, NY: Cornell University Press.

Elder, G. H., Jr. (1986). Military times and turning points in men's lives. *Developmental Psychology, 22*, 233-245.

Elder, G. H., Jr. (1987). War mobilization and the life course. *Sociological Forum, 2*, 449-472.

Elder, G. H., Jr., Caspi, A., & Burton, L. M. (1988). Adolescent transitions in developmental perspective: Historical and sociological insights. In M. Gunnar (Ed.), *Minnesota symposia on child psychology* (Vol. 21). Hillsdale, NJ: Lawrence Erlbaum Associates.

Elder, G. H., Jr., Caspi, A., & Downey, G. (1986). Problem behavior and family relationships: Life course and intergenerational themes. In A. Sorensen, F. Weinert, & L. Sherrod (Eds.), *Human development and the life course: Multidisciplinary perspectives* Hillsdale, NJ: Lawrence Erlbaum Associates.

Elder, G. H., Jr., Caspi, A., & Van Nguyen, T. (1986). Resourceful and vulnerable children: Family influences in hard times. In R. Silbereisen & H. Eyferth (Eds.), *Development as action in context: Problem behavior and normal youth development* (pp. 167–186). New York: Springer.

Elder, G. H., Jr., & Clipp, E. (1988). Combat experience, comradeship and psychological health. In Z. Wilson, Z. Harel, & B. Kahana (Eds.), *Human adaptations to extreme stress: From the Holocaust to Vietnam* (pp. 226–273). New York: Plenum Press.

Elder, G. H., Jr., & Clipp, E. (1989). Combat experience and emotional health: Impairment and resilience in later life. *Journal of Personality, 57,* 311–341.

Elder, G. H., Jr., & Clipp, E. (1988). Wartime losses and social bonding: Influences across 40 years in men's lives. *Psychiatry, 51,* 177–198.

Elder, G. H., Jr., Downey, G., & Cross, E. (1986). Family ties and life chances: Hard times and hard choices in women's lives. In N. Datan (Ed.), *Life-span developmental psychology: Socialization and intergenerational relations.* Hillsdale, NJ: Lawrence Erlbaum Associates.

Elder, G. H., Jr., Liker, J., & Cross, E. (1984). Parent-child behavior in the Great Depression: Life course and intergenerational influences. In P. B. Baltes & O. G. Brim, Jr. (Eds.), *Life-span development and behavior* (Vol. 6, pp. 109–158). New York: Academic Press.

Elder, G. H., Jr., Liker, J., & Jaworski, B. (1984). Hardship in lives: Historical influences from the 1930s to old age in postwar America. In K. McCluskey & H. Reese (Eds.), *Life-span developmental psychology: History and cohort effects* (pp. 161–201). New York: Academic Press.

Elder, G. H., Jr., Van Nguyen, T., & Caspi, A. (1985). Linking family hardship to children's lives. *Child Development, 56,* 361–375.

Eme, R. F. (1979). Sex differences in childhood psychopathology: A review. *Psychological Bulletin, 86,* 574–595.

Emery, R. E. (1982). Interpersonal conflict and the children of discord and divorce. *Psychological Bulletin, 92,* 310–330.

Entwisle, D. R., & Alexander, K. L. (1988). Early schooling as a "critical period" phenomenon. In K. Namboodiri & R. G. Corwin (Eds.), *Sociology of education and socialization* (Vol. 8), Greenwich, CT: JAI Press.

Erikson, E. H. (1959). The problem of ego identity. *Psychological Issues, 1,* 101–164.

Feldman, K. A., & Newcomb, T. M. (1969). *The impact of college on students.* San Francisco: Jossey-Bass.

Greenberg, E., & Steinberg, L. (1986). *When teenagers work: The psychological and social costs of adolescent employment.* New York: Basic Books.

Gunnar-Vongnechten, M. (1978). Changing a frightening toy into a pleasant toy by allowing the infant to control its actions. *Developmental Psychology, 14,* 157–162.

Hagestad, G. O. (1982). Parent and child: Generations in the family. In T. H. Field, A. Huston, H. C. Quay, L. Troll, & G. E. Finley (Eds.), *Review of human development* (pp. 485–499). New York: John Wiley.

Hansell, S., Mechanic D., & Brondolo, E. (1986). Introspectiveness and adolescent development. *Journal of Adolescence and Youth, 15*, 115-132.

Havighurst, R. J., Baughman, J. W., Burgess, E. W., & Eaton, W. H. (1951). *The American veteran back home.* New York: Longsman, Green.

Hendin, H., & Haas, A. P. (1983). *The wounds of war.* New York: Basic Books.

Hetherington, E. M. (1981). Children of divorce. In R. Henderson (Ed.), *Parent-child interaction.* New York: Academic Press.

Hill, R. (1970). *Family development in three generations.* Cambridge, MA: Schenkman.

Hogan, D. P. (1981). *Transitions and social change: The early lives of American men.* New York: Academic Press.

Inkeles, A., & Smith, D. H. (1974). *Becoming modern: Individual change in six developing countries.* Cambridge, MA: Harvard University Press.

Kluckhohn, C., & Murray, H. A. (1965). Personality formation: The determinants. In Kluckhohn, C., Murray, H. A., & Schneider, D. M. (Eds.), *Personality in nature, society, and culture* (2nd ed., pp. 53-67). New York: Alfred A. Knopf. (original work published 1948)

Kohn, M. L. (1977). *Class and conformity.* Chicago: University of Chicago Press.

Kohn, M. L., & Schooler, C. (1983). *Work and personality: An inquiry into the impact of social stratification.* Norwood, NJ: Ablex.

Liker, J., & Elder, G. H., Jr. (1983). Economic hardship and marital relations in the 1930s. *American Sociological Review, 48*, 343-359.

Maccoby, E. E., & Jacklin, C. N. (1983). The "person" characteristics of children and the family as environment. In D. Magnusson & V. L. Allen (Eds.), *Human development: An interactional perspective* (pp. 75-91). New York: Academic Press.

Merton, R. K. (1959). Notes on problem-finding in sociology. In R. K. Merton, L. Bloom, & L. S. Cottrell, Jr. (Eds.), *Sociology today: Problems and prospects* (pp. ix-xxxiv). New York: Basic Books.

Minuchin, P. (1985). Families and individual development: Provocations from the field of family therapy. *Child Development, 56*, 289-302.

Newcomb, T. M. (1943). *Personality and social change: Attitude formation in a student community.* New York: Dryden Press.

Nesselroade, J. R., & Baltes, P. B. (1974). Adolescent personality development and historical change: 1970-1972. *Monographs of the Society for Research in Child Development, 39*(I, Serial No. 154).

Olson, K. (1974). *The G. I. Bill, the veterans, and the colleagues.* Lexington, KY: University Press of Kentucky.

Patterson, G. R. (1988). Family process: Loops, levels, and linkages. In N. Bolger, A. Caspi, G. Downey, & M. Moorehouse (Eds.), *Persons in context: Developmental perspectives.* New York: Cambridge University Press.

Priemus, H. (1986). Housing as a social adaptation process: A conceptual scheme. *Environment and Behavior, 18*, 31-52.

Reese, W. H., & McCluskey, K. A. (1984). Dimensions of historical constancy and change. In K. A. McCluskey & H. W. Reese (Eds.), *Life-span developmental psychology: Historical and generational effects* (pp. 17-45). New York: Academic Press.

Riley, M. W., Johnson, M., & Foner, A. (1972). *Aging and society,* New York: Russell Sage Foundation.

Rindfuss, R. R., Morgan, S. P., & Swicegood, C. G. (1984). The transition to mother-
hood: The intersection of structure and temporal dimension. *American Sociological Review, 49,* 359–372.

Rodgers, W. L., & Thornton, A. (1985). Changing patterns of first marriage in the
United States. *Demography, 22,* 265–279.

Rutter, M. (1979). Protective factors in children's responses to stress and disadvantage.
In M. W. Kent & J. E. Rolf (Eds.), *Primary prevention of psychopathology: Vol. 3.
Social competence in children.* Hanover, NH: University Press of New En-
gland.

Rutter, M. (1982). Epidemiological-longitudinal approaches to the study of development. In W. A. Collins (Ed.), *Minnesota symposia on child psychology* (Vol. 15,
pp. 105–144). Hillsdale, NJ: Lawrence Erlbaum Associates.

Ryder, N. (1965). The cohort as a concept in the study of social change. *American
Sociological Review, 30,* 843–861.

Schaie, K. W. (1965). A general model for the study of developmental problems.
Psychological Bulletin, 64, 94–107.

Schaie, K. W. (1984). Historical time and cohort effects. In K. A. McCluskey & H. W.
Reese (Eds.), *Life-span developmental psychology: Historical and generational
effects* (pp. 1–15). New York: Academic Press.

Simmons, R. G., & Blythe, D. A. (1987). *Moving into adolescence: The impact of
pubertal change and school context.* New York: Aldine.

Snow, M. E., Jacklin, C. N., & Maccoby, E. E. (1983). Sex-of-child differences in father-
child interaction at one year of age. *Child Development, 54,* 227–232.

Stouffer, S. A., Lumsdaine, A. A., Lumsdaine, M. H., Williams, R. M., Jr., Smith, M. B.,
Janis, I. L., Star, S. A., & Cottrell, L. S., Jr. (1949). *The American soldier: Combat
and its aftermath* (Vol. 2). Princeton, NJ: Princeton University Press.

Stouffer, S. A., Suchman, E. A., DeVinney, L. C., Star, S. A., & Williams, R. M., Jr.
(1949). *The American soldier: Vol. 1. Adjustment during army life.* Princeton, NJ:
Princeton University Press.

Sundt, E. (1980). *On marriage in Norway* (M. Drake, Trans.). New York: Cambridge
University Press. (Original work published 1855)

Terman, L. M. (1925). *Genetic studies of genius: Vol. I. Mental and physical traits of a
thousand gifted children.* Stanford, CA: Stanford University Press.

Terman, L. M. (1947). *Genetic studies of genius: Vol. IV. The gifted child grows up.*
Stanford, CA: Stanford University Press.

Thomas, W. I. (1909). *Sourcebook for social origins.* Boston: Badger.

Thomas, W. I., & Thomas, D. S. (1928). *The child in America.* New York: Alfred A.
Knopf.

Thomas, W. I., & Znaniecki, F. (1918–1920). *The Polish peasant in Europe and
America* (Vols. 1 & 2). New York: Octagon Books.

van der Kolk, B. A. (1987). The psychological consequences of overwhelming life
experiences. In B. A. van der Kolk (Ed.), *Psychological trauma.* New York: American Psychiatric Press.

Volkart, E. H. (1951). *Social behavior and personality: Contributions of W. I. Thomas
to theory and research.* New York: Social Science Research Council.

Waller, W. (1940). *War and the family.* New York: Dryden Press.

Weiss, R. (1979). Growing up a little faster: The experience of growing up in a single-parent household. *Journal of Social Issues, 35,* 97–111.

Werner, E. E., & Smith, R. S. (1982). *Vulnerable but invincible: A study of resilient children.* New York: McGraw-Hill.

Wolpert, J. (1966). Migration as an adjustment to environmental stress. *Journal of Social Issues, 22,* 92–102.

7

Schizotaxia as an Open Concept

Paul E. Meehl

AUTOBIOGRAPHICAL PROLOGUE

Born in Minneapolis (1920), an only child of affectionate and proud middle-class parents, I had a relatively happy childhood that was traumatically interrupted at age 11 by my father's suicide. At age 14, suffering considerable psychic distress, I read Menninger's *The Human Mind*, which had a tremendous healing influence and changed my vocational goal from lawyer to psychotherapist. Entering the University of Minnesota the year Murray's classic *Explorations* was published, I found myself majoring in a psychology department that was strongly behavioristic, quantitative, "tough-minded," and rather anti-Freudian. Coming to the field via my high school psychoanalytic reading, this academic environment forced me to think hard and long about methodological questions that most psychologists take for granted. My book on prediction (1954) was a good book partly because of the cognitive dissonance history behind it. Despite the overall flavor of the Minnesota department during my BA and PhD student days (1938–1945), chairman Richard M. Elliott urged us to read Allport and Murray, and a young instructor, Robert E. Harris, "spoke Murray-ese" in characterizing personalities. To this day I find it natural to think of my students, colleagues, and patients in terms of the Murray needs. (I once surprised a sociologist patient by interpreting his behavior as excessively controlled by *n Counteraction*.)

While my early research was on latent learning in rats and on the MMPI, I retained my teenage psychodynamic interest and so took the trouble to have an analysis (85 hours with a Vienna-trained Freudian and 300 with a Radovian), then did a couple of controls and attended a continuous case seminar. My supervisor introduced me to Sandor Rado's little known writings on schizotypy, and about the same time the genetic evidence was becoming impressive, I was treating schizotypal and neurotic patients and was struck by the differences between them. I had as a graduate student read Rosanoff's early work on twins and had imbibed broadly "hereditarian" views from Donald G. Paterson and comparative psychologist William T. Heron. I concluded, partly from the quantitative research but also, some think strangely, from my therapeutic experience, that schizophrenia was a hereditary neurological disease, a view that shocked most psychologists when I propounded it in my American Psychological Association (APA) presidential address (1962b). I am gratified to see that this heretical conjecture has now become a commonplace among informed persons.

From 1955 to 1970 I did a lot of empirical research on this theory, almost all unpublished, because I realized it didn't really *prove* much of anything. I thought—and still think—that what we needed to test a dominant gene theory of a pervasive schizotaxic defect were (1) better indicators, closer to the DNA than to psychometrics or social behavior, such as psychophysiology and soft neurology, and (2) mathematically stronger taxometrics for combining indicators. So I have devoted recent years to the invention of several such taxometric methods, which I conjecture are better than most of the conventional cluster algorithms. All of my work has been influenced by contact with philosophers of science in the Minnesota Center for Philosophy of Science, of which I was a cofounder (with Herbert Fiegl and Wilfrid Sellars) in 1953. Much of the sequel reflects that intellectual influence. I have sometimes regretted becoming a clinical psychologist, because the field's scientific quality is so poor compared, say, to genetics or statistics. But in recent years I have found it possible to work on problems of psychopathology along a mixture of genetic and mathematical lines, which for a person of my tastes and talents is not a bad compromise. By and large, I am having fun at it, and—as my parents taught me by precept and example—if you're not having fun, you might just as well be dead. By far the largest part of my adult behavior has been controlled by a fusion of *n Cognizance* and *n Play*, with assists from *n Recognition* and *n Autonomy*. Readers interested in more details may consult my autobiography (Meehl, 1989).

THE DIAGNOSTIC PROBLEM: TWO CLINICAL CASES

To motivate a discussion that will be largely methodological, I begin with two brief clinical examples. These were patients seen in the Tuesday morning Grand Rounds in the department of psychiatry, a year or so ago, and I write from memory without having gone back to study their charts. As you will see from how I use them, it is not important whether my recollections are entirely accurate, since my discussion is about a loose and debatable syndrome with considerable sign and symptom substitutability. The first patient is a 40-year-old male who presented with complaints of mild confusion, "a dizziness in the head," and inability to work because of "trouble with the hands and feet." On admission the examining resident recorded cataleptic-like partial paralysis of all four extremities, minimal clouding, and anxiety normal for the symptoms. The paralyses disappeared for some hours, then reappeared for a couple of hours and were not clearly in evidence when see in the case conference, although there was a hint of waxiness manifested as slow drop. The patient walked with a somewhat retarded gait, and there was a little stiffness when the examiner handled his arms. There was nothing diagnostic about his interview behavior other than a couple of odd semantic choices, noted by some of us but not by others. Unfortunately, the patient had completed no psychometrics and was subsequently discharged wtihout having done so. I included "atypical catatonic schizophrenia" in my differential diagnosis, but only two other clinicians present agreed with me that this should even be considered. The appropriate affect in the interview and the absence of any clear-cut thought disorder despite the ± odd semantics that some observers didn't agree were particularly odd) and a previous history of adequate work and social adjustment made the schizophrenia possibility seem reaching far out in left field to most of those present.

In the second case I again found myself in the minority (this time a somewhat larger one), the patient being a 30-year-old female who presented with complaints of anxiety and depression and who had for some years lived partly in a childlike, dependent way upon her parents and since then alone on relief because she was unable to hold a job and also was almost phobic about leaving her apartment. The history was of a chronically withdrawn, listless, marginally functional introverted person without any psychotic signs either in the history or when seen. She had been in therapy with several practitioners, one of whom was present at the conference and reported that she was a very difficult patient to deal with as she elicited many countertransference problems on his part. While he didn't know how to diagnose her, he was convinced that she was a hard case with a poor outlook for change. Several of us were inclined to such diagnoses as "borderline" (Kroll et al., 1981) or "Hoch-Polatin Syndrome," a suggestion that engendered a heated debate about whether there was such an entity, and if so, what did it have to do with schizophrenia? There were claims and counterclaims from our fallible memories as to what the follow-up data showed on the original cases described in Hoch and Polatin's classic article (Hoch, Cattell, Strahl, & Pennes, 1962; Hoch & Polatin, 1949). Those who recalled (correctly) that 40% were subsequently hospitalized (one to nine times) and 20% developed a florid schizophrenia construed this as supporting the entity's reality. Opponents urged that this "*only* one in five" figure tended to cast doubt on Hoch and Polatin's concept.

This second patient's mother had at one time been hospitalized in a state hospital for several months, where she had received shock treatment, but—to my chagrin, because it happens constantly in case conferences—the presenting resident had not taken the trouble to find out what the mother's diagnosis was. Here also we obtained no psychometrics, and I have chosen both of my examples partly for this reason. The question is not whether the minority clinicians were right in thinking that these two patients might have been schizophrenes but to illustrate a ubiquitous problem in understanding the concept of psychiatric diagnosis. The conference majority was right in arguing that neither of these patients showed much *descriptive* resemblance to the paradigm patients labeled "schizophrenic" by the great Eugen Bleuler (1911/ 1950) or much less the "textbook" syndrome delineated by the equally great but (in some circles) much maligned Emil Kraepelin (1909–1913/1971). Aside from the diagnostic merits, especially because (as so often happens) there was no elicitation of sufficient additional material, either historical or psychometric, to warrant pursuing the discussion, what were we disputing about? In order to know what additional evidence we would need, and why, one must first ask what the argument was about, what the issue was.

Some would say that such a dispute is merely semantic, a matter of words, a view that I wish to combat vigorously as being a kind of pseudosophisticated cop-out common in social science. I wish I could devote a whole chapter to this one mistake, but I confine myself to expressing with Sir Karl Popper (1959) my agreement with Immanuel Kant, who said, "I for my part hold the very opposite opinion, and I assert that whenever a dispute has raged for any length of time . . . there was, at the bottom of it, never a problem about mere words, but always a genuine problem about things." There are, of course, pointless semantic disputes in social science, but this is not one of them. There are two main goals involved here. The practitioner wants a diagnosis because he believes, perhaps wrongly, that having it will help him deal more effectively with the patient's problem, to make a prognosis and to select treatment. The other goal is that of the theoretician. For example, a clinician doing research in the behavior genetics of schizophrenia is asking a theoretical question that comes down, ultimately, to a question of causality. With regard to prognosis and treatment it is not immediately obvious that the introduction of the diagnostic rubric "Hoch-Polatin Syndrome" will be helpful even if the entity does exist, first, because practitioners who use this concept usually report that the drug treatments of choice for florid schizophrenia (phenothiazines) are not effective with this syndrome, a clinical impression that fits the growing theoretical conviction among psychopharmacologists that these drugs are not antischizophrenic drugs but antipsychotic drugs. Second, there is the fact that the psychophysiology and soft neurology of schizophrenia do not disappear in drug-induced remissions. The prognostic implications for a patient who is clearly unlike Kraepelin's *dementia praecox* cannot be directly transferred to such an atypical form.

Furthermore, it is not known to what extent predictions, including "treatment of choice" predictions, are better mediated by the introduction of such a rubric than by straight statistical prediction from the relevant diagnostic data, that is, by bypassing the nosological taxon. It is interesting that psychiatrists tend to take this mediation for granted, as do psychologists sympathetic to the categories of DSM-III, despite the absence of either mathematical or empirical proof to that effect. My colleague and former student Will Grove has shown in recent mathematical and Monte Carlo work that it is only under certain fairly extreme conditions of taxonic validity and low symptom correlation that the introduction of this mediating category can be expected to improve upon a straight statistical prediction from the evidentiary base.

THE METACONCEPT "TAXONICITY"

A more general question that one might expect to have been settled long since, philosophically and mathematically, but that I find is not, is what do we *mean* when we postulate a taxon (disease entity, type, species, "natural kind") as a way to conceptualize the relationship between a set of signs, symptoms, life history facts, and test scores? What does it mean to say of a data domain in psychopathology that the latent structure is taxonic rather than factorial? I believe that bipolar affective illness and schizophrenia are true taxa, whereas garden-variety borderline intelligence and high social introversion are not. The latter being dimensional in nature, any class words or categories we might use, as when in ordinary speech we use the category term "introvert," are merely convenient demarcations of a continuous region in the descriptor space. It turns out that to construct a definition of "taxonicity" is a good deal harder task than one might have supposed.

In my seminars in philosophical psychology and classification in psychopathology, we have to deal with the metaquestion, what *is* taxonicity? When is an alleged taxon really a taxon, rather than an arbitrary class, perhaps even one that the classifier himself treats as somehow "nonreal"? Students want to be given a clear idea of what a taxon is before leaping into the mathematics, or even considering the general methodology of how one goes about searching for taxa. This is particularly true of students who have been indoctrinated with a philosophy of science that is at least a half century out of date! While it is true in some sense that definitions, being stipulations about the use of language, are "conventional," it is not true that in any respectable science they are "arbitrary." As Carnap pointed out in his paper on the probability concept (Carnap, 1945), one should perhaps use the term "explication" for the kind of definition that occurs in empirical science. The stipulation about the choice of a *term* is a rather minor and uninteresting aspect of the conceptual problem of definition, that is, the formulation of a *concept* that will be theoretically powerful rather than useless or counterproductive. I have found it pedagogically more effective to go directly to a consideration of empirical examples from fields like medicine and genetics, sometimes with but often without the taxometric math, explaining only preliminarily that the metaquestion, what is a taxon? will be clarified as we proceed. This is sometimes referred to by logicians as an implicit or contextual definition, rather than an explicit one in the old-fashioned sense. I hope this does not sound obscurantist—definitely not my intellectual style. I will therefore do here briefly the same thing I do to satisfy the inquiring students, where the incomplete satisfaction may lead you to reflect further on the taxonicity concept and perhaps tempt those with mathematical expertise to make contributions that are sorely needed.

There are roughly three ways of explicating the open concept "taxonicity." They are not mutually incompatible, but their precise relationships remain unclear. The first way proceeds by offering rough synonyms and familiar examples, and this sometimes turns out to be adequate as a basis for developing the statistics of a taxometric search method. A taxon is a class, that is, a collection of individuals (stones, honeybees, mental patients, daffodils) that is—in some sense to be explained—not arbitrary. It is often convenient for ease of communication and administrative purposes, especially where a yes or no pragmatic judgment must be made as to a proposed action, to demarcate regions on a continuum or in a continuous descriptor space by a class name, without any intention of claiming that the demarcation is other than arbitrary. ("Arbitrary" here does not mean whimsical or totally unmotivated; it has to do with certain utility considerations.) When we classify some students as "under-achievers" or say that a person is "obese," we are aware that this is a category term used for short to refer to some region of a quantitative dimension. So terms like "introverted," "bright," "energetic," "underweight," "clumsy," and "dominant"—in fact, almost all of the trait names in ordinary English, as well as most of them in the technical language of psychopathology—are shorthand for regions on a quantitative dimension or volumes in a descriptor hyperspace.

When we attribute empirical taxonicity to a concept, we have in mind something stronger than that, although it is difficult to say precisely in what that stronger meaning consists. In ordinary language we say that we are intending to refer to a *natural kind*, such as a biological species, a disease entity, a personality type, a Mendelizing mental deficiency syndrome, a "qualitative" as contrasted with a merely "quantitative" difference between groups of individuals. To use an expression from Plato, "We want to carve nature at its joints." One sometimes hears reference to a taxon, species, or disease entity as presenting a question of kind and not of degree, but this locution is somewhat careless; what one should instead say is "a difference of kind *as well as* degree," since obviously some of the indicators of membership in a taxon are themselves matters of degree. (When the point is pressed by careful inspection, they almost always are.) It discourages me to find that even graduate students sometimes offer the cliché objection to a concept like schizophrenia or sociopathy, "How can you talk about schizophrenia as an entity when there are all degrees of its symptoms and traits?" This illustrates how even bright people can be led to say dumb things by undergraduate miseducation. Meningitis is a disease entity with a characteristic pathology, and nobody familiar with it would deny that it is a genuine categorical entity in a way that obesity or borderline IQ are not entities. Patients with meningitis have fever, headache, clouding, Kernig's sign, Brudzinski's sign, and so forth. Some of these indicators of the meningitis entity are quantitative, others qualitative (although even Kernig's and Brudzinski's signs *could* be considered merely extreme degrees of leg or neck stiffness!). The confusion here is failing to distinguish between the question whether an indicator is quantitative and whether the set of indicators reflects an underlying causal state of affairs that defines a nonarbitrary class. *Whether the fallible indicators of a putative taxon such as a disease entity, personality type, or biological species are singly qualitative or quantitative in character tells us nothing about the presence or absence of a latent taxonic structure.*

Sometimes this rough synonyms-cum-examples explication of taxonicity suffices to get on with the scientific job. But in other contexts—including, alas, psychopathology—it is rarely sufficient. Reflection on the classification of Mendelizing mental deficiencies and disease entities in organic medicine has led me to focus attention on *causal agency* as a criterion. Mendelizing mental deficiencies may be only slightly distinguishable, if at all, by psychometric patterns, and distinguishable with somewhat higher accuracy by certain anatomical correlates in skin, bones, hair, and the like. These pathological taxa are often specified with high precision when we know the biochemical path, sometimes even the chromosomal locus and codon substitution of a mutation. In stressing causation I have no wish to dogmatize by imposing this semantic preference upon others who experience it as narrow. In teaching or discussing research plans with colleagues, I therefore attach the adjective "causal" to the noun "taxon," since it doesn't matter whether you and I prefer the same semantics so long as we understand each other. In organic medicine and genetics, the taxonicity of a disease entity is closely tied to the notion of specific etiology, but unfortunately that notion is not as clear-cut as one might initially suppose. I have elsewhere set out an explication of *strengths of causal influence* (Meehl, 1977), and I find that scholarly clinicians in my environment use the term "specific etiology" for only the first three strongest causal influences and resist using it for weaker ones. (I may add that most physicians, including scholarly ones, have not reflected much on these matters.) Assume we have set up criteria for an identifiable syndrome of indicators (itself a part of the task of taxometrics). Let us refer then simply to "the probability that Individual X develops the disease." We presuppose that Mackie (1965, 1974) calls a "causal field," such as that the individual receives sufficient calories to stay alive to adulthood and similar kinds of things usually not mentioned as part of the equation. Given that (usually unmentioned) causal field, we imagine a causal equation (not a mere statistical prediction function, although if known it would serve that job beautifully) that gives the probability of disease as a function of causal influences. Suppose one of these causal influences is intrinsically dichotomous, that is, a qualitative, present-or-absent factor, such as whether there is or is not a mutated gene at the Huntington locus. If the probability function equals 1 with that factor present and zero with it absent, we could take the factor in question out of the equation and treat it as a multiplier having the two values 1 and zero. Then regardless of the joint values of all the other causal factors that might, for instance, influence the intensity or age of onset or the rapidity of course or the preponderance of certain elements of the syndrome over others, we have a necessary and sufficient qualitative condition. The dominant Huntington mutation is an obvious example.

Suppose we have an intrinsically dichtomous causal factor such that the disease probability is zero if the factor is absent but is not equal to 1 with the factor present (whether disease occurs being dependent upon other factors); we then speak of a *qualitative sine qua non*, of a necessary but not sufficient condition for the disease. Clinicians readily agree that these are both cases of specific etiology.

Finally, suppose there is a causal agent that is not intrinsically dichotomous but quantitative in character, where the probability of disease is a step function of this agent, such that to the left of the step it has the value zero and then to the right of the step it has a non-zero value that may, however, not be flat but continue to rise as a function of the combined action of the other causal variables. Here, although the factor is not intrinsically dichtomous or qualitative in nature, I find most scholarly clinicians of my acquaintance willing to label this as specific etiology.

But any "weaker" influence than that, such as the most powerful single factor (e.g., caloric intake as a factor in obesity), they think should merely be seen as a case of strong influence and not labeled specific etiology. You should not assume from these examples that the notion of specific etiology has to be closely tied to the organic medical model. A specific major life history event would do as well, the only problem there being that it is difficult to show that there are many such. For example, if Freud's early theory (Freud, 1896/1962) about the specific life history events pathogenic for hysteria and obsessional neurosis had been empirically correct, rather than a mistake on his part between historical events and infantile fantasy, they would have been perfectly good examples of specific etiology. You recall he thought that a condition for either of these neuroses was a prepubescent sexual experience involving overt genital friction. If the patient was passive and the affects of fear and disgust predominated, the later consequence would be hysteria; if the patient played an active role, was the seducer, and the affect at the time was mainly one of pleasure, we have the antecedent for an obsessional neurosis. This, he thought, was why hysteria was commoner in females. Now that event was not a germ, or a gene, or even a mechanical trauma like the popular "being dropped on the head as a baby." But if it had held up empirically, it would be a perfectly good example of specific etiology.

To give a nonmedical example of the taxonicity problem, as an undergraduate I was acquainted with a number of Trotskyists (Minneapolis was one of the centers of the Trotskyist movement in the 1930s and 1940s), and Trotskyism is a very tight syndrome. It is a clearer taxon than many of the taxa of psychopathology, including even the good ones, let alone the rather arbitrary ones sometimes found in DSM-III. I found two signs that were jointly pathognomonic of Trotskyism as a political syndrome. If a person said that (1) the Soviet Union was a workers' state and (2) Stalin was a counter-revolutionary bureaucrat, I could be 100% sure he was a Trotskyist, and a dozen other traits could then be predicted with high confidence. Being a Trotskyist is not due to a germ or a gene, but it's a nice statistical taxon. In some instances, it would not be due to a specific etiology, because one of these events might be reading a certain book; another event might be having married a Trotskyist. Etiology here is not specific, even though each of the candidate causes may have an almost dichotomous character.

In discussing with my colleague Auke Tellegen causal taxonicity as a fruitful concept for analytical purposes and for evaluating taxometric search methods, I have come to use the phrase "Tellegen case" for a puzzling kind of example. Suppose that a federal judge, in his infinite wisdom, decides that the borderline IQ kids in special schools must be mainstreamed in an affluent Minneapolis suburb such as Edina. If one were to administer an omnibus intelligence test to the Edina pupils, given these circumstances, one would get a clear, unmistakable strong taxon from the data, no matter which of the available taxometric methods was employed. You don't need any research to figure that one out from the statistical armchair. But if we are working in the borderline IQ range, avoiding Mendelizing or karyotypic mental deficiencies or developmental anomalies like microcephaly, we are simply dealing with the low end of the polygenic distribution of the heritable component of g, plus environmental deprivation effects. So category words like "dull," "normal," or "borderline" are only loose class names for *regions* on the intelligence dimension. Tellegen points out that this is a pseudotaxon, not a true taxon in any interesting sense, causal or otherwise. He goes on to point out that several—perhaps all— taxometric methods would tend to yield this misleading result.

He makes a good point, and the Tellegen case is an important test case to reflect upon in discussing the metatheory of taxometrics. But the example doesn't trouble me as much as it does him. For one thing, suppose we adopt a convention that "interesting" or "real" taxonicity means causal taxonicity and combine that stipulation with the above mathematical relations, so that we require a dichotomous or step function causal agent responsible for producing the taxon. Then, while the Tellegen case is not a true taxon from the standpoint of a geneticist or developmental psychologist, it is a taxon from the standpoint of a political scientist or jurisprude. In those disciplines, an injunction by a federal court is a powerful causal agent, not a matter of degree; that is, the judge has either issued an injunction regarding educational mainstreaming, or he hasn't. It seems arbitrary to say that we can only identify taxonicity with causality at one level in Comte's famous pyramid of the sciences. For example, to say that Freud's specific etiology of hysteria doesn't count because it's a life history event, and we only count genes or germs, would be quite arbitrary. Higher up in the pyramid of the sciences, we deal with the disciplines of sociology, economics, political theory, and law, and for scholars in those disciplines concepts like "Trotskyism" or "bankruptcy" have a taxonic character.

Second, it is a mistake to require of any statistical method aimed at identifying a substantive—especially causal—state of affairs in the empirical world that should be capable of functioning as a litmus test of theoretical truth or falsity, as a kind of automatic truth-grinding machine for "verifying" causal conjectures. It is perfectionistic to demand that of any taxometric search method. If a taxometric method reveals that 10% of Edina schoolchildren belong to a low IQ taxon in the hypothetical Tellegen case, we remind ourselves that taxometric investigation always involves an interplay between the statistics, which may be a programmed algorithm and in that sense "mechanical," *and all relevant theory and evidence.* There is a temptation— which I do not attribute to Tellegen—for social scientists to treat statistical methods as if they were automated truth-grinding machines. One must consider all relevant aspects of construct validity given by the item content, psychometric, demographic, and life history facts about the individuals, where the sample was obtained from, and whatever general psychological theory and even commonsensical knowledge is available. Our Edina researcher, having identified the 10% low-IQ taxon members, could easily discover a big explanatory fact about them by checking their home addresses, which would (unlike those of the complement class) be outside Edina. No sane investigator would ignore this information or fail to follow it up by inquiry.

A third approach to Tellegen's problem focuses on the mathematics, saying stipulatively, "A set of numerical data is formally, numerically taxonic if and only if they satisfy such and such taxometric equations." In explaining my taxometric methods to graduate students, I begin with a convention: "For the next two hours, we will call a class of patients taxonic if their indicator scores act configurally like Meehl's taxometric bootstrapping methods say they should." Adding a small amount of interpretative text to tie the mathematical machinery to empirical data is an accceptable explication of theoretical concepts, employed in all sciences. But if you do it that way, the question arises, what is the relation between numerical taxonicity (satisfying the postulates of a certain formal calculus) and the interesting substantive questions about causality, which is what we're up to in much of our psychopathology research?

Considering a set of quantitative fallible taxon indicators, starting the reasoning with the taxon members already specified, it is easy to go in that taxon-to-indicator direction. Good indicators of the taxon will be those measures that when distributed separately for the taxon members and the complement class yield two clearly separated (although overlapping) unimodal frequency curves. Imagining ourselves to have Omniscient Jones's knowledge of the latent situation, we assert, "There is some attribute A that is either intrinsically qualitative (yes/no character) or is a quantitative attribute with respect to which the probability of taxon membership is a quasi step function with $p = 0$ to the left of the step. A may be a life history event, an inner state or structure, even a manifest disposition. When we partition the population into the two sets A and $-A$, then the quantitative indicator X_1 will show two unimodal distributions, as will indicator X_2, and so on for all of the indicators that have taxonic validity."

Going in this direction, it's easy. But when we don't have Omniscient Jones's knowledge and have to start with a set of fallible quantitative indicators, how do we define taxonicity? It won't do to say that taxonicity exists if there is a way to partition the population into two subpopulations satisfying the above distribution criteria, because there will always be a way to do that, in fact a very large number of such ways. The existence of a large number of such possible partitions does not depend upon the existence of a taxon since it can, of course, be achieved in a hyperspace of purely factorial ("dimensional," "noncategory") data, provided the indicators are correlated. All we have to do is divide the group at an arbitrary cut on any valid indicator, and when we distribute the other fallible indicators within the two resulting subpopulations, what we get will "look rather taxonic."

Statisticians writing about the "decomposition problem" bypass this troublesome point by simply referring to the decomposability of a manifest frequency distribution into weighted sums of component distributions. But such a mathematical decomposability will always exist, and in a very large number of ways. I am not relying here on the cardinality of the continuum or other such mathematical nicety. I mean that even if we confine all numbers to integers (for example, we don't express any individual's IQ with decimals), there are not an infinite number but an extremely large number of ways to decompose any well behaved frequency distribution. For example, imagine a smooth curve based upon a billion cases that can be exactly graduated (no frequency "error" in the unit intervals) by a frequency function $f(x)$. Choose an arbitrary taxon rate P lying in the probability interval $0 < P < 1$. Define another arbitrary frequency function $g(x)$. Then define, in terms of these, a function

$$h(x) = \frac{f(x) - Pg(x)}{Q}$$

Then if $f(x)$ and $g(x)$ are well behaved frequency functions, so will $h(x)$ be. Since we can choose $g(x)$ in many ways and still satisfy the conditions for being a frequency function, and we can assign the arbitrary taxon rate P in many ways, we can therefore derive our $h(x)$ in many ways. But from the above equation we have immediately

$$f(x) = Pg(x) + Qh(x)$$

That is, the manifest frequency function $f(x)$ is decomposable. If we restricted the choice of $g(x)$ to, say, Pearson's 12 curve types and carried their parameters out to two decimal places, and the same for the arbitrary P, there are over 10^{11} possible decompositions of the manifest frequency function $f(x)$. So the decomposability of a single indicator variable cannot be a test of latent taxonicity, since the answer to the decomposability question is always affirmative. Of course, we concocted a hokey function $h(x)$ so that it *would* serve as a component, but that's not an objection to my point, since if $g(x)$ is a "plausible" frequency function to start with, there needn't be anything outlandish about $h(x)$. The point is that we have not given a mathematically rigorous criterion of taxonicity when we simply say, "Imagine the manifest frequency function to be decomposable into two functions when the latter are appropriately weighted by taxon and complement frequency constants." In order to give a formal defintion of taxonicity in terms of the decomposability criterion, one must impose some additional constraints upon what kinds of functions will be admitted as candidates. We would like to make some sort of link, even if it's only a loose one, between a formal crtierion of taxonic structure and a "theoretically interesting" concept of taxonicity (e.g., causality? developmental origin? source?). We would hope to attain partial insight into what it means to be a "true taxon" or "natural kind" by contemplating the properties of the formalism. Could we motivate the choice of a mathematical generating procedure by reference to a suitably broad specification of how natural kinds, so to speak, "come into being"?

   It naturally occurs to one that perhaps Karl Pearson's famous but little used family of curve types might serve this heuristic role (Craig, 1936; Cramer, 1946; Elderton & Johnson, 1969; Johnson & Kotz, 1970; Kenney, 1939; Pearson, 1894, 1895; Rietz, 1927; Stigler, 1986). Pearson starts with the old notion that the probabilities of a number of causal factors, operating positively or negatively and independently of one another, yield on a particular occasion (say, the measurement of a length of a table or the determination of a person's height by his genes) when $p = q$ a frequency polygon $(p + q)^n$ extremely close to the Gaussian function. If we allow an asymmetry between p and q, we get frequency polygons of varying amounts of skewness. Then Pearson further relaxes the conditions for generating the terms of the series for the discrete case by allowing p to vary as we draw, say, marbles from an urn that contains a mix of white and black marbles in a certain proportion. He opts for the obvious setup of a finite urn sampled without replacement, so that the probability of drawing a white marble in a given point in drawing m marbles depends upon what proportion of those left in the urn are white and therefore depends upon where I am in the sequence and how many white marbles I have drawn up to this point in the drawings. As is well known, a finite urn model sampled without replacement yields us a discrete series somewhat different from the binomial, symmetrical, or skewed series, called the hypergeometric series. By considering the slope connecting two points in the polygon and some high school geometry and algebra, Pearson shows that the slope expressing the difference in height of successive terms of the hypergeometric series per unit increment on the abscissa is equal to the height of the midpoint multiplied by a fraction whose numerator contains the distance from the mode of the polygon in the first degree and whose denominator is a quadratic in that distance. Moving to the continuous case from this frequency polygon, he obtains the differential equation

$$dy/dx = y(m - x)/b_o + b_1x + b_2x^2)$$

It turns out that by suitable assignment of the four parameters of this "generalized frequency function," individual differences data from a wide variety of measures in the biological and social sciences can be satisfactorily graduated.

Pearson was mainly interested in heterogeneity and considered that if you could not closely graduate a set of data from the biological or social sciences by appropriate assignment of the four parameters in his generalized frequency function, this would suggest that you had a population mixture of two natural kinds, and you should attempt to decompose the manifest frequency function into two component functions appropriately weighted by the taxon rate. To a psychologist there is another likely source of maldistribution that, so far as I am aware, did not interest Pearson, namely, a systematic bias, when constructing a psychometric device such as a personality inventory, in the distribution of item difficulties on the underlying psychometric factor. It is easy to see this if, for instance, in building a scale of paranoid sensitivity, a clinician was pretty good at inventing items for individual differences in the nonpathological range, of the sort that go with social introversion and the like, and was also expert at describing psychotic distortions but had trouble thinking up item content in the borderline region (e.g., in early schizophrenia or in a severe neurotic with social phobic distortions not quite amounting to ideas of reference, but close to it). Then if the true distribution of paranoid sensitivity closely fitted one of Pearson's 12 curve types, an inventory used to measure it with poor representation of items in that borderline region would not be satisfactorily fitted by a Pearson curve.

It is well known (Pearson proved it in his original paper) that it is impossible to assign parameters to two Gaussian functions so that their weighted sum will be Gaussian, except for the degenerate case where they have the same mean and standard deviation but merely different sample sizes. I do not have a rigorous proof, but looking at Pearson's equation above, it seems obvious (and my statistician friends agree with this) that a more general statement is that no weighted sum of two Pearsonian functions can be Pearsonian. That interesting mathematical fact suggests a line of reasoning connecting Pearson's curve family with our intuitive idea of a natural kind, and perhaps connected with a dichotomous or step functional causal originator of a curve of individual differences among organisms. If your frequency data cannot be satisfactorily graduated (not merely a significant chi square on frequency discordance, but not even a "close" fit), this suggests that your data have originated in a latently taxonic causal situation. If one can decompose a non-Pearsonian manifest distribution into two Gaussian (or nearly Gaussian) components, this is usually taken as quite impressive corroboration of the taxonic conjecture, although of course it does not constitute a deductive proof. Suppose we find that a decomposition of one fallible indicator's non-Pearsonian distribution into two Pearsonian components is possible, and then we examine a second quantitative indicator and find that we can decompose it into two components (although their Pearson types may not be the same as the first). If the compositional weights assigned are approximately the same for the two indicators, this would constitute a strong corroboration of the taxonic conjecture.

There is a troublesome point here arising from the way in which Pearson derived his function via the hypergeometric series. In the case of the symmetric or asymmetric binomial, it is easy to think of physical circumstances in which multiple causes operate in the way the mathematical model says, and also cases in which the causes are not independent. But the idea of sampling from a finite urn without replacement has, so far as I know, no plausible physical realization in social or biological science. However, you can't go from Pearson's generalized function back to the hypergeometric series. You can only go in the other direction. The movement from the hypergeometric series to the generalized frequency function did not, in Pearson's derivation, consist solely in moving from the discrete to the continuous situation. The discrete case formula for the slope of the polygon segment has an inner structure involving certain required relationships among four numbers (the number of marbles in the urn, the proportion of white marbles, the number of marbles thus far drawn, and the proportion of those drawn that are white). But when Pearson moves to the continuous case, he pays no attention to those interrelationships. He simply observes that in the discrete setup the variable x (distance from the mode of the frequency polygon) appears in the first degree upstairs and as a quadratic downstairs. In that sense, therefore, the Pearson generalized function is more than a continuous form of the discrete; it is also a generalization freed of certain internal constraints upon the way in which the discrete case coefficients were arrived at from the finite urn model. So Pearson's generalized frequency curve does not require the idea of sampling marbles from an urn without replacement as its "structural" or "generative" basis. The easiest way to see that, other than contemplating the discrete case coefficients, is to learn that Pearson is able to fit a U curve to data that require it, with his generalized function. But that is impossible with the hypergeometric series, because it is what the engineer calls "restorative." That is, if, as you draw your set of marbles, you are running ahead of the game in the proportion of whites, the probability of a white falls below that of the initial urn parameter value, and if you are running behind expectancy in terms of the original urn content, your odds of drawing another white marble go up. That means that at any point of the drawing, there is a restorative tendency pulling you back toward the middle, that is, toward the white marble expectancy of the urn before you started drawing. Therefore, the hypergeometric series has to be "constricted" in comparison with the binomial of the same initial white marble rate. Such a restorative generating process cannot, of course, yield a U-shaped distribution, where the ends have higher probabilities than the middle region.

What one would like would be to find the "most general" way of reaching Pearson's generalized frequency function and then to examine that generative process with an eye to the question what kind of physical generative process, giving rise to individual differences among organisms, would correspond to this mathematical generative rule? I have not done a literature search, but query and correspondence with statisticians lead me to the conclusion that nobody has as yet been interested to attempt this most general investigation. I repeat, the point is not to produce a rigorous deductive argument that any time you can fit data with a curve from the Pearson system you can dismiss taxonicity, and any time you can't you can infer taxonicity. That is a philosophical mistake, whatever the mathematician might make of it. It goes without saying that there is no such thing as an absolutely necessary deductive proof of any substantive theory, especially a theory about causal origins, from a mathematical statement of the observable data. That's just not the way any empirical science works. But it would be interesting to know how the most general setup capable of yielding Pearson's function might be restated in terms of the most general kinds of imagined physical processes or entities we could cook up. From a Popperian point of view—or Wesley Salmon's principle of "Damn

Strange Coincidence" (Salmon, personal communication, 1980; 1984)—it might turn out that such a general, almost metaphysical statement of the generative conditions for a Pearsonian frequency curve of individual differences, the mathematics being interpretable by a very general embedding text (referring in highly abstract ways to unspecified kinds of repeated events occurring together and the like), could corroborate substantive taxonic conjectures by an empirical finding that two or more quantitative indicators (1) are each distributed non-Pearsonian but (2) can each be decomposed into two Pearsonian components (3) having component weights the same (within tolerance) for all the indicators.

In almost any discussion of research strategy or data interpretation, one will hear plausible statements like the following: "You cannot study the genetics of schizophrenia until agreement exists on a *definitive* set of diagnostic signs." "To add a new symptomatic indicator to the list constituting a syndrome, or to justify a shift in the diagnostic weights within the received list, either (1) is an arbitrary redefinition or (2) requires nonsymptomatic criteria to validate it." "To rediagnose a case because its subsequent clinical course disconfirms expectation is an arbitrary [or, 'circular'] act." "To say that 'true schizophrenia' refers to the genetically determined cases and all others are phenocopies is viciously circular." "We cannot assign differential diagnostic weights to the elements of a syndrome unless we have an external criterion, as in neuropathology." "Since all classifications are arbitrary anyway, and mental patients differ from normal persons in ways that exist in all degrees, it makes no scientific sense to ask whether an entity like schizophrenia 'really exists,' and the use or avoidance of this concept is a matter of preference only." "It is inadmissible to explain a given symptom as caused by a disease D unless we can define the term 'D' independently of its symptoms. Otherwise we would be mixing empirical relationships and meaning stipulations." "Any diagnostic cutting score on a continuous indicator variable will be arbitrary, a matter of semantics or convenience." "I can find you a so-called 'schizophrenic' who is more similar symptomatically to some manic-depressives than to most schizophrenics, which proves there is no such entity as schizophrenia." "To speculate that a particular person has the disposition to schizophrenia even though he has survived the morbidity risk period without becoming clinically schizophrenic is scientifically meaningless."

None of these familiar remarks is expressed in technical philosophese, but they are all methodological in nature. *And they are all erroneous.* The last one, for example, imposes a criterion of empirical meaningfulness whose grave disadvantages were already shown by logician Carnap more than 50 years ago (Carnap, 1936–1937/1953, pp. 461–463), when the philosophy of science was far more "operational" and "positivistic" than today. I doubt one could find a single contemporary logician or historian of science who would accept the remarks quoted (Meehl, 1972c, 1986).

SYNDROME AND DISEASE: METACRITERIA
FOR ASSIGNING WEIGHTS

Let's go back to Kraepelin. In the 1899 (sixth) edition of his textbook of psychiatry (although he had adumbrated it in the fifth edition 3 years earlier), he sets out for the first time his concept of the entity *dementia praecox*. It was a composite of entities previously described by himself and others, namely, the *demence precoce* of Morel in 1857, the catatonia or *tension insanity* of Kahlbaum in 1874, the hebephrenia of Hecker in 1871, and Kraepelin's own concept of *dementia paranoides*. As you know, this synthesis involved at least as much emphasis upon history as upon symptomatology in that it was a presumably endogenously determined dementia occurring in adolescence and young adulthood and running a malignant course, the latter big fact differentiating it from the favorable prognostic outlook of the other great psychotic group that we now call the major affective disorders. What Kraepelin calls "*the* common characteristic" of dementia praecox—and I take it, since he was a compulsive Teutonic nosologist, he means the *only* common characteristic—is set out briefly and with little descriptive precision, namely, "a peculiar destruction of the internal connections of the psychic personality." It is true that in subsequent editions of the textbook he no longer made early life onset or terminal dementia strictly *definitive*, since he was forced to admit that some cases that met the rest of his criteria made an apparent clinical or social recovery, and that some patients first showed manifest illness in their 30s or even 40s. But the point is that two aspects of history, onset and course, played a core role in his conception of the disease. Bleuler (1911/1950) extended Kraepelin's conception, and, as I read him, considerably more than most British and Continental (or conservative American) psychiatrists are willing to admit. Thus, for example, he flatly states, both in the 1911 classic and in his *Textbook of Psychiatry* (1924), that nearly all cases of chronic intractable hypochondriasis are in fact schizophrenes.

Karl Menninger complained years ago of psychiatrists who rediagnosed patients they had at first labeled dementia praecox or schizophrenia when the patient appeared to make a good social and even clinical recovery. Today we have pretty well accepted the rule of thumb "one third." That is, of patients having a clearly recognizable florid schizophrenia attack, we can expect one-third never to recover from the attack, one-third to recover but have one or more subsequent attacks, and one-third to recover and remain well. Bleuler said that perhaps a fifth of patients make a social recovery, but while he held that Kraepelin was overly pessimistic and succeeded in influencing Kraepelin in this respect in his subsequent editions, Bleuler does make the flat statement— and he had seen not hundreds but thousands of schizophrenic patients and had been able to follow their course over many years—that he had never seen a case that he thought when first carefully diagnosed was an unquestionable schizophrene who upon making what we would ordinarily call a clinical recovery had a complete restitutio ad integrum. In fact, he said, a good clinician does not usually have to look very closely at a "recovered schizophrene" to see unmistakable residues of the disease.

How do we go about deciding when history, as distinguished from the presenting syndrome and the psychometrics, deserves a high weight or even, as clinicians who rediagnose on the basis of long-term course, a definitive status? Whatever else you can say about this problem it is not "merely semantic," and it ought not to be whimsical or arbitrary. The logical positivists' point about the conventional character of definitions has been abused by some psychologists in a way that logicians would not countenance, namely, arguing that because a definition is ultimately stipulative about the use of language, that therefore one definition is just as good as another. As far as I'm aware, no logician, not even the Vienna positivists in their 1928 heyday, maintained such a silly thesis. I put it to you that the evidentiary weight that history deserves among our diagnostic criteria rests epistemologically upon precisely the same basis as neurology or mental status or biochemical tests or an MMPI profile; to wit, it is a portion of the evidence whose relevance must be decided empirically, that latter including corroborated causal theory, if such exists. I have heard psychologists poke fun at psychiatrists for modifying diagnoses in the light of course, as if this were some kind of vicious circularity. They are mistaken in this. The epistemic situation of a diagnostician in the absence of a well confirmed causal theory of a disease entity is exactly analogous to that of a psychometrician factor analyzing an omnibus intelligence test, even though the mathematics has a different structure. You start with the initial observation that certain signs, symptoms, test scores, and life history facts show a non-chance tendency to be associated in the population of patients and normal people. In organic medicine, the fact of the existence of things that "run together" (the Greek for these words being *syndrome*) is usually fairly obvious, and physicians have identified such entities many centuries before Karl Pearson invented chi square and the correlation coefficient. Doing it without formal statistics and frequently with reliance upon one's clinical memory means, of course, that some pseudosyndromes will be identified. But that fact does not disprove the basic epistemic point that when symptoms S1, S2, $S3_n$ . . . are found empirically to cohere, so that when patients have a pair of them they are likely to have several of the others, we conclude that we are onto some kind of disease entity. As I have pointed out elsewhere (Meehl & Golden, 1982), there isn't anything metaphysically profound or methodologically suspect about this. It's close to common sense and the universal experience of medical practitioners. Dr. Fisbee discovers a new syndrome not in the books, consisting of headache, fever, pink ears, and purple tongue. Initially all he has is the statistical confluence of the signs and symptoms. But he also has a sensible medical conjecture, namely, there is something going on inside the patient that gives rise to this syndrome. He doesn't believe that the pink ears are themselves directly causative of the purple tongue or the headache, and so he conjectures—a plausible conjecture warranted by the whole history of medicine since Hippocrates—that these things that go together do so because of a common cause, and that that common cause is not witchcraft or sunspots but an inner state of some sort. In organic medicine that state is called *pathology.*

Now the question is, which signs, symptoms, test scores, or history facts ought to receive more weight in diagnosing the new entity? In medicine that is ultimately decided by the correlation each of them has with the defining pathology. If two similar pathologies are associated with different etiologies (as, for example, two different germs causing meningitis), the weighting of symptoms will also take that different etiology into account. The problem in "functional" mental disorders is that the clinicopathological conference does not have somebody who comes in with the patient's psychic institutions on a tray, or with slides, the way they do in internal medicine, and who points to the "holes in the patient's superego" or the "latent homosexual bubbles from his id." The closest analogy to the pathologist's report on tissue is trait organization and psychodynamics; the analogy to the etiology is genes and the social learning history (Meehl, 1973b, p. 287). Until a well corroborated causal theory of something like schizophrenia or the sociopathic personality is available, we cannot offer *criterial* definitions of the sort we do in neurology or internal medicine, where one says that whatever may be the symptoms and signs, a necessary condition to have paresis is the characteristic (I was taught *unique*) cortical changes of the paretic brain and the presence of *Treponema pallidum* as the causal agent. We do not have the equivalent of this in psychopathology.

Does this mean it is impossible to say anything rationally persuasive about the differential weights for elements of the syndrome and facts of the life history, in discussing an entity like schizophrenia? It is easy to become discouraged and think this, but things aren't quite that bad. I look again to organic medicine for enlightenment, recognizing that some modifications—especially souping up the mathematics—will be necessary. In the delineation of medical syndromes, including those for which the pathology and etiology are unknown or speculative, one is struck by an interesting historical fact. A medical writer does assign more diagnostic weight to some facts than others, which is puzzling when he has no pathological, defining criteria against which to validate them. Suppose I say that Fisbee's Syndrome has as elements purple tongue, pink ears, fever, and headache, but that the pink ears, while perhaps not pathognomonic, are "almost invariably present," whereas the fever may be minimal or absent. This seems a strange thing to say if at this stage of my knowledge all I have to *constitute* Fisbee's Syndrome is its signs and symptoms. This kind of epistemic situation leads some hard-nosed behaviorists to say that the syndrome is circularly defined, which is a stupid thing to say, because the *fact of the syndrome* is a statistical fact, not a definition. When we "define" the syndrome, if we are careful, we scrupulously refrain from a literal identification of the disease with its signs and symptoms. Such an identification would be impossible here, since it would mean that none of the elements listed could ever be missing. That would require that the pairwise correlation of the elements be perfect in order for a syndrome to exist. Since that is plainly false for several thousand well understood diseases, it would be a foolish move to say that a syndrome can only exist if its elements are pairwise perfectly correlated. Most syndromes in organic medicine are like syndromes in psychopathology, namely, they are "loose syndromes" (Meehl, 1973a). That is a fact of nature, not a matter of clinicians' carelessness, laziness, or illogicality. *The background conjecture is the same in psychopathology as it is in organic medicine, even though the theoretical entities differ, and psychologists have been forced to develop more sophisticated search methods than Hippocrates or Osler.*

Basically, the notion is simply that if two things go together in a nonchance way and cannot (on common sense or theoretical grounds) plausibly be supposed to be causing each other, then there is some third thing that causes each of them and brings about their covariation. It is that unknown latent something that we have in the back of our minds when we undertake research on a syndrome so as to understand it better. We anticipate that when we understand it well enough, we will be able to substitute an explicit definition, *in these causal theoretical terms*, for the implicit or contextual definition we have to offer initially by referring to the syndrome's internal statistics. It puzzles me that some psychologists have a hard time grasping this simple methodological point. I have heard it said that to invoke schizophrenia as a cause of hallucinations is circular or, even worse, like explaining a hysterical symptom in terms of witchcraft. The trouble with those fetching analogies is that they are themselves circular, because they presuppose a negative answer to the question whether there is some shared pathology and etiology in cases of schizophrenia. The trouble with the witchcraft theory of a paralyzed arm is not methodological but factual; that is, there aren't any such things as witches. The witchcraft analogy could be used in this way to disparage the biochemist's view that milk is curdled by little creatures called *Lactobacillus bulgaricus*, holding that the latter concept is no more methodologically respectable than the medieval housewives' view that milk is curdled by the brownies. Such malicious analogies are useless, and I have found that pseudosophistication is far worse than naivete because it's harder to cure. The reason we prefer the *Lactobacillus bulgaricus* to the brownie theory is simple—namely, there *are* tiny organisms that secrete the enzyme that curdles milk, and there *aren't* any brownies. If there were any brownies, it would be perfectly all right to explain things by invoking them.

The prevailing theory of schizophrenia when I was a student was that the specific etiology that would some day become the "operational definition" of the disease was something about having a battle-ax mother, a historical event whose residues are now preserved in the patient's schizoid psyche. The statistical evidence having largely discredited that theory (which has nothing wrong with it had it turned out to be factually correct), we now have good support for a different theory, namely, a schizophrenic genetic makeup, whether a major locus, or two, or polygenic with a threshold being still a matter of empirical dispute (Gottesman & Shields, 1972, 1982). If we remain stuck at our present level of information for some time, where evidence is clear to an unbiased mind that the thing is heavily genetic, but we don't know the biochemistry, or even whether a major gene is involved, how would we go about assigning weight to a historical fact, such as unusual shyness in school or—a favorite one with me that emerged from my colleague Garmezy's research years ago—doing well in school until you hit fractions in the third grade and then rapidly declining in school performance? Or how about having a first-degree relative diagnosed schizophrenia? Or a complete symptomatic recovery, where even Bleuler might be hard put to point to the residual scarring?

Well, if that's all we know, we have to rely upon the internal statistics of the syndrome, of course including psychometrics and ward behavior as part of the data. The first question to ask is a mathematical one, namely, is this entity taxonic, that is, does it represent a *type* or *taxon* (a natural kind), or are we merely locating the patient in a hyperspace defined by the relevant continuous descriptors? I would like to think that I have solved the statistical problem of answering that question with some of my own recent taxometric methods, but that would be a bit on the grandiose side. I will content myself with saying that *some such methods* as those that my colleague Robert Golden and I have been working on in recent years will provide the answer (Gangestad & Snyder, 1985; Golden, 1982; Golden, Campbell, & Perry, 1987; Golden, Gallob, & Watt, 1983; Golden & Meehl, 1978, 1979, 1980; Golden, Vaughan, Kurtzberg, & McCarton, in press; Meehl, 1973a, 1979; Meehl & Golden, 1982). The question as to the precise relationship between satisfying statistical criteria of latent taxonicity and corroborating an interpretive text speaking about causes presents grave difficulties, but I am optimistic. Whether you happen to like cluster analysis or latent class analysis and, if the latter, whether you are favorably impressed with such of my methods as have yet been published, is not the point. I only want to persuade you that the essential idea of establishing taxonicity by means of a suitable type of cluster or latent class algorithm corresponds, in a modern sophisticated way, to the historical fact that physicians identified many real diseases before the creation of modern pathology and bacteriology by such greats as Virchow and Koch. The metatheoretical reasoning in taxometrics is essentially the same as in factor analysis, multidimensional scaling, and other psychometric procedures that infer the operation of latent causal entities by studying the statistical structure of covariant facts. Having said this against abusers of the tricky word "circularity," let me say equally clearly that I do not wish to exaggerate the power of purely correlational methods, especially those confined to cross-sectional data, in testing substantive causal theories. Adding the time dimension (we don't let the causal arrow operate backward in time!) and, even more, including in our evidence portions of the theoretical network tested in other ways (e.g., experimentally, or derivable from some other discipline such as genetics) are usually necessary in resolving theoretical disagreement arising from purely correlational information. Of course everybody (except perhaps B. F. Skinner) agrees that one of the merits of a good theory is suggesting new facts to collect or new ways of analyzing old facts.

THE THEORY OF SCHIZOTAXIA

Let me take my theory of schizotaxia as an example (Meehl, 1962b, 1972a, 1972c). I conjecture the existence of a *schizogene* (a few of us, especially in Minneapolis, are not convinced that the major locus theory has been slain) that is an autosomal dominant completely penetrant for an endophenotypic neurological trait I label *schizotaxia*. This is a special kind of neural-integrative defect (about which I have a detailed physiological conjecture) that is, strictly speaking, *all* that can be "inherited." I do *not* say that schizotypy (the personality makeup predisposing to schizophrenia) is inherited, although that statement is commonly attributed to me in general and abnormal psychology textbooks. Schizotypy as a personality makeup is based upon social learning by an organism with the schizotaxic central nervous system (CNS) defect. Schizophrenia is a decompensation of the schizotypal personality that, given the available genetic statistics, I assume occurs in only around 10% of them. I do not look upon schizotypy as a kind of "attenuated schizophrenia," which I think inappropriate for a sophisticated genetic-learning theoretical model. Therefore I also tend to avoid the common locution "spectrum disorder." An analogy: Consider gout, whose sine qua non is an elevated plasma uric acid titer. Less than 10% of men having the gout genome and therefore the elevated uric acid titer develop clinical gout; no one knows why. If we take the medieval physician's tetradic definition of "inflammation" (rubor, dolor, turgor, and calor), we do not expect the gout-free monozygotic (MZ) twins of clinically gouty males to have "just a teeny bit of gout." We do not anticipate their being ill with a member of a gout specrum. What we do anticipate in an MZ twin, and in a sizeable number of dizygotic (DZ) twins, is the elevated uric acid titer.

There is nothing mysterious about this, statistically or causally. It's simply that the closer we are in the causal chain to the DNA, the larger the correlation between a fallible indicator and the mutated gene becomes. One therefore expects the psychophysiology and "soft neurology" of schizotaxia to be more powerful indicators of the schizogene than, say, social anhedonia or subtle semantic manifestations of thought disorder. Since on such a theory there are several presumably polygenic potentiators of schizophrenic illness in the schizotypal personality (I have elsewhere listed a dozen or so, each of which I would bet on with high confidence, purely from my clinician's armchair), we have no way of knowing in advance which of these polygenic potentiators is more causally significant, and therefore we do not have any *theoretical* basis for assigning to some of them more diagnostic weight than others.

I no longer anticipate any molar behavioral indicator, psychometric or interview, to be pathognomonic of schizotaxia, although I do still believe in a one-way pathognonicity (that is, an inclusion test) in the characteristic schizophrenic thought disorder. The example I gave in my 1962 APA presidential address of a patient who, asked why he was in the hospital, said, "Well, doctor, naturally, I'm growing my father's hair" seems to me as good today as it did then, as would that of a patient who, when told by the examiner "I sometimes have trouble following your talk," replies with "Oh, yes, doctor, that's because I often speak Echo Monster Head Affair Language." But the *absence* of thought disorder, even of a subtle type hard to detect on interview or psychometrically, is not, I believe, valid as an exclusion test for schizotaxia. Of course, many competent clinicians would reject it as an exclusion test even for schizophrenia of the relatively intact paranoid variety.

It may be that a sufficiently subtle and mathematically souped-up measure of semantical or syntactical aberrations will someday be a powerful sign of the taxon, but I'm inclined to doubt it, and nobody has yet succeeded in devising one. One ingenious and indefatigable researcher, Oltmanns, after several years of work along the "subtle semantic" cognitive slippage line, has for the time being abandoned that approach to finding strong schizotypal indicators (Berenbaum, Gottesman, & Oltmanns, 1985; Kagan & Oltmanns, 1981; Neale, Oltmanns, & Harvey, 1985; Oltmanns, personal communication, May 19, 1987; Ragin & Oltmanns, 1986). I confess to some resistance in accepting this conclusion, partly on (weak) theoretical grounds, partly because of the central role of associative loosening in Bleuler's minimally theoretical clinical description of the diagnosable syndrome. It is puzzling that a core feature of the disease should be totally absent in compensated schizotypes, so I persist in entertaining a faint hope that we haven't hit upon a sufficiently sensitive (schizospecific!) way to measure it.

The main problem with molar indicators of compensated schizotypy is their "causal distance" from the DNA. Speaking physiologically, we deal with molar outputs that result from numerous serial and converging chains of brain processes, acting as potentiators or inhibitors of one another, sometimes involving two-way influence (positive or negative), presenting possibilities of step-functions and sign reversals, and with the parameters of *all* their linkage functions having large normal range (polygenic and acquired) individual differences. Speaking psychologically, anything molar has a complex learned form and content, with individual differences arising from the different life histories superimposed on (and partly due to) genetic differences. If we did not have available the mass of inconclusive or inconsistent studies to confuse us, we should be able to predict their messiness from our clinical armchairs. Consider, for example, the salient trait of anxiety proneness. Psychodynamically, one thinks immediately of the 20 or so defense mechanisms that the anxiety signal puts into action and realizes that all 20 can plausibly be supposed to have different influences, qualitatively and quantitatively, on various cognitive functions. We cannot even assume that all schizotypes will be made anxious by the same social stimulus, or that, if made so, they will engage the same defense mechanism at different anxiety levels or in different social contexts. The obfuscating role of problematic auxiliary theories, including minitheories of psychometrics, is so great that the conceptual task of parsing studies verges on the impossible (Meehl, in press).

I do not suggest that we cease inquiry into molar level indicators, since a few of them may turn out well despite these pessimistic considerations. "Chaotic sexuality," for example, while listed in my schizotypal checklist (Meehl, 1964) as a fairly important indicator of decompensated schizotypy, I should not have expected to show up in the compensated range, but Frost and Chapman (1987) looks encouraging.

We want to select indicators of the schizotypal personality (Gunderson, Siever, & Spaulding 1983; Meehl,1962b, 1964, 1972a, 1972b, 1972c; Morey, Waugh, & Blashfield, 1985; Rado, 1956, 1960; Rado & Daniels, 1956; Siever & Gunderson, 1983). If one is unpersuaded that there is such an entity, then say merely "the schizophrenia-prone person" (Chapman & Chapman, 1985, 1987). We are faced with a vast, confusing, and often inconsistent literature that contains several hundred candidates for indicator status. One has the impression that whether a certain line of investigation has been pursued did not depend solely on satisfactory replicability. We should not reject purely clinical suggestions in the early literature merely because, when Kraepelin and Bleuler were writing, present day standards of "hard data" quantification and statistical method had not yet evolved. It's one thing to ask whether the observations of an astute and seasoned clinician have been subjected to modern quantitative scrutiny. It's another—smacking of perfectionist, nay-saying scientism—to say that if that has not been done, that we can relegate these impressions to the trash can.

The choice of indicators for further research ought to be based upon a combination of skilled clinicians' consensus (I never lightly dismiss anything the great Bleuler says in his 1911 classic) with what quantitative replications exist, plus a liberal dose of theory. The trouble with this latter is that we have had a great proliferation of theories in the 90 years since recognizing dementia praecox as a diagnostic entity. I have read somewhere that if you count minitheories, there are over 100 published theories of schizophrenia. It's discouraging that none of them has commanded even a preponderance of assent. If we press the point, about the only thing we can say for sure about schizophrenia theory is that there is something genetic about its etiology. We are almost at the stage where a second conjecture commands sizeable assent, namely, it is in some sense a "neurological" disorder. In my APA presidential address over a quarter century ago (Meehl, 1962b), I concluded by predicting that taxonomic statistical methods applied to carefully chosen fallible indicators would show that schizophrenia is fundamentally a neurological disease of genetic origin. That was rank heresy in the psychological profession (and even to a considerable extent in psychiatry) in 1962, and I am in the pleasing position of seeing (if I see straight) my rash prophecy increasingly confirmed. I hope to present details of my current theory of schizophrenia in an issue of Dr. Millon's journal, so I shall only adumbrate that fuller presentation here.

My strategy is different from that followed by almost all previous theoreticians. The usual approach to this puzzling disease has been to focus attention upon one striking feature of the phenotype, chosen by its relative specificity or its qualitatively striking character or its social importance. One then takes this "core, striking" phenomenological feature as basic and attempts to derive the rest of the syndrome from it. This can be done in psychological (behavioral or experiential) terms, or it can be done by identifying the allegedly core feature with some specific region of the brain or some component of the body chemistry and then working back from that conjectured physiological core to attempt derviations of the rest of the loose syndrome. I think this strategy is a mistaken one, and that's why none of these theories has commanded the assent of more than a small minority of practitioners and researchers at any given time. When you approach it this way, you have a fairly satisfactory "explanation" (although sometimes rather tautological) of the one big feature that you selected for attention as being the essence of the disease, but then when you start trying to explain the other elements of the syndrome that, even if not statistically as core as yours, you have to admit are fairly high-weight indicators and certainly have a frequency sufficient to require any theory to explain them plausibly, you have to do an awful lot of fancy footwork and ad hockery, which theorists of other persuasions find implausible.

I think that the psychological source of this strategic mistake is a simple one, namely, that most of us hear about the schizophrenia syndrome in an abnormal psychology class as undergraduates. Many of us first heard it earlier, as sophomores, when described in lecture and several pages of text in a general psychology class. So that by the time we are practitioners and researchers, we have become thoroughly accustomed to this collection of signs, symptoms, traits, and life history characteristics. For this reason, "familiarity breeding blindness," we are unable to take a fresh look, and we have come to take what is really a very odd, heterogeneous collection of aberrations for granted. Clinicians don't realize, unless they force themselves to step back and try to be naive observers who never heard of this strange entity before, what a phenomenologically unconnected, qualitatively diverse range of aberrations constitute the loose syndrome at the descriptive level. I won't try to prove it here, but if you will reflect, I think you will agree that this is truer of schizophrenia than it is of, say, the major affective disorders or anxiety neurosis or organic brain syndrome or even the psychopath. A layman could derive much—I am inclined to think almost all—of the syndromes of hypomania or depression if asked to imagine how he would think, feel, and act if he were a lot sadder than he's ever been or "up"more than he's ever been. But if you try this with schizophrenia, selecting something like, say, an extreme of social introversion, and expect a layman or a personality psychologist to derive from that, thinking phenomenologically or behavioristically, the body image distortion, the soft neurology, the hypohedonia, the subtle semantic aberrations, or psychophysiological indicators like the eye-tracking anomaly or reduced secondary inhibition of the P50 auditory evoked potential, he would not be able to do it. My point is that we should take that qualitative diversity seriously as the *first big fact that must be faced in adopting a strategy of theory construction.*

Let me give some examples of the wrong strategy that go very far back (except for my own 1962 mistake), so hardly anybody today would have any investment in them. While I was an extern in the early 1940s, psychiatrists in my surround were talking about the probable crucial role of what was then called the reticular activating system (RAS) in the etiology of schizophrenia. Why were they talking about this? Well, its very existence as a discrete anatomical system had only been demonstrated in the late 1930s, and that interesting finding from the neuroanatomist was combined with the obvious clinical fact that many schizophrenes show a deviation from the norm in their general level of arousal. The majority were on the low side, with some chronic deteriorated back ward schizophrenes almost as vegetable-like as a severe organic brain syndrome patient; others, especially in the early stages (and dramatically in the syndrome of *catatonic raptus*), showed a hyperaroused state. I'm not saying that it was stupid to call attention to this interesting possibility. I'm merely illustrating what I call the "specific defect" error in strategy. One could understand *some* psychometric and psychomotor characteristics on the basis of aberrations in the arousal system. But when one asked why should arousal result in the unique kind of thought disorder that is not found in an excited manic or a hyperaroused anxiety neurosis, or what arousal should have to do with the interpersonal aversiveness so characteristic of this disease, or even why it should be that some of the severest shattered mentation with gross thought disorder should be found in calm patients (I view the characteristic thought disorder in a nonconfused, nonexcited state as one of the two pathognomonic inclusion tests for schizophrenia), it was hard to explain these things on the arousal basis.

Then I remember a suggestion current around 1940 that the basic problem was a disturbance of carbohydrate metabolism, sugested by the apparent efficacy of insulin treatment and the tendency of some schizophrenes to gobble sweets (one thinks of schizotype Hitler!) and the fact that the brain doesn't know how to utilize anything but carbohydrate in its energy consumption. Or again, because of the spread of interpersonal aversiveness that is *socially* the most outstanding feature (we notice that more than we do soft neurology in our relations with other persons), and assuming that aversiveness ultimately comes down to a matter of conditioned anxiety, we had theories shortly after World War II that focused upon some quantitative aberration in the anxiety parameter (say, the steepness of the conditioned anxiety gradient). This works fine for social fear, but when one considers that potent anxiety reducers like Valium don't do anything for schizophrenia, that relatively nonanxious chronic schizophrenes are likely to show more severe thought disorder than acutely anxious early stage cases, and that one can think of many neurotics who manifest extremes of anxiety more than the great majority of schizophrenes but who do not show even a hint of schizoid cognitive slippage, or any of the psychophysiological or soft neurology features of the syndrome, this conjecture requires more extensive ad hockery than we want to permit.

Coming closer to home, in 1962 under the influence of my Rado-trained analyst (from whom I learned a great deal about schizotypy), I attached more diagnostic importance to hypohedonia than I now think appropriate, and I even made what I now view as a foolish, unplausible attempt to derive the schizophrenic syndrome from a genetic hedonic deficit. I believe that all such theories are bound to fail.

If we begin by focusing our attention not on a particular facet of the syndrome that has high statistical occurrence or clinical importance or social impact or striking quality but instead attend to the near ubiquity of the defect, we come to a different kind of theory. I do not of course maintain that absolutely everything you can study in schizophrenes is impaired, but I suggest to you that *almost* everything is impaired to some extent, even those functions that Bleuler in his monograph describes as not so, such as attention (cf. Knight, 1984). We don't have to decide exactly which subset of all of the hundreds of empirical findings in the literature will hold up under efforts of quantitative replication to make the general statement that many, many things are haywire in these people compared to how many different kinds of things are haywire in neurotics, those with major affective disorders, or psychopaths. In almost all behavior domains or sectors and at all levels of molarity from tendon reflexes up to the most integrative, complex, learned social behavior, if you look carefully, the schizophrene is likely to show some departures, large or slight, from the norm. That to me is the big fact, and the one that suggests the kind of theoretical strategy I favor. The most obvious, straightforward conjecture suggested by ubiquity of aberration at different levels of molarity and different life sectors is that *whatever is wrong with the schizotaxic CNS is wrong throughout; that is, the schizotaxic nervous system is aberrated in every anatomical region and at all levels, from the sacral cord to the frontal lobes.*

What might this defect be? It is not a defect of inputting, nor storage, nor retrieval, nor of insufficient complexity, all of these being defects that would prevent the extraordinary intellectual achievements of some world-renowned schizotypes (e.g., Newton, Goedel). I conjecture a quantitative aberration in the synaptic transmission function called *hypokrisia.* Consider a pattern of arrival times for presynaptic spikes at the terminal knobs, representing this pattern over the synaptic scale by a point in the synaptic signal space whose coordinates are arrival times at the knobs. Assuming concurrent stimulation of the axon hillock, each such point is associated with a Lorente de Nó optional transmission probability. These probabilities define a hypersurface in the synaptic signal space. My conjecture is that this hypersurface is both (1) elevated and (2) flattened—exaggerated but with fewer differential hills and valleys—in the schizotaxic CNS. This results in single-unit "synaptic slippage," which in turn causes slippage in intermodule control functions, and so on up the hierarchy of CNS systems. The hypokrisia itself I attribute to a deficient amount of some substance X whose function is to stabilize the cell membrane or facilitate its repolarization in stimulated subregions in the orthotaxic brain. So you see I am doing precisely what disciples of Skinner consider a cardinal sin, to wit, reattributing to the CNS innards a descriptive property of the behavior, by generalizing Bleuler's fundamental trait of *associative loosening* to the physical system underlying associations, specifically, functional connections at the synapse. Contrary to the Skinnerians, while the history of science shows examples where this kind of partly repeated attribution at another causal level has been useless, in other cases (e.g., magnetism, gas pressure, population genetics) it has been extremely profitable and turns out to be the literal truth of the matter. Strangely enough, while Bleuler does mention several phenomena of soft neurology in his chapter on the physical symptoms of the disease, he does not (so far as I can find) connect these with that "loosening" he believes to be fundamental at the molar level of behavior and experience.

How this loosening in synaptic control will affect a given molar level and behavior domain cannot be rigorously derived without knowing details of the CNS systems of molar domains among normals, which we do not presently have. Hence, explanations of why some cognitive functions are more impaired than others in the experimental literature of psychologists studying schizophrenia are usually premature and result in what appear to be inconsistent findings (Knight, 1984). But I suggest that less detailed, broadly characterized trends are understandable. Why does a ubiquitous integrative defect require less ad hockery than that required by theories that focus on a specific domain or subsystem and are then faced with the terrible task of deriving the qualitative diversity of consequences? The methodological point involved here is this: Because of the syndrome's diversity, playing it in the customary way requires *many different unrelated ad hoc auxiliaries* (Meehl, 1978). It might seem that postulating a ubiquitous defect throughout the nervous system at all levels and in all domains would be in the same boat with regard to ad hockery, but this is not true. Because instead of having the former difficulty, how to derive dissimilar symptoms $S_1, S_2, \ldots S_n$ from special defect D_s? we have the opposite problem in my kind of theory, why doesn't ubiquitous defect D_u impair all functions (levels, domains) equally? But this second question is much less embarrassing. The reason is that we already have independent knowledge, apart from psychopathology, concerning many of the required auxiliary hypotheses. Also, the general fact of partially independent and variably influenced subsystems is well known outside of psychopathology, so it is not ad hoc as a general principle. Classical psychometrics provides the paradigm. For example, in omnibus intelligence tests we have a general intelligence factor, several group factors, specific factors, and error in our psychometric equation. We don't have to know anything about schizophrenia or about abnormal behavior to know that common knowledge and a huge mass of psychometric research on abilities and personality traits shows that whatever may be the detailed character of the cerebral subsystems involved, it is an empirical fact that a general factor, even if as powerful as we find in something like g, does not saturate all kinds of performances equally. This kind of standard psychometric model is the model we should adopt in thinking upon findings like soft neurology in the schizotype. This view, which, I repeat, *does not involve assuming anything beyond what we already know from a huge mass of data about the psychology of individual differences among normals,* leads to expectations that a ubiquitous CNS aberration (1) should influence all, or nearly all, levels and sectors somewhat, (2) should influence some levels and sectors more than others, and (3) should be statistically "fuzzy" because of individual differences in group factors and specifics. There is nothing ad hoc about any of these expectations.

One would like to say a little more than this about different behavior domains, and I think that we can make some plausible predictions of a probabilistic nature as to which domains we expect to be more impaired, *on the average.* We expect to have more impairments among domains (1) involving relatively distant subsystems and hence spike transmissions as the main process, (2) requiring complex integration of spike-transmitted outputs from diverse controlling subsystems, (3) demanding finely tuned multiple control by several converging subsystems as in (2) (this a conjecture that might be expressed mathematically in terms of values of the partial derivatives of multiple input control functions), (4) providing rare opportunity for developing corrective or substitute adjustments (for example, not like the color blind who learn to rely on other cues), (5) where growth of a molar aberration is autocatalytic because two or more functions interact with positive feedback (for example, we have distorted social cognitions leading to aversive drift leading to further distorted cognitions, etc.), (6) where person and environment interactions are like the intrapersonal situation (5), and (7) where the external reinforcement schedule is highly stochastic. Thus the most stochastic of all reinforcement schedules in human life, as I pointed out in my 1962 lecture, is the social, and hence it is not surprising that the most dramatic impairment in the schizotype often is in the interpersonal domain.

It would be pretentious to undertake any kind of high-level quantification of the above list. But I think the reader will agree with me that it is at least not empirically empty of consequences. So my contention is that the postulation of a ubiquitous integrative neural defect such as schizotaxia (whether or not its micro level is spelled out in detail, as in my concept of hypokrisia) does not involve the tremendous amount of unrelated ad hockery needed in going from a more special defect of a particular subsystem like the reticular or the limbic or the dopamine or whatever; rather, it appeals to already independently known facts about individual differences such as are familiar from classical psychometrics. Deriving the aversive drift and the hypohedonia from the concept of hypokrisia is a much more complicated—and, I admit, loose—derivation that I do not have space or courage to present here but will try to do in a longer paper now in preparation.

My colleagues in behavior genetics are puzzled by my avoidance of the term "penetrance" in discussing the theory of schizophrenia (Meehl, 1962b, 1972a, 1972c, 1973a). They sometimes think I dislike the concept because it is an abusable fudge factor, but that is not my point at all. There is nothing wrong with a fudge factor if the relation of the number of equations to the number of unknowns makes the penetrance coefficient overdeterminable from the data. While I sometimes allow myself to speak of "clinical penetrance," by which I mean the proportion of schizotypes who develop a diagnosable clinical schizophrenia, this is a harmless concession to the conventional speech of geneticists, and I have a methodological reason for preferring a different terminology. Genetics texts introduce "penetrance" first and then define "expressivity" as a secondary, derivative notion—that is, "*If* it shows in the phenotype, *then* by how much quantitatively?" This order is both epistemologically and mathematically backward. The proper prior concept is expressivity, the quantitative distribution of an indicator among subjects having the schizoid genotype. This distribution is an objective fact about the empirical world, although we may have a hard time ascertaining it, whereas the penetrance coefficient is the result of our choice of cutting score. The only nonarbitrary penetrance is 100, that is, when the two expressivity distributions have zero overlap. There are as many penetrances as there are cutting scores for a single quantitative indicator.

But the situation is worse than that, because most syndromes—certainly all syndromes in psychopathology—are fairly loose in the statistical sense; so we first have arbitrary penetrance cuts on each trait, and then we have a system of such cuts assigned over the several traits of the phenotypic syndrome. That's a different situation from having a scarlet eye color in the fruitfly.

In my theory, what the schizogene does is to produce a certain aberration in the synaptic control parameters, an *endophenotypic* trait at the level of a single nerve cell, found throughout the CNS of schizotaxic persons. That is *all* the schizogene directly produces causally. In textbooks and articles I am said to hold that what is inherited is the schizotypic personality, but I never committed such an absurdity, and I think my writing on that is clear. All that is, strictly speaking, inherited is the schizotaxic brain, upon which the schizotypal personality develops by a complicated process of social learning. The endophenotype is in turn expressed, in varying quantitative amounts, by various psychophysiological and soft neurological exophenotypic indicators. Whether any of the latter are truly pathognomonic for the schizotaxic brain I do not know. But I take it for granted that the longer the causal chain and the more different kinds of causal links are in that chain between the DNA and an exophenotypic manifestation, the lower the statistical "pathognomicity." It is theoretically unlikely, on a model such as this, that one could invent, say, a psychometric measure of cognitive slippage or hypohedonia that would have quasi-pathognomonic status with respect to the dominant schizogene I conjecture, or, in a polygenic model, a high correlation with the polygenic variable or high sensitivity for having passed a polygenic threshold of the kind conjectured by Gottesman and others.

I find some behavior geneticists, even those whose Ph.D. is in psychology, minoring in genetics (and almost always among those where it goes the other way), still refer to "the trait" in discussing schizophrenia or schizotypy. This is an unfortunate usage because schizophrenia and schizotypy are *loose syndromes*, composed of elements some of which have no content overlap with the others. This is partly what makes schizophrenia so baffling (and interesting!) compared, say, with the major affective disorders. There isn't anything behaviorally in common between subtle semantic or syntactical aberrations in speech, extreme social aversiveness, and a tendency to hear voices—let alone a ± dysdiadochokinesia or the famous reduced specific dynamic action of protein that the Worcester group found when they fed schizophrenia patients a meat breakfast! Even the psychophysiological and soft neurology indicators, which I am happy to see have now been revived in research interest and are spoken of more commonly among clinicians (they went in abeyance during the heyday of psychodynamic and social views of schizophrenia), are far from perfectly correlated. Why should we be surprised at this? It *would* be surprising if the correlation between different neurological and psychophysiological indicators was feeble compared with that between social and personality measures, which attain the values they do as the end result of a long stochastic process involving thousands of life experiences in social learning, whereas the former are closer in the causal chain to the schizogene and influenced by fewer nuisance variables. We take the existence of group and specific factors as a matter of course in all domains of psychometrics, whether we're studying intelligence or mechanical ability or social effectiveness or whatever. We should also assume, given the terrible complexity of the brain, that there are neurological equivalents of group and specific factors, involving different cerebral subsystems, despite our conjecturing a pervasive CNS functional aberration (analogous to Spearman's g), as in my theory.

Considerations of this sort also lead me to avoid the term "modifier" in expounding my theory. If the schizogene gives rise, either by a biochemical lesion or, as I think less likely, but a live option, a fine structure, microanatomic aberration (e.g., something funny about the distribution of terminal knobs over the synaptic scale), we have a brain that is predisposed to certain quantitative aberrations in the acquisition of all sorts of behavioral first-order dispositions such as social habits, verbal, perceptual, and motor skills, and so forth. The same group and special factors that would appear in a factor analysis of abilities, skills, and personality traits in a normal population clear of schizotypes will be operating to produce individual differences within the schizotypal taxon and will thereby lead to some indicators being more statistically high-weight for the schizogene than others. You don't need any research to know this a priori. It would be a miracle if it were not the case, extrapolating from our general knowledge of psychology, physiology, and the statistics of individual differences. In my theory of schizotaxia, the basic neural integrative deficit leads, by a chain of reasoning that I cannot develop here, to the prediction of *aversive drift*, and this aversive drift would have *on the average* a greater push in the highly stochastic domain of interpersonal reinforcement schedules than in, say, the simpler high-probability ones of reaching for a seen object or even working on crossword puzzles.

On the other hand, the polygenic system for garden-variety, normal range individual differences in social introversion, which is now well corroborated by numerous investigations, presumably operates in a quite different way, having no overlap with the causal chain involved in schizotaxic aversive drift. Similarly, polygenes for the general intelligence factor initiate another complex *but parallel* causal pathway. There isn't anything in the theory that suggests that these pathways overlap or that the genes for intelligence somehow get in the way of the schizogene's effecting the aversive drift. Even social introversion, which must be involved in some complicated way with the tendency to aversive drift, is not something that *intervenes* in the causal chain between the gene and the phenotypic expression, as in textbook examples of epistasis or polygenic modifiers. Rather, we have a schizogene leading via social learning processes to more or less specifically schizotypal personality traits *themselves manifest in the phenotype.* (Consider, for example, the "friendly schizotype" we have all seen, who interacts more than a normal person, and far more readily than a nonschizoid introvert, with inappropriate social approaches to total strangers.) Finally, whether a schizotype makes his way in the world or ends up in a mental hospital might be dependent upon his IQ, which is a cluster of traits hvaing, again, negligible overlap with schizoid cognitive slippage or schizoid aversive drift or garden-variety nonschizoid introversion. The point is that these are exophenotypic dispositions controlled by different genetic systems that do interact with the environment and alter the probability of decompensation into a clinical schizophrenia. That causal situation is so different from what is implied by the geneticist's term "modifier" that we need a separate word to designate the change in illness probability, and that's why I prefer the word "potentiator." One consequence of this kind of reasoning is a research strategy that focuses heavily on family studies of neurological and psychophysiological indicators that have been shown to be related to schizophrenia risk, in preference to the more clinically relevant abnormalities of interpersonal behavior.

ENVIRONMENTAL INFLUENCES AND COMPLEXITY OF THE CAUSAL CHAIN

The methodological difficulties in attempting to infer causal influence from the kind of reconstruction of a life history that we ordinarily have available in clinical work are illustrated beautifully (and discouragingly) by the ascendance and decine of the concept "schizophrenogenic mother." After World War II, when I was a young clinician, the notion that one or another kind of battle-ax mother (described in a variety of ways but at least recognized by all as malignant) played a crucial role in the development of schizophrenia was taken seriously by my fellow students and teachers. This was true even in the Midwest, which was less psychodynamic than either coast, where the doctrine was taken as almost axiomatic. In recent years, partly as a result of the adoption studies but also due to the general decline in psychodynamic emphasis in favor of biological approaches to psychopathology, many psychiatrists and psychologists (the majority in my environment) have concluded that the notion of a schizophrenogenic mother is totally without merit. I believe both the old position and the new one are mistaken, and it is useful to examine how these two opposed mistakes have come about.

I begin with the older one. Suppose that there is no such personality type as the schizophrenogenic mother, however described. Putting it more strongly, assume that, typology aside, the behavior of mother has literally zero influence upon whether a child with the genetic disposition to schizophrenia subsequently develops the clinical illness, a doctrine with which I must disagree although I grant that it is closer to the truth than the purely environmental interpretation that used to prevail. How did such a notion arise and capture the allegiance of so many clinicians? I remember that during the 1950s, my reading of the genetic data then available, combined with the rather feeble and inconsistent results of efforts to support the schizophrenogenic concept by quantitative studies, led me to question increasingly the alleged impact of the mother's child-rearing practices and attitudes. Students and colleagues strongly committed to the notion expressed bafflement upon hearing my skepticism, knowing that I was doing quite a bit of psychotherapy at that time and that a sizeable fraction of my patients were schizotypes. "Surely your schizotypal patients bring out material like mine do, unless you are somehow blind to it or turning it off by your interview tactics." It wasn't that my schizotypal patients didn't talk about their childhood families (including their mothers) pretty much the same way the psychodynamic literature reports from other therapists. Rather, it was that my Minnesota training from hardheaded skeptics like Donald G. Paterson and Starke R. Hathaway, not to mention Bill Heron in comparative psychology, had sensitized me to the grave dangers of the anecdotal method, as the old animal psychologists used to call it. I was uncomfortably aware that the anecdotal method does not cease to be anecdotal when we rechristen it with the honorific phrase "clinical experience." I did not doubt, and I do not doubt now, that seasoned clinicians know a lot of things that fresh-baked ones and laymen don't know, but I was properly educated to realize that experienced clinicians also "know" all sorts of things that are not true (Meehl, 1987). Absent quantitative research, one cannot be confident as to what part of clinicians' lore is valid and what part is superstition. It is easy to list from the armchair, simply relying upon our general knowledge of the psychology of testimony and the fallibility of human observation and memory, not to mention the recent research on the inefficiency of many human cognitive processes involving complex judgments, at least seven factors that could give rise to the concept of the schizophrenogenic mother from one's clinical experience, even if the notion, as I am presuming arguendo, was totally devoid of merit. I list the factors briefly without argument, since they are all obviously possible and seen to be antecedently probable as soon as one writes them down:

1. Mother actually behaved ambivalently, inconsistently, and unlovingly because she herself was schizotypal, and this historical fact appears in the patient's psychotherapy productions even though the fact was devoid of causal influence on his illness.

2. Since our schizophrene was schizotypal as a child, he was not a rewarding child for the caregiver, who consequently developed ambivalent attitudes toward him, which are now reported in therapy.

3. The child experienced quite normal child-rearing attitudes and practices, which, of course, invariably included some inconsistencies and a mixed positive

and negative social reinforcement schedule, but being schizotypal he experienced them as more aversive and cognitively misinterpreted them more than a normal or neurotic child would have.

4. Our adult schizophrene remembers selectively and distortedly his childhood experiences of mothering, which were not in fact unusual.

5. Although none of the above factors was operating initially in the sessions, the therapist, because of his theoretical orientation, reinforces talk along the lines of the schizophrenogenic mother, probably overtly, certainly in subtle ways. Thus, for instance, he will show more interest in an episode about bad mothering than he will in an episode about bad teaching in junior high school.

6. Because of his theoretical commitments, the therapist remembers episodes selectively and distortedly, although a content analysis of the patient's discourse would not show it to be different from a randomly chosen nonschizophrenic patient.

7. The therapist construes correlations from listening to the content as "obvious" instances of psychological causality, forgetting that while nonchance covariations prove that some kind of causation, in one direction or another, is at work, they do not tell us without further argument what is causing what.

It's important to realize that none of these seven factors leading to a net therapist impression about schizophrenogenic mothers is incompatible with any of the other six. So it is possible, and I should think to any sophisticated psychologist highly likely, that all of them are at work. Speaking dichotomously, in terms of "Did the patient's mother act schizophrenogenically by my criteria or not?" and imagining that each of these seven methodological bloopers generates a spurious 10% increment in the apparent frequency of such mothers among schizotypal patients, we can easily reach an impression that 70% of our patients had such mothers. If the kinds of things we're listening for appeared in, say, one third of our neurotic clientele, then adding 70% to 30% we might say with a straight face that our clinical experience as psychotherapists proves that 100% of schizophrenes had such mothers.

It is not difficult to concoct reasonably good quantitative tests of these alternatives, although some of them involve quite a bit of effort and it's probably not worth the trouble in today's climate. Example: Our second misleading factor is that a normal mother is simply reacting to the troublesome features of a schizotypal child. On this hypothesis, while a good measure of maternal attitudes and child-rearing practices would show significant differences between the mothers of subsequent schizophrenes and mothers of normal controls, we might expect to find similar sizeable differences in the attitudes of mothers of brain-damaged children whose pathology arises from birth injury and the like, over which the mother had negligible influence; at least one study found that to be the case. Of course that doesn't prove the negative, but it does mean that any investigation of this question by quantifying maternal attitudes has to include other kinds of pathological children in addition to normals, as controls. For example, suppose we have developed sufficiently powerful psychophysiological and soft neurology indicators of the schizogene that we can identify which of a proband's siblings are schizotypes. (It obviously won't do on any sophisticated theory, not just mine, to classify those siblings who are not diagnosably schizophrenic as normal, since the decompensation rate is, on a dominant gene theory, as low as 10%.) We could compare the proband's, the compensated siblings', and normal siblings' retrospections of mother's behavior, both toward them and the preschizophrenic proband, by content analysis of interviews or perhaps even by a sufficiently sensitive and reliable memory-based questionnaire.

Now let's look at the other side of the coin. Biotropes tend to assert that we now *know* that maternal attitudes and child-rearing patterns have zero influence on schizotypal decompensation probability. Being a psychologist, I cannot believe this, on extrapolative theoretical grounds. We have here an interesting methodological problem involving a principle the logicians call "the Total Evidence Rule" for empirical questions. I emphasize that it is a rule of inductive logic, not a particular (debatable) philosophy of science position. It is a principle that I find social scientists sometimes tend to ignore. Beginning with the admitted fact that the concordance even for MZ twins is only around 50 to 60% (depending on Weinberg adjustment and other sample differences), *something* environmental must account for the difference between those who become schizophrenic and those who remain compensated. If we don't believe it's a virus or sunspots or witchcraft, what on earth might it be? One can divide the environmental influences, without being able to specify them individually or even in narrow subcategories, into two broad classes: (1) environmental stressors on the adult as precipitators of illness, and (2) environmental shapers in the childhood developmental period that yield an adult schizotypal organization more or less susceptible to stress. I cannot think of any good theoretical reason, nor am I aware of any hard quantitative data, that would lead me to prefer current stressors over childhood shapers, or the other way around. It has not been easy to show an effect of current stressors as precipitators for schizophrenia, and that debate continues, just as it does for adult precipitators of depression, a more likely candiate for such influence. But the Total Evidence Rule does not permit me to reason as if I *had no other information* about how the human mind is shaped by experiences. Merely because I am talking about schizophrenia, a mental disease, I cannot elect to ignore any general information we have about how persons become the kind of adults that they are. From common sense and everyday observation, not to mention literally thousands of research studies by developmental psychologists and others, we know that adult personality is influenced in a variety of ways, sometimes greatly and other times slightly, by the threefold influences of one's childhood, "precept, example, and reward," as our grandparents would have called them. Children raised in German households do not grow up speaking French. Catholics usually come from Catholic households. People's table manners, their political and religious ideas, their notions of what is a normal kind of family relationship, their ways of handling forbidden wishes, whether of a sexual or aggressive nature, their expectations of other human beings' trustworthiness, their altruisim or egotism, their avocational interests, their degree of sociability, their way of expressing aggression or countering it— these and hundreds of other aspects are influenced by identification or model- ing, by differential reinforcement, and even, although less than it used to be supposed, by verbal instruction as to "how one ought to be." The notion that because we have moved into the domain of psychopathology, all of what we know about social learning goes by the board, just doesn't count anymore, seems to me preposterous on the face of it. To take a simple example, while schizophrenia is a genetically determined neurological disease, it has a *content*, and that content is socially learned. As Bleuler says, "You can't have a delusion about Jesuits if you never heard of Jesuits!" It would be strange to say that while we can infer directly from the MZ twin concordance data that whether you become schizophrenic or not, given the schizotaxic genotype, depends upon nongenetic factors, yet those nongenetic factors do not include *anything* about the way the primary nurturing figure treated you during the early stages of development. I can't believe that as a psychologist, and it's going to take a tremendous mass of powerful, clearly interpretable, and consistent data of a negative sort to persuade me of any such strange doctrine. I shall listen open- mindedly to such negative evidence, but I am going to require that it make a very strong case before I buy it. So, for example, the fact that my colleague Heston's adoptees (Heston, 1966, 1970) show a Weinberg-adjusted lifetime risk not different from that of cases reared by a schizophrenic mother is not a strong refuter, when one computes the confidence belt for a proportion based on $N = 47$.

The very imperfect MZ concordance is puzzling given the sparsity and feebleness of environmental factors and presents a major conceptual problem. This does not depend upon whether one is betting on a major locus or a polygenic theory. I suggest that it becomes somewhat less puzzling if we think about the psychodynamics of an individual from an idiographic viewpoint, given Freud with a big dash of Allport, and some Murray in between. Efforts to find environmental correlates of higher risk have quite understandably focused on what we might call "generic factors," such as infantile illness or injury, school experience, social class of parent, and the like. On my view of the disorder, I would assign a crucial role to the occurrence of certain sorts of adverse events, some of which are essentially independent of the personal characteristics and social status or other demographic features of the individ- ual, literally matters of "bad luck" or "pure chance," that are sequenced, highly autocatalytic, and represent extreme examples of divergent causality (London,

1946; Meehl, 1978, p. 809). Something takes place that was not even unconsciously produced or rendered probable by the behavior of the schizotypal individual, a pure happenstance that altered his momentary psychological state and hence his readiness to misperceive along certain lines; then someting else takes place, equally independent, in both the causal and statistical senses, of the first event, that impacts him because of an idiographic significance *that it would not have for another equally schizoid person*, and that it would not even have for this individual, despite its special idiographic content, if he were not in the state he's currently in. Since such events and states as social misperception and social anxiety are two-way autocatalytic (the more you distort, the more frightened you become, and the more frightened you become, the more you tend to distort), it doesn't take any fancy, implausible ad hockery to understand how one member of a MZ twin pair may fall ill and another one remain well despite sharing not only the specific schizogene but also all of the potentiating polygenes. Sometimes schizophrenic decompensation is the absorbing state of a random walk (Meehl,1978, pp. 811–812). *The conventional social science search for the standard familiar generic variables will not elucidate such processes.* To exemplify this, I cannot do better than quote a previous paper of mine.

> Consequently we should set our switches in advance not to be completely baffled by a paradox: Failure to find positive environmental correlates of decompensation, despite the clearly established power of environmental influences collectively as shown by the genetic statistics themselves. I don't think it will be too hard for a genetically oriented psychotherapist to make sense of these facts, scientifically frustrating though they would be. Neither a rough measure of familial puritanism, nor a measure of a schizotypal mother's differential seductiveness as between two MZ twin boys, covers the possibility of a critical event such as Twin *A* receiving a completely unexpected low grade in his physical education class (due—let's really run it into the ground—to a clerical error!) several months following his first heterosexual experience. It doesn't take much for a schizotypal mind to connect up these two happenings in some sort of crazy, hypochondriacal, and guilt-ridden fashion. *Without anything else* being "systematically" different between him and his MZ co-twin, his aberrated CNS may take it from there and snowball it into a psychosis that appears, say, a year later. I do not myself find this kind of "happenstance" at all implausible, and therefore I was pleased to see our authors' explicit emphasis upon "chance" factors in their discussion of the environment. The causal model for an integrated theory of schizophrenia would surely involve social feedback loops, autocatalytic processes, and powerful critical episodes initiating chains of divergent causality, perhaps the most important of this third kind of causal meaning of interpersonal events *that may have the same sort of "average value," parametrically speaking, for both members of a discordant MZ pair.* Thus, for example, 6 months after our hypothetical Twin *A* in the preceding example has schizotypically concluded that "sexual drainage" caused him to fail the gym course, both twins are present at a dinner table conversation. The father says, innocently and with no notion of his

critical schizophrenogenic role, "If there is anything I cannot stand, it is a boy who is a sissy." Now the schizotypal snowball really gets going for Twin A, whereas father's casual remark has negligible psychological significance for co-twin B (who has neither failed in gym nor visited a prostitute). I find it hard to think of any kind of statistical analysis of case history material or neighborhood characteristics that would tease out this kind of thing. And if one combines these "chance" factors with the possibility (some would say likelihood) that the schizogene(s) can "switch on and off" as a function of intercurrent biochemical states, quite possibly including states induced by momentary stressors, the elements of "psychological-social coincidence" can loom very large indeed. Every psychotherapist who has treated schizophrenics knows that the patients themselves sometimes connect a momentary resurgence of anxiety or confusion with what would to a normal mind be a very minor happenstance; and while I certainly do not wish to rely heavily on these anecdotal connections (see *supra*), neither would I be willing to dismiss them as of no evidential weight. Following close upon father's "sissy" remark, random episode E_1 (a waitress momentarily ignores him in favor of a customer that she knows well) ticks off in our Twin A a 2-hour increase in the blood level of norepinephrine. Due to his oddball dietary obsessions, which in turn went back to his reading a pamphlet (which didn't *happen* to fall into co-twin B's hands) at age 14, he also is running an unusually high level of organic acid X at the time. These concurrent alterations in the intracellular milieu of the schizogene, and note that they are neither physiologically nor psychologically related, nor attributable to any *systematic* characteristics of the environment, "switch on" the cerebral schizogenes and as a result the patient undergoes an increase in his pan-anxiety, his anhedonia, and his tendency to cognitive slippage. The last straw: While he is in this state, which is a deviation from his usual schizotypal norm, his girlfriend breaks a date with him, speaking rather roughly on the telephone (because she is embarrassed, and in order not to feel defensive she becomes aggressive). *Result*: Snowballing in the aversive direction, dangerously consolidating the mixed-up schizoid complex: "I am bad and weak because being sexually drained I have become a sissy as my father said, which is why waitresses prefer others to me, as does my girlfriend, and hence all women. I'm a hopeless nothing." Twin A is now well on the way to clinical decompensation. (Meehl, 1972a, pp. 404–406)

I must emphasize that envisioning these kinds of "idiographic unpredictabilities" and even after-the-fact "unexplainabilities"—not quite the same thing, as Scriven and others have convincingly shown—does not require that we postulate any sort of radical biological or psychological indeterminism. We just have to recognize unblinkingly the rather obvious fact that even a so-called "thorough, in-depth" life history is extremely deficient as regards details, and that we have nothing to guarantee that this deficiency could be made up by *any* amount of ingenuity or expenditure on the part of an investigator concerned to reconstruct the past. The kinds of "influences," "variables," and "factors" that social scientists are usually able to assess are almost always, when carefully scrutinized, classes of variables or kinds of episodes. In terms of learning theory, we deal in most psychological and sociological research with parameters of the elaborate "social Skinner box" that constitute a person's nurturing environment and adult life. The numbers we can correlate with outcome (e.g., psychosis) are in the nature of average values; they do not point to what may be critical events but rather to stochastic features of discriminative and eliciting stimuli or schedules of reinforcement contingencies.

If I were to present an engineer or physicist with a "molar" problem involving a chair made out of a specific kind of metal, riveted or welded in a specified way, telling him I was going to catapult it from the roof of the physics building at 12:32 P.M., in a direction so it would land on the stone steps of the administration building, and require him to predict whether and how it would fracture, he would probably decline the invitation. A fortiori, he would decline if the object to be catapulted were a century-old oak-case grandfather clock! But that, brethren, is about the situation when we are trying to understand why Twin *A* became schizophrenic and MZ Twin *B* did not.

I may conclude this discussion of "chance" factors determining which twin decompensates by quoting from my paper read at the 1971 MIT Conference on Prospects for Schizophrenia Research, where I said:

> But that there are *some* schizophrenics who act more like *some* anxiety-neurotics than they do like *other* schizophrenics is an important fact to think about and to explain. It is, however, very weak evidence against anybody's theory of schizophrenia, genetic or otherwise. I understand from the mathematicians that there is a clear negative answer to this question; and it is found, for example, in the theory of certain stochastic processes such as random walks. Whether a particle pursuing a random walk ends up (after a specific finite time) in a so-called "absorbing state" [= a state that it cannot leave] is a "dichotomous end-result" comparable to whether a schizotype ends up in a state hospital, enters and leaves, or wins the Pulitzer Prize for poetry; but the mathematics of such situations teaches us that it would be a mistake to presume a dichotomous etiological basis for this important outcome difference. In that connection, I mention in passing that we should not assume, even in the case of MZ twins, that a clinical discordance must always have some "big" life-history factor discernible. That Twin *A* becomes schizophrenic and Twin *B* remains "healthy" may be a random walk problem—I myself would bet that *many* of them are. (Meehl, 1972a)

Some of my biologically oriented psychiatry colleagues don't like examples like this; they ask me how anybody could go about checking on such idiographic hypotheses in a scientific way. All I can say is that this is a problem with the usual psychiatric case history that has been with us for many years and that we have become accustomed to it. But that doesn't mean we should ignore its highly problematic status. The usual psychiatric case history that talks about the patient's parental home in a superficial way and mentions that a relative died of a brain tumor and when the patient flunked a certain course in school is simply not capable of getting at the kind of thing hypothesized in my preceding example. I do not look upon it as a defect at a conjecture aimed at accounting for such a big paradox as that between the moderate MZ concordance and the relative absence of strong environmental correlates of illness that one may have great difficulty unscrambling it. Even a Popperian, while insisting that a theoretical conjecture should be testable (although not necessarily at this time in this state of the art), does not require that a conjecture concerning a *particular* event should always be testable after it has happened. Thus, for example, we have a rather mild windstorm that does very little damage anywhere in the vicinity except that farmer Jones's silo fell down. We know enough about the general propeties of silos and the laws of mechanics and the properties of winds to come up with some plausible explanations of what might have been the cause for this particular silo's falling down in such a mild storm. But it will usually be the case that we are unable to reconstruct the causal chain from the remnants well enough to decide among these competing alternatives.

The ordinary psychiatric history, or even one filled out by a psychotherapist on the basis of extensive contact and psychoanalytic kind of anamnesis, could be analogized to the following example for an animal psychologist: You are told that Rat R came from a bright strain of the Wistar stock, lived in the Minnesota lab for 3 months, and then was sold to the Kansas lab. This rat received an adequate amount of bran mash both places, but also vitamins in Minnesota. There are three litter mates, two living and well; one has an ear infection and shows equilibrium disturbances. Rat R has been subjected to considerable experimentation in three apparatuses, two of which are the T-maze and the Skinner box, the third unknown. The exact experimental regime is undetermined, except that the experimenter is known to be interested in problems of discrimination learning. At the present time, this rat seems unable to form a simple form discrimination and also shows face washing, defecation, and excitable behavior generally when placed in a Skinner box with the light on. Query: What exactly is the trouble with Rat R, and how did it originate? I would be inclined to take the position of Skinner when he is fending off complaints about applying certain principles in nonexperimental contexts, namely, that you attempt to corroborate regions of the theoretical network by experimental or, lacking that, statistical research, but you do not require that the scientist, in offering a plausible explanation of a complicated particular event, should always be able, so to speak, to "prove the whole theory over again" afresh. Of course, all of these considerations become rather pointless if what occurs is a more or less random turning on and off of the schizogene, analogous to what we assume takes place in the major affective disorders.

Suppose the essential features of my theory were to be corroborated by multiple lines of taxometric investigation. What then would be the clinical situation? For one thing, on such a theory one does not anticipate persistence of long-term outcome as a highly valid indicator of the taxon, certainly not the quasi-pathognomonic role it played with Kraepelin and still does with some old-fashioned clinicians. On the other hand, one might anticipate a predictive value for early life history data. On my theory, garden-variety social introversion, a nontaxonic factor distinct from schizoid autism and known to be highly heritable, is a strong potentiator of decompensation in the adult schizotype. It might also be a predictor of adverse long-term outcome, *but not because it is anything specific to schizophrenia,* just as in our competitve extrovert culture I daresay extreme social introversion potentiates low IQ as a predictor of economic failure, but that doesn't tell us anything about the relationship between the polygenic introversion variable and the heritable component of *g*. Those who don't understand my theory expect me to say that the severity of a soft neurological or psychophysiological indicator of the schizoid taxon should be predictive of outcome, and they are puzzled when I say not at all, and that I would be disappointed if that should be the case. The confusion arises from a failure to realize that one must think differently about taxometrics than about factor analysis or multidimensional scaling of continuous variables. Take, for instance, the SPEM (Smooth Pursuit Eye-Movement) psychophysiological aberration, which has been shown in several laboratories to be a powerful indicator of schizotaxia, possibly having a valid positive rate pushing 90% at the expense of negligible false-positives (provided one excludes remitted manic depressives who are on lithium). This test remains positive on schizophrenes in remission and has been shown to have a fairly high incidence in their first-degree relatives. Since all such "integrative" functions are good bets on my theory, I expect this one to become shortly a part of our diagnostic armamentarium. The parameter distributions of these eye movement curves are bimodal, but there are still individual differences within the pathological group (Iacono, 1988).

Why should one expect, on a major locus genetic model, the quantified SPEM defect to be correlated with clinical severity or malignant course? All one can say taxometrically is that the higher the deviant score, the more *confidence* one can have in the taxonic classification of the individual. But this is totally different from the notion that whatever polygenic or environmental variables produce individual differences within the taxon (as also among normals) should be correlated with severity of the neural integrative defect. It's a different way to think, and one has to get used to it.

Given the MZ concordance of 55% or less, one expects to find some strong environmental influences determining which schizotypal twin falls ill. With rare exceptions (e.g., seasonality, birth weight, maternal exposure to influenza), efforts to identify such generic potentiating factors have not turned up much. How is this possible, given the sizeable MZ discordance? *Something* must be making the difference, so where could it be if not "in the environment"? Two possibilities suggest themselves. It may be that the schizogene turns on and off randomly, or at least not in response to the kind of environmental factor we usually study in social science. It may, for example, respond to a minor alteration of diet occurring in hot weather—hardly likely to be found in the typical psychologist's or sociologist's candidate list of "environmental influences." Examples are known in medical genetics. Speaking against this hypothesis is the fact that schizophrenes in remission show psychophysiological and soft neurological aberrations, as do many of their first-degree "normal" relatives, children at genetic risk, and preschizophrenic children (Fish, 1975, 1977, 1984; Freedman, Adler, Baker, Waldo, & Mizner, 1987; Heinrichs & Buchanan, 1988; Iacono, 1988). A gene turn-on theory cannot handle this, unless we ad hoc it by postulating a *second* major gene that's responsible for producing episodes of schizotypal decompensation. The other explanation, which I think more plausible, is that a series of adverse events occurring close in time and idiosyncratic in their psychodynamic import *just happens* to befall the unlucky twin (Meehl, 1962a, 1972a, 1972c). He's the victim not of such standard social science systematic factors as rejecting mother, bad school, infectious disease, social class, or whatever, but simply of the binomial theorem.

METATHEORY OF OPEN CONCEPTS

What do I mean in speaking of schizotaxia as an *open concept*? While this terminology was introduced by the late philosopher of science Arthur Pap (1953) in 1951, the concept is older, having been formulated by Rudolf Carnap in his classic paper on testability (Carnap, 1936–1937/1953). The theoretical entity named by an open concept term is defined implicitly or contextually; in a developed discipline like genetics or chemistry, by the mathematical formalism and an interpretative text. But the interpretative statements in that text are rarely explicit definitions and almost never "operational" definitions in the conventional sense. The nomological network consisting of the words and the math (and maybe some diagrams or Tinkertoy models) *jointly* (1) define the theoretical terms and (2) make assertions about the theoretical entities' causal and compositional relations, a heretical thesis propounded by Cronbach and myself in 1955 that I gather is now accepted by most knowledgeable psychologists.

A beautiful example of an open concept in the life sciences is the gene. It was contextually defined until Crick and Watson made the theoretical breakthrough that enables us now to define it explicitly as a *cistron* consisting of a certain sequence of *codons*. This is not an operational definition but an explicit definition *in other theoretical terms*, in this case terms of organic chemistry.

This is not the place, even were it within my technical competence in philosophy of science, to present a detailed explication of the metatheory of open concepts as it has been worked out by logicians and philosophers of science over the past half century since Carnap's classic paper (but those who are interested may see Meehl, 1972c, p. 21, references). Essentially, the advance made over a simplistic operationism about *concepts* (and a corresponding strict verifiability criterion of scientific meaning for theoretical *statements*) was the recognition that many scientific concepts are not originally introduced by explicit definitions, stating the necessary and sufficient conditions for a concept's applicability to a particular, but rather by a collection of statements (in a logical form called by Carnap "reduction pairs") that represent different observational avenues to deciding on the applicability of a concept. Which one of these is chosen will depend upon the context, and it may sometimes not be possible to use one, so we use another. Thus, for instance, whether an electric current is flowing in a wire is sometimes decided by observing whether there is a deflection of a compass needle in its vicinity; on another occasion we ascertain whether when the wire is cut and the ends placed in a suitable solution, one gets a deposit of, say, silver at the cathode; and on still another occasion, we determine whether it will heat a filament. We do not explicitly define the concept "electric current" by conjoining these three indicators. That is, we do not say, "An electric current *is* (or *consists of*) . . . ," but we say that it is appropriate to assert that a current is flowing when one of these test conditions is applied and the specified test result is observed. The fact that this is not an explicit definition of the full semantic content of the term "electric current" and that the list of indicators is indefinitely extensible is the first kind of openness that was expounded by Carnap in his paper and elaborated by Pap (1953, 1958). In addition to the extensibility of the indicator list, there is a second kind of openness that arises when the theoretician makes a weaker claim in that the test observation relevant to decision is only probabilistic, so that observing or not observing the test result in the test condition raises or lowers the odds but does not definitively prove or refute the attribution. When this softened form is used, as is almost always the case in the life sciences and sometimes even in the inorganic sciences, there is no longer a strict deduction running from the result of one of the indicator tests to another, as there was in the original formulation where probability is not involved. So even with a stipulated list of indicators that we have for some reason decided not to expand further, there is an element of looseness, especially as applied to individual patterns of indicators where some are present and some are absent, the typical situation in making a diagnosis in medicine or psychopathology. Finally, a kind of openness that is not discussed by Carnap and Pap but is of great importance in studying the historical development of a discipline is that the long-term aim of much research is to be able to offer an explicit definition of the theoretical entities that in the early stages are defined implicitly or "contextually" by their role in this network of connections among observables. Thus, for instance, from Mendel until Crick and Watson, the term "gene" was defined implicitly by reference to its role in a statistical system that has an input side (ancestry) and an output side (phenotypic traits). Prior to Crick and Watson's discovery, one could not say in explicit terms just *what the gene is*; one only said it was a something, presumably of a physical nature, that had a location (shown by linkage statistics) at a certain place on the chromosome, and that it was the causal ancestor of a chain of events in the development leading to various phenotypic manifestations. In drawing a diagram to illustrate the nomological network metaphor, where one connects the concepts represented by open circles with lines or strands of the net, where the nodes of the net are the theoretical entities and the strands of the net are their functional or compositional relations, I was struck by an analogy between those open circles and the vacuous eyes that used to appear in the Little Orphan Annie cartoons of my youth. So I dubbed this third kind of openness "Orphan Annie's Eyes," meaning that one of our long-term scientific aims is to learn enough about the *innards* of an implicitly defined theoretical entity—what parts or substances it is composed of, and how they are put together—so that while still using the contextual definition for many purposes (especially technological ones), we can also provide an explicit theoretical definition of the entity in terms of its inner nature (Meehl, 1977; Meehl & Golden, 1982).

When we offer a list of symptoms, signs, character traits, life history events, and psychometric scores as relevant to diagnosing schizotaxia, the imperfection and extensibility of that list represent openness of the first kind. When we go on to say that no one of these indicators is two-way pathognomonic (even the thought disorder is not quite that), we are referring to openness of the second kind, the stochastic as contrasted with the nomological character of the strands connecting the nodes of the theoretical net. Suppose someone then asks, "Well, all right, I understand that you don't offer a strictly operational definition that would enable us to tell for certain whether a particular individual is or is not a schizotype, and that you don't expect to be able to do that until research is farther along than it is today; but surely you must have some sort of theoretical conjecture as to just what this schizotaxic defect consists of in its own nature?"

One might justifiably decline to answer that on the grounds that it is premature and speculative. In thinking about my theory of schizophrenia, I am a Popperian and not shy about conjectures, as long as I have some notions about how you might ultimately go about testing them, even if you can't do so today. When one even says something as vague as "a genetically determined neural integrative defect," despite the vagueness of that language, it is the beginnings of filling in Orphan Annie's Eyes. It excludes, for instance, the notion that schizotypes have the same CNS parameters as normal people but have merely acquired some undesirable ways of behaving and experiencing through aversive social conditionings. And when one states further that, whatever the inner nature of that integrative defect may be, it is the specific defect that predisposes to schizophrenia rather than, say, to dyslexia or stammering or tone deafness or the hereditary kind of spelling defect, he has further narrowed down the concept. One must realize that various degrees of filling in Orphan Annie's Eyes can exist, depending on the theorist's speculative daring, all within the contextual framework given by the *implicit* mode of definition. A Minnesota colleague who goes along with my conjectures that schizophrenia represents the decompensation of the schizotypal personality, that the schizotypal personality is the personality that develops by the process of social learning on a schizotaxic brain, and that the schizotaxic brain is characterized by a specific kind of neural integrative defect that is hereditary, may or may not go on to conjecture with me what the inner neurophysiological nature of that integrative defect is. So two theorists may agree about the schizotaxia concept as an open concept specified by its role in the network but may disagree when it comes to closing the third kind of openness by different ways of filling in Orphan Annie's Eyes. My theory starts at the molar level with the open concept of schizotaxia, defined implicitly by its role in a loose and highly incomplete nomological network (clumsy but more accurately, "stochastological network," in Meehl, 1978). The defining contextual strands include the soft neurology and psychophysiology of schizophrenia, with a weak assist from other "organic" correlates (see, e.g., Shattock, 1950); the admittedly variable but, taken as a whole, convincing "cognitive" aberrations (Knight, 1984); and the presence of these phenomena in relatives, which combined with the clearly genetic etiology leads us to attach the adjective "heritable" to the phrase "neural integrative defect" in defining schizotaxia. So at this level we have a syndrome plus a partial, but specific, etiology. Orphan Annie's Eyes are nearly empty, except perhaps for the semantic overtones of "neural" together with "soft neurological," which suggest a "promissory note" about future discovery—something aberrant about how the brain works that is not merely unfortunate *learned content*. Then comes the conjecture that the integrative defect is ubiquitous, something haywire throughout the CNS, a functional parameter deviant for every neuron, not something only in the limbic system, the RAS, or the proprioceptive system. Next we identify this functional parameter aberration with reduced signal selectivity (hypokrisia) at the synapse. Finally we conjecture that the hypokrisia is due to a biochemical deficiency of a substance whose function in the orthotaxic brain is to resist spread of depolarization of the cell membrane, and that a dominant mutation is responsible.

The methodological point is that at each stage of this progressive conjectural filling in of Orphan Annie's Eyes, a theoretician may call a halt and say that he will go along with me so far but no farther. His dealing with the first two aspects of openness will be unaffected by this disagreement as to the conjectured filling in of Orphan Annie's Eyes. I should emphasize, finally, that in the theory of open concepts, philosophers of science have not meant to suggest, certainly not since Pap's elaboration (1958) of the Carnap paper, that such openness is only characteristic of the "soft" sciences. A fair statement of the consensus is from a remark made to me in discussion by the late Imre Lakatos: "All concepts are open, it's just that some are opener than others!"

If you can't tolerate working with open concepts, you should study something else instead of psychopathology. The opposite mistake is to wallow in them, a distressing tendency of our age's intellectual fecklessness and subjectivism. What you should do with an open concept is to recognize its openness and use appropriate methods, particularly statistical ones, to tighten it up, keeping in mind Aristotle's dictum in the *Ethics* that one should insist on precision in concepts insofar as the nature of the subject matter permits. I hope I am pursuing that line in my current thinking about taxometric research on the theory of schizophrenia. I might reassure you on this score by pointing out that if you are clever and lucky in your choice of taxometric indicators, moderately valid indicators can be combined in sets of a half dozen or so to yield diagnostic probabilities as attached to individuals in the high .90s. This is plenty good enough both for clinical work and for the testing of strong genetic models.

IMPLICATIONS FOR THE CLINICAL EXAMPLES

Where do these considerations leave us with respect to the clinical examples with which we began? The answer is obvious: They leave us up in the air as to the merits. Both parties to the dispute are wrong methodologically if they claim to settle the merits on present evidence. In our first patient, an attenuated waxy flexibility and faint semantic oddities do not rule in schizotypy, let alone schizophrenia, and his previously adequate life adjustment does not rule it out. Ditto the pan-anxiety, introversion, passivity, and dependency of our second patient. The pro-schizotypal diagnosticians who rely on the follow-up statistics of Hoch and Polatin's cases are making too much of the 20% schizophrenic outcome; those who emphasize the majority that do not develop subsequent florid schizophrenia are making too much of that fact. It's a free country, and everyone is entitled to bet on his own horse. As Mark Twain says, "A difference of opinion is the essence of a horse race." I am not criticizing those who disagreed or those who agreed with me for placing clinical bets, as long as we all realize that the assignment of relative weights to life history factors and the defense of such an entity as the Hoch-Polatin syndrome on the basis of long-term outcome are at present subjective judgments and will remain so until more powerful indicators of the schizotypal taxon are available.

In our clinic we have begun (not consistently, alas, but frequently) to run some of the soft neurology tests, especially the SPEM, on patients in whom there is this kind of diagnostic disagreement in case conference. It is only by a certain loosenesss that we refer to a "pathognomonic" sign or symptom, even when looking to the future. Proof in empirical knowledge is, as the logician reminds us, a matter of degree. All knowledge of empirical matters is only probable, although there are sometimes such mountains of tightly interconnected evidence that we find it impossible *psychologically* to doubt it. We do not countenance the conjecture that the sun is Apollo's chariot or a gigantic red-hot cannonball, but in theory even such quasi-certain knowledge as we have that the sun is a ball of hot hydrogen is open to revision.

THE SUPER BOOTSTRAPS THEOREM

We do, nevertheless, speak of certain signs, symptoms, or biochemical tests in organic medicine as pathognomonic. There is an interesting epistemological question here, namely, how can we get to quasi-certainty, which is what is claimed for a two-way pathognomonic sign, starting out with fallible indicators of an open concept? That deserves a lecture by itself, but the short answer is that we conduct a successful "bootstraps" operation on a set of fallible indicators, and we often conclude, as knowledge advances, by changing the relative weights, as in some of the symptoms (e.g., expansive delusions) of general paresis. (Actually, Noguchi and Moore did not find the spirochete in the brain of every single paretic they studied, although some clinicians think that.) Years ago, I proved a paradoxical theorem in my early work on taxometrics, which I deliberately christened with a challenging name: the Super Bootstraps Theorem (Dawes & Meehl, 1966; Meehl, 1965, p. 37 ff.; 1973c, pp. 216–217; Meehl & Golden, 1982, pp. 143–144). Suppose we have three fallible quantitative indicators of a conjectural latent taxon such as psychopathy or schizotaxia or cyclothymia. Applying certain coherency or consistency tests to the internal statistics of these three indicators may justify entertaining, until further notice, a high confidence that the latent structure meets certain mathematical conditions (which I will not here discuss), such as relative independence of the indicators within the inferred latent categories. Given satisfaction of our consistency tests, we believe we have a fairly accurate estimate of the taxon base rate in a specified population. We infer, for instance, that 30% of the patients in a general psychiatric outpatient clientele are schizotypes, even if they present with pseudoneurotic or pseudopsychopathic symptoms, traits, or signs. Then one can optimize a cutting score on each indicator and can compute the inverse probability, for any given sign pattern, of taxon membership for each subject. The optimal cut having led to three dichotomous signs, we have thereby defined eight pattern "cells," for each of which a taxon probability is computable. The point is that while these must be fairly valid in order to warrant the whole business, they need not be highly valid or anywhere near pathognomonic, *either singly or collectively*. We do not know, even for sign patterns all three plus or all three minus, which *individual* is a taxon member; and for weaker patterns, such as $x^+y^+z^-$, we have only moderate betting odds for each individual. Nevertheless, for each cell we can infer with a small error tolerance what the *proportion* of taxon members in that cell must be. What I showed in the Super Bootstraps Theorem (see Appendix) is that if we now consider a fourth quantitative indicator v, which Omniscient Jones knows has two distributions with zero overlap, we can try various cutting scores on v, each defining a dichotomous sign v^+/v^-, and can count the proportion of individuals per cell that is v^+. We then compute the discrepancy between the v^+ rate per cell and that cell's Bayes's Theorem taxon rate, computed on the three fallible signs. What the theorem shows is that it is impossible to match these frequencies over the eight cells (for that matter, over even two cells, but the more the better!) unless the optimal cut on v which achieves that matching is infallible.

This strange result is nothing more than high school algebra and formalizes what physicians have been doing for centuries when they altered their subjective nonstatistical "clinical" weights on the basis of further experience. That's the kind of procedure that leads us to find a genetic marker for a hereditary disorder where we don't know the biochemistry, let alone the chromosomal locus. So it is not fanciful to imagine that within the next 10 years, even if no lucky or clever biochemist finds the "purple spot" for schizotaxia in paper chromatography, that several psychophysiological and soft neurological indicators will be found, via the Super Bootstraps Theorem, to be quasi-pathognomonic. When that happens—I say *when* and not *if*, advisedly—we should be prepared to find patients presenting with a wide spectrum of social and psychological traits and symptoms, despite their genetic homogeneity as revealed by these nonbehavioral markers. Personally I think to say that this will happen within 10 years is being pessimistic; I would guesstimate 5. At that point one will know with some statistical precision what role such life history facts as age of onset, number and duration of episodes, and Kraepelin's malignant final outcome should be assigned.

There is a theoretical reason for expecting long-term course and outcome to have a privileged indicator status. If the defining pathology-cum-etiology is a fine structure brain condition of genetic origin, we do not expect it to change. If biochemical, that depends on whether we have an off-and-on setup or a steady state modifiable (if at all) by a specific therapeutic intervention. If Thorazine acts mainly as an antipsychotic, ameliorating Bleuler's accessory symptoms but leaving the soft neurology relatively untouched, we expect to find signs of the latter in first-degree relatives who have never become schizophrenic, and we do. This indicates a perdurable "something haywire in the brain" that persists despite fluctuations in clinical status, whatever complex of causal factors superimposed on the schizotaxic neural integrative defect is responsible for decompensations and remissions. But while these considerations may heighten the prior (thinking Bayesian) for giving a high diagnostic weight to outcome, leading to our being more easygoing in criticizing research along those lines, ultimately the matter is empirical. When enough replicable findings are in, course and outcome will be given whatever indicator weight the taxometric bootstrapping assigns to them. Whether, or to what extent, very strong theoretical arguments, including content validity, should be allowed to countervail the taxometrics is a difficult question I shall not discuss.

BIOTROPES AND SOCIOTROPES

Although I am a practitioner of psychoanalytic and rational-emotive therapy, I have said nothing about psychodynamics, which may seem unbefitting a book honoring Henry A. Murray. But that is not because I dismiss the psychisms at work in schizophrenia; rather, it's that I take them for granted. You see, we Minnesota clinicians firmly resist classification as biotropes *versus* sociotropes, an easy conventional dichotomy we consider simplistic. "The mind is the brain functioning" is for some psychologists a mere cliché, whereas we take it seriously. The theory of schizotaxia as an inherited neurological defect does not contradict a single psychodynamic truth about schizophrenia. Psychodynamics is concerned with learned social and intrapsychic *content*, with perceptual, cognitive, affective, and motivational states and events. They are molar level entities—psychisms—and the dispositions to these psychisms are acquired and activated by life experiences, especially with other persons. The mathematical parameters of the several acquisition and activation functions involved are deviant in the schizotaxic brain, and this constitutes the specific etiology of schizophrenia. But we do not liquidate molar level explanations in favor of brain language. It was a mistake in the 1930–1960 period to ignore the soft neurology or explain it away as due to anxiety or withdrawal. It would be a similar mistake today for biotropes to explain catatonia in purely neurological terms, which Bleuler easily refuted in his masterly *Theory of Schizophrenic Negativism* (1912). Catatonic phenomena are purposive, as when we understand such "opposite" behaviors as negativism and command automatism or mutism and echolalia, as the patient's fluctuating modes of disengagement from his social surround. Similarly, the delusion of the end of the world, sometimes found in the early stages of schizophrenic decompensation, can be interpreted as the symbolic and intellectualized expression of the patient's realization that he is undergoing a withdrawal of cathexis from the internal representations of social objects. The anhedonia, Rado's pain-dependent pleasure, and Bleuler's cardinal trait of ambivalence I subsume under the general heading of ambivalence combined with aversive drift, which is an intermediate level psychism. But I can't derive aversive drift in psychodynamic terms; rather, I move down to a neurological level of explanation in terms of (+) and (−) reinforcement centers in the brain. Again, while the uniquely schizophrenic semantic slippage may depend for its *possibility* rather directly on synaptic slippage, *when* it occurs and with what psychic *content* involves the particular patient's psychodynamics. As Bleuler would say, there is a primary "associative loosening," but the resulting thought sequence is catathymically determined. It often seems that the genetic and physiological revolution in psychotherapy has led some biotropes to disbelieve in the reality of mind, but I assure you that I am not among them.

REFERENCES

Berenbaum, H., Gottesman, I. I., & Oltmanns, T. F. (1985). Formal thought disorder in schizophrenics and their twins. *Journal of Abnormal Psychology, 94*, 3–16.

Bleuler, E. (1912). *Theory of schizophrenic negativism* (W. A. White, Trans.). New York: Journal of Nervous and Mental Disease Publishing Co. (Reprinted 1970 by Johnson Reprint Corporation, New York)

Bleuler, E. (1924). *Textbook of psychiatry* (A. A. Brill, Ed. and Trans.). New York: Macmillan.

Bleuler, E. (1950). *Dementia praecox* (J. Zinkin Trans.). New York: International Universities Press. (Original work published 1911)

Carnap, R. (1936–1937). Testability and meaning. *Philosophy of Science, 3*, 420–471; *4*, 2–40. Reprinted in H. Feigl & M. Brodbeck (Eds.), *Readings in the philosophy of science* (pp. 47–92). New York: Appleton-Century-Crofts, 1953.

Carnap, R. (1945). The two concepts of probability. *Philosophy and Phenomenological Research, 5*, 513–532. Reprinted in H. Feigl & M. Brodbeck (Eds.), *Readings in the philosophy of science* (pp. 438–455). New York: Appleton-Century-Crofts, 1953.

Chapman, L. J., & Chapman, J. P. (1985). Psychosis proneness. In M. Alpert (Ed.), *Controversies in schizophrenia.* New York: Guilford Press.

Chapman, L. J., & Chapman, J. P. (1987). The search for symptoms predictive of schizophrenia. *Schizophrenia Bulletin, 13*, 497–503.

Craig, C. C. (1936). A new exposition and chart for the Pearson system of frequency curves. *The Annals of Mathematical Statistics, 7*, 16–28.

Cramer, H. (1946). *Mathematical methods of statistics.* Princeton, NJ: Princeton University Press.

Cronbach, L. J., & Meehl, P. E. (1955). Construct validity in psychological tests. *Psychological Bulletin, 52*, 281–302.

Dawes, R. M., & Meehl, P. E. (1966). Mixed group validation: A method for determining the validity of diagnostic signs without using criterion groups. *Psychological Bulletin, 66*, 63–67. Reprinted in P. E. Meehl, *Psychodiagnosis: Selected Papers.* Minneapolis: University of Minnesota Press, 1973.

Elderton, W. P., & Johnson, N. L. (1969). *Systems of frequency curves*. London: Cambridge University Press.

Fish, B. (1975). Biologic antecedents of psychosis in children. In D. X. Freedman (Ed.), *Biology of the major psychoses* (pp. 49–83). New York: Raven Press.

Fish, B. (1977). Neurobiologic antecedents of schizophrenia in children. *Archives of General Psychiatry, 34,* 1297–1313.

Fish, B. (1984). Characteristics and sequelae of the neurointegrative disorder in infants at risk for schizophrenia: 1952–1982. In N. F. Watt, E. J. Anthony, L. C. Wynne, & J. E. Rolf (Eds.), *Children at risk for schizophrenia: A longitudinal perspective* (pp. 423–439). New York: Cambridge University Press.

Freedman, R., Adler, L. E., Baker, N., Waldo, M., & Mizner, G. (1987). Candidate for inherited neurobiological dysfunction in schizophrenia. *Somatic Cell and Molecular Genetics, 13,* 479–484.

Freud, S. (1962). Further remarks on the neuro-psychoses of defence. In J. Strachey (Ed. and Trans.), *The standard edition of the complete psychological works of Sigmund Freud* (Vol. 3, pp. 157–185). London: Hogarth Press. (Original work published 1896)

Frost, L. A., & Chapman, L. J. (1987). Polymorphous sexuality as an indicator of psychosis proneness. *Journal of Abnormal Psychology, 96,* 299–304.

Gangestad, S., & Snyder, M. (1985). "To carve nature at its joints": On the existence of discrete classes in personality. *Psychological Review, 92,* 317–349.

Golden, R. R. (1982). A taxometric model for detection of a conjectured latent taxon. *Multivariate Behavioral Research, 17,* 389–416.

Golden, R. R., Campbell, M., & Perry, R. (1987). A taxometric method for diagnosis of tardive dyskinesia. *Journal of Psychiatric Research, 21,* 101–109.

Golden, R. R., Gallob, H. F., & Watt, N. F. (1983). Bootstrapping conjectural indicators of vulnerability for schizophrenia. *Journal of Consulting and Clinical Psychology, 51,* 937–939.

Golden, R., & Meehl, P. E. (1978). Testing a single dominant gene theory without an accepted criterion variable. *Annals of Human Genetics London, 41,* 507–514.

Golden, R., & Meehl, P. E. (1979). Detection of the schizoid taxon with MMPI indicators. *Journal of Abnormal Psychology, 88,* 217–233.

Golden, R., & Meehl, P. E. (1980). Detection of biological sex: An empirical test of cluster methods. *Multivariate Behavioral Research, 15,* 475–496.

Golden, R. R., Vaughan, Jr., H. G., Kurtzberg, D., & McCarton, C. M. (in press). Detection of neonatal brain dysfunction without the use of a criterion variable: Analysis of the statistical problem with an illustrative example. In P. Vietze & H. G. Vaughan, Jr. (Eds.), *Early identification of infants at risk for mental retardation*. Orlando, FL: Grune & Stratton.

Gottesman, I. I., & Shields, J. (1972). *Schizophrenia and genetics, a twin study vantage point*. New York: Academic Press.

Gottesman, I. I., & Shields, J. (1982). *Schizophrenia, the epigenetic puzzle*. New York: Cambridge University Press.

Gunderson, J., Siever, L., & Spaulding, E. (1983). The search for a schizotype: Crossing the border again. *Archives of General Psychiatry, 40,* 15–22.

Heinrichs, D. W., & Buchanan, R. W. (1988). Significance and meaning of neurological signs in schizophrenia. *American Journal of Psychiatry, 145,* 11–18.

Heston, L. L. (1966). Psychiatric disorders in foster home reared children of schizophrenic mothers. *British Journal of Psychiatry, 112,* 819–825.

Heston, L. L. (1970). The genetics of schizophrenia and schizoid disease. *Science, 167,* 249–256.

Hoch, P. H., Cattell, J. P., Strahl, M. O., & Pennes, H. H. (1962). The course and outcome of pseudoneurotic schizophrenia. *American Journal of Psychiatry, 119,* 106–115.

Hoch, P., & Polatin, P. (1949). Pseudoneurotic forms of schizophrenia. *Psychiatric Quarterly, 3,* 248–276.

Iacono, W. G. (1988). Eye movement abnormalities in schizophrenia and affective disorders. In C. W. Johnston & F. J. Pirozzolo (Eds.), *Neuropsychology of eye movements.* Hillsdale, NJ: Lawrence Erlbaum Associates.

Johnson, N. L., & Kotz, S. (1970). *Distributions in statistics: Continuous univariate distributions-I.* New York: John Wiley.

Kagan, D. L., & Oltmanns, T. F. (1981). Matched tasks for measuring single-word, referent communication: The performance of patients with schizophrenic and affective disorders. *Journal of Abnormal Psychology, 90,* 204–212.

Kenney, J. F. (1939). *Mathematics of statistics, Part II.* New York: Van Nostrand.

Knight, R. A. (1984). Converging models of cognitive deficit in schizophrenia. In W. D. Spaulding & J. K. Cole (Eds.), *Theories of schizophrenia and psychosis. Nebraska Symposium on Motivation 1983, 31,* 93–156. Lincoln, NB: University of Nebraska Press.

Kraepelin, E. (1971). *Dementia praecox and paraphrenia* (R. M. Barclay, Trans.; G. M. Robertson, Ed.). Huntington, NY: Robert E. Krieger. (Original work published 1909–1913; original translation of selected portions published 1919)

Kroll, J., Sines, L., Martin, K., Lari, S., Pyle, R., & Zander, J. (1981). Borderline personality disorder. *Archives of General Psychiatry, 38,* 1021–1026.

London, I. D. (1946). Some consequences for history and psychology of Langmuir's concept of convergence and divergence of phenomena. *Psychological Review, 53,* 170–188.

Mackie, J. L. (1965). Causes and conditions. *American Philosophical Quarterly, 2,* 1–20.

Mackie, J. L. (1974). *The cement of the universe: A study of causation.* Oxford: Oxford University Press.

Meehl, P. E. (1954). *Clinical versus statistical prediction: a theoretical analysis and a review of the evidence.* Minneapolis: University of Minnesota Press.

Meehl, P. E. (1962a). Psychopathology and purpose. In P. Hoch & J. Zubin (Eds.), *The future of psychiatry* (pp. 61–69). New York: Grune & Stratton.

Meehl, P. E. (1962b). Schizotaxia, schizotypy, schizophrenia. *American Psychologist, 17,* 827–838.

Meehl, P. E. (1964). *Manual for use with checklist of schizotypic signs* (Report No. PR-73-5). Minneapolis: University of Minnesota, Research Laboratories of the Department of Psychiatry.

Meehl, P. E. (1965). *Detecting latent clinical taxa by fallible quantitative indicators lacking an accepted criterion* (Report No. PR-65-2). Minneapolis: University of Minnesota: Research Laboratories of the Department of Psychiatry.

Meehl, P. E. (1972a). A critical afterword. In I. I. Gottesman & J. Shields (Eds.), *Schizophrenia and genetics: A twin study vantage point* (pp. 367–416). New York: Academic Press.

Meehl, P. E. (1972b). Reactions, reflections, projections. In J. N. Butcher (Ed.), *Objective personality assessment: Changing perspectives* (pp. 131–189). New York: Academic Press.

Meehl, P. E. (1972c). Specific genetic etiology, psychodynamics and therapeutic nihilism. *International Journal of Mental Health, 1*, 10–27. Reprinted in P. E. Meehl, *Psychodiagnosis: Selected Papers*. Minneapolis: University of Minnesota Press, 1973.

Meehl, P. E. (1973a). MAXCOV-HITMAX: A taxometric search method for loose genetic syndromes. In P. E. Meehl, *Psychodiagnosis: Selected papers* (pp. 200–224). Minneapolis: University of Minnesota Press.

Meehl, P. E. (1973b). Why I do not attend case conferences. In P. E. Meehl, *Psychodiagnosis: Selected Papers* (pp. 225–302). Minneapolis: University of Minnesota Press.

Meehl, P. E. (1977). Specific etiology and other forms of strong influence: Some quantitative meanings. *Journal of Medicine and Philosophy, 2*, 33–53.

Meehl, P. E. (1978). Theoretical risks and tabular asterisks: Sir Karl, Sir Ronald, and the slow progress of soft psychology. *Journal of Consulting and Clinical Psychology, 46*, 806–834.

Meehl, P. E. (1979). A funny thing happened to us on the way to the latent entities. *Journal of Personality Assessment, 43*, 563–581.

Meehl, P. E. (1987). Theory and practice: Reflections of an academic clinician. In E. F. Bourg, R. J. Bent, J. E. Callan, N. F. Jones, J. McHolland, & G. Stricker (Eds.), *Standards and evaluation in the education and training of professional psychologists: Knowledge, attitudes, and skills* (pp. 7–33). Norman, Oklahoma: Transcript Press.

Meehl, P. E. (1989). Autobiography. In G. Lindzey (Ed.), *History of psychology in autobiography* (Vol. VIII, pp. 337–389). Stanford, CA: Stanford University Press.

Meehl, P. E. (in press). Why summaries of research on a psychological theory are often uninterpretable. In R. Snow & D. E. Wiley (Eds.), *Strategic thinking: A volume in honor of Lee J. Cronbach.*

Meehl, P. E., & Golden, R. (1982). Taxometric methods. In P. Kendall & J. Butcher (Eds.), *Handbook of research methods in clinical psychology* (pp. 127–181). New York: John Wiley.

Morey, L. C., Waugh, M. H., & Blashfield, R. K. (1985). MMPI scales for DSM-III personality disorders: Their derivation and correlates. *Journal of Personality Assessment, 49*, 245–251.

Neale, J. M., Oltmanns, T. F., & Harvey, P. D. (1985). The need to relate cognitive deficits to specific behavioral referents of schizophrenia. *Schizophrenia Bulletin, 11*, 286–290.

Pap, A. (1953). Reduction-sentences and open concepts. *Methodos, 5*, 3–30.

Pap, A. (1958). *Semantics and necessary truth.* New Haven, CT: Yale University Press.

Pearson, K. (1894). Contributions to the mathematical theory of evolution. *Philosophical Transactions of the Royal Society of London* (A), *185*, 71–110.

Pearson, K. (1895). Contributions to the mathematical theory of evolution, II: skew variation. *Philosophical Transactions of the Royal Society of London* (A), *186*, 343–414.

Popper, K. R. (1959). *The logic of scientific discovery.* New York: Basic Books.

Rado, S. (1956). *Psychoanalysis of behavior.* New York: Grune & Stratton.

Rado, S. (1960). Theory and therapy: The theory of schizotypal organization and its application to the treatment of decompensated schizotypal behavior. In S. C. Scher & H. R. Davis (Eds.), *The out-patient treatment of schizophrenia* (pp. 87–101). New York: Grune & Stratton.

Rado, S., & Daniels, G. (1956). *Changing concepts of psychoanalytic medicine.* New York: Grune & Stratton.

Ragin, A. B., & Oltmanns, T. F. (1986). Lexical cohesion and formal thought disorder during and after psychotic episodes. *Journal of Abnormal Psychology, 95,* 181–183.

Rietz, H. L. (1927). *Mathematical statistics.* Chicago: Open Court.

Salmon, W. C. (1984). *Scientific explanation and the causal structure of the world.* Princeton, NJ: Princeton University Press.

Shattock, F. M. (1950). The somatic manifestations of schizophrenia. A clinical study of their significance. *British Journal of Psychiatry, 96,* 32–142.

Siever, L., & Gunderson, J. (1983). The search for a schizotypal personality: Historical origins and current status. *Comprehensive Psychiatry, 24,* 199–212.

Stigler, S. M. (1986). *The history of statistics: The measurement of uncertainty before 1900.* Cambridge, MA: Harvard University Press.

Appendix

Proof of Super Bootstraps Theorem

For a given cut on v, defining a sign $v(+)$, let

$p_i(+)$ = Observed $v(+)$ probability among cases in cell i,
$p_j(+)$ = Observed $v(+)$ probability among cases in cell j.

Inferred from patterns of fallible indicators (x, y, z) are latent taxon-rates in cells i and j,

$$p_i = \text{Latent taxon-rate in cell } i$$
$$p_j = \text{Latent taxon-rate in cell } j$$
$$\text{Let } p_t = \text{Valid } v(+) \text{ rate in taxon class}$$
$$p_c = \text{False } v(+) \text{ rate in complement class}$$

Then, expressing the matching of latent taxon-rate with observed $v(+)$ rate in latent terms,

$$p_i(+) = p_i p_t + q_i p_c = p_i$$
$$p_j(+) = p_j p_t + q_j p_c = p_j$$

Subtracting,

$$p_i(+) - p_j(+) = p_t(p_i - p_j) + p_c(q_i - q_j)$$
$$= p_t(p_i - p_j) - p_c(p_i - p_j)$$
$$= (p_t - p_c)(p_i - p_j) = p_i - p_j \text{ Matched, by hypothesis}$$

Dividing by $(p_i - p_j)$, which will rarely $= 0$,

$$p_t - p_c = 0$$

which is impossible unless $p_t = 1$, $p_c = 0$, that is, new indicator v is infallible when optimally cut.

303

8

The Life of Henry A. Murray:
1893–1988

James William Anderson

Henry A. Murray died on June 23, 1988, at the age of 95. The obituary in the *New York Times* (June 24, 1988) quoted a 1981 appraisal of Murray's work, written by Joseph Adelson of the University of Michigan. "Not since William James has there been an American psychologist so versatile," Adelson commented, "nor has anyone else written with equal verve and boldness."

I was fortunate to know Murray during the last 15 years of his life. I worked with him for two summers, 1975 and 1977, as a research assistant and became his friend. Although not living in Cambridge, I visited him regularly, sometimes for casual talks, other times for formal interviews on topics about which I was curious, such as the development of the Thematic Apperception Test and his involvement with psychoanalysis. From the beginning of my relationship with him, I was aware of his importance in the field of psychology, and I almost always took careful verbatim notes during my talks with him, or tape-recorded them.

My purpose in this chapter is to try to give a sense of how he experienced his life by relying largely on his comments, in his talks with me and in his two autobiographical papers, about his personal life, the major developments in his career, and the people he had known. I will have less to say about his specific contributions to psychology because several excellent accounts of his work are available (see Hall & Lindzey, 1957; Maddi & Costa, 1972; White, 1981).

"AN AVERAGE, PRIVILEGED AMERICAN BOY"

Henry Alexander Murray was born on May 13, 1893, in a stylish brownstone at 54 West 59th Street in New York City. His family was conservative, Republican, Episcopalian, and moderately wealthy.

His father, Henry Alexander Murray, Sr., was a Scot who was born in Australia because *his* father, a British Army officer, was stationed there. When Murray Sr. was a child, his father died, and his mother took the family back to Great Britain. They were poor. Murray Sr. was educated at a school for boys from impoverished but good families, Christ's Hospital in London, but never attended a university. After his mother's death, Murray Sr. moved to the United States to make his fortune and had great success: He found a job with the Mutual Life Insurance Company in New York City, and although he was never an outstanding businessman, he married the boss's daughter (Murray, 1967, pp. 295–296).

Fannie Morris Babcock was from an English background; all of her ancestors had come to the American colonies in the 17th century. For years Murray kept in his living room a portrait of an ancestor on his mother's side, Adam Babcock, painted by John Singleton Copley, one of the most prominent artists of the Revolutionary War period. Her father, Samuel D. Babcock, a successful financier, was president of the Mutual Life Insurance Company and the source of the family's wealth. An imposing man with a gray beard, he was a presence in the family as Murray was growing up. Murray commented to me once that he disagreed with Freud's suggestion that the image of God is based on the father. He argued, instead, that it is based on grandfathers, on older family patriarchs. In any case, as a child he pictured God as looking like his grandfather.[1]

Murray had the childhood of "an average, privileged American boy" (Murray, 1967, p. 298) at the turn of the century. He attended an exclusive preparatory school, Groton. His family built a summer home in Wave Crest, on Long Island, in 1899. It was large enough and imposing enough that it eventually became the clubhouse of a country club.[2] Murray considered it unusual that someone from his background would become a psychologist. When he taught abnormal psychology at Harvard in the 1930s, there would be a small number of students in the class who stood out, on the basis of their "clothes and manner," as being "preppies." When he got to know these students, he invariably found they had particular problems that had driven them to study abnormal psychology. For example, their parents might be divorced. Or, frequently, "they weren't admitted to the club they wanted, and that's why they were interested in abnormal psychology, to find out what was wrong with them."[3]

Murray's own childhood appears on the surface to have been quiet and uneventful. In contrast to the preppies who later took his course on abnormal

FIGURE 8.1 Summer home built in 1899 by Murray's parents in Wave Crest, on the southern shore of Long Island.

psychology, his family remained intact, and while an undergraduate at Harvard he became a member of A.D., one of the most prestigious clubs. But he is able to point to three difficulties he encountered that may help explain why he was disposed to choose psychology for his lifework.

The first and most important is his troubled relationship with his mother, which Murray (1967, pp. 299–300) analyzed in his main autobiographical paper. He was convinced that when he was a young child, his mother failed "to bestow a sufficiency of emotional nurturance." (No doubt his personal experience played a part in his later coining the term "nurturance," which has become widely used.) At first he tried to protest with "spectacles of hypersensitive grief," but his efforts "led only to frustration and shame." Finally, "with some of the murderous resentment of an abandoned child," he gave up on the relationship and concluded that he and his mother "were now dead to each other." From this experience he developed "a marrow of misery and melancholy," in other words, a feeling of depression so deep that it felt as if it were inside his bones. Although this feeling was "repressed by pride and practically extinguished in everyday life by a counteracting disposition of sanguine and expansive buoyancy," it remained under the surface throughout his life and produced "an affinity for the darker, blinder strata of feeling," an affinity that made him receptive to depth psychology.

The second difficulty was his stuttering, which began at age 7 or 8. "I stammered so badly," Murray recalled, "that they let me off reciting in school."[4] He let his stuttering interfere with his life as little as possible, but it must have contributed to a nagging feeling that he was not the same as other boys. During his adulthood his stuttering gradually diminished to the point at which, in his later life, only a hint of it was noticeable.

The third difficulty had to do with his eyes. As a small child he had a mild internal strabismus; in other words, his eyes were crossed. When he was 9 years old, he was subjected to an operation. But unfortunately, the surgeon cut too many muscle fibers, and Murray was left with the opposite defect, an external strabismus. This abnormality was less obvious, but it made it impossible for him to focus both eyes simultaneously on a single object. Although Murray did not make the connection for years, his external strabismus rendered him unable to play sports requiring hand-eye coordination with any skill. In a milieu in which sports were of great importance, this difficulty was by no

FIGURE 8.2 Murray at the age of 20 months (January 12, 1895) with his mother, Fannie Morris Babcock Murray.

means trivial. Murray had many memories of "humiliating incidents," such as striking out while playing baseball or missing an easy catch (Murray, 1967, pp. 301–302).

In thinking over his experiences with sports, Murray saw them as illustrating his "very strong achievement motive"; he would not let himself be defeated by his visual handicap. During his childhood his "first priority" was football, but in addition to his problems with catching the ball, he was not particularly fast or heavy. He became an expert at calling signals. In those days, the quarterback called the signals and blocked; he rarely handled the ball. "It was a mental thing that got me on the team, even though I wasn't very good," Murray recalled. At Groton, where nothing was more important than football, he became the starting quarterback. Curiously, Murray found that he never stuttered when calling signals.[5]

Murray (1967, p. 297) remembered his father as being "a positive univalent figure in my mind, a dependable guide and teacher in the Hellenic mode." He described him as "an unself-centered, even-tempered, unpretentious, undemanding, acquiescent, firm yet unauthoritarian, jolly father." Murray elaborated: "He wasn't competitive. He didn't have extravagant ambitions. He married the daughter of his boss and was given a job in the bank which didn't call for much originality or zest." Murray saw himself as being very different from his father. "I was imbued with a good deal of the opposite," he said. "I thought it was much better to do one thing very well than a lot of things moderately well. His view was, 'Don't try to be the champion of the world. Don't try to do many things.'" As a child, Murray was preoccupied with sports and was an intense competitor. Not only did his father not pressure him to succeed, but, as Murray recalled, "It didn't seem to make a great deal of difference to him whether I won or lost."[6]

Murray (1967, p. 297) had a more "ambivalent" attitude toward his mother than his father; she was "more often the focus of attention, affection, and concern" and also "more resented." "Of the two, she was the more energetic, restless, enthusiastic, enterprising, and talkative . . . also the more changeable, moody, and susceptible to melancholy." Murray saw himself as being similar to his mother in all these respects except for one: "Like my fortunate father, I have never been plagued by endogenous anxieties and worries."

When Murray later encountered psychoanalysis, he was attracted to its emphasis on the unconscious, but one reason he had reservations was the centrality, in psychoanalytic theory, of the Oedipus complex. "Freud's psychology," Murray suggested, "was for people like Freud: those who have a terrific unshakable attachment to the mother and a seething hostility to the father."[7] Freud's concept of the Oedipus complex rang true for people whose personal experience it matched. But Murray hardly had an "unshakable attachment" to his mother. He had a troubled relationship with her, which had led him to develop "the conviction that I could get along well enough with a minimum

FIGURE 8.3 Murray at the age of 16 (1909) with his father, Henry A. Murray, Sr., and his younger brother, Cecil Dunmore Murray.

amount of aid, support, appreciation, recognition, or consolation from others," particularly his mother. And his kindly father did not fit Freud's image of the "threatening, awesome, high and mighty judge" (Murray, 1967, pp. 297, 300). "My mother and father," Murray commented, "just didn't at all fit the Freudian scheme."[8]

After reading an earlier paper that I wrote about him (Anderson, 1988), Murray pointed out that while I had given due attention to the influence of his parents, I had underemphasized his relationship with his sister and brother.[9]

Murray's sister, Virginia, was born in 1890. "She was willful, active, bright, and had a sense of humor," Murray recalled. "Because she had this advantage of almost four years, she did a lot of bullying of me." Their relationship finally changed when Murray was 10 years old. "We were crossing the Atlantic. We got in a fight until I got her shoulders down. From then on everything was different."[10]

Although they no longer had physical fights, they continued to quarrel throughout their lives. She married a businessman named Robert Low Bacon. "Due to her influence," according to Murray, "her husband changed professions and went into politics."[11] He became a congressman from Rhode Island and served several terms. She and her husband were staunch Republicans. Murray was a Democrat and an enthusiastic supporter of Franklin D. Roosevelt. "We would get into terrible political arguments," Murray added.[12] Murray's widow Nina mentioned to me that in the later years—Virginia lived until 1980—there was still some visible antagonism between the brother and sister, and Virginia sometimes took a critical, condescending attitude toward him.

Murray had a more affectionate relationship with his brother, Cecil Dunmore Murray, nicknamed Mike, who was born in 1897. "We were very close, my brother and I," Murray said. "I was sort of paternal towards him, perhaps too much so." Like his older brother, Mike attended Groton and Harvard. "He was naturally very good with machinery, all kinds of applied sciences," Murray explained. "His ability with machinery led him to aviation." Mike left college during the war to join the Naval Air Corps. He became a hero during the war and was awarded the Congressional Medal of Honor. After the war he graduated from Harvard and then went through medical school.[13]

"He had a tendency to follow what I had done," Murray said. Mike went into psychiatry, in part because of his older brother's interest in psychology. Murray saw this choice as a "mistake because that wasn't the way his mind worked. He was very good at dealing with scientific things but only average with psychic things." Mike died tragically of Hodgkin's Disease in 1935 at the age of 37.[14]

"OFTEN IN THE DEAN'S OFFICE
BUT RARELY ON HIS LIST"

Murray graduated from Groton School in 1911 and from Harvard University in 1915. Throughout these years he was an indifferent student. When I was looking through some of his memorabilia with him, I came across a monthly report from Groton dated November 20, 1909. Murray received an "average mark," and his rank was 16th in a class of 25. At the bottom, Endicott Peabody, the school's legendary headmaster, had written a laconic remark: "My impression is that he could stand a good deal higher if he would." While at Harvard, Murray, whose concentration was in history, had little interest in academic work. In later years he liked to joke, "I was often in the dean's office but rarely on his list." He explained, "I was called in by the dean two or three times for my studies being low and my absences being high."[15]

Murray had virtually no exposure to psychology while an undergraduate. He went to the first meeting of a course taught by Hugo Münsterberg, the German-trained psychologist, and he quickly decided "It's not for me." His memory was that the lecture dealt with "the anatomy of the ear"; Murray did not see how the topic had much relevance to the psychological life of human beings.[16]

At Groton, Murray had a brief flirtation with religion. While taking long, lonely runs, he enjoyed nature and thought, "There must have been a God who made all this beauty." For 2 or 3 months he even considered becoming a minister and going to Labrador as a missionary. During his first months at Harvard, he had some interest in Unitarianism. He shared his enthusiasm with Peabody, who besides being headmaster was an Episcopalian priest. Peabody's comment about Unitarians was "But there are so few of them." Murray considered this comment to be ludicrous.[17] He was searching for truth; what did it matter how many Unitarians there were?

Murray soon gave up all religious belief. His view in the later years was that "it is all imagination." He was convinced that people had created all ideas about the Deity, but he considered religion to be "fascinating" because he saw it as "a tremendous bridge to the imagination," that is, it illustrated how people felt on the inside and what they desired.[18]

The image of Murray as a mediocre student might suggest that he cared little for achievement during his preparatory school and college years. But in fact, his achievement motive was as strong as ever; he expressed it in athletic competition. In fact, as the captain of the Harvard crew, he was one of the most visible and admired members of his class. Rowing is still a major sport at Harvard, but in his era it had the importance of today's professional football. Large crowds attended the races, and the Boston and New York newspapers gave detailed, daily coverage to intercollegiate rowing.

"In college," Murray wrote (Harvard College Class of 1915, 1965), "my two fields of concentration had been rowing and romance . . . ; rowing ended with a flunk in the finals at New London . . . , but, on the morrow, I received a more than compensating A in romance" (pp. 366–367). His collegiate rowing career ended with a defeat in the annual Harvard-Yale race. The day after the race, he proposed to a young woman from Boston named Josephine Lee Rantoul. She accepted, and they were married a year later, in 1916. Josephine was avidly interested in medicine. At the time of their courtship and afterward, she did volunteer work in the outpatient department of a hospital.[19] As a woman from the upper class, she would not have considered becoming a physician or a nurse. But she was pleased that Murray went on after graduation to Columbia's College of Physicians and Surgeons.

FIGURE 8.4 Murray with his future wife, Josephine Lee Rantoul, in 1915 during their engagement.

In medical school, Murray became serious about his studies for the first time, worked tirelessly, and ended up graduating, in 1919, first in his class. When, late in his life, he looked back at this period, however, he felt he had been "sleep-walking." It seemed to him that he had hardly been aware of himself and his surroundings. He had been going through life "as if it were a play." "The way I became conscious," Murray said, was through his talks with another medical student, Alvan Barach, "who was very subjective and was very concerned with his own feelings." His relationship with Barach also prompted Murray to question some of the prejudices of his class; Barach was Jewish, and

Murray had assumed from his family and acquaintances a vague anti-Semitism. He went on to have an intimate, lifelong friendship with Barach. Barach became a prominent physician and researcher; he specialized in respiratory disease and helped develop the oxygen tent.[20]

After finishing medical school, Murray stayed at Columbia and received an MA in biology in 1920. Then he did a 20-month surgical internship at Presbyterian Hospital in New York City.

In 1921 Franklin D. Roosevelt had an attack of infantile paralysis and was taken to Presbyterian Hospital. George Draper, a specialist in the illness, was in charge of the case, but Murray, as a young intern, spent more time with the patient than the experienced physicians. Nearly every day during Roosevelt's 6-week hospitalization, Murray drew his blood and had talks with him. Both were graduates of Groton and Harvard, and they had numerous interests in common. Murray recalled that Roosevelt was not interested in the medical findings but wanted instead to discuss other matters, for example, his collection of naval memorabilia. Murray found Roosevelt "very talkative" and was particularly impressed that he saw "no evident depression." Historians have noted that Roosevelt seemed extremely unusual in avoiding the depression that is usually associated with suffering from a disabling disease such as infantile paralysis, but they have wondered whether Roosevelt might have put on an optimistic front for his family and friends. Murray believed that his experience with Roosevelt virtually proves that Roosevelt did not experience any significant depression.[21] Roosevelt may have had reasons for feigning confidence in front of those close to him, but, Murray noted, "A person doesn't hide things from a young doctor. Nothing can be gained for his pride in anything to do with a young fellow who doesn't know anything. There wasn't any special reason why he should show off in front of me." Murray saw Roosevelt's reaction to his illness as being indicative of "his nature."[22] Roosevelt showed the same optimism during the economic depression of the 1930s and the world war of the 1940s as he had exhibited during his personal crisis in 1921.

Murray also formed one other conclusion on the basis of his experience with Roosevelt in 1921. It is common for a person with infantile paralysis to develop "an ambitious set of fantasies and goals," presumably as a way of combating depression. Murray was convinced that Roosevelt generated the goal of becoming president of the United States "right there in the hospital while he was lying in bed."[23]

After his internship, Murray did research on physiological ontogeny, studying the development of chicken embryos. He spent 4 years at the Rockefeller Institute in New York City and then continued his research at Cambridge University in the laboratory of Frederick G. Hopkins, who later won a Nobel Prize. He received his Ph.D. in biochemistry from Cambridge University in 1927.

A "PROFOUND AFFECTIONAL UPHEAVAL"

During his years as a student of biochemistry, Murray made steady, gradual progress in his research and published 21 articles in scientific journals. But at the same time he was undergoing what he later described as a "profound affectional upheaval" (Murray, 1967, p. 290). He encountered, for the first time, a whole new world of which he had never before dreamt, the inner world of the human mind. He found himself "in a blaze." Great works in the humanities helped precipitate his newfound interests. While reading *Moby*

FIGURE 8.5 Henry A. Murray in midlife (photograph by Fabian Bachrach).

Dick, he found himself "being witched, illumined, and transfigured by the magic of another's art" (Murray, 1951/1962, p. 62). For the rest of his life, he was a fervent admirer and student of Melville. The novels of Dostoevsky, Tolstoy, Proust, and Hardy also spoke to him, as did the music of Beethoven, Wagner, and Puccini. He not only read the poetry of E. A. Robinson and saw the plays of Eugene O'Neill but also became friendly with these two men and other figures in the arts. Murray later speculated that his "emotional potentialities had been denied adequate participation" in his biochemical work. He was ready to be receptive to a disciplline that would make use of both his passion for exploration and his newly discovered fascination with what William James had called "the darker, blinder strata of character" (Murray, 1967, pp. 291, 293).

During this period, Murray first encountered depth psychology. One evening in 1923 he bought a copy of Carl G. Jung's *Psychological Types*, just published in English translation. "I read it all night long and all the next day," Murray later recalled.[24] Jung demonstrated to Murray that it was possible to study, and to make sense of, the psychological terrain that Murray had recently discovered. Murray experienced the book as "a gratuitous answer to an unspoken prayer." "The transaction with Jung," he wrote, "led to an omnivorous and nourishing procession of readings through the revolutionary and astonishing words of Freud and his disciples, heady liquor for the young chemist" (Murray, 1967, p. 289).

An exciting, upsetting development in his personal life interacted with the changes in his intellectual life. Two or 3 weeks after reading *Psychological Types*, he met Christiana Drummond Morgan, a married woman 4 years younger than himself.[25] She was an amateur artist, intuitive and sensitive. The inner world of the mind, with which Murray was just becoming familiar, was her métier. She was also deeply interested in Jungian psychology. Already, at this point, she had a familiarity with Jung's published works. Later she had an analysis with him and became, in Murray's phrase, a "semi-Jungian" psychotherapist (Murray, 1976, p. 520).

Murray fell in love with Morgan and found himself in a painful, wrenching dilemma. He abhorred the idea of divorce. He was deeply fond of his wife and did not want to be separated from her, and they also had a child, Josephine, who had been born in 1921. But he could not stand giving up Morgan.

In 1925 Murray visited Jung "supposedly to discuss abstractions; but," he wrote, "in a day or two to my astonishment enough affective stuff erupted to invalid a pure scientist" (Murray, 1940, p. 153). "I saw him every day for three weeks," Murray said, "and we went sailing down the lake and stayed at his retreat on the lake and talked all the time." Jung struck Murray as being "very natural and very friendly." "Jung didn't believe in a regular systematic way of going about things," Murray noted. "He would cut the time short or long depending on the circumstances." Jung also talked freely about himself. For

FIGURE 8.6 Christiana Drummond Morgan in 1937.

example, Jung told Murray that the central idea of *Psychological Types* stemmed from "his wife's reaction to his behavior in a group." His wife "would often object to what he said as lacking sensitivity to the feelings of people he was talking to." Jung tried to figure out why he and his wife would react differently to people, and he developed his first two personality types, the thinking and feeling types. "So his wife represented feeling, and he represented thinking," Murray noted. "It developed in that way. Real people in real circumstances."[26]

Murray was awed by Jung. "This first encounter with an analytical psychiatrist of the new order," Murray (1967) wrote, provided him "with an exemplar of genius that settled the question of his identity to come" (p. 291). Murray had found his vocation; he decided to become a depth psychologist.

In looking back, Murray felt he was so impressed with Jung largely because Jung was the first person he had ever met who was in touch with the unconscious. "When I went to him I was completely ignorant . . . so that every time he opened his mouth he surprised me because he had something new to say." Murray met with Jung another six or seven times over the years and corresponded with him. As time went on and Murray's "critical faculty developed," Murray found that Jung "said a lot of things that weren't true. And he wasn't at all critical. . . . He'd believe anything I told him that was along the lines that he liked."[27]

Murray saw Jung's reaction to *Explorations in Personality* as being characteristic. "The only thing he picked out of it was that we found the Catholics showed the fewest neurotic symptoms and then the Protestants about in the middle and the Jews the most. And he loved that about the Catholics." In Murray's view, Jung fastened on that one minor conclusion because it seemed to support Jung's bias about the advantages of spirituality. "He turned out to be much more religious than I thought," Murray added, "and I think in the later years he went the way most people do. . . . They begin to think about the afterlife and that kind of thing."[28]

In Murray's 1925 meeting with Jung, the most crucial question that arose was Murray's conflict over his involvement with two women. Jung revealed in their very first talk that he had faced the same conflict, and he had solved it by openly maintaining his relationships with both his wife and Toni Wolff. Murray decided to adopt Jung's solution. Jung pointed out the difficulties. "You have no idea what problems you're going to run into," he said. In Murray's view, Jung was discouraging in order to make sure Murray's relationship with Morgan was not just a "momentary flirtation." Murray noted in looking back at his talk with Jung that his relationship with Morgan lasted for more than 40 years. "As things go in this world, that was close to permanent."[29]

After his meeting with Jung, Murray put Jung's solution into effect. His relationship with his wife was not simply *pro forma*. He was deeply attached to her and appreciated her. He described her to me as somebody who "loved people and they loved her." "She was a great person, very active in joining all kinds of caring and helping organizations." When she died in 1962, he noted, 600 people attended her funeral. Murray also valued her skill as a wife and mother. But, he added, she "had few intellectual interests, almost nil."[30]

In contrast, he and Morgan "talked alike and thought alike." They shared a passionate interest in the inner world. "Christiana and I were the only ones who had that to that extent and reveled in it and got our nourishment from it and wrote about it and lectured about it," he added. "It's perfectly possible to go about your professional work and you get on all right with your wife." But in encountering Morgan, he believed, he had happened upon a rare and unexpected opportunity. They had "the same way of looking at things." It all came together: "being in love with your work and your lover and the theories."[31]

Murray looked on 1925 as "the year of my rebirth." Even as he was completing his work in biochemistry, he found, with the aid of Jung, "a path of deeper joy and my veritable identity." "I returned to America bent on a new profession, medical and academic psychology combined" (Harvard College Class of 1915, 1965, p. 367). Morton Prince, the Boston psychiatrist who was best known for his work on multiple personality, was in the process of forming the Harvard Psychological Clinic. Murray applied to be his assistant. Even though Murray had had no formal education in psychology whatsoever, Harvard's president, A. Lawrence Lowell, chose him for the job. The psychologists at Harvard also approved his faculty appointment as an instructor of psychology.

"THE GREAT, HAUNTINGLY RECURRENT PROBLEMS"

In 1927 Murray began at the clinic. In 1928 Prince became ill, and Murray became a candidate to be his successor. Rodney G. Triplet (1983, p. 151), in archival research for his dissertation on Murray and the clinic, discovered a number of previously unknown facts; Murray himself was unaware of many of them. Triplet found that Edwin G. Boring and his fellow Harvard psychologists opposed Murray's appointment as director of the clinic. They argued that when Murray became Prince's assistant, they had assumed his Ph.D. was in psychology; they had had no idea his degree was in biochemistry. They also voiced their concern over Murray's interest in the psychodynamic psychology of Freud and Jung. President Lowell, however, was responsible for the final decision. He chose Murray as the new director of the clinic. Murray also received an appointment as assistant professor of abnormal and dynamic psychology.

If the objections of Harvard's psychologists suggest they were less than enthusiastic about Murray, he was even more critical of them and, for that matter, of all of academic psychology.

Murray left behind a career as a biochemical researcher and became a psychologist because he had a passionate need to understand the inner workings of the mind. He assumed that psychology was "the science which describes people and explains why they perceive, feel, think, and act as they do" (Murray, 1935/1981, p. 338). He later described what he saw as the goal of the personality psychologist, or in his terminology, the personologist:

> A personologist wants to know why man, "like an angry ape, plays such fantastic tricks before high heaven"; why he laughs, blasphemes and frets, cheers at a spangled cloth and bleeds for a king; why he blushes over four-letter words and hides his

genitals, and falls in love with so and so and later strangles her; why he mourns in isolation, lacerates himself with guilt, invents a purgatory and a paradise. (Murray, 1940, p. 150)

When Murray entered academic psychology, he found a field that focused on "measuring the lawful relationships of narrowly restricted forms of animal behavior, of physiological processes in general, and of the simplest sensory and sensorimotor processes of human beings in particular" (Murray, 1967, p. 305). Psychologists, he quickly noticed, paid no attention to "the phenomena that intrigued" him (Murray, 1940, p. 154). He continually observed "a mountain of ritual bringing forth a mouse of fact more dead than alive" (Murray, 1967, p. 305). Murray was not just disappointed with academic psychology; he was disgusted with it. And he was not a person to keep his opinions to himself. "I was a very obnoxious person," he said, "because I didn't have any respect for the psychology that was taught and for the people who taught it."[32] He published a paper in 1935 asserting that academic psychology "has contributed practically nothing to the knowledge of human nature." "It has not only failed to bring light to the great, hauntingly recurrent problems," he argued, "but it has no intention, one is shocked to realize, of attempting to investigate them" (Murray, 1935/ 1981, p. 339). Boring, who was then chairman of Harvard's Department of Psychology, looked at the paper and advised Murray "never to let anyone see it." Boring told him, "If you publish it, you'll be ostracized in the APA all your life."[33] Boring's prophecy proved to be wrong. The American Psychological Association bestowed one of its highest honors on Murray in 1981, the Award for a Distinguished Scientific Contribution (Haydn, 1970, p. 124).

Murray believed that psychoanalysis had far more to offer than the academic psychology of the day. "The technic of research, many of the revealed facts, and a few of the theories advanced by psychoanalysts," he wrote in the 1935 paper, "represent the weightiest contribution ever made within a short space of time to an understanding of human nature" (Murray, 1935/1981, p. 341). He made every effort to learn about psychoanalysis. He was one of the central figures in a 10-person group that founded the Boston Psychoanalytic Society in 1928, and he hosted the society's seminars at the Harvard Psychological Clinic (Hendrick, 1961, pp. 14, 32). He had a 9-month training analysis with Franz Alexander from 1931 to 1932, saw control cases under the supervision of Hanns Sachs, and became an accredited member of the American Psychoanalytic Association and the International Psychoanalytical Association in 1933.

Murray's analysis with Alexander was a disappointment. "I thought, 'He's a good fellow and quite able but second order'" in comparison to Jung, Murray recalled. "What Alexander said, after Jung, was either old hat to me, something I knew already, or something quite ordinary." Murray felt that he did not "resonate" with Alexander, and he found himself "not involved" with him. "It was like going to a play and not being involved in the play and being able to make comments on the scenery in the theater." In looking back, Murray realizes that he did not "reveal" himself to Alexander.[34] The best indication that the analysis stayed on the surface is that Murray's relationship with Morgan never received serious consideration. Murray mentioned the relationship near the beginning of the analysis, and Alexander referred to it as a "narcissism *á deux.*" Alexander's remark is critical in two ways. In calling the relationship narcissistic, he was saying that it was selfish. In using the phrase "*á deux,*" he was alluding to the psychiatric term "*folie á deux,*" which means a shared delusional system, and thereby implying that the relationship was pathological. Murray decided early in the analysis not to expose his dual relationship with his wife and Morgan. "I could see right away that he wasn't the kind that would appreciate the best reason for my doing it."[35]

Murray's experience of doing psychotherapy and psychoanalysis was somewhat more successful. In all, he estimates that he treated about 15 patients extensively. Most of his therapeutic work took place from 1932 to 1935. His experience with patients increased his respect for psychoanalytic theory. He noted, for example, that two or three of his patients who had hysterical symptoms produced "dreams and associations which were almost identical to some that are found in the psychoanalytic literature" (letter to J. W. Anderson, November 9, 1982). He was also impressed with Sachs's supervision. Sachs "proved time and time again that he could predict my patients' trends several days or even weeks before they were exhibited." It occurred to Murray that "a theory that can do this is valuable" (Murray, 1940, p. 156). Murray, however, did not find it personally rewarding to treat patients; he preferred creating ideas and conducting research (Murray, 1967, p. 300).

Murray accepted "a large part (more than half) of the psychoanalytic scheme" (Murray, 1940, p. 152). Psychoanalysis, in contrast to academic psychology, paid attention to the complexity and depth of human nature and never slighted unconscious forces. But Murray resented the view of many psychoanalysts that one must "swallow the whole indigestible bolus" (Murray, 1940, pp. 152, 157). He found most of the Boston psychoanalysts to be intolerable. They acted, in his opinion, like "zealous disciples"; they did not take a scientific approach (letter to J. W. Anderson, November 9, 1982). Psychoanalysis had an enormous effect on Murray. But he decided to go his own way. He created his own point of view, informed by psychoanalysis, rather than becoming a part of the psychoanalytic movement.

"TO ILLUMINATE THE UNCONSCIOUS PROCESSES"

Murray set out to develop a new approach to the exploration of human nature. In contrast to academic psychology, which he considered to be obsessed with obscure and irrelevant phenomena, he was determined to study the most important dimensions of personality. And he saw himself as different from the psychoanalysts in that he was attempting to devise a systematic method for investigating personality, while they were attempting to cure neurotic disorders and learned about psychology only as a by-product of their therapeutic work.

He believed that to understand personality, he had to learn about "the darker, blinder strata"; consequently, he faced the problem of gaining access to the very aspects of personality that were most hidden. It occurred to him that projection might provide the answer. He noted, he later told me, that in primitive religions "objects of awe are endowed with anthropsychic—not anthropomorphic—qualities." A hurricane might have aims that would be to the benefit or detriment of the worshiper. But that aim comes from the worshiper; it is not held by the hurricane. Understanding the aim can tell the observer about the hopes and fears of the worshiper. Murray saw projection as "the best way of learning about somebody next to his being aware and anxious to tell you."[36]

In an early experiment (Murray, 1933), he looked at "the effect of fear on suspicion of hostility." At lunchtime he had his daughter and a group of girls who were playing with her look at a series of pictures. He asked the 11-year-old girls to rate each one on the basis of how malicious or kindly the person in the picture seemed to be. In the evening, the girls played a frightening game called Murder while the house was pitch black. Immediately after the game, he had them rate the pictures again. "They saw much more maliciousness than usual," he noted. The pictures were no different than they had been at lunchtime. The additional attribution of maliciousness was coming from the girls."[37]

"Then I got around to the point where I thought it wasn't enough to know about one variable," Murray recalled. He thought of looking at fantasies. But it was difficult to gather fantasies; merely asking someone for his or her fantasies did not work well. One of Murray's students, Cecelia Roberts, faced the same difficulty as she tried to gather fantasies from blind people and sighted people in order to compare them. She tried to get her son to tell her his fantasies. "He wasn't being productive; he thought it was silly to tell his mother what his fantasies were," Murray said. "She had a book and asked him to tell a story about one of the pictures." Her son responded by making up a rich, imaginative story. When Roberts told Murray about this experience, he capitalized on it and started working on the Thematic Apperception Test (TAT).[38]

In 1934 Murray and his colleagues put together the first set of TAT cards. He took them with him during a visit with his mother in the country. "I showed her five of them in an offhand way," he recalled. She told story after story that "reflected her continued grief"; her husband—Murray's father—had died 2 months earlier. At the time she was putting on a facade of being over her mourning, and she had no idea that the stories were about herself. Murray felt "guilty" because he had unintentionally induced his usually introverted mother to reveal so much about herself. But this experience—with his very own mother—convinced him of the power of the TAT.[39]

When Murray completed the paper that introduced the TAT (Morgan & Murray, 1935), he not only included Morgan's name as a co-author but listed her as the senior author. Although Murray talked over all of his work with her, she took only a "mild" interest in the TAT.[40] Her chief involvement was drawing some of the pictures and administering the test one time to a fascinating anorectic patient whom she was treating. Murray put her name on the paper in an unsuccessful attempt to "encourage" her to become more involved with the TAT. She did not want to have her name on the paper and became increasingly irritated as letters poured in asking her questions about the TAT.[41]

Murray had little patience in later years with psychologists who viewed the TAT as a test of behavior. "My idea was to illuminate the unconscious processes—that were repressed—of which the subject was not aware," he pointed out. "That was the whole point of it."[42]

"A GOING CONCERN"

Murray, of course, was not interested only in developing tools for research. His goal was to explore personality holistically. He believed that one of the shortcomings of the usual attempts at "representation of the personality"— psychobiographies and clinical case studies—is that a single author produces them. "My point," he explained, "is that a person is different in different contexts and with different people at different times." He saw the necessity of having a group of personologists working together, studying the same subjects.[43]

Perhaps Murray's greatest accomplishment was developing the Harvard Psychological Clinic into such a "creative environment," to use Donald Mac-Kinnon's phrase. MacKinnon (1982) tried to define the common ingredient that made the clinic, Murray's Office of Strategic Services (OSS) assessment program during World War II, and Kurt Lewin's various research centers so successful. He concluded that it was "the presence of a highly intelligent, highly original charismatic leader who had attracted a group of intelligent, energetic, and devoted co-workers who were fiercely loyal to their leader and deeply committed to furthering the goals which he set for them, which they set jointly, and which they also set for themselves" (pp. 12–13).

Murray commented to me once that the clinic seemed to function most efficiently when he was clearly in charge. He also found that he felt best when he was in a leadership role. He saw this as being one of "the manifestations of narcissism": one feels "healthier and better off" when one is a leader.[44]

Robert W. White, an early graduate student in the clinic and then the only faculty member there in addition to Murray, was especially impressed by the variety of workers at the clinic. In addition to Murray and the graduate students, "there was a male Freudian analyst and a female Jungian analyst with their respective patients, there were a sociologist and two anthropologists, and there were representatives of literature, craftsmanship, and other interests unusual on a scientific team" (White, 1987, p. 17). The Jungian analyst, of course, was Christiana Morgan.

Murray liked to include individuals who were exceptional but who would not usually be welcome at a research center located in an academic department of psychology. The most striking example of a person like this is Erik H. Erikson. When Erikson came to the United States in 1933, he had training in psychoanalysis in Vienna but had never attended a university. Murray invited him to participate in the work of the clinic.

One time Murray gave me his impressions of Erikson during that period. Erikson "hadn't had any big recognition yet," Murray recalled, "so he was uncertain of himself. I recognized right away that he was very talented." Murray placed him on the Diagnostic Council. The five people on the council were responsible for rating the subjects in the clinic's large research project on a number of different variables. It turned out that Erikson's ratings consistently disagreed with those of the other members of the council. "But then when he described his own personal experiment," Murray went on, "everybody thought he was very subtle and very clever." Murray believed that Erikson was never very effective at working with a group of people. "These are the secondary characteristics of genius that may or may not be there," he added.[45]

Interesting visitors also contributed to the atmosphere of the clinic. Jung, Adler, Janet, and Rank all gave talks or had lunch at the clinic.[46] Some frequent visitors from outside psychology were Felix Frankfurter, Conrad Aiken, Katherine Cornell, Bertrand Russell, Paul Robeson, and Alfred North Whitehead (Triplet, 1983, p. 157).

Teaching was an important responsibility of Murray's. His chief course, offered each year, was "Abnormal and Dynamic Psychology." A large number of students were attracted to this course. In 1930 the dean of the Faculty of Arts and Sciences, Clifford H. Moore, undertook an investigation of the course. He was afraid that something must be wrong since so many students were interested in the course. For example, there was the possibility that Murray might be grading the students too leniently. Nothing untoward was found during the investigation (Triplet, 1983, p. 159). Most likely the course was so popular because Murray was a dynamic, committed teacher and because many students wanted to learn about the new psychology.

Despite Murray's apparent success at Harvard as a researcher and teacher and as the director of the clinic, he found himself on the verge of being ousted in 1936. He was aware he did not get along well with the other psychologists at

Harvard. "I didn't have too much respect for them, and they certainly didn't have respect for me, but we agreed to disagree," he commented. The faculty had lunch together each week, and "psychoanalysis versus psychophysics was brought up every time." Professor C. C. Pratt "believed we wouldn't get anywhere in psychology," Murray recalled, "until we had reduced mental processes to physics."[47]

The Harvard Psychological Clinic was located at 64 Plympton Street, while Emerson Hall, in Harvard Yard, housed the rest of the department. "If you were two or three blocks from Emerson Hall, where the psychophysicists were, you had a good deal of independence," he noted.[48] Not only were his courses popular, but graduate students flocked to the clinic. Statistics from 1936 indicate that Murray had nearly as many graduate students working with him as all the rest of the faculty members put together (Triplet, 1983, p. 248). "How could they help being put out?" Murray asked. "This outsider who doesn't know anything comes in and gets a house to himself and pretty soon it's a going concern."[49]

Harvard's president, James Bryant Conant, set up a committee to review Murray's appointment in 1936. The members of the committee were Boring, Karl S. Lashley, and Gordon Allport from the Department of Psychology; Stanley Cobb, professor of neuropathology in the Medical School; and two deans, Charles Sidney Burwell and George David Birkhoff. It was apparent from the beginning that Lashley would be Murray's chief antagonist. An adherent to an extremely narrow and rigid brand of experimental psychology, Lashley had come to Harvard in 1935 from the University of Chicago with, as Murray put it, "a tremendous chip on his shoulder and distaste for anything to do with psychoanalysis."[50] While in Chicago, Lashley had started an analysis with Franz Alexander but had quit in a rage after a few sessions. After this abortive experience with analysis, he had tried to get Alexander fired from his adjunct professorship at the university and had become a bitter and outspoken opponent of psychoanalysis. The committee solicited letters about Murray's stature as a psychologist. Among the psychologists who wrote in support of him were B. F. Skinner, Kurt Lewin, and William McDougall (Triplet, 1983, pp. 243–244, 248, 253).

The committee met on December 23, 1936, to make its decision. According to Murray, who did not attend the meeting but heard about it from some of the participants, the discussion turned into a bitter argument. At a crucial moment, Allport stood up for Murray and said he was a rare and exceptional scholar like Harvard's first professor of psychology, William James. Lashley responded by attacking James; he called him "the worst thing ever to happen to psychology." Lashley had chosen just the wrong point to make. Conant knew little about psychology but revered William James. "I've been told he was the best professor ever here," he commented. There was so much anger by the end of the meeting that Conant had to ask everyone to shake hands.[51]

The committee was deadlocked in its vote. Allport, Cobb, and Burwell were in favor of granting Murray tenure. Boring, Lashley, and Birkhoff voted to terminate him (Triplet, 1983, p. 253). Murray, of course, learned about the tie vote, but he did not know who had supported him and who had opposed him. He was surprised to learn decades later, when he read Triplet's dissertation, that Boring had voted against him. He felt betrayed and told me Boring had always said "he was doing what he could for me."[52]

The disagreement over Murray came down to a question about whether or not his approach was a legitimate part of psychology. Allport wrote to Conant in support of Murray:

> It must be borne in mind that Murray is working in an almost virgin territory where chicanery and system-making have always prevailed. He brings a more critical mind to his subject than did Charcot, Prince, Freud, or Jung. . . .
> I earnestly hope that you will not now permit the humanistic tradition in psychology at Harvard to be imperiled and destroyed. The critical standards of the "exact sciences," admirable in their own right, are not catholic enough in outlook to serve as the norm for the newer science of the human mind.

Lashley wrote Conant an angry letter, charging Murray with "intellectual dishonesty" in his use of statistics and "a supercilious attitude" in his approach to validation. He argued that "stripped of his verbiage, his major concepts are elementary and his elaboration of them is in terms of orthodox psychoanalytic theory." Lashley concluded that disagreement over Murray's reappointment resulted from "the conflict between the older humanistic and philosophical psychology and the attempt to evolve a more exact science through an objective and biological approach." Allport and Lashley both felt so strongly that Allport threatened to resign if Murray were not retained and Lashley threatened to resign if Murray were not "fired" (Triplet, 1983, pp. 256–257).

Boring suggested a compromise, according to which Murray would be promoted to associate professor but not given tenure. The chief difficulty was that university funds could not be used to help support the clinic if Murray were not tenured. The Rockefeller Foundation had been subsidizing the clinic. Conant conferred with Alan Gregg, director of the Foundation's Medical Sciences Division, and felt confident that the Foundation's support would continue. On March 17, 1937, Conant appointed Murray to two 5-year terms as an associate professor. Lashley was enraged and insisted that his professional integrity would be jeopardized by Murray's new appointment. He finally agreed not to leave Harvard when Conant offered to name him to a research professorship and to excuse him from all administrative and teaching responsibilities within the department (Triplet, 1983, pp. 257–259).

For the rest of his life, Murray deeply appreciated Allport's loyal support during his reappointment crisis. And one would think that they also would have been close friends and allies, since they were the only senior faculty members interested in personality psychology and, in addition, they shared a humanistic perspective. But it would be more accurate to describe them as rivals during their many years together on the Harvard faculty. M. Brewster Smith (1971) has published an account of a seminar in which Murray, Allport, and Kurt Lewin presented and debated their perspectives. Murray and Allport are outspoken about their differences with each other. Murray criticizes Allport for limiting himself to that which is "conscious, voluntary, and rational or self-consistent and coherent" and for leaving out the "vast Sargasso Sea of [the] id" (pp. 359–360). Allport is no more conciliatory in his comments on Murray. He criticizes Murray's "excessive geneticism" and calls his theory of needs "too arbitrary" (p. 360).

Murray's attitude toward Allport came out in his commentary to me on Allport's meeting with Freud. Allport often told the story of how he visited Freud shortly after graduating from college (Elms, 1972). Allport told Freud about seeing a 4-year-old boy on the tram who seemed to have a "dirt phobia." Throughout the trip, the boy kept complaining that he did not want to sit in a seat because "it was dirty," and he did not want to sit next to a man because "he was dirty." Freud then said to Allport, "And was that little boy you?" Allport thought Freud "definitely wrong" and saw his comment as one reason for dismissing his point of view. Murray said, "I haven't been able to make out surely yet what this is about." Murray went on:

> Why should he think that was a stupid thing to say? It was a very clever thing to say because that's just what Allport is. I mean, he is a very fastidious person; he is very clean himself. And everything is very nice and orderly. He isn't compulsive, or he isn't neurotic or anything like that. But he is just very strong on the side of gentility and being very clean, and his desk was always perfect. . . . Freud just hit him right on the head, right on the nose.

Murray added that the meeting did not cause Allport to dismiss Freud's view; Allport had already given up on psychoanalysis because he "doesn't like anything to do with sex . . . and the unconscious." "He thought of consciousness as large and the unconscious as a little bit of a thing down here."[53]

Murray also had an opportunity to visit Freud. In 1937 he was in Vienna and hoped to find a way to get an appointment with Freud. To his surprise, he received an invitation at his hotel to visit Freud. He was not even aware that Freud knew who he was, let alone that he was in town. Almost the first words out of Freud's mouth, when they began their talk, were "Why didn't I get an honorary degree at the Harvard Tercentenary and Jung did get one?" Murray realized that Freud had wanted to see him to ask him this question. Murray explained that the psychology faculty had voted; Freud had received the most votes, and Jung had come in second, but Erikson had pointed out that Freud was ill and could not possibly make the trip to Cambridge to receive an honorary degree. Freud seemed pleased with Murray's explanation. What struck Murray was that "it turned out he cared a lot." "The old rivalry" between Freud and Jung was still alive in Freud's mind.[54] Murray went on to talk with Freud for about 2 hours; his impression was that "we got along very well." "I liked him very much, all the way through. That was something very natural, to expose to me this jealousy he had about Jung." Freud seemed to Murray to be "a warm, cordial person." "I think he's a person who has a lot of very human qualities," Murray added, "and they're very conscious to himself."[55]*

"A MULTIFORM METHOD"

In 1938 Murray's most important work, *Explorations in Personality* (Murray et al., 1938), was finally published. A group of personologists under his leadership studied 51 college-aged men. Murray devised a personological system to use in analyzing the subjects. Some of his best known concepts, including his taxonomy of needs and types of "press," are a part of this system. Murray and his co-workers used 25 procedures in studying each subject, including standard procedures such as interviews and new ones such as Erikson's Dramatic Productions Test. Several of the researchers studied each of the subjects, and one researcher then wrote a lengthy case study of the subject.

In his conversations with me, Murray underlined the central ideas behind *Explorations in Personality*, as well as his later personological work (Anderson & Murray, 1977). His ultimate goal was to develop a comprehensive personological system, one that could adequately deal with the complexity of an individual. The system presented in *Explorations in Personality* was meant as a first attempt, a provisional system. He believed in studying the subjects with a "multiform method." To avoid the limitations inherent in having one researcher, there would be a number of researchers. To avoid the limitations inherent in using one procedure, there would be a number of procedures. And to avoid the limitations of studying just one subject, there would be a number of subjects. After studying all of the subjects, the researchers would then ask, how effective is the personological system at representing the personalities of the subjects? The personological system would then be revised on the basis of the answer to that question. Then—and Murray saw this as the heart of his plan—the whole process would be repeated again with another group of subjects. His hope was to devise increasingly powerful personological systems by carrying out a succession of research projects.

*Here and throughout the paper, I have deliberately refrained from analyzing the part his personality played in his way of relating the experiences of his life. For two psychobiographical perspectives on Murray, see Elms, 1987, and Anderson 1988.

After completing *Explorations in Personality*, Murray did begin another large-scale study. His collaborators included, in addition to White and Morgan, Leo Bellak, Elliot Jacques, Silvan Tomkins, Frederick Wyatt, and Daniel Horn (Murray, 1967, p. 305). He had great expectations for this research, but World War II intervened. First, he had to scale down the project. And then, in 1943, when he began his work with the OSS Assessment Staff, he left Morgan to try to salvage at least a part of the research. The result was "A Clinical Study of Sentiments" (Murray & Morgan, 1945), an analysis of how the 11 subjects who had been studied felt about four topics: war, religion, their parents, and sex. Murray commented to me several times about his regret that in the rush to finish the work, his and Morgan's collaborators were not given credit for their part in the research.[56]

During the war, Murray served in the Army Medical Corps as a major and, eventually, a lieutenant colonel. He was head of the assessment program of the OSS, the predecessor of the Central Intelligence Agency. The program's mission, he later wrote (Harvard College Class of 1915, 1950), was "to devise and administer a system of procedures for judging the suitability of men and women who had been recruited for a wide variety of secret assignments, many of which were perilous missions in territories occupied by the enemy" (p. 234). The book *Assessment of Men* (Office of Strategic Services Assessment Staff, 1948) reports on this work. Psychologists associated with assessment centers have commented to me that Murray's work is considered seminal in their field.

"MY BODY OF UNFINISHED AND UNFINISHABLE WORKS"

After the war, Murray returned to Harvard. In 1947 he finally received tenure, along with the title, lecturer on clinical psychology. In 1951, at the age of 58, he was named professor of clinical psychology.

One of the central questions that those interested in Murray's life ask is, "Why did he achieve so little in the years after the war, in comparison to his contributions up to that time?" Robert W. White (letter to J. W. Anderson, March 13, 1988) gave me his answer:

> After the great success of *Explorations* and the huge personal satisfaction of leading such a distinguished crew in the assessment program, I think he never again was as happy and satisfied with what he could accomplish. He disassociated himself from the clinical training program we had started, presided over a talented but small research group in a separate house, drove them at times mercilessly to produce (I'd guess) another great coup, and of course could not reinstate the drama of his first two creations. He wrote some brilliant papers, but struggled apparently in vain to achieve a coherent systematization of personology. It's hard to hit two mountaintops in a lifetime.

Murray's achievements in the later years would seem impressive for someone who had not accomplished what he had earlier in his career. He joined with Clyde Kluckhohn, Talcott Parsons, O. Hobart Mowrer, and Allport in forming Harvard's Department of Social Relations. The department championed an interdisciplinary approach to the social sciences for 23 years before it was merged with the Department of Psychology in 1972. He coedited an influential text that exhibited this approach (Kluckhohn & Murray, 1948). He was ahead of his times in working on social issues; he was concerned in particular with the dangers of overpopulation and nuclear war. And he published several papers that established his reputation among Melville scholars.

But in Murray's own view, he managed to finish only a small part of what he had set out to achieve. When I worked with him in the 1970s, he had hundreds of pages of partly written manuscripts and thousands of pages of notes for other enterprises. Three of his most important projects were as follows:

(1) A biography of Melville: He had worked intermittently for 40 years on Melville and drafted many chapters for a biography, in various versions, but he could never qutie bring himself to put his work into final form.

(2) The TAT-II: He developed a revised version of the TAT. The pictures included color and brought out the subjects' organizational abilities more than the original TAT did. He did some experimentation with the TAT-II but did not feel it was finished.

(3) His "personological theoretical system": Murray worked at devising a final personological system that would go far beyond the system presented in *Explorations in Personality*. He wrote about aspects of it (Murray, 1959, 1968) but did not complete it.

His explanation to me about his failure to complete his work was "I was never in a hurry to publish. I'd gone ahead as if I've got five or six years [at least] ahead of me." He felt there was always more time, and if he waited he would develop increasingly better ideas. He relied on a kind of "creative evolution."[57]

The 1960s was a decade of endings for Murray. He retired from Harvard in 1962, and his wife, Josephine, also died in that year. He was terribly depressed after her death. One of his students told me Murray "turned old overnight." "He would cry all day, and he would leave meetings because he was overwhelmed by his grief" (Arthur Couch, personal communication, October 30, 1981). In 1967 Christiana Morgan died. She had suffered for years from heart disease, and, in Murray's words, "Finally, with the lethal mounting of ventricular fibrillations, Christiana Morgan chose her best-loved Caribbean beach, St. John's Island, as locus of her demise" (Murray, 1976, p. 521).

Murray also experienced a new beginning in the 1960s; he married Caroline (Nina) Fish in 1969. He saw his second marriage as the most rewarding

FIGURE 8.7 Murray with his second wife, Nina (Caroline Fish Murray), in 1975.

experience of his later years. He told me in my very first talk with him (in my paraphrase): "If you get into your late 70s and you're debating whether you should get married again—do it!"[58]

Murray hated old age. For someone who took so much pride in his acute intelligence, it was especially painful to observe some decline in his abilities. He showed me a letter he was writing to a friend in which he diagnosed himself as having "senile arteriosclerosis" on the basis of "the hard fact that it now takes me 5 times longer than it did formerly to write a publishable page or write a letter . . . , but I am slowed down, partly incapacitated, in *all* other functions, even toddling and babbling (and slobbering)!" He added, "But please don't infer from this that I am now set to acquiesce with grace to the fiery furnace's consumption of my body in the company of my body of unfinished and unfinishable works" (letter to K. S. Lynn, March 21, 1977). In 1979 he suffered from a series of strokes. In addition to experiencing substantial paralysis on his left side, he became depressed. "The stroke made me aware that I wasn't going to finish anything I had started and my whole life would be a failure," he told me. "[It was] like death to my expectations."[59] Murray also had emphysema during the later years.

FIGURE 8.8 Henry A. Murray in 1985 at the age of 92 (photograph by James W. Anderson).

Despite his indisputable physical problems, those who knew him found him to be sharp, witty, and creative during his 80s and 90s. He exhibited strong emotions—especially warmth and anger, and he remained a brilliant conversationalist. Through hard work with a physical therapist, he even made an amazing recovery from his strokes, although he later had further setbacks. In my last meeting with him, when he was 94 years old, he was physically debilitated, but he was very much the Harry Murray I had known for years, full of life, and with opinions and observations on every subject that came up. He even told me he was having new ideas about different aspects of his life, such as the effect it had had on him to be from a wealthy background.[60]

Murray retained his sense of humor to the end. The psychologist Howard Gardner had a final visit with him just a few weeks before Murray's death from pneumonia. Near the beginning of their talk, Murray said he was not feeling well and expected to begin his "intergalactic trip" that day. Later Murray was telling Gardner how much he appreciated their friendship. Murray commented that he would remember everything Gardner had done for him for the rest of his life. Then Murray chuckled and said that that really was not much of a compliment. He noted that earlier in the conversation he had said he was going to die that day—and now he was saying that he would remember his debt to Gardner for the rest of his life (Gardner, Remarks at Memorial Service, Cambridge, MA, October 3, 1988).

END NOTES

These notes refer to the dates of interviews that the author conducted with Henry A. Murray.

1. 11 April 1981.	16. Ibid.	31. 2 October 1987.
2. 3 October 1987.	17. 11 April 1981.	32. 5 June 1981.
3. 2 October 1987.	18. Ibid.	33. 29 August 1985.
4. 15 July 1975.	19. 26 May 1986.	34. Ibid.
5. 8 June 1981.	20. 2 October 1987.	35. 28 May 1986.
6. Ibid.	21. 22 May 1981.	36. 28 May 1973.
7. Ibid.	22. Ibid.	37. Ibid.
8. 22 May 1986.	23. Ibid.	38. Ibid.
9. 3 October 1987.	24. 26 May 1986.	39. 31 December 1973.
10. 22 May 1986.	25. Ibid.	40. 2 October 1987.
11. 30 April 1984.	26. Ibid.	41. 25 January 1987.
12. 22 May 1986.	27. 19 August 1975.	42. 28 May 1973.
13. 30 April 1984.	28. Ibid.	43. 4 August 1977.
14. Ibid.	29. 26 May 1986.	44. 11 November 1982.
15. 2 October 1987.	30. Ibid.	45. 18 July 1975.

46. 11 April 1981.	51. 18 August 1976.	56. 22 May 1986.
47. Ibid.	52. 29 August 1985.	57. 11 April 1981.
48. Ibid.	53. 31 July 1975.	58. 28 May 1973.
49. Ibid.	54. Ibid.	59. 11 April 1981.
50. 31 July 1975.	55. 29 August 1975.	60. 3 October 1987.

REFERENCES

Anderson, J. W. (1988). Henry A. Murray's early career: A psychobiographical exploration. *Journal of Personality, 56,* 139–171.

Anderson, J. W., & Murray, H. A. (1977). *Suggested procedures for devising—and criteria for evaluating—a personological system.* Unpublished manuscript.

Elms, A. C. (1972). Allport, Freud, and the clean little boy. *Psychoanalytic Review, 59,* 627–632.

Elms, A. C. (1987). The personalities of Henry A. Murray. *Perspectives in Personality, 2,* 1–14.

Hall, C. S., & Lindzey, G. (1957). *Theories of personality.* New York: John Wiley.

Harvard College Class of 1915. (1950). *Thirty-fifth anniversary report.* Cambridge, MA: Cosmos Press.

Harvard College Class of 1915. (1965). *Fiftieth anniversary report.* Cambridge, MA: Harvard University Printing Office.

Haydn, H. (1970). Portrait: Henry A. Murray. *American Scholar, 39,* 123–136.

Hendrick, I. (Ed.). (1961). *The birth of an institute.* Freeport, ME: Bond Wheelwright Co.

Kluckhohn, C., & Murray, H. A. (Eds.). (1948). *Personality in nature, society, and culture.* New York: Alfred A. Knopf.

MacKinnon, D. W. (1982, August). *Environments that favor creativity.* Paper presented at the annual convention of the American Psychological Association. Washington, DC.

Maddi, S. R., & Costa, P. T. (1972). *Humanism in personality: Allport, Maslow, and Murray.* Chicago: Aldine, Atherton.

Morgan, C. D., & Murray, H. A. (1935). A method for investigating fantasies: The Thematic Apperception Test. *Archives of Neurology and Psychiatry, 34,* 289–306.

Murray, H. A. (1933). The effect of fear upon estimates of the maliciousness of other personalities. *Journal of Social Psychology, 4,* 310–329.

Murray, H. A. (1940). What should psychologists do about psychoanalysis? *Journal of Abnormal and Social Psychology, 35,* 150–175.

Murray, H. A. (1959). Preparations for the scaffold of a comprehensive system. In S. Koch (Ed.), *Psychology: A study of a science* (Vol. 3, pp. 7–54). New York: McGraw-Hill.

Murray, H. A. (1962). "In nomine diaboli." In R. Chase (Ed.), *Melville: A collection of critical essays* (pp. 62–74). Englewood Cliffs, NJ: Prentice-Hall. (Original work published 1951)

Murray, H. A. (1967). The case of Murr. In E. G. Boring & G. Lindzey (Eds.), *A history of psychology in autobiography* (Vol. 5, pp. 285–310). New York: Appleton-Century-Crofts.

Murray, H. A. (1968). Components of an evolving personological system. In *International encyclopedia of the social sciences* (Vol. 12, pp. 5–13). New York: Macmillan & Free Press.

Murray, H. A. (1976). Postscript: Morsels of information regarding the extraordinary woman in whose psyche the foregoing visions were begot. In C. G. Jung, *The visions seminars* (pp. 517–521). Zurich, Switzerland: Spring Publications.

Murray, H. A. (1981). Psychology and the university. In E. Schneidman (Ed.), *Endeavors in psychology: Selections from the personology of Henry A. Murray* (pp. 337–351). New York: Harper & Row. (Original work published 1935)

Murray, H. A., & Morgan, C. D. (1945). A clinical study of sentiments. *Genetic Psychology Monographs, 32*, 3–311.

Murray, H. A. (1938). *Explorations in personality*. New York: Oxford University Press.

Office of Strategic Services Assessment Staff. (1948). *Assessment of men*. New York: Rinehart & Co.

Smith, M. B. (1971). Allport, Murray, and Lewin on personality theory: Notes on a confrontation. *Journal of the History of the Behavioral Sciences, 7*, 353–362.

Triplet, R. G. (1983). *Henry A. Murray and the Harvard Psychological Clinic, 1926–1938: A struggle to expand the disciplinary boundaries of academic psychology*. Unpublished doctoral dissertation, University of New Hampshire, Durham, NH.

White, R. W. (1981). Exploring personality the long way: The study of lives. In A. I. Rabin, J. Arnoff, A. M. Barclay, & R. A. Zucker (Eds.), *Further explorations in personality* (pp. 3–19). New York: John Wiley.

White, R. W. (1987). *A memoir: Seeking the shape of personality*. Marlborough, NH: Homestead Press.

9

Henry Murray's Legacy: An Epilogue

Robert A. Zucker

It has been 10 years since the first Murray Lectureship and 50 years since the publication of *Explorations*. At the time of this writing it is the ninety-fifth year since Harry Murray's birth and the thirtieth year since I first met him; it is also the year of his death. As the one member of the Lectureship committee who knew him in a sustained way, my editor-colleagues have agreed that it would be most appropriate for me to end this volume with a commentary on his legacy. To what extent have his life and his work had any bearing on the psychology of today; to what extent might they have an influence on psychology hereafter?

It is a temptation to provide an overarching evaluation, either positive or negative, about Murray's impact upon the current personological scene; neither is likely to be correct. As Fredrick Wyatt (1988) noted in his presentation at the APA Symposium on Murray, there were clearly ways that Murray's conceptual edifice was a product of the physicalism and factualism of its time, even as it attempted to transcend these frameworks. What then is still enduring?

There are at least three different levels at which this question can be addressed. First, there is the influence of Murray the teacher/mentor/leader, whose power frequently loomed large—if not larger than life, at least larger than that of ordinary men—and whose impact was significant on a cadre of psychologists whose work continues on into the present day. Perhaps out of the origins of high privilege—as James Anderson describes in the previous chapter—perhaps out of the force of intellect and personality that showed early on in his childhood, and perhaps out of his capacity to generate and describe visions of the great landscapes of mankind (Murray, 1960, 1962), Murray was repeatedly able to assemble groups of highly talented and creative scholars (Murray, 1938; Office of Strategic Services Assessment Staff, 1948). They interacted and produced while with him, and thereafter developed significant research lines of their own, which had clear ties to the experience (White, 1963). The Murray Lectureship is continuing testimony to that capacity as well, since many of the lecturers had that direct contact (Rabin & Zucker, 1988).

There is a second level of influence, that of the longer term, substantive impact of Murray's ideas and lifework. In the spirit of irreverence that was also Murray's, we take his dedication in *Explorations* as a standard against which to judge his contributions. Therein he acknowledges "Morton Prince, who had the vision, raised the endowment and was the first director of the Harvard Clinic, Sigmund Freud, whose genius contributed the most fruitful working hypotheses, Lawrence J. Henderson, whose expositions of scientific procedure established a methodological standard, Alfred N. Whitehead, whose philosophy of organism supplied the necessary underlying generalities, and Carl G. Jung, whose writings were a hive of great suggestiveness" (Murray et al., 1938, p. v).

Murray fares well on all counts, although some of his contributions are less visible than others. The accuracy of his vision is strikingly communicated in one of his later but less well known writings entitled "Vicissitudes of Creativity" (1959).[1] In the paper, Murray anticipates Maddi's Murray Lecture (1984); Maddi talks about the investigation of potentiality rather than actuality; Murray some 25 years before sees the investigation of the creative process as one in which psychologists "may be engaging in more enlightened endeavors to transform the place and the society in which we live" (Murray, 1959, p. 118).

Ever wedded to what we now call a biopsychosocial perspective, Murray reiterated the interplay of mental and physiological events:

> Although what Darwin called "accidental variations" are dependent on chance encounters among different genes, the crucial determinant is something else, namely the inherent capacity of genes—as well as numberless other entities—to participate in the composition of new and valued generating entities. . . . when we study creative processes we are focussing not on some sort of epiphenomenon that occurs only in the minds of a few "born" geniuses, but on processes that carry on, like coral insects, secretly and unobtrusively on all levels. (Murray, 1959, p. 104)

Nonetheless, he reminded the reader that the obverse, literary and religious language, was equally vital, and suggested "that when the physiologist, the psychologist and the poet begin to talk corresponding languages we shall be on

---

[1]Of the many papers one might choose to illustrate this point, I've selected this one in particular because it is of some sentimental significance to the Michigan State University Lectureship (Murray delivered the paper here in 1958).

our way to a genuine understanding of human nature" (Murray, 1959, p. 106). Gilligan, Brown, and Rogers clearly are part of this heritage.

Murray's preoccupation with systems and with across-system relationships is as relevant in this era (Hoffman, 1981; Levine & Fitzgerald, in press; Miller, 1978) as it was when he grappled with these issues in his discussion of the organism and its environment in 1938, when he dealt with issues of levels of influence from culture to constitution in 1953 (Murray & Kluckhohn, 1953), and in the late 1950s and early 1960s when he addressed the issues of interdependence and independence of systems at the dyadic/interpersonal level (1963). And although the need-press schema as an explicit conceptual framework in which to view behavior has fallen into disuse, notions of transactional processes between self and environment are as common today in longitudinal research (Rutter, 1987; Sameroff, 1975) as they are in the consulting room (Langs, 1976; Stone, 1984). In all of these regards, Murray's vision continues to be relevant into the 1980s.

Although not strictly a methodological contribution, Murray's development, with his long-time colleague/friend/companion Morgan, of the Thematic Apperception Test (TAT) was a major advance in being able to access and objectify unconscious content (McClelland, 1958). The TAT's continued utility as a research instrument in motive research, as well as its remaining one of the most widely used measures in clinical assessment practice (Sweeney, Clarkin, & Fitzgibbon, 1987), testifies both to the power of this contribution and to the importance of the content domain that it accesses.

Murray did not only theorize about environmental press; he also created it, by way of the development of structures for work, in at least three different settings that have thereafter had a major influence upon the field of personality. The creation of a model for the assessment and conceptualization of personality using multiple measures, multiple methods, multiple assessors, and a diagnostic council was first practiced in the Harvard Psychological Clinic of the 1930s. Murray and his colleagues, but most especially Donald MacKinnon, used and expanded that model when they ran the Office of Strategic Services center for the selection of intelligence agents during World War II (Office of Strategic Services Assessment Staff, 1948). MacKinnon thereafter moved those procedures to Berkeley, where they were institutionalized within the Institute of Personality Assessment and Research (IPAR), which itself has been the home of much of what is regarded as central within the field of personality research in the last generation.[2] What is less well known is that these procedures are the intellectual forebears of Assessment Center methodology (Bray & Grant, 1966; Huck, 1973), one of the most common techniques

---

[2]Runyon is the most recent IPAR member to have presented at the Murray Lectures; Jack Block was the first.

used for the identification of managerial talent on the modern business scene, which Bray (1982) has estimated is responsible for the assessment of several hundred thousand persons annually.

Murray's legacy extends to another work structure, Harvard's now defunct Department of Social Relations, a department that he, Allport, and Kluckhohn began in the late 1940s. For close to 20 years this setting was able to institutionalize the training of multidisciplinary scholars and to support the pursuit of interdisciplinary research. The setting was one of a small number that institutionally legitimated a point of view that we now take for granted as part of our working vision, namely, that psychological study must also be psychosocial study; and it is equally clear to anyone who knew Murray that he would have added "It must also be biopsychosocial," although he would have managed to convey this with a more felicitous turn of phrase.

* * * *

There is another level of Murray's influence that is less obvious to those who only knew the public man or met him through his writing; that is the impact of his life upon those around him. It would be easy to paint a romanticized picture of this aspect of his life; there is much that he did and was that radiated power and charm. But such a sketch would be as inaccurate as a rendition of *Explorations* that catalogued only half a dozen needs, had no conception of press, and ignored the dynamic interplay between conscious and unconscious forces in determining life trajectory. In addition to his graciousness, he had the capacity to be cutting and controlling; he knew how to lead and nurture, but he also had difficulty legitimating the competence of others who might challenge or disagree. The external evidence suggests he was better at nurturing his working environment than he was his home, at least during his first marriage. The details of his relationship with Christiana Morgan remain unclear, although indirect textual evidence from the creativity paper (Murray, 1959, pp. 112–115) strongly suggests that the relationship was exceptionally vital and in its own way both powerfully curative and possibly central to his affectional and creative well-being.[3] The relative lack of published work in psychology,

---

[3]The text referred to here ostensibly deals with one of Murray's patients, but the intimate events described and the obvious passion attached to the account reads more like a love story than a clinical account. Other elements in the account also lend credence to this conclusion: for one, the implausibility of a patient's *repeated* return to a former therapist, particularly when his posttherapy life is so satisfying that the motivation to return is unexplainable; for another, the fact that the ex-patient finds more in a dyadic intimate relationship than he ever did in treatment fits more with Murray's own life experience than it does with the notion of a devoted patient's wish to return and confide in a treatment that failed; and for still another, several of the other incidental details (e.g., that the female member of the partnership had already undergone a psychoanalysis) are consistent with known details of the Murray-Morgan involvement. Taken together, I have concluded that Murray in this instance decided, like Freud, to use himself as a disguised case history, and in so doing gives us a more unguarded sense of his life than would be accessible by way of a formal autobiographical account.

coupled with the volume of unfinished manuscripts, remains a puzzlement as well, especially when it is coupled with the apparent lack of publishing blocks during his brief biochemistry research career.

With all these complexities, Harry Murray remained a powerful figure long after he had retired; his Cambridge home continued to be a place to be sought out, not only to touch living history but also as a place where ideas still ruled. Even in his 92nd year he served as a consultant/participant to a television special on the life of Melville (the special was also dedicated to Murray). In these last few years he remained incisive in his vision and sparkling in his imagination; he continued to have the capacity to make little observations that were a window into a giant and colorful world of myth and fantasy and liveliness. There is a way that this constant delight in life, shown in later years, was his greatest gift to those that were close to him; it suggested that after all, he had been successful in dissolving some of the marrow of misery in his bones.

Some of Harry Murray's legacy is in what we remember, and some is in what we use; that is a part of the mainstream of our work. For this, we do not even need to remember, because it is a part of us.

REFERENCES

Bray, D. W. (1982). The Assessment Center and the study of lives. *American Psychologist*, 37, 180–189.

Bray, D. W., & Grant, D. L. (1966). The Assessment Center in the measurement of potential for business management. *Psychological Monographs*, 80 (Whole No. 625), 1–27.

Hoffman, L. (1981). *Foundations of family therapy*. New York: Basic Books.

Huck, J. R. (1973). Assessment centers: A review of the external and internal validities. *Personnel Psychology*, 26, 191–212.

Langs, R. (1976). *The bipersonal field*. New York: Jason Aronson.

Levine, R. L., & Fitzgerald, H. E. (Eds.). (in press). *Analysis of dynamic psychological systems*. New York: Plenum Press.

Maddi, S. R. (1984). Personology for the 1980s. In R. A. Zucker, J. Aronoff, & A. I. Rabin (Eds.), *Personality and the prediction of behavior* (pp. 7–41). Orlando, FL: Academic Press.

McClelland, D. C. (Ed.). (1958). *Motives in fantasy, action and society*. Princeton, NJ: Van Nostrand.

Miller, J. G. (1978). *Living systems*. New York: McGraw-Hill.

Morgan, C. D., & Murray, H. A. (1935). A method for investigating fantasies: The Thematic Apperception Test. *Archives of Neurology and Psychiatry*, 34, 289–306.

Murray, H. A. (1959). Vicissitudes of creativity. In H. H. Anderson (Ed.), *Creativity and its cultivation* (pp. 96–118). New York: Harper & Brothers.

Murray, H. A. (1960). The possible nature of a "mythology" to come. In H. A. Murray (Ed.) *Myth and mythmaking* (pp. 300–353). New York: George Braziller.

Murray, H. A. (1962). Prospects for psychology. *Science, 136*, 483–488.

Murray, H. A. (1963). Studies of stressful interpersonal disputations. *American Psychologist, 18*, 28–36.

Murray, H. A. (1938). *Explorations in personality*. New York: Oxford University Press.

Murray, H. A., & Kluckhohn, C. (1953). Outline of a conception of personality. In Kluckhohn, C., & Murray, H. A. (Eds.), *Personality in nature, society, and culture* (2nd ed., pp. 3–32). New York: Alfred A. Knopf.

Office of Strategic Services Assessment Staff. (1948). *Assessment of men*. New York: Rinehart.

Rabin, A. I., & Zucker, R. A. (1988, August). *Further explorations in personality*. Paper presented at the American Psychological Association symposium, The Murray Tradition: The 50th Anniversary of *Explorations in Personality*, Atlanta, GA.

Rutter, M. (1987). Psychological resilience and protective mechanisms. *American Journal of Orthopsychiatry, 57*, 316–331.

Sameroff, A. (1975). Transactional models in early social relations. *Human Development, 18*, 65–79.

Stone, L. (1984). *Transference and its context*. New York: Jason Aronson.

Sweeney, J. A., Clarkin, J. F., & Fitzgibbon, M. L. (1987) Current practice of psychological assessment. *Professional Psychology: Research and Practice, 18*, 377–380.

White, R. W. (Ed.). (1963). *The study of lives: Essays in honor of Henry A. Murray*. New York: Atherton.

Wyatt, F. (1988, August). *Psychoanalytic ideas in "Explorations" and subsequent developments in psychoanalysis*. Paper presented at the American Psychological Association symposium, The Murray Tradition: The 50th Anniversary of *Explorations in Personality*, Atlanta, GA.

Index